Elder Law

by

NANCY R. GALLO, J.D.

DELMAR
CENGAGE Learning™

Australia • Brazil • Japan • Korea • Mexico • Singapore • Spain • United Kingdom • United States

Elder Law
Nancy R. Gallo

Vice President, Career and Professional
Editorial: Dave Garza

Director of Learning Solutions: Sandy
Clark

Acquisitions Editor: Shelley Esposito

Managing Editor: Larry Main

Senior Product Manager: Melissa
Riveglia

Editorial Assistant: Lyss Zaza

Vice President, Career and Professional
Marketing: Jennifer McAvey

Marketing Director: Deborah Yarnell

Marketing Manager: Erin Brennan

Marketing Coordinator: Jonathan
Sheehan

Production Director: Wendy Troeger

Production Manager: Mark Bernard

Senior Content Project Manager: Betty
Dickson

Senior Art Director: Joy Kocsis

Senior Director of Product
Management for Career, Professional,
and Languages: Tom Smith

Production Technology Analyst: Thomas
Stover

For product information and technology assistance, contact us at
Cengage Learning Customer & Sales Support, 1-800-354-9706

For permission to use material from this text or product,
submit all requests online at **www.cengage.com/permissions**
Further permissions questions can be emailed to
permissionrequest@cengage.com

Library of Congress Control Number: 2008932897

ISBN-13: 978-1-4018-4257-4

ISBN-10: 1-4018-4257-7

Delmar
Executive Woods
5 Maxwell Drive
Clifton Park, NY 12065
USA

Cengage Learning is a leading provider of customized learning solutions with office locations around the globe, including Singapore, the United Kingdom, Australia, Mexico, Brazil, and Japan. Locate your local office at
www.cengage.com/global

Cengage Learning products are represented in Canada by
Nelson Education, Ltd.

To learn more about Delmar, visit **www.cengage.com/delmar**

Purchase any of our products at your local bookstore or at our preferred online store **www.cengagebrain.com**

Printed in the United States of America
2 3 4 5 6   26 25 24 23 22

Dedication

*This textbook is dedicated to
my parents and favorite elders,
Dr. James M. and Nancy V. Gallo.*

Contents

CHAPTER 3 Life Planning: Advance Directives for Health Care, Euthanasia, and Physician-Assisted Suicide 65

CHAPTER 7   Financial Planning 193

CHAPTER 12 Legal Aspects of Funeral Planning 325

Preface

It is not the years in your life, but the life in your years that matter.

Abraham Lincoln

This country's senior citizens are part of America's fastest-growing population. This group includes baby boomers who were born between 1946 and 1964, a period described as America's baby boom. The first boomers have become eligible for Social Security benefits, with huge numbers of boomers expected to follow in the coming years. Contrastingly, children under 15 years of age constitute less than 25 percent of the U.S. population. America's senior citizens will continue to develop physical, emotional, and legal needs particular to their age group. The expected growth in the area of elder law is related directly to the increase in America's elderly population.

While the practice of elder law is poised to become one of the nation's top priorities, attorneys, paralegals, social workers, and professionals in the growing geriatric specialties need to be schooled in this specialized area of the law. Law schools and paralegal programs across the country are recognizing the population numbers and financial opportunities available for practitioners who meet the needs of a population that will increase with the graying of the baby boomers.

Although some people think that elder law is only about wills, trusts, and estate planning, an elder law practice can help clients in many related areas and encompass so much more. For example, while traditional estate planning emphasizes what happens to an individual's property after death, *elder law issues more typically emphasize life planning before death.*

The purpose of this text is to focus on the elder law client as a *whole* person with the many questions and problems that go with and *beyond* wills, trusts, and estate administration. This textbook was written to be used primarily in elder law classes. It was designed to meet the needs of students studying law, social work, family structure, and any of the geriatric specialties and to be used as a resource by graduate students.

Defining elder law is a complicated task. Legal issues pertaining to the elderly encompass a lengthy list of topics. Topics relevant to elder law include housing options, age discrimination, the economics of retirement, disability law, bankruptcy, estate planning, institutionalization, fraud issues, Social Security, Medicare, marriage, grandparenting, health care issues, abuse, the Americans with Disabilities Act, guardianships, insurances, senior living facilities, funeral planning, and the ethical issues related to all of those topics. Some or all of these topics will play a role in client representation.

Morality issues also are a large part of elder law practice. Unfortunately, the question of whose social and moral responsibility it is to care for the nation's elderly is not always met with enthusiasm. For example, it may seem obvious that adult children should be held accountable for their elderly parents' care. However, a majority of states have found it necessary to impose a statutory duty on adult children to provide financial assistance to their indigent parents. Five states have gone further and imposed the duty on grandchildren. This mandated imposition of what many view as a moral duty might be viewed as pragmatic and fiscally wise by states that do not want to become the financial caretakers of their aging citizens. This statutorily mandated duty only begins to touch on the many divergent legal issues that pertain to the elderly population.

Not all topics in this text are the exclusive domain of the elder population. In fact, most of the topics apply to the needs of younger individuals as well. For example, all three of this country's most highly publicized right-to-die cases involved women in their 20s and 30s.

CONTENTS OF THE TEXT

Chapter 1 introduces the reader to the daily world of two paralegals working with a solo practitioner in a firm specializing in elder law. Readers follow newly graduated paralegal Luke Andrews as he is guided through a busy elder law practice by longtime paralegal Rena Buss and attorney Tara Jensen. This chapter includes a review of the medical problems that the elderly face and the way those medical problems can affect legal representation. In addition, office design used to promote a more therapeutic-centered practice is explained.

Chapter 2 begins with a review of the last will and testament. This subject was chosen for one of the beginning chapters because for many people, long-range life planning begins with the notion that they should consider drafting a last will and testament. This often brings a client to an attorney's office to begin what may be a frightening process. The chapter covers the necessary steps in the preparation of a last will and testament. Some readers may have already completed a course in wills and trusts or estate administration. If so, the information in this chapter, which is presented from an older clients' perspective, may be a different view of the topic. For the reader who has not taken a course in elder law, the chapters are written to facilitate the learning of new legal terminology and concepts.

Chapter 3 explores the high-profile topic of advance directives for health care, often called living wills. The life-and-death drama of Theresa Schiavo's case has served as a "lightning rod" for many Americans. Not since the cases of Karen Ann Quinlan and Nancy Cruzan have living wills been the topic of so many conversations. Surprisingly, as of 2005, only 10 percent of Americans had signed a living will; but the Schiavo case has served to encourage many more to do so. This chapter also covers the topics of euthanasia, physician-assisted suicide, and Dr. Jack Kevorkian.

Chapter 4 reviews the subject of guardianships and conservatorships. The chapter explains why, in most cases, guardianships happen when clients fail to utilize legal planning tools. When to seek a guardianship and how to undertake the legal process are covered in detail. The chapter also focuses on the many important topics involving the role of a caregiver.

Chapter 5 covers the topic of trusts and the increasing role they play in life and tax planning for the average American. For example, the chapter focuses on the use of a special needs trust to assist an elderly father planning for the continuing care of his mentally challenged adult son in the event of the father's death.

Chapter 6 delves into the topic of love and relationships among older Americans. Somewhat surprisingly, senior citizens make up the fastest-growing segment of the adult population living together without being married. Senior citizens also marry and divorce, and the chapter discusses the impact that marriage and divorce may have on the elderly. Chapter 6 also discusses the importance of legal planning in fostering harmony among merging families.

Chapter 7 explores the financial planning and retirement options available to America's oldest citizens. This chapter asks the difficult questions to which many clients want easy answers (e.g., whether Social Security will be a social entitlement program a client should depend on or whether Social Security benefits will go by way of the dinosaur). The topics of viatical death benefits and reverse mortgages are presented. The plusses and minuses of long-term care insurance also are discussed. In addition, Chapter 7 deals with the topics of Medicare and Medicaid. This chapter explains the important role that legal professionals can play in planning the best (and legally permitted) results for clients fearing the complete loss of assets when faced with the cost of nursing home care.

Chapter 8 investigates the numerous housing options available to the elderly. The options cover many scenarios and funding options. The chapter also reviews living trends. Specifically, contractual issues pertaining to elder care housing are discussed. The chapter also covers legislative guidelines for elder housing.

Chapter 9 deals with the fact that statutorily, federal age discrimination in employment legislation can be applied to any claimants over the age of 40. This means that the pool of possible claimants will reach a large portion of the population in upcoming years. The steps of bringing and defending age discrimination in an employment lawsuit are presented.

Chapter 10 explores the unfortunate fact that the incidence of elder abuse (mental, physical, and economic) has been increasing. The statistics and definitions are discussed, as is how to recognize elder abuse. The chapter also covers stopping the abuse, reporting the abuse, and punishing the perpetrator.

Chapter 11 investigates the status of grandparent visitation rights in the post-*Troxel* era. A parent's ultimate right to make decisions regarding his or her child versus a grandparent's right to developing a familial relationship with the family's youngest generation is discussed in detail from different perspectives.

Chapter 12 delves into funeral planning and its legal and financial ramifications. During a time of emotional pain and personal loss, many families are asked to make decisions about a funeral. This chapter emphasizes the legal, ethical, and financial minefields that can be avoided when people are armed with knowledge about planning a funeral.

SPECIAL FEATURES

A key component of each chapter is the Ethics Alert scenario that highlights the ethical dilemmas that support staff working in an elder law practice may face. Each chapter concludes with the Chapter Summary, Key Terms, Chapter Review Questions, Helpful Web Sites, and Endnotes. Key Terms include a list of new vocabulary words introduced in the chapter. Helpful Web Sites is a list of sites pertaining to the chapter's content. Finally, the Glossary provides definitions for the reader. Learning elder law terms should help the reader confidently navigate the field of elder law.

INSTRUCTOR'S MANUAL

Instructors utilizing the text have a helpful selection of ancillary materials, including an *Instructor's Manual* with a Suggested Elder Law Course Syllabus, Elder Law Course Lecture Outline, answers to the Chapter Review questions and Test Bank. The Test Bank has a variety of true-false, multiple choice, and fill-in the-blank questions for each chapter, as well as midterm and final exams. Any professor who adopts this textbook may call or e-mail the author to ask questions or offer suggestions. She would be pleased to discuss the material and to connect with her colleagues and readers from across the country. The author, Nancy R. Gallo, J.D., can be reached at (973) 300-2181 or at ngallo@sussex.edu.

Online Companion™

The text's Online Companion™ is a no-cost benefit to students and instructors who want to look beyond the textbook for more material. One feature in particular is the Web sites from the Helpful Web Sites section of each chapter; they are active links available through the Online Companion™. The Online Companion™ can be found at www.paralegal.delmar.cengage.com in the Online Companion™ section.

Web Page

At <http://www.paralegal.delmar.cengage.com>, you will find valuable information such as hot links and sample materials to download, as well as other Delmar, Cengage Learning products.

Please note that the Internet resources are of a time-sensitive nature and URL addresses may often change or might be deleted.

ACKNOWLEDGMENTS

I wish to thank my wonderful husband and children for always supporting my endeavors. Dale, Alyssa, Tara, James, and Luke, I am thankful each day that we are teammates in life.

I wish to acknowledge the assistance and support of three wonderful paralegals and former students: Julie Deitz, Cheryl Krouse, and Jennifer Smith.

I am grateful to the following reviewers who gave their time so generously and provided such helpful comments on the manuscript of this textbook:

Anne Conti
Hilbert College
Hamburg, NY

George Guay
Canyon College
Caldwell, ID

Deborah Howard
University of Evansville
Evansville, IN

Erin Jensen
St. Cloud State University
St. Cloud, MN

Nancy Simmons
St. Louis Community College at Meramec
St. Louis, MO

I also wish to acknowledge the warm support and assistance of the staff at Delmar, Cengage Learning.

Table of Cases

1

The Elder Law Practice

▓ OBJECTIVES_____

After completing this chapter, you will be able to:

- Explain the development of elder law.
- Identify the special needs of the elderly client.
- List and describe the health problems of the elderly.
- Describe the different kinds of professionals that aid an elderly client.
- Identify the ethical concerns in an elder law practice.

INTRODUCTION

America's ever-increasing elderly population has developed legal needs particular to their age group.[1] This changing demographic has spawned the creation of the Elder Law specialty as a legal practice constantly evolving to meet this population's concerns. Legal issues of importance to the elderly client often focus on personal independence and decision making. For example, the right to care for oneself in one's own home is often a continuing concern for elderly clients. The right to make personal financial and health decisions (including end-of-life decisions) is often discussed

"Old age is an excellent time. My goal is to say or do at least 1 outrageous thing every week."

MAGGIE KUHN, FOUNDER OF THE GRAY PANTHERS

with legal counsel. Usually discussed with each elder law client is the preserving of any assets built during the client's lifetime and the desired distribution of those assets after the client's death.

Elder law practice typically emphasizes life planning *before* death, unlike traditional estate planning that generally emphasizes what happens to an individual's property *after* his death. Unfortunately, elder law practitioners are often asked to help clients who have failed to plan for their old age.[2]

Legal issues pertaining to the elderly encompass almost an inexhaustible list of topics for the elder law attorney and his support staff. Elder law practice is not only about providing efficient estate tax planning advice (e.g., focusing on the least amount of federal and state taxes being paid after a client's death). Pertinent and related elder law topics that may play a role in client representation include but are not limited to the following:

- Government benefits
- Housing options
- Age discrimination
- Economics of retirement
- Disability law
- Bankruptcy
- Estate planning
- Institutionalization
- Fraud issues
- Social Security, Medicare, and Medicaid
- Marriage
- Grandparenting
- Health care issues
- Abuse
- Guardianships and conservatorships
- Senior living facilities
- Funeral planning

Elder law practitioners should be prepared for ethical issues relating to any of those topics.

The most holistic elder law practices use a network of allied professionals to provide the most cost-effective and productive service to their clients. This means using the services of geriatric managers, life care planning specialists, financial planners, and accountants.[3] It is also a practice area that constantly evolves as myriad changes in federal and state law occur. For example, the Deficit Reduction Act of 2005 heralded significant changes in elder law practice in the asset retention area (e.g., Medicaid planning).

Law schools and paralegal programs across the country should recognize the potential financial opportunities available to practitioners who decide to meet the needs of a client population that will explode with the graying of America's baby boomers.[4] The practice of elder law is poised to become one of the nation's top priorities because of this population boom and burgeoning need. That being said, attorneys, paralegals, social workers, and professionals in the growing geriatric specialties will need to be schooled in this specialized area of the law.

Population Growth

Population aging is a worldwide phenomenon. Like other developed countries, the United States is no longer a nation of youth. In fact, children under 15 years of age constitute less than 25 percent of the American population.[5] California is home to the largest population of residents 65 years and older, followed by Florida, New York, Texas, and Pennsylvania. Half of older Americans live in nine states: California (3.6 million); Florida (2.8 million); New York (2.4 million); Texas (2.1 million); Pennsylvania (1.9 million); and Ohio, Illinois, Michigan, and New Jersey (each with more than 1 million).[6]

In 1995, the 65- to 74-year-old age group (18.8 million) was eight times larger than in 1900; the 75- to 84-year-old age group (11.1 million) was 14 times larger; and the 85-plus age group (3.6 million) was 29 times larger. Statistically, a child born in 1995 can expect to live 75.8 years, about 28 years longer than a child born in 1900.[7] There were approximately 35 million people age 65 and older in the United States by 2000. This number increased from 1900 by 10 times. It has been predicted that one in five people in the United States will be 65 years or older by 2025. By 2002, 50,364 people were aged 100 or older, a 35 percent increase from 1990. Interestingly, the actuarial tables, which are based on mortality tables and used by the insurance industry to estimate how long people will live, were recently changed for the first time in two decades. The new charts go up to 120 years compared to the old tables, which stopped at 100 years.[8]

By 2025, the 78 million adults comprising the group called the baby boomers will begin to hit age 85 and it has been estimated that nearly nine million Americans will be over age 85.[9] Unfortunately, as many as half of those over age 85 will have some cognitive deficit before they die.[10] Refer to Exhibit 1–1 to view this population increase.

Older Americans are mostly women because women have a longer life expectancy—living an average of six years longer than men. Almost half of women 65 years and older are widows. According to the 2000 United States Census, the ratio of men per 100 women steadily declines from 92 men per

Age Discrimination In Employment Act Of 1967

A federal government act that provides protection to certain applicants and employees 40 years of age and older from discrimination on the basis of age in hiring, promotion, discharge, compensation, or terms, conditions, or privileges of employment.

100 women aged 55 to 64 to 46 men per 100 women aged 85 and over. The median income of the country's 65-year-olds was $19,436 for men and $11,406 for women.

When Is Someone Considered Elderly?

There is no one particular age when a person should automatically be defined or described as elderly. Such a description is very subjective, is stereotypical, and is based on highly individualized personality and health-related factors. However, both the federal and state governments have established specific age requirements for citizens to become eligible to receive age-related governmental protections and benefits.

For example, the federal government's **Age Discrimination in Employment Act of 1967** is a federal government act that provides protection to certain applicants and employees 40 years of age and older from discrimination on the basis of age in hiring, promotion, discharge, compensation, or terms, conditions,

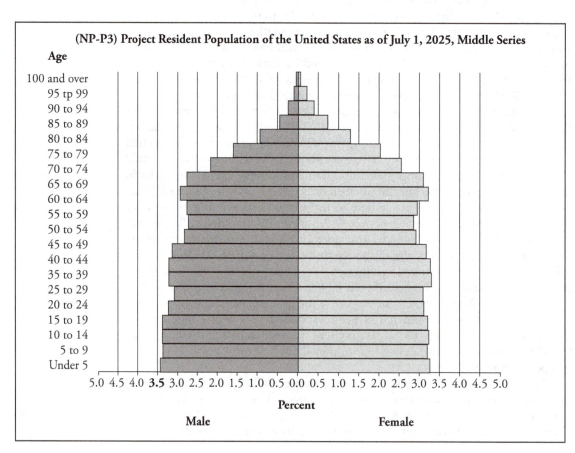

EXHIBIT I–I   Projected Population of the United States 2025

or privileges of employment. The federally created **Age Discrimination Act of 1975** prohibits discrimination on the basis of age in programs and activities receiving federal financial assistance. The Act, which applies to all ages, permits the use of certain age distinctions and factors other than age that meet the Act's requirements. Another federal law which is geared to seniors only is the **Older Americans Act (OAA)** which provides that states *must* offer eligible seniors assistance with their everyday needs or face federal funding cuts. Different types of assistance include housing assistance; health and wellness programs; senior legal aid; employment programs; tax relief; reduced transportation fares; tuition-reduced education; and recreation, leisure, and entertainment cost reductions.

The federal government's Social Security retirement benefits and Medicare eligibility ages may be considered an elder benchmark. Some state benefit programs may include job assistance and tax rebates beginning at age 55. Another informal example is the membership criteria for the largest private organization geared to older Americans, AARP (formerly known as the American Association of Retired Persons). AARP accepts members at age 50.

CREATING THE RIGHT OFFICE ENVIRONMENT

A law firm paralegal or office manager may be asked to assist in the design or renovation of the office space of an elder law practice. It is important to look to the demographics of a firm's clientele. The same research that provides suggested guidelines for assisted living facilities may be very helpful in finding the optimum law office design.[11] Even a law firm's geographic location can have an impact on client comfort. For example, a highly congested and high traffic area may make it difficult for some elderly clients to navigate their way to the office. Will handicap accessibility be important? Obviously, stairs may make it difficult, if not impossible, for some clients to visit a law office. Conference rooms and offices on a ground level are advisable. Does available parking accommodate the firm's older clients? Covered parking could be advantageous in certain areas of the country. Is the parking lot and walkway paving in good condition? Can a client be dropped off at the law firm's front door? Are the law firm's exterior signs easily found? Striving for compliance with the Americans with Disability Act usually ensures that the office is accessible to a firm's elderly and possibly impaired clients.

Many elder law clients travel to an elder law firm with a family member. However, it may not be wise for the family member to remain with the elderly client during an office visit. The question of which person is the client and issues of undue influence may become a concern during the visit. A firm may want to set up a family waiting area equipped with toys, a television, and reading materials to make waiting family members or friends comfortable.

Age Discrimination Act Of 1975

Prohibits discrimination on the basis of age in programs and activities receiving federal financial assistance.

Older Americans Act (OAA)

A federally created act that provides that states *must* offer eligible seniors assistance with their everyday needs or face federal funding cuts.

Researching issues involving cognitive disorders such as Alzheimer's disease and other forms of dementia reveal that individuals with those conditions feel safer and more comfortable in a calm, less stimulating environment. This means that an office that feels more homelike and less like a bustling law office is usually best.[12]

One suggestion for facilitating an office visit with a client suffering from a cognitive disorder is to pipe in calming music or sounds of nature in the waiting area. Of course, the music should not be piped into a private office where it could disturb a hearing-impaired client meeting with his attorney. Difficulties with depth perception often go hand in hand with cognitive disorders, and the design of an office that emphasizes contrasting solid colors can assist with perception difficulties. Carpets should be low-pile and wall-to-wall to eliminate a tripping hazard. Floors should not be slippery and thresholds should not be too tall for clients who may not be able to raise their feet high enough. Wheelchair-bound or physically impaired clients should be able to navigate the floor and the doorways. Lighting should minimize glare, and task lighting can be used where documents must be read. Clients suffering from hearing loss may speak loudly or may need to be spoken loudly to. Therefore, private offices should be well insulated. Elderly clients may use the arms of an office chair to help them stand. All office chairs should be able to withstand such use.[13] Elder law attorneys and their paralegals will need to travel to the clients occasionally. For example, clients unable to travel may be in a hospital, nursing home, or private home. In these cases, an attorney should travel with a portable desktop to facilitate the signing of documents.

Tea and Sympathy: Practicing Therapeutically

Legal talent must coexist with compassion. Attorneys, paralegals, and support staff working in an elder law practice need to understand the special needs of the older client. Paralegals and support staff are often the first contact a client has with a firm. All firm members should be patient, sensitive, and good listeners and have a personality that fits well with older clients. A firm can facilitate the appearance of a friendly and warm office by including the staff's family photographs, plants, and flowers in the office décor. Such items can be conversation starters with new clients. Politeness and respect for elders should be emphasized. Older clients should be called by their surnames. Telephone calls confirming appointments and mailed directions for getting to the office are helpful. Clients may have physical or mental difficulties that make helping them with their legal issues a bit daunting. A major concern is that many clients have varying degrees of vision problems. Documents may need to be prepared in a larger font size to accommodate the reading of the documents by sight-impaired clients. Basic white paper and a large grip black ink pen also assists readability.

Some elder law practitioners have even been known to keep a drawer full of glasses with different prescriptions for those clients who forget their own glasses.[14]

While many legal practices may have considered how the law can and does impact a client's emotional and psychological well-being, others are touting the development of what is being called a *new* legal and psychological hybrid generally known as **Therapeutic Jurisprudence**. Therapeutic Jurisprudence is defined as the melding together of a client's legal and psychological issues by his attorney and the firm's legal support staff to better serve the client's needs.

therapeutic jurisprudence

The melding together of a client's legal and psychological issues by his attorney and the firm's legal support staff to better serve the client's needs.

The concept is really about moving beyond appellate opinions and legal issues and getting to the emotions behind a client's legal problems. Although they are not alone in facing emotion-laden issues, elder law attorneys certainly face their fair share. They and their staff need to be aware of the psychological state of their clients and their clients' families when they come to the law firm for assistance.

Unfortunately, some attorneys may be aware of the emotions and psychological ramifications being experienced by their clients but are unprepared to deal with such personal issues adequately. Experts in the field have suggested that practitioners should practice law in a way that promotes healthy benign closure to the issues. This does not mean that the untrained should attempt to practice psychological counseling. However, it does mean that attorneys and their staffs need to recognize that some elderly clients feel overwhelmed by the legal system and rejected and abandoned by family. A client who feels such a sense of loss and helplessness, in particular, needs to feel that his attorney and the attorney's support staff are doing their best to understand his needs and emotional pain. Experts suggest that pointing out that other clients have had it worse or trying to joke or ignore the problem make clients feel *ignored, minimized,* or *wrong*. Such a negative result will certainly impede the successful completion of a case.[15]

Some elder law firms are managing the art of satisfying client expectations by using what has been called a **personalized legal plan**.[16] Such personalization should be useful in any area of practice. A personalized approach means leaving behind the assumptions of the attorney and the attorney's support staff and clients. It means asking the client probing questions to determine his goals for the attorney and the law firm handling the client's case. The pursuit of such client goals and legal access has prompted the American Bar Association's Commission on Legal Problems for the Elderly to advocate streamlining the administrative processes of the Social Security system to provide due process and favorable decisions as quickly as possible. The American Bar Association also has promoted the idea that senior citizens would have better and more economical access to the legal system with the increased use of dispute resolution and avoidance of the court system whenever possible. A checklist may be used throughout the firm's representation of the client to make sure everything is being done to meet the client's goals.

personalized legal plan

The development of a personalized approach to satisfy client expectations by determining the client's goals for the attorney and the law firm handling the client's case.

The personalized legal plan can reach optimum efficiency with the *narrative approach*. The legal profession's use of the narrative approach stems from the narrative medicine movement. The movement teaches physicians to listen to their patient's stories as a diagnostic tool. The legal profession also must be in tune with a client's story and concerns in order to understand how to help.[17] Of course, reaching a client's goals also fosters client satisfaction and is a positive reflection on the law firm. Refer to Exhibit 1–2 to read suggested interview questions that can help personalize client representation.[18]

SENIOR BENEFITS

■ **state units on aging**
state agencies that are empowered to administer, design, and advocate programs and services for their elderly citizens.

Every state and territorial government has enacted legislation creating agencies that are empowered to administer, design, and advocate programs and services for their elderly citizens. The Area Agencies on Aging (AAA) are public agencies serving the needs of senior citizens within a defined geographic area. Generically, these agencies may be called **state units on aging**; but each state and territory has its own name for its particular agencies. The foundation of each state unit on aging is the federal legislation called the Older Americans Act (OAA). The OAA was enacted in 1965 and amended in 2000. The Act mandates and funds the community-based programs administered by the AAA. The federal government's Department of Health and Human Services along with the national

---

EXHIBIT 1–2   EVALUATING ELDERLY CLIENTS

1. Medical/Health information (if the client wants to share)

2. Demographics (age, gender)

3. Medical problems

4. Healthcare providers

5. Medications

6. Psychosocial information

7. Living arrangements (lives alone, uses assisted living, is married, etc.)

8. Emergency contacts

9. Function information

10. Hearing and vision impairments, if any

11. Mobility (unassisted, cane, etc.)

12. Cognitive status

13. Community transportation (drives, uses public transportation, etc.)

ELDER LAW PRACTICE

A Paralegals Role

Rena knew it was time to increase the office staff. Her lunch breaks were down to 10 minutes and on the way to nonexistent.

The piles of clients' files did not bring the words *neat and organized* to mind. After working 20 years as a paralegal in a variety of law offices, Rena knew it was only a matter of time before a deadline was missed and trouble came to the law office of Tara Jensen, Esq.

"I *have* to talk to Tara again," Rena thought. Never having been the type of woman "to put off until tomorrow what you can do today," Rena practically leapt at Tara when she walked in later that day after visiting clients at a local nursing home.

"We have to talk," Rena announced ominously.

Tara knew by Rena's face that they would not be chatting about that year's fashions.

"Okay. Give me a minute to take my coat off, and I'm all yours," Tara quickly responded. Since it was after office hours, Tara stayed in the small reception area and plopped down on the sofa in the cozy waiting area.

Joining Tara, Rena said, "Even if it isn't in this year's budget, we need help now before a statute of limitations date is missed, something worse happens, or I go crazy. And not necessarily in that order!" Rena could see that Tara was becoming resigned to the fact that her one attorney and one paralegal office emphasizing a comfortable and family atmosphere needed to get bigger.

Nodding in unison with her own comments, Tara said, "I know, I know. I thought we could keep it small. Who knew that our elder law practice would fill such a need?" She continued, "We could just say no to new clients, but we are needed *and* are making money." "My dad always says there is nothing like making money doing good work for people who need you, and boy is he right," Tara added.

Tara continued, "When I left my old firm, I wanted to start a solo practice that emphasized a comfortable environment for my elderly clients. I bought this little house to create a homey atmosphere. I just felt it was going to fill a niche. It did, and having you join me a year later made all the difference." Laughing now, Tara added, "I'm going to blame you for us growing so much!"

Laughing herself, Rena responded, "You know, I've been in the legal field over 20 years and I have seen a lot of different office environments; but our clients sure appreciate this one. I knew when I was looking for a change and interviewed with you that this would be a different experience."

As pragmatic in business as she was caring for clients, Tara said, "Look, I know that adding another paralegal can mean more revenue. I just want a family feel at the firm."

Looking around the cozy living room turned reception area, Rena answered, "I think that's up to us, and I'll do whatever you need to help keep the place like it is—*but* please, only more organized."

Smiling, Tara said, "Okay, let's start by putting feelers out to the local college's paralegal program. Maybe we can get a referral from one of the professors there. Who knows, we may just find a graduate ready to take on the world."

(continues)

ELDER LAW PRACTICE *(continued)*

Luke Enters the Picture

A few weeks later Luke Andrews jumped off his Kawasaki and walked with a slight limp into the reception area of the law firm on the busy corner of Main and Henderson Streets. He had been working as an aide in a rehabilitation clinic while studying for his nursing degree when a motorcycle accident derailed his plans.

Facing the fact that the physical strain of nursing would hinder his nursing career, Luke had redirected his studies and graduated from his local community college's two-year paralegal program. He had spent the last few weeks interviewing for positions in corporate legal departments, law firms, and at the county courthouse. Although he had been thrilled to be offered two positions, neither felt right to him. He told one firm he was not interested, but held off responding to the second offer until after his interview with Tara Jensen.

As usual, Tara was out visiting clients. Rena was asked to do a preliminary interview. After all, Rena would probably be the one working closest with the new paralegal. Rena was sitting at her desk, answering the occasional telephone call and trying to tell Luke what it was like working with an older clientele. "You see Luke," Rena began, "working in an elder law practice means having to understand the special needs of the older client."

Luke responded, "I've been told that I'm real good with the older folks. The gang at the rehab clinic just loved me because I listened to their stories."

A knowing smile creeping across her face, Rena said, "That's great, but our clients may have physical or mental difficulties that makes helping them with their legal issues a bit more daunting. There may be warring factions within a family. A major concern is that many of our clients have vision problems. In fact, Tara read about an elder law practitioner who kept a drawer full of glasses with different prescriptions for clients who forgot their glasses. Tara started doing the same thing here."

Rena explained, "Of course, when I first started working here I thought we had more than our fair share of forgetful clients when I opened what I thought was a drawer full of lost and found glasses."

Smiling broadly, Tara had walked in the rear entrance and overheard Rena's last comment. Tara chimed in, "We do have to deal with our share of forgetful clients; and having patience is more than a virtue around here—it's a necessity."

"Hello, I'm Tara Jensen. You must be Luke Andrews."

Luke quickly answered, "Yes, ma'am, that's me" as he jumped up and offered his hand to Tara.

Tara answered, "No need to "ma'am" me. I go by Tara around here. But our older clients respond wonderfully to good old-fashioned politeness, so you can "ma'am" them all you want." She added, "So, Rena, have you been scaring Luke? I've had three recommendations from his law professors at the college; we don't want to scare him off with too much of a reality dose this early!"

"Well, I didn't mention the office rattlesnake yet," Rena answered laughing.

"Okay, let's go to my office and you can tell me why I should hire you," Tara declared.

Twenty minutes later Tara had heard the story of Luke's life *and* was convinced that he would be a good fit for the office. Luke happily accepted Tara's offer of full-time employment starting next Monday morning.

Administration on Aging and the Centers for Disease Control and Prevention are the umbrella agencies for the state- and community-based programs. Refer to Exhibit 1–3 for a chart showing the network of national and state agencies serving the needs of the nation's elderly.

Each state's unit on aging is the state agency designated to implement services for their state's senior citizens. Portions of the OAA can be read in the Elder Law Online Supplement. Each state unit on aging has the mission of protecting the civil rights, entitlements, and services that should be provided to the nation's most senior citizens. For example, state units on aging administer home- and community-based senior programming with the goal of preventing institutionalization unless absolutely necessary. State units on aging also are excellent clearinghouses for information important to seniors. State units on aging also may administer senior legal services, advocate insurance issues, and provide protective services for abused seniors.

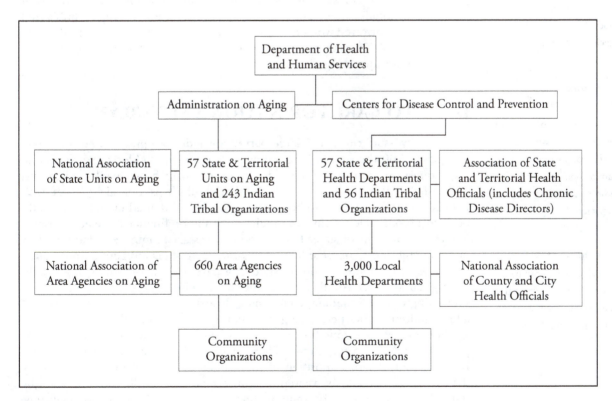

EXHIBIT 1–3 Network of Agencies Serving the Needs of the Nation's Elderly

Protective Services for Seniors

ombudsman

a person who has the power to investigate official misconduct, help fix wrongs done by the government, and sometimes prosecute wrongdoers.

Each of the 50 states provides for the protective services of an **ombudsman** for its institutionalized elderly. Each state also has a legal process for initiating a **public guardianship** or **public conservatorship** for elderly adults with no willing or responsible family members or friends who can serve in that capacity. An ombudsman is a person who has the power to investigate official misconduct, help fix wrongs done by the government, and sometimes prosecute wrongdoers. A guardian is a person who has the legal right and duty to take care of another person or that person's property because he cannot. The arrangement is called a guardianship. A **conservator** is a person who has the continuing permission of another person to handle that person's personal and financial decisions.

Seniors Becoming Empowered

public guardianship

a guardianship of last resort when there are no willing and appropriate family members or friends who can serve. The government is then called upon to act as a surrogate decision maker.

The larger the elder population pool, the greater their political power. For example, AARP helps keep those topics that are especially important to the senior population in the forefront of the American political landscape.[19] Not all topics discussed by senior citizens are the exclusive domain of the elder population. In fact, most topics covered in this textbook apply to the needs of younger individuals as well. For example, all three of the most highly publicized *right-to-die* cases involved women in their twenties and thirties. These are the well-known cases of Theresa Schiavo, Nancy Cruzan, and Karen Ann Quinlan, discussed in an upcoming chapter.

DUTY TO CARE FOR NATION'S ELDERLY?

public conservatorship

provided by the states for elderly adults with no willing or responsible family members or friends who can serve in that capacity.

Morality issues can play a large part in any elder law practice. For example, the question of who should have a duty to care for one's elderly relatives is one such question. Unfortunately, the question of whose legal and moral responsibility it is to care for the nation's elderly is not always met with enthusiasm. It may appear to be a natural conclusion that adult children should be held accountable to care for their medically or financially needy parents. However, a majority of states have found it necessary to impose a statutory duty on adult children to provide financial assistance to their indigent parents. Such laws have raised the question of whether a parent's abandonment of his child during childhood would release the adult child from such filial duty. Interestingly, the Canadian courts have heard such questions and released adult children abandoned during their minority from all filial responsibility.

conservator

a person appointed by a court to make personal and financial decisions for another person.

Some states have gone further and imposed such a duty on grandchildren to provide for their grandparents. These states include Alaska, Arkansas, Iowa, Louisiana, and Utah. Imposition of what some may view more as a *moral* duty than a *legal* duty could be viewed as a pragmatic and fiscally wise approach by states that do not want to become the financial caretakers of their aging citizens.

Refer to Exhibit 1–4 to read a sample of a state statute that imposes a duty of parental care on an adult child and provides criminal sanctions for children judged to be failing to fulfill parental obligations.[20]

EXHIBIT 1–4   SAMPLE DUTY OF CARE STATUTE

N.J.S.A. 2C:24-8. Abandonment, neglect of elderly person, disabled adult; third degree crime

    Except as otherwise provided by law, an adult child shall, to the extent of his or her ability, support a parent who is in need and unable to maintain himself or herself by work.

- A person having a legal duty to care for or who has assumed continuing responsibility for the care of a person 60 years of age or older or a disabled adult, who abandons the elderly person or disabled adult or unreasonably neglects to do or fails to permit to be done any act necessary for the physical or mental health of the elderly person or disabled adult, is guilty of a crime of the third degree. For purposes of this section "abandon" means the willful desertion or forsaking of an elderly person or disabled adult.

- A person shall not be considered to commit an offense under this section for the sole reason that he provides or permits to be provided nonmedical remedial treatment by spiritual means through prayer alone in lieu of medical care, in accordance with the tenets and practices of the elderly person's or disabled adult's established religious tradition, to an elderly person or disabled adult to whom he has a legal duty to care for or has assumed responsibility for the care of.

- Nothing in this section shall be construed to preclude or limit the prosecution or conviction for any other offense defined in this code or in any other law of this State

---

SEEKING PERSONAL INDEPENDENCE

One of the most pressing legal questions that clients face as they age deals with their personal independence. How long they will be able to take care of their personal and financial needs without some level of assistance is an issue of huge importance for clients. These issues involve whether some sort of a guardianship may be necessary. Unfortunately, issues of personal wellness and health care often become regular topics as clients age. Will a client be able to make his own health care decision until he dies? Unfortunately, dying peacefully in one's sleep at 98 years of age happens to only a fortunate few. Too often life issues may not be able to be made competently. This scenario can then lead to legal conflict. Very often issues regarding daily care arise months or years prior to an end-of-life issue. This may involve legal questions involving asset protection, Medicaid eligibility, estate planning, and nursing homes.

MEDICAL PROBLEMS AND THE ELDERLY

Legal practitioners embarking on a career in elder law practice need to learn the language of aging particular to their clients. For example, legal practitioners must learn medical terminology so they are prepared to deal with their clients' experiences.

Nearly *all* elderly Americans will experience some type of chronic health condition in their last years of life. In fact, statistics show that Americans with chronic illnesses will spend *two or more years* at the end of their lives unable to help themselves with their *routine* activities of daily living. In addition, most Americans live out the end of their lives in hospitals, being cared for by paid professionals rather than loved ones in the comfort of their own home or a family member's home.[21]

The good news is that Americans are staying healthier and living longer. The average life expectancy for American women is 77; for American men, it is 75.[22]

Historically, this was not always so. An American male in 1900 could expect to live to 47 years of age. Death in 1900 occurred quickly and from illnesses such as pneumonia, tuberculosis, diarrhea, and from injuries. Typically, women cared for their sick family members at home.

ELDER LAW PRACTICE

Mr. MacGee, an octogenarian and retired teacher, is in the hospital with a broken hip. Normally a very active and competent person, Mr. MacGee is his wife's chief caregiver. Mrs. MacGee is in the early stages of Alzheimer's disease. Mr. MacGee is worried about his wife's care because she is home alone.

Without local family, Mr. MacGee did not know who to call and sought the help of his attorney. His attorney, Tara Jensen, Esq., quickly sought permission from Mr. MacGee to call some neighbors and distant family members about Mrs. MacGee. Tara Jensen also asked permission to get in touch with both of the MacGees' doctors, their stockbroker and financial planner, their insurance broker, the local social worker, and Mrs. MacGee's geriatric manager. Experience has taught Tara Jensen that elderly clients have varied needs and that an attorney is just one member of that team.

The MacGees are not wealthy, but they have a wealth of overlapping issues. Given this scenario, what are some likely legal issues?

Analysis: One concern is likely to be about paying for nursing home care and rehabilitation if they should become necessary for one or both MacGees. This includes issues of Medicare, Medicaid, and possibly long-term and supplemental health insurance. The MacGees may have to sell their home. There are ways to preserve the MacGees' home and still have Medicaid pay for nursing home care, and this point would have to be investigated. Whether powers of attorney and wills are in place and whether a trust of some sort is appropriate also should be discussed. All of these issues are reviewed in upcoming chapters.

Death in the new millennium is more complicated than it was in 1900. A patient facing death today may need many different types of services and care. Chronically ill patients at the end of their lives often need both conventional health care that concentrates more on curative issues and the treatment of symptoms and comfort-oriented palliative care.

Mental Illness and the Elderly

Living longer means that the onset of age-related mental illness may increase. Statistically, 50 percent of people who develop dementia also develop a treatable **psychosis** or **depression**. Such dementia leads to problem behaviors that ultimately result in institutionalized care over home-based family care.

Suicide, the eleventh leading cause of death in the United States, is very common among older people. Approximately every 83 minutes one adult 65 years of age or older commits suicide in the United States. Statistics show that elderly people kill themselves at a higher rate than any other segment of the population. According to the National Institute of Mental Health, people 65 years and older account for almost 20 percent of all suicides although they make up only 13 percent of the population. Why is this happening? The relationship between specific illnesses and rates of suicide is important to consider. Not surprisingly, depression, bipolar disorder (manic-depressive) illness, and severe pain are associated with the largest increase in suicide rates.[23] Additional chronic illnesses including seizure disorder, congestive heart failure, and chronic lung disease also play a part in suicide among the elderly.

Mental health experts have warned that a national crisis in geriatric mental health care is on the horizon. The increase in the number of baby boomers is projected to raise the 1970 number of four million elderly to 15 million by 2030. This generation has a strong history of substance abuse (illicit substances, alcohol, and prescription drugs), which may increase the rate of mental illness as a group.[24]

Medical services, community services, support systems, and training programs concentrating specifically on geriatric mental health nationally have been called *nonexistent* and a potential *disaster*.[25] The suggested remedy is the training and education not only of health care professionals but also of lawyers and their staff, law enforcement officers, letter carriers, public workers who come in contact with the elderly, and the community at large so that people in need of help can be identified and assisted even if they are too ill to seek help themselves.

Dealing with Cognitive Disorders

Dementia is a general term used to describe a mental illness associated with the impairment of an individual's brain function. Along with persistent impairment of brain function, dementia may bring a decline of memory and one or more of the following mental processes: language, visual spatial ability,

psychosis

a mental disorder characterized by symptoms such as delusions or hallucinations that indicate impaired contact with reality; any severe form of mental disorder.

depression

the condition of being sad or despondent.

dementia

a general term used to describe a mental illness. It is a persistent impairment of brain function with a decline of memory and one or more of the mental processes of language, visual spatial ability, personality, cognition, calculation, and judgment.

■ **Alzheimer's Disease (AD)**

a type of dementia that accounts for 50 to 75 percent of all dementias

personality, cognition, calculation, and judgement. The key feature of dementia includes cognitive deficits in multiple areas, including memory loss with progressive deterioration. Such cognitive impairment typically interferes with activities of daily living. Dementia affects approximately eight percent of the population over the age of 65.[26] **Alzheimer's disease (AD)** (a type of dementia) reportedly is responsible for 50 to 75 percent of all dementias, but there are at least 50 others. Hardening of brain arteries (i.e., vascular disease) accounts for another 20 percent. It has been estimated that AD, the eighth leading cause of death in the United States in 2006, affected 4.5 million people in the United States in 2000 and is anticipated to increase to more than 13 million by 2050. This will put huge demands on the health care system.[27]

Alzheimer's is typically described as a disease of the elderly. This is only partially true. Younger people can be stricken by the disease, although it is more typically diagnosed in patients over 60 years old. Many people with AD are not immediately and specifically diagnosed with the disease because a person cannot have an absolute diagnosis of Alzheimer's until an autopsy is performed. However, improved diagnostic testing can now identify the first signs of the sticky deposits in the brain that are thought to be the underlying reason behind AD. The best available diagnosis of the disease is usually based on criteria from the National Institute of Neurological and Communicative Disorders and Stroke-Alzheimer's Disease and Related Disorders Association. Refer to Exhibit 1–5 to review the criteria.

AD may progress at vastly different rates for different individuals. The duration of the illness generally lasts anywhere from 3 to 20 years. The classic symptoms are often described medically as developing in three stages. The symptoms begin as a loss of recent memory and good judgment. A person with

---

EXHIBIT 1–5   DIAGNOSTIC CHARACTERISTICS BASED ON DSM-IV

Cognitive changes

- Memory impairment

- At least one of the following:
  - Problems with language
  - Problems doing motor activities with functional motor system
  - Inability to recognize or identify an object with functional sensory system
  - Difficulties with executive function

The features must negatively impact social participation or work in a meaningful way.

There must be a meaningful change in function.

Course: Gradual onset and progressive decline in cognition

Cause: The features of the condition are not due to another cause (e.g., cerebrovascular accident, depression).

mild AD may be able to live alone, but problems will likely arise when he is faced with more complicated activities such as money management. A person with *moderate* Alzheimer's has difficulty living alone. Both recent and remote memories are affected, and the person may have problems in orientation to time or season. Functional problems at this stage include driving a car safely and behavioral problems including agitation and aggression. These problems result in additional caregiving burdens. *Moderately severe* dementia is characterized by a need for help in performing activities of daily living (e.g., bathing and using the toilet). This stage often involves severe behavioral problems, the likelihood of wandering off alone, and changes in the ability to be mobile and continuing worsening of language and memory. The final state is *severe dementia.* This stage often involves the inability to sit up, smile, or be mobile. Language is often limited to few or no words per day. Tragically, advanced cases need complete assistance with all activities of daily life.

There are different types of care available for Alzheimer's patients. However, in the advanced stage of AD, patients' needs often exceed the in-home caregivers' abilities and nursing home care becomes necessary. In fact, AD has been cited as the most common cause for entry into a care facility.[28] Although there is no one way to care for an Alzheimer's patient, loved ones must choose the most appropriate treatment in consultation with the patient's caregivers. Attention needs to be focused on caregivers who may be taxed beyond their ability. Caregiving burdens have been found to affect caregivers by negatively impacting well-being, increasing fatigue, causing social isolation, leading to depression, and increasing health care utilization.[29]

CARING FOR THE ELDERLY

Unfortunately, the boom in longevity is often accompanied by illness and the immediate need for personal caregiving. Illnesses may be life-threatening or chronic. The growth in chronic illnesses has focused caregivers and legal practitioners on the question of how to provide long-term care for anyone suffering from chronic illnesses.

First, who are most likely going to be caregivers? The families of the elderly do approximately 80 percent of the unpaid care of the nation's oldest citizens. In fact, very often only one family member takes on the role of the primary caregiver. One-quarter of people caring for elderly relatives do so from a distance.[30]

The vast majority of that care is done by female family members and most likely by a daughter. Statistically, the duration of the caregiving averages 4.5 years. AARP has estimated that the financial value of this unpaid care may reach $287 billion annually. Smaller family sizes and changed family structures (increases in single people living alone and the high number of divorces) are leaving a smaller group of potential family caregivers. Unfortunately, family caregivers eventually may be unable to care for elderly family members at home when problem behavior develops. For example, 50 percent of patients with some type of dementia develop a psychosis or depression that can lead to problem behavior and eventual institutionalization.

The assistance of a **geriatric care manager** may be helpful in determining the appropriate care plan for an elder. The geriatric care manager should conduct a complete and professional assessment of a patient's condition. The assessment should provide guidelines as to what type of care a patient requires and, specifically, whether that care can be provided by family members. The assistance may be used on an ongoing basis or in troubleshooting solutions as problems occur.

The **Family and Medical Leave Act (FMLA)** provides a federal safety net for working Americans who need to take time off from work to care for a family member suffering from an illness or who have their own medical condition to deal with. There are some caveats.

Some states have legislation providing a state version of the FMLA. The state versions may go into effect only after a worker has used all of his time off under the federal FMLA but still needs additional time off to care for a family member. Refer to the FMLA in the Elder Law Online Supplement.

The Shadow of Long-Term Care

The majority of older Americans will need some type of assistance with their daily lives before they die. Long-term care of some kind will be needed by two out of every three Americans 65 years and older. Working in an elder law practice most likely means visiting clients in their homes, at assisted living facilities, in nursing homes, and in hospitals. Slightly more than 50 percent of those people receiving assistance with their daily lives will still be in their own homes. A common problem is that many people assume Medicare, the federal health care program for the elderly, will pay for long-term in-home care. In fact, Medicare does not pay for home health aides or adult day care. Approximately 20 percent will live with their caregivers in their homes or the caregivers will move into the care recipient's home. Between four and five percent of all Americans over 65 years of age are living in assisted living and nursing homes.[31]

ELDER ABUSE

An important issue in the United States is elder abuse. The exact number of elder abuse incidents is not known; but within the last decade, it has been estimated that on an annual basis, the number of victims of physical and mental elder abuse has reached 820,000. This number does not include those seniors who self-inflict abuse due to mental illness. Self-inflicted abuse raises the number

▓ geriatric care manager

a person who conducts a complete and professional assessment of a patient's condition and provides guidelines as to what type of care the patient requires and, specifically, whether that care can be provided by family members.

▓ Family And Medical Leave Act (FMLA)

provides a federal safety net for working Americans who need to take time off from work to care for a family member suffering from an illness or who have their own medical condition to deal with. Some states provide a state version.

to an estimated two million victims.[32] Sadly, the perpetrators are typically family members or caregivers. The physical and mental demands of caregiving may be one important reason for caregivers' losing control and becoming perpetrators of such unforgivable violence.

Just as some state laws mandate the reporting of suspected child abuse, some states also mandate the reporting of suspected elder abuse. An attorney or a paralegal who suspects such abuse is occurring is in a position that requires the reporting of such abuse.

PARENTING ISSUES THAT NEVER REALLY END

Not all elder law issues with clients will involve the client solely. For example, an elderly client may be the parent of a minor child or the client may have an adult child who is mentally or physically challenged. In either case, the elderly client will likely need assistance in the eventual transfer of his parental responsibilities to another designated guardian. Financial planning may involve a trust as an appropriate mechanism for the transfer and preservation of the elderly client's assets to his children. Grandparents' rights are another issue involving children that an elder law practice may handle. Visitation and custody issues involving grandchildren may arise.

In fact, early 21st century data showed four million children living with a parent in a grandparent'(s) home and 1.4 million children being raised solely by a grandparent without the presence of a parent.[33]

RECOGNIZING THE FIRM'S CLIENT

Who is the law firm's client in an elder law practice? It may seem like a simple question, but it can lead an attorney and a paralegal through an ethical minefield. Many senior clients first come to a law firm with an adult child or a caregiver. The child or caregiver may insist on staying with the senior during the appointment with the attorney. The problem with this scenario is that the senior may not feel comfortable complaining about his child/caregiver while that person is in the office.

On the other hand, a senior may only be comfortable with his child/caregiver close by and insist that the child/caregiver stay during the meeting with the attorney. The problem with this scenario is the possibility of dominance or undue influence on the part of the caregiver/child if that person is the main recipient of the elderly client's estate. Another problem is that even the innocent child/caregiver may appear to have been unduly influenced or dominated. Obviously, all of the scenarios tests the attorney's ability to deal with everyone involved.[34]

SUMMARY

The explosive growth in America's senior population has fueled the development of elder law practice. Traditional estate planning emphasizes what happens to an individual's property after death, but elder law practices more typically emphasize life planning before death.

Defining elder law is a complicated task; there is no exact definition. Pertinent and related elder law topics include government benefits law; housing options for seniors; age discrimination; the economics of retirement; disability law; bankruptcy; estate planning; institutionalization; fraud issues; Social Security; Medicare; Medicaid; marriage; grandparenting; health care issues; abuse; the Americans with Disabilities Act; guardianships and conservatorships; insurances; funeral planning; and, of course, ethical issues for legal professionals working in elder law. Some or all of these topics may play a role in the representation of a client by a law firm. Therapeutic Jurisprudence can be applied to an elder law practice. It is defined as the melding together of a client's legal and psychological issues by his attorneys and the firm's legal support staff to better serve the client's needs.

The federal Older Americans Act provides that states *must* offer seniors who need assistance with their everyday needs or face federal funding cuts. Different types of assistance include housing assistance; health and wellness programs; senior legal aid; employment programs; tax relief; reduced transportation fares; tuition-reduced education; and recreation, leisure, and entertainment. This statutorily mandated duty only begins to touch on the myriad legal issues that pertain to the elderly population. Every state and territorial government has enacted legislation creating agencies that are empowered to administer, design, and advocate programs and services for their elderly citizens. These agencies may generically be called state units on aging.

Unfortunately, this century's boom in longevity is often accompanied by illness and an immediate need for personal caregiving. Illnesses may be life-threatening or chronic. Living longer means that the onset of age-related mental illness may increase. The growth in chronic illnesses has caregivers and legal practitioners focusing on the question of how to provide long-term care for anyone suffering from chronic illness. Families of the elderly do approximately 80 percent of the unpaid care of the nation's oldest citizens. In fact, very often only one family member takes on the role of the primary caregiver. One-quarter of people caring for elderly relatives do so from a distance. The duration of the caregiving averages 4.5 years. It has been estimated that the financial value of this unpaid care reaches $287 billion. The FMLA provides a federal safety net for working Americans who need to take time off from work to care for a family member suffering from an illness or who have their own medical condition to deal with.

KEY TERMS

Age Discrimination Act Of 1975	dementia	Older Americans Act (OAA)
Age Discrimination In Employment Act Of 1967	depression	ombudsman
	Family And Medical Leave Act (FMLA)	palliative care
Alzheimer's Disease (AD)		personalized legal plan
conservator	geriatric care manager	psychosis

REVIEW QUESTIONS

1. What was a major cause for the development and growth of the practice of elder law?

2. What areas of law meld together and are emphasized in a typical elder law practice?

3. What type of personality traits would be helpful to someone interested in entering the elder law field?

4. How can an elder law practitioner create a law office that is elder law client-friendly?

5. What can an elder law practitioner do to conduct a more therapeutically centered legal practice?

6. What types of programs offer assistance to America's elderly citizens?

7. What are the ramifications for people living in a state that imposes a duty to care for their elderly relatives?

8. What types of medical problems affect the nation's elderly?

9. What types of mental health problems affect the nation's elderly?

10. What ethical concerns, if any, could a lawyer or a paralegal have if an elder law client arrived at a law office accompanied by one of his adult children?

ETHICS ALERT

The question of who the firm's client is often arises in an elder law practice. For example, a son may bring his elderly father to a law firm for legal representation and insist on being involved in every step of the representation. If the son pays the attorney's fees, does that make the son the firm's client? Is the firm representing only the father? Is the firm representing both the father and the son? Should the attorney and paralegals share the father's information with the son? What if the father is impaired in some way? Does that matter?

HELPFUL WEB SITES

ADMINISTRATION ON AGING <HTTP://WWW.AOA.GOV> This agency oversees state and area agencies.

NATIONAL ASSOCIATION OF AREA AGENCIES ON AGING <HTTP://WWW.N4A.ORG> This association focuses on state and local aging programs.

ALZHEIMER'S ASSOCIATION <HTTP://WWW.ALZ.ORG> This site provides information about Alzheimer's disease.

NATIONAL FAMILY CAREGIVERS ASSOCIATION <HTTP://WWW.THEFAMILYCAREGIVER.ORG> This site offers caregivers an information resource.

NATIONAL CAREGIVERS LIBRARY <HTTP://WWW.CAREGIVERSLIBRARY.ORG> This is a research site.

NATIONAL INSTITUTE ON AGING <HTTP://WWW.NIA.NIH.GOV> This Web site is a clearinghouse for information on the aging process.

NATIONAL ASSOCIATION OF PROFESSIONAL GERIATRIC CARE MANAGERS <HTTP://WWW. CAREMANAGER.ORG> This site is designed for geriatric care professionals.

ALZHEIMER'S FOUNDATION OF AMERICA <HTTP://WWW.ALZFDN.ORG> This Web site provides information on Alzheimer's disease.

NATIONAL ACADEMY OF ELDER LAW ATTORNEYS, INC. <HTTP://WWW.NAELA.COM> This Web site focuses on the elder law speciality.

TRANSFORMING PRACTICES <HTTP://WWW.TRANSFORMINGPRACTICES.COM> This Web site states that it's purpose is to explore sources of meaning and pleasure in law practice.

NORTH STATE COOPERATIVE LIBRARY SYSTEM <HTTP://WWW.NSCLS.ORG> This organization has established a technical assistance program available nationally to all legal services, public interest, and pro bono attorneys who seek to enforce federally mandated rights against state governments and their agencies.

ENDNOTES

[1] The Institute for Continuing Legal Studies, *Updates in Elder Law Seminar*, New Brunswick, NJ, July 12, 2006.

[2] *<http://www.pbs.org/independent lens/sunset story/graying.html>*

[3] The role of a life care planning specialist is that of an advocate for an individual in need of assistance. This specialist studies and summarizes the medical, educational, vocational, physiological, and daily living needs of an individual and projects long-term costs of care and rehabilitative needs if applicable.

[4] There was a marked rise in the U.S. birth rate from 1946 to 1964. With this rising tide, the population increase is described as the baby boom and the children born during this period are called baby boomers. The explanation for this population boom is generally considered to be people's desire to have children before or after separations caused by war (the Second World War; the Korean War; and to a lesser extent, the Vietnam War). From *Sociology, Understanding a Diverse Society*, Second Edition, by Margaret L. Andersen and Howard F. Taylor, Wadsworth Cengage Learning, 2002, page 85.

[5] United States Census Bureau (2000).

[6] United States Department of Health and Human Services (2002).

[7] Hawkins, Barbara A., "Living Long, Aging Well," *Research & Creative Activity*, Vol. XXIV, Indiana University (2001).

[8] American Council on Life Insurance (2007).

[9] Ash, Lorraine, "Living Alone with Relish," *Daily Record*, March 22, 2004, page A6.

[10] Hawkins, Barbara A., "Living Long, Aging Well," *Research & Creative Activity*, Vol. XXIV, Indiana University (2001).

[11] Noland, Roberta, "Not All Office Environments Are Created Equal: Designing with Clients in Mind," *The National Paralegal Reporter*, October/November 2005, page 10.

[12] Morgan, Rebecca, "The Practical Aspects of Practicing Elder Law," *Family Law Quarterly*, Vol. 38, No. 2, Summer 2004.

[13] Segal, Troy, "Designed for a Comfortable Fit," *ABA Journal*, January 2000, page 76.

[14] Morgan, Rebecca, "The Practical Aspects of Practicing Elder Law," *Family Law Quarterly*, Vol. 38, No. 2, Summer 2004.

[15] Keeva, Steven, "Emotional Subtext," *ABA Journal*, December 2003, page 85.

[16] Carter, Terry, "Tell Us What You Want," *ABA Journal*, March 2006, page 27.

[17] Keeva, Steven, "What's the Story," *ABA Journal*, October 2004, page 88.

[18] "Therapeutic Interventions for Seniors," *Drug Store News*, Fall 2003, page 11.

[19] *Caring for Your Parents*, AARP Publication (2004).

[20] N.J. STAT. § 2C:24-8 (2006).

[21] *Caring for People with Alzheimer's Disease: A Manual for Facility Staff*, Second Edition, Lisa P. Gwyther, American Health Care Association and Alzheimer's Association (2001).

[22] American Council on Life Insurance (2007).

[23] Reisberg, B., and Kluger, A., Assessing the Progression of Dementia: Diagnostic Consideration. In Salzman, C. (ed.), *Clinical Geriatric Psychopharmacology*, Third Edition, Baltimore, MD, William & Wilkins, 1998, pages 432–462.

[24] Reisberg, B., and Kluger, A., Assessing the Progression of Dementia: Diagnostic Consideration. In Salzman, C. (ed.), *Clinical Geriatric Psychopharmacology*, Third Edition, Baltimore, MD, William & Wilkins, 1998, pages 432–462.

[25] Evans, D. A., Funkenstein, H. H., Albert, M. S., Scherr, P. A., Cook N. R., Chosw, M. J., Herbert L. E., Hennekens, C. H., and Taylor J. O., "Prevalence of Alzheimer's Disease in a Community Population of Older Persons: Higher Than Previously Reported," *JAMA*, Vol. 262, 1989, pages 2661–2556.

[26] Richards, S. S., and Hendric, H. C., "Diagnosis Management and Treatment of Alzheimer Disease," *Archives of Internal Medicine*, 1999, page 159.

[27] *Caring for People with Alzheimer's Disease: A Manual for Facility Staff*, Second Edition, Lisa P. Gwyther, American Health Care Association and Alzheimer's Association, 2001.

[28] Cummings, J. L., "Alzheimer's Disease," *New England Journal of Medicine*, 2004, pages 56–67.

[29] Bullock, R., "The Needs of the Caregiver in the Long-Term Treatment of Alzheimer Disease," *Alzheimer Disease and Associated Disorder*, 18 Suppl. 1, 2004, pages S17–S23.

[30] Caring for Your Parents, *AARP Publication* (2004).

[31] United States Census (2000).

[32] National Elder Abuse Incidence Study, Department of Health and Human Services, Administration on Aging, 1998.

[33] Grandparents Raising Grandchildren: Implications for Professionals and Agencies, Purdue University Cooperative Extension Service, National Conference, January 12, 1999.

[34] Podgers, James, "Who Is the Client?" *ABA Journal*, January 2004, page 49.

Online Companion™
For additional resources, please go to
http://www.paralegal.delmar.cengage.com

CHAPTER 2

Life Planning: Drafting a Last Will and Testament

■ OBJECTIVES

After completing this chapter, you will be able to:

- Identify last will and testament drafting requirements.
- Describe the testate versus intestate scenario.
- Explain the consequences of not following drafting requirements.
- List the steps of the probate administration process.
- Understand the significance of applicable statutory and common law authority.
- Define terminology associated with will creation and estate settlement.
- Identify and explain the roles of participants involved in will creation and probate administration.
- Describe questionable will creation.
- List the grounds for contesting a will.

"Father Time is not always a hard parent, and, though he tarries for none of his children, often lays his hand lightly upon those who have used him well; making them old men and women inexorably enough, but leaving their hearts and spirits young and in full vigour. With such people the grey head is, but the impression of the old fellow's hand in giving them his blessing, and every wrinkle, but a notch in the quiet calendar of a well-spent life."

CHARLES DICKENS

INTRODUCTION

last will and testament

A document in which a person directs how her property is to be distributed after her death.

will

The shortened term commonly used when referring to a last will and testament.

A **last will and testament** is a document in which a person directs how her property is to be distributed after her death. If all necessary formalities have been completed in the creation of the will, the legal system will help carry out the wishes of the person making the last will and testament. The legal system's process for recognizing a last will and testament's validity is called probate. A **will** is the shortened term commonly used when referring to a last will and testament. A will should be reviewed periodically to ensure its continuing accuracy.

Approximately 40 percent of Americans over 45 years of age have never drafted a will. Anyone with minor children, part of a nontraditional household, or a couple remarried with children from a previous marriage can benefit from taking the legal precaution of writing a will. A client does not have to have a large estate to benefit from life and estate planning, including the drafting of a will. In fact, more than one-third of Americans with investment portfolios of $10 million or more do not have wills.[1]

Some individuals may seek the security of drafting their wills as young adults. Other individuals may be emotionally wary of facing issues involving their death. Others may see the need for a will, but they have difficulty completing the business details of life. Still others may experience their first serious thoughts of writing a last will and testament after a life-altering experience. Perhaps, a marriage, a birth, an illness, a death, or a national emergency will be the impetus for realizing that it is time to come to terms with the natural progression of life. When an individual realizes that she is not going to live forever, it may jolt the person into serious thoughts about her future and that of her family. These thoughts often lead to the acknowledgment that a will is necessary, followed by the decision to seek an attorney's assistance. On occasion, elderly clients may have their first contact with an attorney when they finally decide to seek assistance drafting their will.

In general, a client's estate includes all of her assets, less all debt, plus death benefits from all life insurance policies not held in an irrevocable trust. Trusts will be discussed in Chapter 5.

client interview questionnaire

An information tool used by an attorney. It focuses on *all* aspects of life and estate planning when the attorney conducts an extensive and thorough client interview.

Once a client retains an attorney, the attorney should take the opportunity to complete an extensive and thorough client interview. A will may be the primary reason that a client comes to a law office; but if an attorney wants to do a thorough job, she should suggest that the client focus on *all* aspects of life and estate planning. Up-to-date estate plan documents maximize the chances that a client's wishes with respect to medical and financial affairs will be carried out in the event of the client's death or disability. Refer to Exhibit 2–1 to review a sample **Client Interview Questionnaire** that may be used to prepare for the drafting of a client's will and estate plan.

The legal requirements for properly executing a will vary from state to state. Some states follow the Uniform Probate Code (U.P.C.), and other states have enacted more state-specific legislation and follow their state's common law decisions. The U.P.C. is a uniform compilation of laws drafted to promote efficiency and uniformity among adopters. The U.P.C. has been adopted by at least 18 states.

Some readers of this textbook may have previously experienced an estates and trusts course. If so, this chapter will serve as a review of material covering issues of last wills and testaments. Readers who have not studied estates and trusts in depth should find this chapter and the upcoming chapter about trusts a helpful introduction to the material and a necessary part of gaining an understanding of elder law issues.

DRAFTING A WILL

The person who writes her own will is called the **testator**. Today, whether in a U.P.C. state or not, generally three elements must be present when a person writes a will. If any one of these elements is missing, the validity of the testator's will may become suspect. First, the testator must fully understand the legal consequences of writing a will. This first element is referring to the testator's mental intent to complete the act of writing her will. Second, the testator must know the full extent of her property. (The old-fashioned term *bounty* is often used in the explanation of this second element.) Third, the testator must know the names of the proper recipients of her property. (The proper recipients are usually considered the testator's family members). The second and third elements refer to the mental **capacity** of the testator. For example, is the testator aware that she owns stock in a certain company and does she know its value? Is the testator aware that her home is worth $500,000 dollars, not $50,000 dollars? Does the testator clearly communicate her wishes?

There are basically 3 types of bequests made by a testator in a will:

1. **General bequest**
2. **Specific bequest**
3. **Residuary bequest**

A general bequest is defined as any gift given by will. A specific bequest is defined as a gift named and identified in a will. A residuary bequest is defined as a gift given via a will after all general and specific bequests have been made. Other terms such as **beneficiary, devisee, and legatee** describe a person who inherits property through a will.

An *apportionment clause* included in a will can state from where any federal or state estate taxes due will be paid. This means that any tax burden can be apportioned among the beneficiaries and the residuary clause if the testator so

testator
The person who writes her own will.

capacity
A testator's mental ability to sign a will; the legal term used to identify whether a person is mentally competent.

general bequest
Any gift given by a will.

specific bequest
A gift named and identified in a will.

residuary bequest
A gift given via a will after all general and specific bequests have been made.

beneficiary, devisee, and legatee
A person who inherits property through a will.

lapsed

Refers to a devisee who predeceases a testator.

ademption

A situation when the testator has devised personal or real property to a beneficiary, but that property has been sold, given away to another, or lost.

real property

Land and things affixed to or growing on the land.

personal property

All things not considered real property, including intangibles (i.e., shares of stock and bank accounts).

tenancy in severalty

Ownership by one person. Also known as sole ownership.

sole ownership

Ownership by one person. Also known as tenancy in severalty.

joint tenancy

Where two or more owners have equal interests in acquired property at the same time and if one owner dies, that person's ownership interests automatically pass to the other owner without going through probate. This is usually known as right of survivorship.

chooses. Without such a clause, the applicable state statute applies. Some state statutes look completely to the residuary clause, or states following the U.P.C. apportion equally with a *pro rata* split among all beneficiaries.[2]

Generally, the law of wills followed across the country requires a devisee to survive the testator in order to take the bequest (i.e., the devise) from the will. If the devisee predeceases the testator, the gift is considered **lapsed**. The death of a devisee prior to the death of a testator can be problematic because the bequest to the deceased devisee may then be considered null and void in certain states. An exception to a lapsed bequest is created if a state has an *anti-lapse statute*. In such a case, the anti-lapse statute usually provides that a lapsed gift can pass only to the children of a deceased devisee. The ramifications of an anti-lapse statute can be avoided if the testator requires her beneficiaries to survive her; otherwise, a lapsed gift will result. Another problematic situation that is disappointing to a beneficiary is when the testator has identified the property to be given to the beneficiary, but the property has already been sold, given away to another, or lost. This situation describes what is technically known as an **ademption**. Once an ademption has occurred, the property is gone and the beneficiary cannot receive property the testator no longer possessed at her death.

Property Ownership and Wills

Both **real property** and **personal property** can be owned. Real property is defined as land and things affixed to or growing on the land. For example, buildings are considered affixed to land. Personal property is defined as all other things not considered real property, including *intangibles*. Examples of intangibles include shares of stock and bank accounts. Intangible property has no physical existence; rather, it represents the right to receive a tangible thing that may have value. Examples of tangible personal property are a client's recreational vehicle and jewelry. Real property can be owned in one of four ways:

1. **Tenancy in severalty** (also known as **sole ownership**)
2. **Joint tenancy**
3. **Tenancy in common**
4. **Tenancy by the entirety**, also known as **community property**

Not all property ownership can be transferred to another via a will.

Tenancy in severalty is defined as ownership by one person. Joint tenancy is defined as ownership of property where two or more owners have equal interests in acquired property at the same time and if one owner dies, that person's ownership interests automatically pass to the other owner without going through probate. This is usually known as a right of survivorship. The last surviving joint tenant is ultimately entitled to sole ownership (i.e., tenancy in severalty). Property owned via a joint tenancy cannot be transferred through a will.

Tenancy in common is defined as ownership interest in land by two or more persons called tenants in common that can be passed on to heirs or otherwise disposed of. Each tenant in common may own equal or unequal interests that are separate and undivided in the property. However, unlike joint tenants, a tenant in common owns a specific portion of the property and there is no right of survivorship; in addition, the property may pass to heirs. Each tenant in common usually shares any profits proportionate to her ownership. A joint tenancy or tenants in common ownership position may be turned into a sole ownership or tenancy in severalty. Joint tenants or tenants in common must file a *petition to partition* the real property. This may be done by agreement or through a court order following the filing of a petition seeking a partition.

Tenancy by the entirety is ownership similar to joint tenants, except that the owners must be husband and wife. Neither spouse has a share of the land because both hold the entire land as one owner. These definitions vary slightly in different states. A married couple would also want to determine if any property they own is subject to community property statutes. The subject of community property is covered in Chapter 6 as part of the discussion on overlapping marriage and elder law issues.

Another way to describe a type of real property ownership is to state the type of estate the real property is. Generally, an estate is described as a **fee simple absolute** or a **life estate** or a **tenancy for years**. Fee simple absolute is defined as a full estate in land with no ownership limitations. It is also called a fee simple estate, estate in fee, or a fee. This type of ownership provides the owner an unqualified and unlimited ownership interest.

A life estate is an ownership interest in property that lasts until a named person(s) dies. For example, a life estate would be created if a grandmother gave her grandson the deed to her home but retained the use of all or part of her home via that deed until her death. A life estate can be created via a will or a deed, and such an estate may be gifted or sold but will end when the original life estate tenant dies. The deed with the life estate should be recorded in the county where the property is located. Obviously, such a life estate would make the sale of the house less attractive to purchasers outside the grandmother's family, but the grandmother would likely be assured that she has a place to live. There is also a possible tax benefit when a life estate is created. For example, the grandmother should file a federal gift tax return when she transfers her home to her grandson and her life estate is created. If the grandmother later dies and her grandson sells the house, he will benefit from what is called a *stepped-up basis*. This means that the difference in the sales value of the house between the day the grandson receives the house and a future sale date (if the grandson sells the property) will be the amount used to compute the grandson's capital gains. A larger capital gain results in a higher capital gains tax. Tax savings are discussed further in Chapter 7.

---

tenancy in common

Ownership interest in land by two or more persons that can be passed on to heirs or otherwise

tenancy by the entirety

Legal ownership providing that property will pass solely to the surviving spouse.

community property

A person has a right to 50 percent of all of her spouse's assets from the day the couple is married and can be held liable for 50 percent of all of her spouse's debts as well.

fee simple absolute

An unqualified and unlimited ownership

life estate

An ownership interest in property that lasts until a named person(s) dies.

tenancy for years

Created when a lessor (landlord) and lessee (tenant) agree on a specific stated period for a lease to be in effect.

elective share statutes

Statutes that permit a spouse to take what she receives from a will.

pretermitted spouse statutes

Statutes that apply to spouses who have *not* been mentioned in their spouse's will.

forced share

Refers to the situation when a spouse is permitted to take a larger share when mentioned but left very little in a spouse's will.

trust

A legal mechanism by which one or more persons hold legal title to money or property for the benefit of another who holds equitable title.

testamentary trust

A trust included in a will and designed to take effect after a testator's death.

pretermitted child statutes

Statutes that give children born after the execution of a parent's will and not provided for in the will a share in the deceased parent's estate.

A tenancy for years is created when a lessor and a lessee agree on a specific stated period for a lease to be in effect. A lessor is another way of describing a landlord, and a lessee is another way of describing a tenant. Ownership of real property is transferred through a written, signed document called a deed. The deed is evidence and proof of ownership. The recording of a deed provides a chain of title to property.

Marriage and Wills

Two types of statutes pertain to wills that husbands and wives should know about. These include the **elective share statutes** and the **pretermitted spouse statutes**. Collectively, these statutes may be described as *taking against the will*.

Basically, the elective share statute states the following to the surviving spouse: *Take what you received from the will, or you have a choice of taking a statutorily predetermined share after your deceased spouse's debts are paid.*

The pretermitted spouse statutes apply to a surviving spouse who has *not* been mentioned in her deceased spouse's will. This can occur if a testator executed a will and then subsequently married or if while married the testator wrote a will and made no mention of a current spouse. The pretermitted spouse statute states the following to the surviving spouse: *If you are not mentioned in your spouse's will, the law will treat you as if your spouse had no will and died intestate.* The pretermitted spouse then will be eligible to take an intestate share of the testator's estate (which in most states is defined as at least half of the estate). The majority of states also give a spouse an intestate share unless it appears that the omission was intentional. If a spouse is mentioned but is left very little, the majority of states will allow the spouse to take what is called a **forced share**.

In the case of spouses who are marrying for the second (or third, fourth, etc.) time, there may be children from previous marriages to which both spouses wish to leave the majority of their assets. If that is the case, those spouses should create a **trust** instrument. A trust is an arrangement by which one person holds legal title to money or property for the benefit of another. A trust can be simple or complicated. A trust may be a separate legal document or may be incorporated into a client's will. When a trust is incorporated into a client's will, it is called a **testamentary trust**. The majority of states also have **pretermitted child statutes** that give children born after the execution of a parent's will and not provided for in the will a share in the deceased parent's estate. Minor children should not be left their inheritances outright. This forces the court to appoint a trustee for the property and may not result in the best investment options. Instead, any inheritance to a minor should be placed in a trust and an appropriate trustee appointed to direct the trust.

The drafting of different types of trusts can be part of estate planning. The topic is particularly important in elder law practice, and Chapter 5 is devoted to a general overview of the subject.

EXHIBIT 2–1   CLIENT INTERVIEW QUESTIONNAIRE

1. Client Name

2. Date of Birth

3. Social Security Number

4. Citizenship

5. If testator is a U.S. citizen, is citizenship by birth or naturalization?

6. Date/Place/Location of Naturalization Papers

7. Address of Legal Residence

8. Telephone Number

9. E-mail Address and Fax Number

10. Second Home Address

11. Telephone Number

12. E-mail Address and Fax Number

13. Has client executed a will previously?

14. Name of Spouse

15. Spouse's Date of Birth

16. Spouse's Social Security Number

17. Spouse's Citizenship

18. Address or Legal Residence of Spouse

19. Has client been divorced or widowed?

20. Name(s) of Former Spouse(s)

21. Is copy of final judgment of divorce attached?

22. If not, name of state and court of divorce

23. Names of Children

24. Addresses of Children

25. Names of Minor Children

(continues)

EXHIBIT 2–1 CLIENT INTERVIEW QUESTIONNAIRE *(continued)*

26. Name of Mother of Minor Children

27. Named Guardians and Addresses for Minor Children

28. Names and Addresses of Next of Kin

29. Names and Addresses of Grandchildren/Great-Grandchildren

30. Decisions Regarding Domestic Animals

31. Is there a durable power of attorney?

32. Is there a living will?

33. Is there a health care power of attorney? Are there primary and secondary health care proxy designees?

34. Decision Regarding Organ Donation

35. Automobiles Individually Owned

36. Real Property Owned

37. Mortgages: Mortgagee Name and Address

38. Mutual Funds Owned

39. Annuities Owned

40. Pension(s)/Individual Retirement Accounts/401K/403(b)/529 Plan

41. Individual Bank Accounts

42. Joint Bank Accounts

43. Certificates of Deposit

44. U.S. Treasury Funds/Bonds

45. Closely Held Corporate Shares

46. Partnership Interests

47. Sole Proprietorship Interest

48. Stock Options

49. Ownership Interest in Time-Shares

50. Burial Plot(s)/Location of Plot Records

51. Life Insurance

52. Medical Insurance

(continues)

EXHIBIT 2–1   CLIENT INTERVIEW QUESTIONNAIRE *(continued)*

53. Long-Term Care Insurance

54. Homeowner's Insurance

55. Automobile Insurance

56. Marine/Aircraft Insurance

57. Umbrella Coverage

58. Personal Property Coverage

59. U.S. Military Service/Location of Any Discharge Papers

60. Location of Safe-Deposit Box

61. Name(s) of Person(s) with Right to Enter Safe-Deposit Box

62. Assets in Foreign Countries

63. Social Security and Veterans' Benefits

64. Any Other Business Interests

65. Any Ownership Interests in Patents, Copyrights, Franchises, Licenses, Mineral Rights, etc.

66. Any Charitable Pledges

67. Any Pending Litigation

68. Any *Inter Vivos* Trusts Created by Client

69. Advance Gifts and Transfers Planned or Made

70. Named Executor

71. Named Secondary Executor

72. What testamentary trusts have been created and for whom

73. Named Testamentary Trustee(s)

74. Named Guardian(s)

75. Named Designated Beneficiaries

76. Addresses of Beneficiaries

77. Devises to Beneficiaries

78. Residuary Beneficiary

79. Appearance of Client/Evident Testamentary Capacity

80. Location of Tax Return

(continues)

EXHIBIT 2–1 CLIENT INTERVIEW QUESTIONNAIRE *(continued)*

81. Client's Accountant

82. Client's Financial Adviser

83. Client's Insurance Broker

84. Household Furniture/Appliances

85. Fine Art

86. Antiquities

87. Collectibles

88. Jewelry

89. Any judgments against others

90. Any judgments against self/business

91. Other

▦ **intestate**

A person who dies without having drafted a will

▦ **heir**

A person who will inherit property from a deceased person with or without a will.

▦ **distributee**

The term used to describe a person statutorily entitled to a decedent's property through the intestate statutes.

▦ **next of kin**

All persons entitled to inherit from a person who has not left a will.

▦ **intestacy statutes**

Each state's statutes that designate the beneficiaries of an individual who has died intestate.

WITHOUT A WILL: THE LAW OF INTESTATE SUCCESSION

Although drafting a will can provide individuals with control over how their property will be distributed after their death, many still fail to draft a will. Such a person is called an **intestate**. All 50 states consider a person who dies without a will to have died intestate. The proper term for a person who will inherit property from a deceased person with or without a will (both under the common law and in statutes) is **heir**. The term **distributee** also is used to describe a person statutorily entitled to a decedent's property through the intestate statutes. The term **next of kin** or kindred relationship is used to define all persons entitled to inherit from a person who has not left a will. Determining an intestate's next of kin can be done by looking to the consanguinity factors (i.e., blood relationships) of an intestate. For example, a daughter is related by consanguinity to her father and grandfather.

Each state has **intestacy statutes** that designate the beneficiaries of an individual who has died intestate. Such statutes vary from state to state as does the case law regarding intestacy issues. Terms such as *ancestor* and *descendant* can be used to describe family lineage. The term *affinity* describes a family relationship established through marriage.

Failure to have a will may not make a significant difference (e.g., if the decedent would have left her property to the same people designated as beneficiaries in the applicable intestate statutes). However, any real property owned by the decedent outside the decedent's domicile state will pass according to the state's intestate statutes. Without a will, probate courts will have more to say about other issues that can arise after a person dies intestate. Refer to Exhibit 2–2 to review a sample intestate statute.

EXHIBIT 2–2   SAMPLE ARIZONA INTESTACY STATUTE

§ 14-2103. Heirs other than surviving spouse share in estate

Any part of the intestate estate not passing to the decedent's surviving spouse under § 14-2102 or the entire intestate estate if there is no surviving spouse, passes in the following order to the following persons who survive the decedent: 1. To the decedent's descendants by representation; 2. If there is no surviving descendant, to the decedent's parents equally if both survive or to the surviving parent; 3. If there is no surviving descendant or parent, to the descendants of the decedent's parents or either of them by representation; 4. If there is no surviving descendant, parent or descendant of a parent, but the decedent is survived by one or more grandparents or descendants of grandparents, half of the estate passes to the decedent's paternal grandparents equally if both survive or to the surviving paternal grandparent or the descendants of the decedent's paternal grandparents or either of them if both are deceased with the descendants taking by representation. The other half passes to the decedent's maternal relatives in the same manner. If there is no surviving grandparent or descendant of a grandparent on either the paternal or the maternal side, the entire estate passes to the decedent's relatives on the other side in the same manner as the half.

Without a Will, What Happens to Property?

Each state has intestatacy statutes that clearly designate who will inherit property from an individual who has died but failed to leave a will. Without a written will, a judge must get involved and will look to the **degree of relationship** between the decedent and any statutorily designated heirs. Degree of relationship is defined as how closely relatives are related to each other. For example, brothers are related in the first degree; a grandparent and child, in the second degree. The individual who receives the first cut of an estate is a spouse. Next, any children receive a portion of the estate. If children have predeceased the decedent but the decedent has grandchildren, a *per stirpes* **distribution** will occur. *Per stirpes* distribution describes a method of dividing a deceased person's estate by giving out shares equally by representation or by family groups. For example, if John leaves $3,000 dollars to Mary and Sue and then Mary dies leaving her two children (Steve and Jeff), a *per stirpes* division gives $1,500 dollars to Sue and Mary's share would be divided between Steve and Jeff, each receiving $750.

Alternatively, *per capita* **distribution** may occur. If John used the *per capita* division and Mary predeceased both John and Sue, Sue would get the entire $3,000 dollars when John died. If a decedent does not have a spouse or children, the decedent's parents would be in line to receive the estate. Following parents comes any grandparents, followed by siblings. Each distributee statutorily

■ degree of relationship

How closely related relatives are to each other (e.g., brothers are related in the first degree; a grandparent and child, in the second degree).

■ per stirpes distribution

A method of dividing a deceased person's estate by giving out shares equally by representation or by family groups.

◼ *per capita* distribution

A method of dividing a deceased person's estate by giving out shares equally to the surviving beneficiaries.

◼ escheat

The forfeiture of property (including bank accounts) to the state.

receives a designated portion of an estate according to each state's applicable intestate statute. Some states provide that stepchildren and descendants of stepchildren of a decedent may be in line to inherit.

The statutory designation becomes more remote as it is determined which relatives have predeceased the decedent. If it appears certain that there are no named beneficiaries, heirs, descendants, or ancestors (regardless of how remote as long as the connection is proved), any property will **escheat** to the state. This means that the property will be forfeited to the state to do with as it chooses.

Some states that do not include stepchildren or descendants of stepchildren in the original intestate distribution chain provide that stepchildren or descendants of stepchildren of a decedent may be in line to inherit from a decedent's estate as an alternative to escheating to the state. This will occur if the decedent left no descendants, spouse, parents, grandparents, descendants of parents (i.e., siblings, nieces, or nephews), or descendants of grandparents (aunts, uncles, first cousins, or descendants of first cousins).

Ensuring Proper Will Execution

The formal requirements for properly executing a will vary from state to state depending on whether a state has adopted all or portions of the U.P.C. or has more state-specific requirements. Historically, some of this statutory variety developed because much of American law is based on England's legal system and England has had not one, but two statutes dealing with will execution.

Today some states have enacted variations of the two English statutes. The Statute of Frauds is one component of the English Statute of Frauds enacted in 1677 that dealt with wills (and numerous other legal issues). Following England's enactment of the Statute of Frauds, a will had to be written and signed by the testator in the presence of three witnesses for the will to be allowed to transfer land ownership legally. The English Wills Act (enacted in 1837) made the formalities even stricter, but reduced the required number of witnesses to two. Together the two witnesses had to observe the actual signing by the testator, and the testator had to sign the will at the end of the document. Some states now use a version of the Wills Act test by asking whether the testator was conscious of the witnesses signing as such.

The U.P.C. includes what is essentially a modern-day American version of a less strict English Statute of Frauds but leaves the witness number at two, as in the English Wills Act of 1837. The U.P.C. does require a will to be in writing. In fact, the majority of states require a will to be in writing. Generally, the writing may be word-processed, typed, printed, or handwritten (with certain limitations). The U. P.C. does not require that witnesses sign in the testator's presence. This latter U. P.C. position is not followed in all states. For example, in one interesting case, the testator signed his will while in a hospital as a patient. Two witnesses watched the testator sign his name when one witness, a nurse, was called away. While the nurse was gone, the testator and remaining witness signed the testator's will. The nurse momentarily returned and signed the will. Following the testator's death, the execution of the will was questioned because the nurse had left the room while the testator and the other witness signed the will. The court held that the will failed because the nurse did not *literally* see the testator sign.[3] This finding would be unlikely in states following the U.P.C. because U.P.C. Section 2-501 does not require a witness to sign in the presence of a testator.

The U.P.C Section 2-503, can be described as a significant change in the law regarding the legal formalities of wills. It permits a court to dispense with formalities if there is *clear and convincing evidence* that a decedent intended the document to be her last will and testament *even if all formalities were not followed.*

A testator usually must sign her will in order to validate it. However, there are exceptions to this requirement. All states permit another person to sign a will for a testator who is unable to do so. However, the will must be clear that such permission is being given. Attestation clauses facilitate probate by providing *prima facie* evidence that a testator voluntarily signed her will in the presence of witnesses. Such a clause is designed to prevent fraud and undue influence. An attestation clause also permits probating of a will when a witness forgets the circumstances of the will's execution or dies before the testator. On the other hand, self-proving affidavits are sworn statements by eyewitnesses that the will has been duly executed. Self-proving affidavits help ensure that the document presented as a testator's document reflects the complete and true intention of the testator. The term *subscribe* also may be used to describe the signing of a will. Refer to Exhibit 2–4 to read a sample of a self-proving affidavit at the end of a will drafted by Tara Jensen, Esq., for elder law client Henry Buss.

All states require a will to be witnessed by at least two witnesses, except Vermont, which requires three witnesses. The role of a will's witness is to verify that the testator is signing her last will and testament of her own free will. Each witness should be competent to fill that role (i.e., be able to testify as to the testator's mental capacity and the facts surrounding the will's execution). Witnesses should not be a beneficiary under the will, although the U.P.C. does validate wills with witness beneficiaries. This is not the case in some states where such an interested witness would forfeit her devise or bequest.

The best case scenario for the signing of a will has a testator signing her will at the end of the document. However, signature placement elsewhere in the will usually does not invalidate a will *if* the circumstances and the testator's intention can be verified. The witnesses should listen to the testator's responses and be in a position to clearly watch the testator initial each page of the will and sign the signature page. One of the witnesses should read the attestation clause of the will aloud. The reading should be followed by the witnesses watching the testator sign the will and then signing themselves. No state statute specifically requires that the witnesses sign after the attestation clause, but the use of an attestation clause permits the will to be considered duly executed and to be entered into probate *even* if the witnesses cannot be located or have predeceased the testator. A witness's signature on a will does not need to be notarized unless a self-proving affidavit is used.

It is an understatement to say that formal requirements for executing a will vary greatly from state to state. For example, one Texas court allowed a name stamp to be used by the testator to sign his name and found that it did not prevent a will from being considered valid. This would be questionable in the majority of states.[4] Problems can arise because of something as simple as failing to staple a will's pages together. Refer to Exhibit 2–3 to review a summary of the minimum steps that should be taken when formalizing a will.

EXHIBIT 2–3   BASICS OF WILL EXECUTION: LITERALLY PUTTING IT ALL TOGETHER

1. The testator must read and understand the will before signing it.

2. The lawyer should reinforce the seriousness of the signing to all participants, including the testator, witnesses, and notary if used.

3. The lawyer should reinforce for the witnesses and her own satisfaction that all of the elements necessary to prove the testator's mental capacity are present. Several standard questions should be asked aloud, including these: "Do you declare this to be your last will and testament? Have you read it, and do you understand it? Does it dispose of your property in accordance with your wishes?"

4. The testator should sign each page along the margin as well as at the end of the document.

5. The witnesses and notary, if used, should see the testator sign the will.

6. The witnesses should sign in the appropriate spots.

7. All pages of the will should be stapled together.

Safekeeping a Will

A testator's will and important papers should be located as soon as possible after her death. Failure to locate such documents can cause great difficulty for surviving family and friends.

Safekeeping of the will often falls by default to the attorney who drafted it; but according to experts in the field,[5] attorneys should not store clients' wills. However, an attorney storing a document will probably be the professional asked to assist in the estate administration process. Interestingly, some states permit their citizens to file and store wills with the clerk of their local probate court, but most people do not know about this opportunity. The U.P.C. provides for the deposit of a will in court for its safe protection.[6] A will is best kept with the testator in a safe, accessible location. A will should not be stored in the testator's safe-deposit box since a court order may be needed to enter the box after the testator's death. However, a safe-deposit box that is rented by a testator as a joint tenant with a spouse or some other significant person does permit access by the surviving joint tenant.

Less Than Perfect: Questionable Will Creation

Historically, it was popular to write a last will and testament in letter format. A handwritten will is called a **holographic will**. Interestingly, holographic wills have been written on a nurse's slip and an eggshell and even scratched on a tractor fender.[7] In at least one case, a plaster wall was used to write a will. The piece of plaster was eventually recognized as a valid will, but transportation of the will to the surrogate's office destroyed the wall.[8] A significant number of states still accept a holographic will as a valid format, but such a will can be more easily challenged.

A questionable will format is the **oral will**. The oral will is technically known as a **nuncupative will**. The nuncupative will is accepted by a minority of states but only during wartime conditions or from a testator's deathbed. States that do accept a nuncupative will may limit its use to the passing of personal property only; in addition, these states usually require witnesses. The U.P.C. does not permit the nuncupative will format.

Another ill-advised format is the use of joint, or mutual, wills. The sharing of one will by two individuals is likely to invite litigation.

Using Form Wills

A minority of states have statutorily authorized simple fill-in-the-blank will forms. Refer to the Elder Law Online Supplement to review blank wills that have been used in California and Michigan. A great deal of commentary (and quite a few problems) has been written about some form wills because they are typically completed without the aid of professional legal guidance.[9]

How to Change or Revoke a Will

A **codicil** is an addition to a will that changes the will. A better idea is to go through the process of writing an new will rather than attaching a codicil to the original will. In an age of computers and word processing, this is not as difficult as it sounds. A codicil is not the best choice when making changes to a will; if a beneficiary is taken out of a will in a codicil, the beneficiary has standing to challenge the will.

The majority of courts take the position that if a will is not lawfully revoked, it continues until the testator's death. Three legal terms describe the revocation of a will:

holographic will
A handwritten will.

oral will
Technically known as a nuncupative will.

nuncupative will
A type of will accepted by a minority of states but only during wartime conditions or from a testator's deathbed.

codicil
An addition to a will that changes the will.

■ **revocation by a physical act**

A will may be revoked when the testator purposely destroys it.

■ **revocation by operation of law**

A will may be revoked subsequent to a divorce or marriage.

■ **revocation by subsequent writing**

A will is considered revoked when a new will is written.

1. **Revocation by a physical act**
2. **Revocation by operation of law**
3. **Revocation by subsequent** (or *later*) **writing**.

A will is considered revoked by a physical act if the testator purposely destroys it. Revocation of a will by operation of law can occur subsequent to a divorce or marriage. A will is generally considered revoked when a new will is written. The new will should clearly state that the old will is revoked. It is extremely important for any subsequent will to revoke all past wills; otherwise, confusion and legal problems may result.

The burden of proving that a revocation was not intended is on the person making such a claim. This is a heavy burden if the will is damaged or marked as *canceled* or *revoked*. Of course, the suspicion can be claimed that someone damaged or marked up the will so that it would be rejected for probate. However, if the allegedly valid but marked-up, canceled, or revoked will is found in the testator's home or among her effects, it is usually assumed that the testator intended to revoke the will. Evidence that the testator intended to make or did make a new will that was inoperative may throw light on the question of intention to revoke the old one, but it can never revive a will once it has been completely revoked.

To Err Is Human, But Still Unacceptable

Lawyers and their support staff can get into all sorts of difficulties if they fail to follow their particular state's technical requirements for drafting and executing a will. For example, one case ended with public censure of a lawyer who erred with something as simple as names. The attorney in the case wrote valid wills and spelled the clients' names correctly, but he missed the error of the husband signing the wife's will and vice versa.[10] Of course, the attorney in this case carried the weight of complete responsibility; but an eagle-eyed paralegal would have been a great help in catching the error and averting professional disaster for her employer.[11]

A number of will creation and execution scenarios test the outer boundaries of formalities. For example, would a handwritten bequest added after the typed-up portion of a will be valid?[12] The U.P.C Section 2-502 (c) states that if a printed will has handwritten language on it, the testamentary intent can be established for a holographic will by looking at portions of the will that are not in the testator's handwriting. Not all states concur.

Do witnesses have to sign the will before the testator's death? It may seem obvious, but witnesses in the majority of states must sign a will before the testator's death.[13] However, some states stretch that rule. For example, in New Jersey, a court held that a witness could sign an attestation a reasonable time after the testator's death. The definition of what a New Jersey court found reasonable was answered when it was determined in a later case that a witness signing a will 15 months after a testator's death was too long.[14]

Generally well-known rules must be adhered to in the drafting and execution of a will. For example, witnesses to a will should not also be beneficiaries of the will. What happens if a signing witness to a will also is a named beneficiary? The answer depends on the state in which the will was signed. A relatively small minority of states (approximately one-third) allow a witness to be a beneficiary. The majority of states void any devise made to an attesting witness. If the state follows the U.P.C., an interested witness does not forfeit a gift under the will.

What happens if a testator signs an X as her signature? Would a will with only a signed X be valid?[15] What if a testator wrote this in her will:*I revoke the legacy to Judy since I have already given her $5,000 dollars.* However, the testator did not give Judy $5,000 dollars.[16]

Dealing with a Conflict of State Laws

If a question arises of what state laws should be applied to a client's case, the most common conflict of law rule usually directs the questioner to apply the law of the state where the decedent's **domicile** was at her death. A domicile is defined as a person's home state. A person can have only one domicile, but she may have an unlimited number of residences. The location of real property dictates the laws that apply to the disposition of real property. The best-case scenario has a lawyer drafting a will and executing it in a manner that satisfies the formal requirements of wherever a testator owns real property. In addition, if property is owned in a foreign country, a will should comply with any applicable foreign laws.

Usually, under conflict of law rules, the following applies:

1. The laws of the domicile state determine the distribution of personal property.

2. Real property is distributed according to the laws of the states in which the property is located

3. Usually a will is considered valid if it was executed as required where the decedent was domiciled or the state where the will was executed or where the testator was domiciled when the will was executed.

domicile
A person's home state. A person can have only one domicile.

ELDER LAW PRACTICE

Sixty-five-year old Henry Buss is in good health and has the mental capacity to prepare a will. However, Henry knows enough about the law to understand that good intentions do not equal good preparation. He is married to Lila; and they have a minor daughter, Dana. He and Lila have decided to go to an attorney, Tara Jensen, for drafting their wills. Both Henry and Lila, older parents, are most concerned about providing for their daughter. Refer to Exhibit 2–4 to read Henry Buss's last will and testament and note the provisions made for Dana. What problems could arise if Dana survived her parents while she was still a minor and her parents had failed to draft their wills? Each clause of Henry Buss's will is named to ensure easier identification of its purpose.

EXHIBIT 2–4 SAMPLE OF A WILL: LAST WILL AND TESTAMENT OF HENRY BUSS

Exordium Clause

I, Henry Buss, being of sound mind and disposing memory, residing at 568 West Knowles Avenue, New Jersey, I hereby make, publish and declare this document to be my **Last Will and Testament.**

Revocation Clause

1.) I do hereby revoke all former Wills and codicils made by me.

Marriage Clause

2.) I am married to Lila Buss, and have been so married since March 25, 1989.

Children's Clause

3.) I have 1 child, Dana Buss, born October 5, 1993. Dana resides with her mother and me.

Payment of Debts Clause

4.) I direct that all my lawful debts, including funeral expenses, expenses for my last illness, if applicable, and the expense of the administration of my estate, be paid by my Executor named below, or the successor thereof, as soon as practicable after my death.

Burial Clause

5.) I direct that my body be cremated after my death.

Appointment of Guardian and Successor Guardian Clause

6.) If my spouse shall not survive me or is incapacitated, and it is necessary that a guardian be appointed for our children born or not yet born, I name and appoint Karen Richards of Montclair, New Jersey, to be the guardian of Dana and any child or children hereafter born to me, until they have reached majority. If the FIRST guardian shall cease or be unable to serve for any reason, I name and appoint Charlotte Richards of Montclair, New Jersey, as guardian of Dana or any child or children born hereafter, until they have reached majority age.

Appointment of Executor aka Personal Representative Clause
Note that a bond is not required.
Description of Executor's aka Personal Representative's Powers Clause
Successor Executors aka Personal Representatives Named Clause

7.) I appoint and nominate Lila Buss as Executor of this Will, to serve without bond, and I hereby grant full powers and authority to the said Executor to use the fullest discretion in all matters and questions relevant to the carrying out of the matters directed in this Will. If my wife, Lila Buss, shall die before me or shall cease or be unable to serve for any reason, then I appoint and nominate Bradley Ryan of 28 Jefferson Terrace, Oakwood, as Executor of this, my last Will and Testament, with the same conditions as described.

a.) The said powers, authority and discretion shall include (but shall not be limited to) complete authority to sell at public or private sale for cash or credit with or without security and/or to invest, reinvest, mortgage, compromise and settle claims, lease, pledge and dispose of all property, at such time and upon such terms and conditions as she may solely determine. I hereby relieve the other parties to such transactions from all obligations to inquire into the necessity or propriety thereof, or to see to the application of the consideration above. The foregoing power of sale of real estate is given

(continues)

EXHIBIT 2–4   SAMPLE OF A WILL: LAST WILL AND TESTAMENT OF HENRY BUSS *(continued)*

not only for the purpose of the administration of my estate but for the purpose of selling any or all of the same and distributing the proceeds to my residuary beneficiaries herein above set forth if in the judgment of my Executor such action is for best interest of my estate.

b.) To retain as investments, or otherwise, any property owned by me at the time of my death, or distributed by my Executor and to increase the investment in any such property; and to make other investments in, and to exchange any property for, any securities of any corporation; any obligations of any government, state, county municipality or political subdivision or instrumentality, domestic or foreign; any real estate or improvements thereon; any other investment of any kind; all in the absolute discretion of my Executor or my Trustee as may be deemed proper; whether or not any such investments are authorized by law as proper for the investment of trust funds.

c.) To take part in any manner in any reorganization or other corporate change affecting my securities held.

d.) To exercise any privilege to convert any securities into other securities; and to exercise any right to subscribe for any securities; or to dispose of any such privilege or right.

e.) To keep any securities registered in the name of any nominee or in bearer form, my intention being not to require any securities to be registered in the name of my Executor or my Trustee.

f.) To pay over the full net income to the person beneficially entitled, without reserving any sinking fund either to meet the wearing away of premiums of securities received or bought above par or for any other purpose, or in the absolute discretion of my Executors or my Trustees, or to treat the total income received from any assets during the administration of my estate by Executor as income of my residuary estate without apportioning any of it.

g.) To decide whether and to what extent any dividend or other distribution, whether payable in cash, stock, bonds or otherwise, is to be added the principal of the trust or distributed as income thereunder.

h.) Except as otherwise provided above, upon the division of my estate, or the payment of any legacy, or the settling up of the trust or the distribution of any fund, at the option of my Executor or my Trustee, as the case may be, to divide and distribute, in whole or in part, in kind, instead of selling any asset and dividing and distributing the proceeds; and for this purpose to determine the then current market values of the various assets held by my Executor or my Trustee; and to assign and distribute such assets at the values so determined, which shall be conclusive and binding on all concerned.

i.) To make and carry out any agreements relating to any property held by my Executors or my Trustee and to execute any Trustee and to execute any papers on any terms deemed by it exercising any of its powers.

j.) To borrow money from other or from itself, whether to pay taxes, exercise options or subscription rights, pay assessments, or to accomplish any other purpose of any nature incidental to the administration of my estate or of the trust or powers in trust hereunder, and to mortgage or pledge as security therefore any property constituting a part of my estate at any time held by it hereunder.

k.) To determine what expenses, fees, costs and charges of all kind shall be charged against income and what against principal, and to make such charges and elections without the necessity or making reimbursement or adjustment of estate accounts or beneficiaries; shares or in their absolute discretion, to make such adjustment or reimbursement as they may deem advisable.

(continues)

EXHIBIT 2–4 SAMPLE OF A WILL: LAST WILL AND TESTAMENT OF HENRY BUSS *(continued)*

Testamentary Trust for Testator's Child Clause
Appointment of Testamentary Trust Trustee Clause
Successor Trustee Named Clause

8.) If any beneficiary under the Will shall be under the age of twenty-five (25) years at the time he or she becomes entitled to the distribution herein, then the payment of such entitlement shall not be made, but shall be deferred until such beneficiary reaches twenty-five (25) years of age. Such entitlement shall, instead, be held by the Trustee herein appointed under this Will, in trust for and on behalf of that beneficiary. The Trustee is hereby directed to invest the said entitlement in such income yielding ventures as the Trustee may deem proper, and the income as well as such amounts of the principal as are necessary, even to the extent of all, shall be applied to the support, general welfare and education of the said beneficiary until he or she reaches the age of twenty-five (25) years whereupon the remaining principal and income of the trust, if any, shall be paid to the beneficiary.

I appoint Lila Buss of 568 West Knowles Avenue, New Jersey as Trustee under this Will, to act without bond and with full powers. If the first named Trustee shall be unavailable or unwilling or unable to serve for any reason, I name and appoint Bradley Ryan as Trustee under the same powers and condition. I direct that no Executor or Trustee shall be entitled to receive any commissions for acting as such.

Legacies Clause

9.) I hereby give, devise, and bequeath any and all articles of tangible personal property to my wife, provided she survives me. If my wife shall not survive me, I give all such tangible personal property, to my daughter, Dana, if she is my only child, or if more children have been born then the children shall share all of my tangible personal property equally.

Residuary Clause

10.) After my lawful debts are paid, I give all the residuary of my estate to my wife, in the event that my said wife shall predecease me or fails to survive me for sixty (60) days, I give all my residuary estate to my daughter, Dana, or if more children have been born then to my children equally, *per stirpes.*

Simultaneous Death Clause

11.) In the event that my wife and I shall die together as a result of a common disaster, or under circumstances such that it cannot be readily determined who died before the other, it shall be presumed for purposes of this Will and my estate that I died before her.

Testimonium Clause

IN WITNESS WHEREOF, I hereby sign, seal and declare this as my Last Will and Testament on this date, the _____ day of the month of May 2008 in the presence of the subscribing witnesses.

_____
Henry Buss

Self-Proving Affidavit Clause with Required and Witnessing Affidavits
AFFIDAVIT OF ATTESTING WITNESSES
TO THE WILL OF HENRY BUSS

(continues)

EXHIBIT 2–4   SAMPLE OF A WILL: LAST WILL AND TESTAMENT OF HENRY BUSS *(continued)*

Whereupon, the said persons, as each of them individually signed and appended his/her respective name and address to this document, and while being severally sworn, individually and collectively stated under oath, that they witnessed the execution of the Last Will and Testament of HENRY BUSS, the within named Testator, on _____, 2008; that the Testator, in their presence, subscribed to and signed the Last Will and Testament at the end, and, that at the time of the said making of the subscription, he/she declared the instrument to be the Testator's Last Will and Testament; that at the request of the Testator and in the Testator's sight and presence, and in the sight and presence of each other, the said persons witnessed the execution of the Last Will and Testament by the Testator by subscribing their own names as witnesses to it; and that the Testator at the time of the execution of the Last Will and Testament, appeared to them to be of full age and sound mind and memory and was in all respects competent to make a will and was not under any restraint.

Attestation Clause

The SUBSCRIBING WITNESSES FURTHER STATE UNDER OATH that this Affidavit is hereby being executed at the request of HENRY BUSS, the Testator who made the Last Will and Testament; and that at the time of the execution of this Affidavit, the original Last Will and Testament, above described, was exhibited to them and they identified it as such a Last Will and Testament by their signatures appearing on it as subscribing witnesses.

SIGNATURES, NAMES & ADDRESSES OF WITNESSES

Signature   _____

Print Name   _____

Address   _____

Signature   _____

Print Name   _____

Address   _____

Signature   _____

Print Name   _____

Address   _____

STATE OF NEW JERSEY)

COUNTY OF MORRIS) ss.:

On this date, the _____ day of _____ 2007 HENRY BUSS personally appeared before me, a Notary Public duly authorized to administer the oath in and for the above captioned County and State, and the undersigned persons, who are known to me or have been made known to me.

Severally subscribed and sworn to before me on _____ 2008.

_____

Notary Public

CHOOSING THE RIGHT PERSON

personal representative

The person who administers a decedent's estate and is responsible for carrying out the wishes of the decedent's will or is appointed by the court to follow intestate guideline.

executor

A personal representative who manages, administers, and distributes a decedent's estate according to the terms of a will.

executrix

A female executor.

administrator

A personal representative appointed by the state to manage, administer, and distribute a decedent's estate when there is no will.

administratrix

A female administrator.

fiduciary

A person who manages money or property for another person and in whom that other person has a right to place great trust.

Usually one person is named in a will as the person who will ensure that all of the bequests are distributed, that all of the probate property of the testator is transferred, and that all of the estate's creditors and taxes are paid. The U.P.C. uses the term **personal representative** to describe a man or woman who manages, administers, and distributes a decedent's estate according to the terms of a will or the appropriate state statute if the decedent has died testate. Some states call this person an **executor**. Some states have used the old-fashioned term **executrix** to describe a female executor. If there is no will, a court will name a person called a personal representative in U.P.C. states and an **administrator** in non-U.P.C. states to ensure that the estate is properly distributed. Some states have used the old-fashioned term **administratrix** to describe a female administrator. The responsibilities of a personal representative/executor are usually stated in a will. These responsibilities can be reviewed in Article 7 of the Last Will and Testament of Henry Buss in Exhibit 2–4.

A personal representative/executor or an administrator is taking on serious responsibility when he or she accepts the role. This responsibility has been designated by both statutory and common law as a *fiduciary duty*. A **fiduciary** is a person who manages money or property for another person and in whom that other person has a right to place great trust. Fiduciaries are viewed by the courts as having to rise to a higher standard of ethics and *malfeasance* on their part; for example, self-dealing or embezzlement of estate funds is viewed as a particularly heinous deed.

The duties of an executor/personal representative or administrator encompass the details of settling an estate. These details can include:

1. Locating all of the testator's real and personal property.

2. Paying creditors and taxes.

3. Ensuring the smooth transfer of the assets to the heirs as per the will or applicable statute.

4. Locating witnesses to a will.

5. Obtaining death certificates.

6. Hiring professional assistance (e.g., attorneys, accountants, household assistance, appraisers, and/or estate sales personnel).

7. Dealing with financial investments.

8. Contacting beneficiaries.

9. Overseeing the practical maintenance of assets that may include buildings, businesses, and other investments.

A personal representative/executor may have to deal with a will contest. A will contest happens when someone disagrees with the validity of the will and legally claims that the will should be judged invalid by the appropriate court. For example, one claim may be that the testator was improperly influenced by a beneficiary. Contests happen in fewer than three percent of all wills probated.[17]

A prospective personal representative/executor should discuss her duties with the testator before agreeing to act as the personal representative/executor of the testator's estate. Obviously, wills that disinherit close family members and leave inequitable or shocking distributions to others will likely result in discontent and probably lead to lawsuits and hard work for a personal representative/executor. If the nominated personal representative/executor knows that the testator is the type of person to dispose of very little, the personal representative/executor is likely to work harder than she would have liked in organizing the testator's paperwork and property.

An unwilling personal representative/executor fearing personal liability may ask a testator to include a clause in the testator's will that restricts the executor's personal liability, except in circumstances of *gross negligence*. Some states also have statutes prohibiting personal representative/executor liability unless there has been intentional or gross negligence. In addition, both U.P.C. and non-U.P.C. states usually provide that a personal representative/executor may be asked to purchase a bond. Most states require an executor or administrator to post a **bond** to protect the estate. A bond is a document that promises to pay money if a particular future event happens; it also is a sum of money that is put up and will be lost if the event happens. However, the testator can personally waive the bond requirement in her will.

bond

A document that promises to pay money if a particular future event happens; also a sum of money that is put up and will be lost if the event happens.

Most clients choose a trusted relative or friend who the client believes is capable of handling the financial duties of the job. Some states restrict a client's choice by mandating that the executor be domiciled in the same state as the testator. It is always advisable to select an alternate executor. It is allowed but ill-advised to name an executor who also is a beneficiary. This joint position can promote the appearance of conflict of interest.

All 50 states have eligibility requirements for individuals who want to accept a position as a personal representative/executor or administrator. All states require a personal representative/executor or an administrator to be a certain age, have a certain mental capacity, be of sound moral character (e.g., no criminal history), and be able to complete her duties. There are a variety of additional nonresident requirements; however, a nonresident usually can be appointed successfully as a personal representative/executor.

ESTATE ADMINISTRATION

Although a will designates a personal representative/executor or a judge appoints a personal representative/administrator to be in charge of ensuring that an estate is properly dealt with, many personal representatives/executors and administrators seek the assistance of an attorney and the attorney's staff to ensure that the process of settling an estate goes smoothly. The will should provide that the executor is free to hire professional help.[18] Paralegals need to learn the estate administration process because the process entails plenty of client contact, paperwork, and procedural steps that they can handle under an attorney's supervision. A general overview of the estate administration process follows.

Learning the location of a decedent's last domicile is necessary to determine which county court has jurisdiction over a person's probate estate. The administration of estates is under the jurisdiction of state courts whether the factual scenario involves a will or intestacy. The courts having this limited jurisdiction over wills, estate administration, guardianships, and trusteeships may be called a Surrogate's Court, a Chancery Court, or an Orphan's Court depending on the state. This type of court follows the state's procedures; and its powers and responsibilities are described in each state's statutes, court rules, or case law. An official called a Surrogate (or Registrar in some states or Register of Wills in others) is usually not a judge and may be appointed or elected to this position. This office typically provides all of the forms necessary for completing the probate process. The probate process provides the mechanism for a will to be filed officially with the testator's county of domicile and for a testator's or an intestate's property to be legally distributed to her heirs.

A death certificate must be obtained. Funeral directors (if used) typically order these for the family of the deceased. The attorney for the estate should review the death certificate. If she finds an error, the law firm may need to assist in having the certificate amended. For example, simple spelling errors or the wrong residence can have consequences. Multiple copies of the death certificate usually are necessary to probate a will. For example, a death certificate will be needed when dealing with any bank where the decedent had an account.

Initiating Probate

The probating of a will can usually be initiated in at least two ways, but different procedures may be followed depending on individual states. For example, the personal representative/executor may go to a Surrogate's Court alone (i.e., *ex parte*) without notice being given to anyone and request that the will be admitted to probate. Another way that a will can be probated is to give all beneficiaries listed in the will *notice* and apply to have a hearing before a judge. This hearing involves testimony regarding whether the will should be admitted to probate. If a decedent/testator owned real property in a state(s) other than her state of domicile, a secondary probate procedure called **ancillary administration** must be begun in the state(s) where the real property is located. This protects creditors of the decedent/testator in the ancillary state. Ancillary administration usually includes the following steps:

1. Accepting the will in the ancillary state

2. Issuing letters of authority (which may be called Letters Ancillary Testamentary)

3. Paying taxes due to the ancillary state

A separate personal representative may have to be appointed if the ancillary state does not allow the domiciliary personal representative/executor to administer the foreign estate. The U.P.C. gives a domiciliary personal representatives priority of appointment in ancillary matters.

If a will is considered **self-proved**, it usually will be admitted to probate without further proof of proper execution. Self-proving (also called **self-authentication** in some states) is proof that a document is genuine. For example, many states allow a will to be self-authenticated if a notary public, two witnesses, and the testator signed at the same time and place. Self-proving a will saves the time-consuming process of gathering the will's witnesses and having them provide affidavits of authentic execution. If witnesses have scattered since the signing of a will that is not self-proved, a paralegal may be asked to assist in locating them. Once the witnesses are found, they may be deposed in their own county of residence and asked to attest to the authentication of the execution of the will. If the witnesses are deceased, usually the authentication of the testator's and witness's signatures may be proved by another. Finally, then, the will can be admitted to probate. Obviously, self-proving a will at the time it is first signed is more efficient and cost-effective.

If a person dies intestate, her next of kin will need to apply to the appropriate court for **letters of administration**. (Some states use a different term to describe the same thing.) Again, the next of kin can seek out the services of an attorney and her staff to assist with the decedent's estate. Usually the personal representative/administrator of the intestate estate will be asked to file an affidavit acknowledging her fiduciary duty to the estate and to post a bond. In addition, the personal representative/administrator may need to file a separate form requesting *execution of a power of attorney* and a *form of judgment*. The court also may appoint a personal representative/administrator when there is a will but the nominated executor has died or refused to accept the position.

An alternative to letters of administration can occur in most states when the surviving spouse or next closest kin can provide what is generally called an **affidavit in lieu of administration**. This affidavit states that the estate's monetary value does not exceed a certain statutorily designated amount. This amount is typically under $10,000. Such a low estate value means that the estate can be settled more quickly.

ancillary administration

Additional probate administration required to distribute any property owned by a decedent in a state other than the decedent's domiciliary state.

self-proved

Proof that a document is genuine. Also called self-authentication.

self-authentication

Proof that a document is genuine. Also called self-proved.

letters of administration

An appointment by the court granting a named individual as the personal representative/ administrator of an intestate decedent.

affidavit in lieu of administration

An alternative to letters of administration wherein the estate's monetary value does not exceed a certain statutorily designated amount.

The Work of the Estate

Once a will has been admitted to probate or letters of administration have been issued, there can be a long list of duties to which the personal representative/executor must attend. The personal representative/executor may utilize assistance from an attorney and paralegals. Usually there is a deadline for the personal representative/executor to send a copy of the will and probate information to all beneficiaries. All states direct personal representatives/ executors and administrators to pay debts according to their state's *abatement statute*. The abatement statute provides in what order a decedent's assets are used to pay the debts of an estate. Abatement can result in a beneficiary's devise being used to pay debts.

The living joint tenants of bank account owned with the deceased can draw on any bank accounts up to half the amount in the accounts. The other half can be withdrawn only with a *tax waiver*. The personal representative, executor, or administrator can also usually withdraw up to half the funds. The personal representative/executor or administrator usually opens a new checking account to pay the debts of the estate. The personal representative, executor, or administrator can be responsible for claiming any insurance proceeds. Again, a death certificate, a Surrogate's certificate, and the insurance company's own *claim form* must be provided. The personal representative, executor, or administrator will have to transfer to the proper beneficiary any vehicles owned by the testator. This is usually done by presenting a certificate of ownership to the local motor vehicle agency, endorsing the certificate of ownership, and presenting a Surrogate's certificate. Stocks and bonds usually can be transferred by sending the designated transfer agent the stock certificates together with stock powers including affidavits of domicile and Surrogates' certificates. Stocks owned in joint names are not considered probate assets and can be transferred to sole ownership without a Surrogate's certificate. Real estate transfers are done by written deed. Such deeds are generally drafted by an attorney or a title property agency.

Any debts that the estate owes are paid off by the personal representative, executor, or administrator. If the estate does not have enough funds to pay all of the creditors, most states provide a statutory guideline for who gets paid first. Usually a personal representative, executor, or administrator must file a public notice in an *official legal newspaper* so that any outstanding creditors are notified to come forward within a designated period of time (defined in state statutes) to make their claims against the decedent's estate. This is done so that the personal representative, executor, or administrator has to wait only a certain amount of time to distribute the assets of the estate so she can move forward with closing the estate.

The personal representative/executor or administrator also is responsible for filing the final tax return for the decedent and the fiduciary income tax return providing the income of the estate after the death of the decedent. The tax return in the name of the estate is filed using a separate tax identification number with a form supplied by the Internal Revenue Service. Of course, state estate tax forms (if a state has an estate tax) and federal estate tax forms may have to be filed. Again, there are time deadlines for filing estate tax returns.

TRANSFERRING PROPERTY *OUTSIDE* THE PROBATE PROCESS

A person may have a will but still want to transfer her real or personal property without going through the probate process. Reasons for avoiding probate may include the fact that a will becomes a public document filed with the decedent's county of domicile for *anyone to read*. Refer to "Helpful Web Sites" at the end of the chapter to view a site that includes wills of the famous and infamous, including Marilyn Monroe and Chief Justice Warren Burger. In addition, tax savings may be possible when property is not transferred solely through the probate process. The legal mechanisms created to conduct these transfers without going through the probate process are often called **will substitutes**. These substitutes may include trusts; life insurance policies; pensions; retirement or investment accounts; bank accounts; joint tenancy; *inter vivos* gifts; and in the state of Washington, a community property agreement. The state of Washington (a community property state) provides that spouses may draft a community property agreement as a will substitute. The community property agreement upon the death of the first spouse provides that the community estate is transferred to the surviving spouse without going through the state's probate process administration. More about these will substitutes will be covered in later chapters. For example, Chapter 5 concentrates on the creation and uses of trusts. Chapter 7 concentrates on financial planning and retirement issues.

will substitutes
Legal mechanisms created to conduct the transfer of real or personal property without going through the probate process.

Retirement Accounts

Every individual retirement account (IRA) or company retirement plan asks its owner to name a beneficiary on the account's form. Filling in a spouse's name is easy to do and is even easier to forget to change after a divorce or death. A huge mistake is made if minor children are named as beneficiaries or as contingent beneficiaries because a minor cannot legally hold assets in her name. This means that a probate court is forced to name a guardian for the funds inherited outright by minors; typically, a financial institution is named as a guardian. This is an added expense that will chip away at the inheritance. Some states require that any money inherited without specific direction be automatically distributed to a child when she reaches the age of majority. Age of majority is 18 years of age in most states.

Failure to name a beneficiary of investment accounts results in the proceeds of the account going to the owner's estate and if there is a will, being distributed through the residuary clause of the owner's will. An intestate estate provides that those proceeds will be distributed according to the inheritance statutes of each state.

Bank Accounts

Several types of multiple party bank accounts can cause problems if they are not dealt with properly following a death. They are bank accounts that transfer outside the probate process. These bank accounts include the following:

1. Joint and survivor accounts
2. Payable-on-death accounts
3. Agency accounts
4. Savings account trust, also known as a Totten trust

Payable-on-death accounts are not recognized by all states. These accounts are invalid in some states because they are considered a testamentary account not executed with the formalities of a will. The savings account (or Totten) trust is accepted in the majority of jurisdictions.

Life Insurance

Life insurance is another example of an asset that passes outside a will (i.e., outside the probate process). However, it still may still be considered part of the decedent's taxable estate (for both federal and state tax purposes) unless certain precautions are taken.

An unfortunate true case involved a man, his first wife, his second wife, and his stepson. The man had been acrimoniously married to wife one for a short time. The man and wife one divorced. He then went on to be happily married to wife two and to raise his stepson as his own son. The man wanted his second wife to receive the proceeds of a life insurance policy he purchased many years before; and in the case of her death, he wanted his stepson to receive the insurance proceeds. The man made sure that he wrote his intentions clearly in his properly executed will. The will was drafted and signed over a decade *after* his divorce.

Unfortunately, he died without notifying the insurance company that he no longer wanted his *first wife* to be his beneficiary. Quoting from the appellate court's opinion in the case: "Public policy requires that the insurer, insured, and beneficiary alike should be able to rely on the certainty that policy provisions pertaining to the naming and changing of beneficiaries will control except in extreme circumstances. Equity aids the vigilant, not those who slumber on their rights." Indeed.[19]

Most states follow the same position and make an exception only when the owner of the policy made a reasonable attempt to comply with the insurance company's requirements to change the beneficiary but failed. On the bright side, even if most states will not interfere with an insurance contract, they will revoke a will's designation of an ex-spouse as a beneficiary if the will was signed *prior* to a divorce.

CONTESTING A WILL

Disputes regarding wills or intestate estates are begun like other types of civil disputes by filing a complaint. Any questions regarding a will's authenticity, proper jurisdiction, the mental capacity of the testator, or any applicable dispute usually stops the admission of a will to probate. The person filing the lawsuit has the burden of proving her case by *clear and convincing evidence*; in addition, the filer *must be in a position to gain from the will being found invalid.*

A testator who wants to avoid a will contest and all the distress it will cause after her death may include an *in Terrorem* **clause**, also called a no-contest clause, in her will. This clause warns a beneficiary that contesting any of the other devises made to any other beneficiary will cancel the devise made to the contesting beneficiary. The majority of states do not enforce a no-contest clause *unless* there is probable cause for the contest. A minority of states enforce a no-contest clause only when the contesting beneficiary alleges forgery or subsequent revocation by a later will or codicil or the beneficiary is contesting a provision benefiting the drafter of the will or any witness.

> **in terrorem clause**
> A no-contest clause included in a will that warns a beneficiary that contesting any of the other devises made to any other beneficiary will cancel the devise made to the contesting beneficiary.

Defining Mental Capacity

Historically, mental capacity is a concept that goes back at least as far as the ancient Romans. The Romans believed that a will should be recognized only if the testator's wishes were reflected in the will. Any doubts about the testator's mental capacity raised the suspicion that the testator may have been *possessed by the devil* when she wrote the will. Moving forward to the Renaissance period, the emphasis was on an individual losing her decisional rights when the person's sanity was questioned. The requirement for mental capacity was seen as protection for the decedent's family members against the family's **bounty** being transferred outside the family. Bounty is an old-fashioned term meaning a person's assets.

> **bounty**
> An old-fashioned terms meaning a person's assets.

The grounds used to contest a will usually bring forth two types of issues. The first issue involves questions regarding the testator's mental capacity at the time she signed the will. The second issue involves questions of **undue influence** upon the testator by the persons inheriting from the testator. Undue influence is defined as misusing a position of trust or improperly taking advantage of a person's weakness to change that person's actions or decision. A will contest can involve one or both issues.

> **undue influence**
> The act of misusing a position of trust or improperly taking advantage of a person's weakness to change that person's actions or decision; coercion.

Today three elements involving mental capacity must be present when writing a will. If any one of these three elements is missing, the testator's will may be suspect. First, the testator must fully understand the legal consequences of writing a will. Second, the testator must know the full extent of her property. (The term *bounty* is often used.) Third, the testator must know the names of the individuals who are the proper recipients of the testator's property (e.g., the testator's family members). These three elements show the testator's mental capacity. If a testator has three children but at the time of signing her will can remember the names of only two children, this lapse clearly supports a claim that the will may be invalid because of the testator's lack of capacity. The bottom line: Mental competency of the testator at the time she signed her will is a fundamental requirement. Big problems will follow if the testator's mental competency at the time of signing is called into question. A will can still be considered legally valid if the testator's competency did not become questionable until *after* she signed the will.

Defining Undue Influence

Lord Justice Hannen (an English judge who sat on the bench over 100 years ago) was instrumental in defining undue influence as it pertained to the making of a will. Hannen said that *to be unduly influenced in the eye of the law, there must be—to sum it up in one word—coercion.* What would be considered coercion today? A good test is whether such control was exercised over the mind of the testator as to overcome her free agency and free will and to substitute the will of another so as to cause the testator to do what she would not otherwise have done, but for such control.[20]

One particularly suspicious scenario involving undue influence involves a person in a confidential relationship receiving the majority of a testator's estate. A majority of states look to see if the testator is suffering from a weakened mental state (e.g., there may be a question of mental capacity). If that is the case, the burden of proof is with the recipient to prove that there was no undue influence. In several states, a disgruntled would-be beneficiary also would be required to show additional evidence that the beneficiary was active in procuring the execution of the will. In that vein, one California case involved an attorney who opened an office next to a retirement community called *Leisure World.* Apparently, the attorney acquired 7,000 new clients from the nearby community and inherited millions of dollars from the numerous wills he prepared. Not surprisingly, a great deal of litigation followed.

There will be a *presumption* of undue influence if an attorney drafting a will receives a legacy (except when the attorney is related to the testator). The only way to fight such a claim of undue influence is to rebut with **clear and convincing evidence**. Clear and convincing evidence is defined as stronger evidence than a preponderance of the evidence (evidence that something is more likely to be true than false) but not as strong as beyond a reasonable doubt. Beyond a reasonable doubt is the standard of evidence used in criminal cases in American courts.

clear and convincing evidence

The legal standard used in a will contest to gain from the will being found invalid. Clear and convincing evidence is stronger than a preponderance of the evidence but not as strong as beyond a reasonable doubt.

Defining Fraud

Discussing fraud in the context of creating a will usually involves one or both kinds of fraud known as **fraud in the inducement** or **fraud in the execution**. Fraud in the inducement occurs when a person misrepresents the facts with the intent to deceive the testator to influence the testamentary disposition of the testator's property. An example is misrepresenting facts to induce a testator to do the one or more of the following:

1. Execute a new will

2. Include particular provisions in the wrongdoer's favor

3. Refrain from revoking a will

4. Not execute a will

Fraud in the execution occurs when a person misrepresents the character or contents of the document to be signed by the testator, which does not, in fact, carry out the testator's intent. Of course, any will procured by fraud should be suspect and found invalid.

The appearance of fraud may lead to the necessity of a **constructive trust** being created to protect an estate's assets. When on the Court of Appeals bench for New York, Supreme Court Justice Cardozo explained when a constructive trust should be applied. Justice Cardozo said, "A constructive trust is the formula through which the conscience of equity finds expression." Prior to a constructive trust being applied most courts required a plaintiff to exhaust all probate remedies first. Another last-chance remedy is called **tortuous interference with an expected inheritance or gift**. This cause of action requires that the plaintiff prove that the interference involved tortuous conduct such as fraud, duress, or undue influence. The positive side of using a tort cause of action is that **punitive damages** may be recovered under a tort suit but not in a lawsuit seeking to prevent the probating of a will. Punitive damages are defined as extra money given to a plaintiff to punish a defendant and to help keep a particularly bad act from happening again.

ELDER LAW PRACTICE

Mary Loomis and her husband, Harry Loomis, need help to stop what they described to their attorney, Tara Jensen, as a *great injustice* being done by family members. Mary claims that there should be somewhere between two million and three million dollars in her late Aunt Jenny's estate but that her brother and his wife, Martha, *must have done something with the money*. Mary and Harry think that Mary's brother, Ralph, took money from their aunt. Ralph and his wife were chosen as copersonal representatives of their aunt's estate.

Mary thinks that Ralph and Martha took advantage of their aunt during the last few months of her life. Mary cannot accept that her Aunt Jenny would give her primary home and her beach house to Ralph and Martha. Ralph wrote and signed many checks from Aunt Jenny's account. Ralph had power of attorney when Aunt Jenny was alive.

(continues)

---

fraud in the inducement

Occurs when a person misrepresents the facts with the intent to deceive the testator to influence the testamentary disposition of the testator's property.

fraud in the execution

Occurs when a person misrepresents the character or contents of the instrument to be signed by the testator, which does not, in fact, carry out the testator's intent.

constructive trust

A remedy employed by a court to convert the legal title of property into a trust held by a trustee for the benefit of a third party who in good conscience should have reaped the benefits of the possession of the property put into the constructive trust.

tortuous interference with an expected inheritance or gift

A cause of action that requires the plaintiff to prove that the interference involved tortuous conduct such as fraud, duress, or undue influence.

punitive damages
Extra money given to a
plaintiff to punish a
defendant and to help
keep a particularly bad act
from happening again.

ELDER LAW PRACTICE   *(continued)*

Cases involving the issues of undue influence and doubts concerning a testator's mental capacity often find their way to elder law offices. The scenario involving Mary and Harry Loomis is not untypical. What questions should be asked of Mary and Harry? What type of evidence would Tara need to support Mary and Harry's claims? What type of evidence would Ralph and Martha need to refute Mary and Harry's accusations?

Contracts to Make a Will

The U.P.C. attempted to reduce litigation involving contracts to make a will by creating stricter requirements for making contracts relating to wills. The Code did not help in the following case.

CASE LAW *Peter K. Dementas v. Estate of Jack Tallas*

764 P.2d 628; 95 Utah Adv. Rep. 28 (1988)

Case Facts: Jack Tallas, an immigrant from Greece living in Utah, befriended fellow Greek Peter Dementas. Dementas gratuitously helped Tallas for 14 years by driving him to the grocery store, picking up his mail, and assisting him in the management of his rental properties. In a memorandum dictated to Dementas on December 18, 1982, Tallas stated that he was grateful for everything Dementas had done for him over the years and that he believed that Dementas should receive $50,000 upon Tallas's death for all of Dementas' help. Tallas also stated in the memorandum that Dementas would be added to Tallas's will as an heir. Tallas failed to do so. When Tallas died, Dementas filed a timely notice with Tallas's estate. The estate denied the claim, and Dementas filed suit. Dementas lost his case in the lower court, and he appealed.

Issue: Whether the memorandum dictated by Tallas created a binding contract entitling Dementas to $50,000 from the estate.

Court's Reasoning: The contract lacked the consideration necessary to be a binding contract. This is because Dementas helped his friend out of the goodness of his heart without expecting anything in return. The promise to provide for Dementas was not in exchange for legal detriment, i.e., a promise to do work in the future that Dementas was not legally required to do. Dementas' previous work was *past consideration* and past consideration does not create a binding contract.

Holding: The court affirmed the lower court's ruling.

Case Discussion: This case was particularly interesting because it hinged on the intent of the parties involved—the intent of Dementas to help his friend without expectation of reward and the intent of Tallas to reward his friend for years of help. However, intent does not solely create a valid contract nor does the intent to change one's will actually change it. Should Dementas have expected to receive a financial remuneration for helping a friend?

Partial Invalidation of a Will

The following case provides hope for beneficiaries who question the validity of a portion of a will but fear that the entire will be set aside and intestacy will be the result if they seek to set aside the questionable portion.

CASE LAW	*Williams v. Crickman*
	405 N.E.2d 799 (1980)

Case Facts:	This case involved a claim made by a legatee of the residuary clause that a longtime employee of the deceased testator unduly influenced the testator. The legatee claimed that the employee managed to convince the elderly testator to include in her will the option of allowing the employee to buy her farm for a bargain price and that the single paragraph providing this option should be struck from the will. The legatee's position was that if the option was struck from the will, the farm could be sold and the monies from the sale would be distributed through the residuary. The trial court dismissed the case, and the legatee appealed.
Issue:	Whether the court has the power to declare a testamentary instrument partially invalid where only part of the instrument is alleged to be the product of undue influence.
Court's Reasoning:	We agree with the plaintiff. For example, if the contested provision were fraudulently inserted by a third party, the court would have the power to deny probate to that provision alone. Those portions of the will alleged to be the product of undue influence may be stricken and the remainder of the will allowed to stand if those portions of the will can be separated without defeating the testator's intent or destroying the testamentary scheme. Where it can be shown that a part of the will, caused by undue influence, can be separated from the rest, leaving it intelligible and complete in itself, it is held in most states, that only such part of the will as is caused by undue influence is invalid, and the rest is valid.
Holding:	Judgment reversed and remanded for further proceedings consistent with the opinion.
Case Discussion:	Does it appear that an uphill battle would ensue to prove that a testator was only partially influenced?

To Contest the Will Is the Question

Apparently the testator in the next case was aware that the beneficiaries could be a bit ornery. The testator's solution was to include a no-contest clause in his will. The result was the following case.

CASE LAW   *Burch v. George*

27 Cal. Rptr. 2d 165 (1994)

Facts:	Marlene Burch became the fifth wife of Frank Burch in December 1985. In 1988, Frank executed his integrated estate plan, which consisted of a will and a testamentary *inter vivos* trust. The beneficiaries of the trust included Marlene, Frank's elderly mother, his children from a prior marriage, and other relatives. Prior to his death in March 1989, Frank transferred substantial assets to the trust. To discourage litigation over the trust and its distribution scheme, Frank inserted a no-contest clause in the trust instrument. After Frank's death, Marlene petitioned the probate court to determine whether she could, without violating the no-contest clause, proceed with plans to litigate her rights as a surviving spouse to certain assets in the estate under California's community property laws.

Relying on the language of the trust instrument and the uncontroverted declarations of Frank's attorney and one of the trustees of the trust, the probate court ruled, among other things, that Marlene's proposed action would trigger the trust instrument's no-contest clause because Marlene's proposed action would thwart the basic intent of Frank's estate plan. |
| Issue: | Whether a no contest clause is unenforceable against a surviving spouse. |
| Court's Reasoning: | An *in Terrorem* or no contest clause in a will or trust instrument creates a condition upon gifts and dispositions provided therein. No contest clauses are valid in California and are favored by public policy for discouraging litigation and giving effect to the purposes expressed by the testator. We have reviewed the Probate Code and the case law and are unable to find any authority for the proposition that a no contest clause is either invalid or unenforceable against a beneficiary who claims that a will or trust instrument purposes to dispose of property in which the beneficiary allegedly has independent interests. It is Marlene's position that public policy is in favor of deeming a no contest clause unenforceable against a surviving spouse.

We disagree. Both Marlene and the dissent misapprehend the purpose and effect of a no contest clause. Such a clause essentially acts as a disinheritance device, i.e., if a beneficiary contests or seeks to impair or invalidate the trust instrument or its provision, the beneficiary will be disinherited and thus may not take the gift or devise provided under the instrument. Such a clause does not deprive the spouse of his or her community interest in property, nor does it hinder the ability of the spouse to assert such interest. To the extent the spouse believes valid community claims may be made against estate property, the spouse remains free to pursue them at his or option. In doing, so however, the spouse may not retain the distribution conditionally provided for under the estate plan. We see no legal or policy reason that would justify allowing the spouse *to also* take under the instrument in clear violation of the decedent's intentions. |
| Holding: | Court found for the estate. |
| Case Discussion: | The plaintiff in this case was granted her day in court, but she received no special treatment as a spouse of the testator. Did the majority's decision reflect the purpose behind the *in Terrorem* clause? |

Attorney Impropriety?

The lower court in the following case found overreaching on the part of a father-son team of attorneys who had been total strangers to their client before the transaction in question. The Surrogate found the attorneys guilty of constructive fraud. The Appellate Court reversed the Surrogate, and the case was heard by New York's highest court.

CASE LAW *In the Matter of the Estate of Julius Weinstock, et al. v. Usdan*

386 N.Y.S.2d 1 (1976)

Facts:	The decedent was an elderly man, 82 years old, with physical infirmities whose mental acuities were allegedly waning. The decedent showed the attorneys his current will, and they were informed that the decedent no longer wanted to have his bank serve as his executor. The decedent explained that he wanted to avoid the fees the bank would normally expect to receive for serving in such capacity. The decedent also told the attorneys that there had been discussion of the possible appointment of the decedent's daughter and son-in-law as executors because the decedent knew that they would not charge a fee. The younger attorney testified that there was discussion of the appointment of an executor or executors and of the number of executors. The emphasis, however, was always on executors in the plural; yet as the attorneys admitted, they never told the decedent that if they were to be the two executors, each would be entitled to receive full commissions because, as the attorneys knew, the estate would be over $100,000 dollars. The two attorneys ultimately were named in the decedent's will as coexecutors.
Issue:	Whether there was impropriety on the part of the attorneys that reached to the level of constructive fraud.
Court's Reasoning:	While recognizing that the provisions of the Code of Professional Responsibility are not to be elevated to the status of decisional or statutory law, nonetheless the courts should not denigrate them by indifference. That Code contains a precisely pertinent provision. The Code provides *a lawyer should not consciously influence a client to name him as executor, trustee, or lawyer in an instrument.* In those cases where a client wishes to name his lawyer as such, care should be taken by the lawyer to avoid even the appearance of impropriety. The Surrogate found in effect that these attorney-draftsmen were legally responsible for their own designation as co-executors; surely it cannot be said that any care whatsoever was taken to avoid what was at the very least the appearance of impropriety.
Holding:	The order of the Appellate Division should be reversed, and the decree of the Surrogate's Court should be reinstated.
Case Discussion:	What actions, if any, could the defendants in the *Weinstock* case have taken to avoid the appearance of impropriety?

CAN YOU BEQUEATH PERSONAL VALUES?

There is a growing trend to expand the concept of a last will and testament beyond the bequeathing of a person's assets gathered during a lifetime. This trend seeks to document something symbolically larger than a list of material possessions by offering the details of a person's belief system to loved ones. Generally known as an **ethical will** or **family legacy**, it provides personal reflections on a person's life, hopes, and dreams; but it does not carry the same legal status as a properly executed last will and testament.

No less a personality than former president Bill Clinton advises readers in his autobiography that anyone who has reached age 50 should take the opportunity to reflect on the experiences and lessons learned during his or her lifetime for the benefit of his or her children and future generations.[21] The concept of

ethical will or **family legacy**

The offering of the details of a person's belief system to loved ones.

bequeathing your personal values to your loved ones is not new and can be easily traced to biblical times. For example, in the Bible's book of *Genesis,* Jacob gathers his sons before his death to share stories and wisdom. For many years, some hospice programs have offered patients assistance in writing ethical wills as a therapeutic tool for patients and their survivors. The goal is for the terminally ill patient to receive a sense of peace by writing an ethical will.[22]

What are new are the businesses that have sprung up around the idea. Web sites, how-to books, and seminars are all available to help clients write ethical wills. Even professional writers offer their services and will write an individual's entire ethical will for a fee.[23]

THE LAST WORD ON HAVING THE LAST WORD

letter of instruction

A decedent's non-legally binding document giving instructions to family and friends after the decedent has passed away.

Perhaps clients can have the last word with family and friends. This can be done by writing a **letter of instruction** regarding any funeral and burial requests or the people to whom they want specific personal property given. The letter of instruction is not legally binding, and the last will and testament should be the deciding document if there is a conflict. The letter of instruction can include the location of the writer's will. A client also may want to create an "Information Book" to help his or her family, executor, and estate attorney make decisions efficiently. For example, key items in the book may include a net worth statement, a contact list, last wishes, a valuables list, a key documents list, and the location of important files.

SUMMARY

A last will and testament is a document in which a person tells how her property is to be distributed after her death. The legal requirements for properly executing a will vary from state to state. Some states follow the Uniform Probate Code (U.P.C.), and other states have enacted more state-specific legislation and follow their own state's common law decisions. The U.P.C. has been adopted by at least 18 states. Today, three elements must be present when a person writes a will. If any one of these three elements is missing, the testator's will may be suspect. First, the testator must fully understand the legal consequences of writing a will. Second, the testator must know the full extent of her property. (The term *bounty* is often used.) Third, the testator must know the names of the individuals who are the proper recipients of the testator's property (e.g., the testator's family members).

Generally, three types of bequests are made in a will:

1. General bequest

2. Specific bequest

3. Residuary bequest

If the person listed in the bequest predeceases the testator, the gift is considered lapsed. Another problematic situation is when the testator has identified the property and the beneficiary of the particular property, but the real or personal property has been sold, given away, to another or lost. This situation describes what is technically known as an ademption.

All 50 states consider a person to have died intestate when the person dies without having created a will. Each state defines its version of intestacy in its intestate statutes. The proper term for a person who will inherit property from a deceased person (both under the common law and in statutes) is *heir*. The term *distributee* also is used to describe a person statutorily entitled to a decedent's property through the intestate statutes. The term *next of kin* is defined as all persons entitled to inherit from a person who has not left a will. Without a written will, the court looks to the degree of relationship between the deceased and possible heirs. *Per stirpes* distribution describes a method of dividing a deceased person's estate by giving out shares equally by representation or by family groups. Alternatively, per capita distribution can occur. If no relatives are found (regardless of how remote as long as the connection is proved), any property will escheat to the state.

Husbands and wives should know about the two types of statutes that pertain to wills: the elective share statutes and the pretermitted spouse statutes. If a surviving spouse is mentioned in a will but is left very little of a larger estate, the majority of states allow the surviving spouse to take a larger forced share. The majority of states also have pretermitted child statutes that give children born after the execution of a parent's will and not provided for in the will a share in the deceased parent's estate.

The formal requirements for properly executing a will vary greatly from state to state. Usually one person is named in a will as the person who will ensure that all bequests are made and that all property ownership is transferred. This person is called a personal representative in states following the U.P.C.; she is called an executor in other states. Three terms describe the revocation of a will:

1. Revocation by a physical act

2. Revocation by operation of law

3. Revocation by a subsequent (or *later*) writing

Disputes regarding wills or intestate estates are begun like other types of civil disputes by filing a complaint. Questions regarding a will's authenticity, proper jurisdiction, or *any* dispute usually stops a Surrogate (some states use a different term) from admitting the will to probate. Someone who disagrees with the validity of a will and legally claims that the will should be judged invalid is contesting the will. An ethical will, also called a family legacy, provides an opportunity for the writer to provide loved ones with personal reflections on her life, hopes, and dreams.

KEY TERMS

ademption	forced share	punitive damages
administrator	fraud in the execution	real property
administratrix	fraud in the inducement	residuary bequest
affidavit in lieu of administration	general bequest	revocation by a physical act
ancillary administration	heir	revocation by operation of law
beneficiary, devisee, and legatee	holographic will	revocation by subsequent writing
bond	*in Terrorem* clause	self-authentication
bounty	intestacy statutes	self-proved
capacity	intestate	sole ownership
clear and convincing evidence	joint tenancy	specific bequest
Client Interview Questionnaire	lapsed	tenancy by the entirety
codicil	last will and testament	tenancy for years
community property	letter of instruction	tenancy in common
constructive trust	letters of administration	tenancy in severalty
degree of relationship	life estate	testamentary trust
distributee	next of kin	testator
domicile	nuncupative will	tortuous interference with an ex-
elective share statutes	oral will	pected inheritance or gift
escheat	*per capita* distribution	trust
ethical will or family legacy	*per stirpes* distribution	undue influence
executor	personal property	will
executrix	personal representative	will substitutes
fee simple absolute	pretermitted child statutes	
fiduciary	pretermitted spouse statutes	

REVIEW QUESTIONS

1. What are three reasons for drafting a will?
2. What are three reasons for not drafting a will?
3. Describe three types of bequests that may be made in a last will and testament.
4. Describe the steps that should be followed to help ensure that a will is properly executed?
5. What are an advantage and a disadvantage of having an ownership interest in real property with an attached life estate?

6. What options are available to a surviving spouse if the surviving spouse is not mentioned in the deceased spouse's will?

7. Failure to draft and properly execute a will can leave a recently deceased person's family looking to statutory guidelines to determine how the deceased person's estate will be distributed. Explain those statutory guidelines.

8. How does per capita distribution work?

9. What is a better policy to follow than creating a codicil?

10. Explain why personal representatives, executors, and administrators fulfill a fiduciary role.

11. List the usual duties of a personal representative, an executor, and an administrator.

12. What are some examples of will substitutes? How would these be created?

13. Define the three elements of mental capacity.

14. In the context of drafting a will, what would be considered undue influence or coercion?

15. Discuss fraud in the context of drafting a will.

16. Can a valid contract be made that requires a testator to include a particular beneficiary or a specific bequest?

17. What could a writer include in an ethical will?

ETHICS ALERT

Following a busy morning of document preparation, Luke, a paralegal, was ready to forget his paralegal responsibilities for an hour and join Stacy, a paralegal at another local firm, for a late lunch. During their lunch, Stacy shared a recent office experience with Luke. Stacy explained, "This morning I was so surprised to see my boss's name had been added as the main beneficiary to old Mrs. Thompson's will." Stacy has been asked by her boss to be available later that afternoon to witness Mrs. Thompson's new will. What problems, if any, do you see with the facts described by Stacy? Assuming an innocent scenario, what precautions should Stacy's boss take to avoid the appearance of impropriety?

HELPFUL WEB SITES

ASSOCIATION OF PERSONAL HISTORIANS <HTTP://WWW.PERSONALHISTORIANS.ORG> This Web site can be used to locate a personal historian who will write an ethical will for a fee.

NATIONAL ACADEMY OF ELDER LAW ATTORNEYS, INC. (NAELA) <HTTP://WWW.NAELA. COM> This site describes itself as the leading elder law organization in the field.

ASSOCIATED HUMANE SOCIETIES AND POPCORN PARK ZOO <HTTP://WWW.AHSCARES. ORG> The purpose of this organization is to assist pet owners with the planning of long-term pet care after the owner has died.

COURT T.V. <HTTP://WWW.COURT.COM> This site is offered by Court Television and provides the user access to the wills of famous individuals.

ENDNOTES

[1] Roberts, Alison, "Having a Will Is Part of Your Obligation to Family," Daily Record, December 19, 2006, page 7.

[2] U.P.C. Section 3-916 (a) (b).

[3] *In Re Estate of Gasparovich*, 487 P.2d (Mont. 1971).

[4] *Philips v. Najor*, 901 S.W.2d 561 Tex. App. 1995).

[5] The Institute for Continuing Legal Education, Seminar, New Brunswick, NJ, May, 5, 2007.

[6] Uniform Probate Code Section 2-515 (1990).

[7] *In Re Collin*, 1 W.L.R. 1440 (1972).

[8] Dukeminier, Jesse and Johanson, Stanley M., *Wills, Trusts, and Estates*, New York Aspen Law & Business, 2000, page 221.

[9] Beyer, Gerry W., Statutory Fill-in Will Forms, 72 Or. L.Rev. 769 (1993).

[10] *In Re Snider*, 52 N.Y.2d 193, 418 N.E.2d 656, 4337 N.Y.S.2d 63 (1981).

[11] *In Re Grant*, 262 Kan. 269, 936 P.2d 1360 (1997).

[12] *Clark v. National Bank of Commerce*, 304 Ark. 352, 802 S.W.2d 452 (1991).

[13] *In Re Estate of Royal*, 826 P.2d 1236 (Colo. 1992).

[14] *In Re Estate of Peters*, 107 N.J 263, 526 A.2d 1005 (1989).

[15] *In Re Estate of McCabe*, 224 Cal. App. 3d 330, 274 Cal. Rptr. 43 (1990).

[16] *Witt v. Rosen*, 765 S.W.2d 956 (Ark. App. 1989).

[17] The Institute for Continuing Legal Education, Seminar, New Brunswick, NJ, June 20, 2006.

[18] Weston, Liz Pullam, "Executors Can Inherit an Unholy Mess," May 29, 2003 <http://moneycentral.msn.com>

[19] *Cook v. Equitable Life Assurance Society*, 428 N.E. 110, 25 A.L.R. 4th 1153 (1981).

[20] *Lipper v. Weslow*, 369 S.W.2d 698 (1963).

[21] Clinton, William, *My Life*, New York, Alfred A. Knopf, 2004, page 38.

[22] Cheney, Karen, "Gift of a Lifetime," *AARP*, September/October 2004, page 34.

[23] Halpern, Stan, *The Forum*, Vol. B-1, November 8, 2002. Halpern, with the Jewish Ethical Will Society in Boca Raton, Florida., helps draw up ethical wills. During the last few years, he has videotaped the life stories of people that conclude with an ethical will for their children, grandchildren, and descendants. Halpern has made more than 70 such videotapes, he does not charge for his work, and some of the videotapes have aired on local educational television.

Online Companion™
For additional resources, please go to
http://www.paralegal.delmar.cengage.com

3

Life Planning: Advance Directives for Health Care, Euthanasia, and Physician-Assisted Suicide

▨ OBJECTIVES

After completing this chapter, you will be able to:

- Explain the need for advance health care decision making.
- Describe the types of advance health care planning documents.
- Explain the legal issues surrounding euthanasia and physician-assisted suicide.
- Describe palliative care.

INTRODUCTION

Elderly clients often have to deal with more health concerns as they age. Elder law attorneys and their staff should be aware of this fact and foster in their clients a commitment to planning *before* a medical emergency or incapacity strikes. Literally speaking, the need to make life-and-death decisions occurs more than 1,000 times per day in American hospitals and nursing homes.[2] Failure to plan ahead for such unfortunate occurrences generally leaves the client's family addressing incapacity issues while dealing with their loved one's immediate physical and mental health needs.

> "Every human being of adult years and sound mind has a right to determine what shall be done with his own body.[1]"

JUSTICE CARDOZO

PLANNING BEFORE A HEALTH EMERGENCY

■ **advance directives for health care**

Documents that specify an individual's health care decisions and identify who will make decisions for the individual in the event the individual is unable to communicate his wishes to doctors.

■ **health care power of attorney (HCPOA)**

A document that specifies an individual or individuals to carry out the wishes of the principal regarding medical treatments the principal would want if he was unable to share his wishes with health care providers.

■ **durable power of attorney for health care**

A document that specifies an individual or individuals to carry out the wishes of the principal regarding medical treatments the principal would want if he was unable to share his wishes with healthcare providers. The document endures even if the principal becomes mentally incapacitated.

All 50 states allow for documents collectively known as **advance directives for health care** and have statutes that provide the procedural and substantive drafting requirements. Approximately 40 states have forms for drafting advance directives for health care. About 20 states require that these forms be substantially adhered to, but those 20 states still allow additional language to be inserted. It may appear confusing at first since advance directives for health care are known by a variety of names, including advance medical care directive. Some states use a document specifically named an advance health care directive. Some states use the term **health care power of attorney (HCPOA)**. Some states recognize an advance directive written only in a certain format. Yet another option is called the **durable power of attorney for health care**.

Whatever name an advance directive for health care goes by, the primary objective should be the same—to specify an individual's health care decisions and to identify who will make decisions for the individual in the event he is *unable to communicate* his wishes to doctors. Generally, one or two types of advance directives for health care documents are used. The first type is a **living will**. A living will is self-directed and should describe an individual's wishes regarding medical treatments the person would want if he was unable to share his wishes with health care providers. For example, would the individual want artificial means of support? Very often living wills concentrate on prolonging the dying process when a person is fighting a terminal illness. A living will alone may not be as helpful as the creator of the will might have hoped because many living wills are standardized boilerplates that may be open to interpretation. For example, the National Conference of State Legislatures cited the terms *heroic measures* and *terminally ill* used in some state forms as examples of vague wording.

The second type of advance directive for health care document is a **medical power of attorney**. The medical power of attorney document allows an individual to appoint a trusted person to make health care choices when the individual is not able to share his health care choices with health care providers. The living will and the medical power of attorney frequently are merged into one document, which is a good idea if state statutes permit it. A trusted person appointed to deal with such issues can interpret a patient's wishes based on their trusted relationship and mutual knowledge of their beliefs. Very often advance directives for health care specify a *DNR* (Do Not Resuscitate) order. Nearly all states have enacted legislation that allows their citizens to choose to refuse artificial means of support. Inclusion of DNR decisions makes sense when the historical background of advance directives for health care is considered. Such directives were originally advocated by right-to-die groups such as Choice in Dying. However, a national standard dealing with such refusal would be helpful because state standards vary widely.

The purpose of a *medical* power of attorney is clearly different from a **general power of attorney**. First, a medical power of attorney is very *specific* in its purpose (i.e., the making of medical treatment decisions by one person [usually called an **agent**, a **health care proxy**, or a *health care representative*] for another person. The creator of a power of attorney is called the **principal**.

A general power of attorney is usually very *broad* in its purpose (i.e., the handling of general business matters). For example, filing taxes, buying and selling real estate, entering safe-deposit boxes, and dealing with banking matters are permitted by a general power of attorney. An additional power that may be granted to an agent is running a business or employing professionals (such as attorneys and accountants) to assist the agent.

Another type of power of attorney is called the **special power of attorney**. As its name implies, a special power of attorney is usually created to give an agent one special power. For example, the agent may be authorized to represent the grantor at the closing of his home if the owner is out of town. The authority behind a special power of attorney usually ends with the completion of the responsibility.

All three types of powers of attorney (health care, special, and general) can be made a permanent part of a client's life planning file by being designated as *durable*. A **durable power of attorney** remains in effect *even if the creator becomes incompetent*. This is not normally the case with the general or special power of attorney. Incompetence of the creator invalidates those two powers of attorney unless certain language is included to make a power of attorney's effect durable. For example, the statement *This power shall not be affected by my subsequent disability or incapacity* would make a power of attorney durable. When a durable power of attorney is written so that the authority of the **attorney-in-fact** begins at a later time upon the occurrence of a certain event (usually incapacity), the document is called a **springing durable power of attorney**.

Making sure an advance directive for health care is in place can be especially important for an isolated person. An elderly patient who lacks capacity and has no concerned relatives places health care personnel in the perilous position of making uninformed decisions regarding the patient's care. Only 13 states currently have enacted statutes dealing with this issue.[3]

Should Everyone Have An Advanced Directive for Health Care?

Elder law attorneys should ask their clients this question: *What measures do you want taken if you are ever in a permanently unconscious state?* If an advance directive for health care has not been written and a client is terminally ill or is in a permanently unconscious state, the question an elder law attorney should ask a client's family members is this: *What would the patient have wanted under the particular circumstances the patient is in now?*

living will

A document describing an individual's wishes regarding medical treatments the person would want if he was unable to share his wishes with health care providers.

medical power of attorney

A document very specific in its purpose that allows an individual to appoint a trusted person to make health care choices when the individual is not able to share his health care choices with health care providers.

general power of attorney

A document very broad in its purpose that allows an individual to appoint a trusted person to handle general business matters.

agent

The individual appointed to make medical treatment decisions for another person; also known as a *health care proxy*.

health care proxy

The individual appointed to make medical treatment decisions for another person; also known as an *agent*.

principal

The creator of a power of attorney.

special power of attorney

A power of attorney created to give an agent one special power that usually ends with completion of the responsibility.

durable power of attorney

A power of attorney that remains in effect even if the creator becomes incompetent.

attorney-in-fact

The individual who has been given the authority to handle another's affairs.

springing durable power of attorney

A power of attorney that begins at a later time upon the happening of a certain event.

A wide client base is in need of advance directives for health care. Fewer than 10 percent of all Americans have written a living will.[4] Creating such a directive forces the creator to think about intensely personal questions. For example, when should certain therapies be withheld or stopped to allow nature to run its course?

There is no "right way" to create an advance directive for health care. Issues of mental capacity, physical abilities, and quality of life should be pondered. For example, would a client want every possible medical intervention done to resuscitate him at 60, 70, 80, 90, or 100 years old? Clients should consider whether they want to be resuscitated if such medical intervention would mean a return to a conscious life of dementia due to AD or a life suffering the effects of a stroke.

Almost every hospital asks an incoming admission whether the person has an advance directive for health care and if not, whether he would like to sign one. Hospitals cannot refuse admission and insurance companies cannot deny coverage because an individual refuses to sign an advance directive for health care. It is a good idea for an individual to review and possibly rewrite an advance directive every few years.

Clients who have decided to draft a living will also should be asked if they want to sign an advance directive for health care. Some living will forms currently in use apply only when an individual is expected to die within a short period of time and do not allow for the withdrawal or withholding of artificial nutrition and hydration. They do not cover a condition such as a persistent vegetative state, which occurred in both of the well-known cases of Nancy Cruzan and Theresa Schiavo.

The American Medical Society, AARP, and the American Geriatrics Society highly recommend that everyone, regardless of age, take time to prepare a written plan of his preferences pertaining to health care. In its guidelines, the American Medical Society clearly includes its official position regarding the withholding or withdrawing of life-sustaining treatment and clearly supports patient preference in making treatment decisions. Refer to Exhibit 3–1 to read a portion of the American Medical Society's official position. The Uniform Health Care Decisions Act also provides guidance to states drafting statutory guidelines for dealing with health care decisions.

Drafting an advance directive for health care and designating a health care proxy are not the only factors impacting an individual's end-of-life decisions. The best way to comply personally with each state's requirements should be considered. What state a person lives in can make a huge difference in what kind of death the person experiences. For example, differences in state budgets are why some residents are more likely to die in a hospital than at home or in a hospice environment. For example, in a recent year, Mississippi spent 4.2 percent of its long-term health care budget to aid patients who wanted to be treated at home. Compare that number to Oregon spending 50.4 percent of its long-term budget that same year for long-term treatment of patients at home or in a hospice. Oregon is not alone in making such budgetary decisions. California spends, on average, 30 percent of its long-term health care budget on treatment for home and community care.[5] Just as budgets vary greatly, so does the language of the advance directives for health care legislation across the country.

Medical Terminology Used in Advance Directives

Clients may ask their elder law attorneys to review unfamiliar medical terminology particular to advance directives for health care. These medical terms include the following:

- Artificially provided fluids and nutrition
- Cardiopulmonary resuscitation (CPR)
- Life-sustaining measures
- Decision-making capacity
- Terminal condition
- Permanent unconsciousness
- Persistent vegetative state
- Incurable and irreversible chronic diseases
- Whole brain death[6]

EXHIBIT 3–1   E-2-20 WITHHOLDING OR WITHDRAWING LIFE-SUSTAINING MEDICAL TREATMENT

The social commitment of the physician is to sustain life and relieve suffering. Where the performance of one's duty conflicts with the other, the preferences of the patient should prevail. The principle of patient autonomy requires that physicians respect the decision to forego life-sustaining treatment of a patient who possesses decision-making capacity. Life-sustaining treatment is any condition. Life-sustaining treatment may include, but is not limited to, mechanical ventilation, renal dialysis, chemotherapy, antibiotics and antibiotics, nutrition and hydration.

There is no ethical distinction between withdrawing and withholding life-sustaining treatment. A competent, adult patient may, in advance, formulate and provide a valid consent to the withholding or withdrawal of life-support systems in the event that injury or illness renders that individual incompetent to make such a decision. A patient may also appoint a surrogate decision maker in accordance with state law.

If the patient receiving life-sustaining treatment is incompetent, a surrogate decision maker should be identified. Without an advance directive that designates a proxy, the patient's family would become the surrogate decision maker. Family includes persons with whom the patient is closely associated. In the case where there is no person closely associated with the patient, there are persons who both care about the patient and have sufficient relevant knowledge of the patient, such persons may be appropriate surrogates. Physicians should provide all relevant medical information and explain to surrogate decision makers that decisions regarding withholding or withdrawing life-sustaining treatment should be based on substituted judgment (what the patient would have decided) when there is evidence of the patient's preference and values. In making a substituted judgment, decision makers may consider the

(continues)

EXHIBIT 3–1   E-2-20 WITHHOLDING OR WITHDRAWING LIFE-SUSTAINING MEDICAL TREATMENT *(continued)*

patient's advance directive (if any); the patient's values about life and the way it should be lived; and the patient's attitudes towards sickness, suffering, medical procedures, and death. If there is not adequate evidence of the incompetent patient's preferences and values, the decision should be based on the best interest of the patient (what outcome would most likely promote the patient's well-being).

Choosing a Health Care Proxy

An advance directive for health care may not be effective alone because family members do not always agree with what the incapacitated person has written in his directive.[7] The choice of a health care proxy (also known as a health care agent or health care representative) who has similar end-of-life beliefs is one more preventive action that helps ensure that a creator's health care decisions are respected.[8] The most important thing to remember in the choice of a personal health care proxy is to be confident that the person will follow any instructions to the letter, even if the patient's instructions differ with the proxy's personal beliefs. The choice of health care proxy can greatly impact the end-of-life experience for the principal.

ASKING OTHERS TO MAKE A HEALTH CARE DECISION

Today the decisions that a health care proxy makes for an incompetent patient should be accepted by the patient's physician. However, four situations may require institutional (e.g., a hospital) or judicial review and intervention in the decision-making process:

1. No available family member is willing to be the patient's surrogate decision maker.
2. There is a dispute among family members, and no decision maker has been designated in an advance directive for health care.
3. A health care provider believes that the family's decision is not what the patient would have decided if he were competent.
4. A health care provider believes that the decision is not one that reasonably could be judged to be in the patient's best interests.

Refer to Exhibit 3–2 to review a list of the responsibilities of an individual who agrees to be a health care proxy.

EXHIBIT 3–2   THE RESPONSIBILITIES OF A HEALTH CARE PROXY

A health care proxy/agent is normally permitted to do the following:

1. Consent or forbid any medical treatment

2. Hire and fire all medical personnel

3. Determine the best-suited medical facilities

4. Visit the medical facility treating the patient

5. Review any medical records

6. Appear in court proceedings on the patient's behalf to fight for compliance of the wishes of the proxy/agent and the patient's advance directives for health care.

When Does an Advance Directive for Health Care Become Operable?

No advance directive for health care takes effect unless the creator's mental state has deteriorated to a point that he is unable to make decisions for himself. The determination of incapacity is typically decided by the creator's personal attending physician and usually needs to be seconded by another physician.

Most states have laws that do permit the removal of life-sustaining treatment under very limited circumstances. Permanent unconsciousness, terminal illness, or treatment that will only prolong the dying process may trigger the removal of life-sustaining treatment. All states look to what the treatment is and whether the burden of the treatment is outweighed by the benefits and vice versa. If an advance directive for health care is ambiguous or unclear in explaining the patient's treatment wishes, the decision making will be left to a health care proxy (if one was appointed by the patient) or to family or perhaps to the patient's physician. A health care institution may be fined or penalized for not complying with a patient's advance directive for health care. An exception is usually made regarding a patient's wish to remove life-sustaining treatment if the hospital or other health care facility is one with a religious affiliation.

When Does a Durable Power of Attorney End?

The creator of an advance directive for health care can change or revoke his directive if he still has capacity. Depending on the state, the revocation can generally be done by any action, written or oral. It is better if the old written advance directive is destroyed and a new advance directive is written and signed.

Copies of the creator's advance directive for health care should be given to the designated proxy, to close family members, and to the creator's doctors to include with the medical records.

Any type of durable power of attorney ends upon the death of the principal. If a client wants his attorney-in-fact to handle his personal affairs posthumously, the attorney-in-fact must be named as an executor in the client's will. A durable power of attorney also can end if the document is invalidated by a court, the named attorney-in-fact dies or declines the authority, or the principal divorces and has previously named his now ex-spouse as the attorney-in-fact. This last point occurs only in a minority of states.

Practical Advice

A law firm can provide clients with a card stating that the bearer has an advance directive for health care. This is a thoughtful service similar to organ donor cards used across the country. Clients also should be given practical advice to help ensure that their advance directive for health care choices are recognized. For example, clients should be told to keep the number and name of their health care agent/proxy on their person, especially if they travel often. Elder law attorneys should suggest that clients talk with their spouse and adult children about their wishes when they are healthy and more willing to discuss such matters. Clients should be reminded to designate someone as their agent who will accept the position and will understand his role. In particular, clients should be advised to speak with their primary care physician to make sure the physician knows their choices and is supportive of those choices.[9]

Where Should an Advance Health Care Directive Be Kept?

It has been estimated that 35 percent of advance directives for health care cannot be found when needed.[10] The U.S. Living Will Registry has been electronically storing advance directives for health care since 1996. The Registry is designed to provide health care providers with 24-hour document access. According to the Registry, once a person is registered, that person is registered for life. Other states are following the Registry's example. For example, the Secretary of State's office in North Carolina has set up a registry that allows citizens to file up to four different advance directives. The link for North Carolina's registry site can be found in the end-of-chapter section "Helpful Web Sites."

PRACTITIONERS SHOULD BE AWARE OF STATUTORY CHANGES

Changes in the law regarding advance directives for health care have evolved over the last two decades. One change is that all hospitals and nursing homes are now required by federal law to offer living wills as a no-cost service. Changes in *state* laws pertaining to health care directives frequently occur. Practitioners need to be aware that these changes can make an advance directive for health care invalid. For example, Connecticut's first living will statutes permitted a living will to take effect only if a patient was diagnosed with a terminal illness. Originally, a patient in a coma or persistent vegetative state would not have fallen under that state's living will statute. Connecticut's living will statute evolved to include a permanently comatose patient under the definition of having a terminal illness and allowed the termination of artificial feeding under that fact situation.[11]

Another example of evolving legislation occurred when the California legislature changed its advance directive for health care statute and enacted the single document *Advance Health Care Directive* in July 2000. California's *Advance Heath Care Directive* actually consists of four sections, including the *Power of Attorney for Health Care, Instructions for Health Care, Donations of Organs at Death,* and the *Primary Physician* designation. The power of attorney portion allows the creator to designate another person to make decisions about the signer's health care. The *Instructions for Health Care* is very specific as to the types of health care the creator would want in the event he were not able to make such decisions. The type of health care wanted or refused can include both physical and mental health treatment. The *Donations of Organs at Death* section is optional and self-explanatory. The *Primary Physician* section also is optional and allows the creator to appoint a specific physician to make decisions regarding his health care instead of a non-medical professional agent. California's one *Advance Health Care Directive* replaced the need for two documents, a durable power of attorney for health care, and a living will (also formerly known in California as the *Declaration Made Pursuant to the Natural Death Act*). California citizens are required by statute to replace any living wills and durable power of attorneys for health care created prior to 1992 with the four-sectioned *Advance Health Care Directive*.

Unfortunately, state laws often lack enforcement powers if a physician refuses or fails to honor a living will. In this day and age, patients need a backup advocacy plan. Patients need someone to call, someone to be at their bedside to help frame the issues, help clarify their desires, and go to court if necessary. This is where a client's health care proxy is an invaluable asset.

Numerous advance directive ready-made forms are available, but time meaningfully spent thinking about one's wishes, discussing one's decisions with loved ones, and incorporating those thoughts into an advance directive for healthcare is a wiser choice than checking off boxes on a generic form. Elder law clients need to know that each state has its own legal requirements and often its own suggested form. An individual must check with his state statutes (or hire an attorney to do so) to determine if the state is among the minority of states requiring that a particular state-mandated statutory advance directive for health care form be used. Some states (e.g., California, Ohio, Texas, and Vermont) require state statutory forms. Michigan requires the agent's signature on the advance directive. Most states require that the advance directive be signed in the presence of two adult witnesses who are not related or who are directly related to the health care of the person creating the document. Individuals who have multiple residences in different states should complete advance health care directives for each state.

The American Bar Association's Commission on Law and Aging makes available to the public a *Consumer's Tool Kit for Health Care Advance Planning*. This tool kit does not create a formal advance directive for health care; rather, it facilitates in the multistep process of reaching personal decisions regarding advance health care planning.

Elder law professionals also should be aware of the changes wrought by the 1996 passage of the **Health Insurance Portability and Accountability Act (HIPPA)**, the first federal privacy standards designed to limit the information that health care professionals can share, use, and release to others concerning their patients. The goal of this federal legislation is medical records privacy, but the result can prove problematic for an attorney asked to represent an unconscious patient and wade through privacy rules.

Refer to Exhibit 3–3 to read the health care power of attorney that Luke prepared, under Tara's supervision, for their client Juliana Jameson.

▨ **Health Insurance Portability and Accountability Act (HIPPA)**

The first federal privacy standards designed to limit the information that health care professionals can share, use, and release to others concerning their patients.

ELDER LAW PRACTICE

Tara walked from her office to the area shared by Rena, Luke, and hundreds of files. The walls were covered with metal files, and each paralegal's desk was neatly stacked with piles of papers and files.

Tara had just received a telephone call from a client who wanted to come to the office to have an advance directive for health care and a durable power of attorney for health care drafted. Tara had been surprised by the call because the client, Juliana Jameson, had come into the office with her adult children the day before and had shared with Tara and her staff that she was concerned that to write such documents would bring an early death.

"Hey, Rena. You owe me a chocolate bar. Juliana Jameson just called me. She's coming in to have a living will and durable power of attorney for health care drafted."

"I didn't think she'd cooperate," Rena answered.

"I wonder what made her change her mind." Luke pondered aloud.

(continues)

ELDER LAW PRACTICE *(continued)*

"Well, some of our clients do need to come to terms with their belief in superstitions, and I have to do my best to help them help themselves," Tara offered. "Juliana is a strong woman who knows what she wants. I think she finally understands that advance directives for health care are great tools for making sure she gets her way even if she is incapacitated and can't make her feelings known."

Tara continued, "Everyone should spare family members the angst of not knowing what he or she wants when the worst happens."

Luke interjected, "The Terry Schiavo case should act as a reminder that without the proper paperwork in place, your most personal and private life issues could fall into the hands of politicians and the courts."

"It seems to me that an advance directive is just one more way to make sure you don't have to suffer from indecision on the part of loved ones or from medical treatment you'd never permit if you were capable of saying so," Luke added.

"Exactly," Tara answered. "Luke, we've never gone over the process of creating an advance directive for health care, have we?"

"Not quite. We started to discuss it quite a few times; but then the phone rang, a client popped in, or something else interrupted us," Luke answered.

"Okay. I started out learning some vocabulary specific to living wills. Years ago I typed up a list of vocabulary words to remember to review with my clients. Rena, where is that list?" Tara asked. Rena shuffled the piles on her desk and passed a one-page copy of the terms to Luke.

"Thank you, Rena." Tara began, "It helps to remember them by reading them aloud. We can do that right now. Go ahead."

Luke looked doubtful about taking up Tara's valuable time.

She said, "It's okay. I want to train you to really know your stuff. The best way for you to help this firm is to learn, learn, and then learn some more. Okay?"

Luke responded with a definite "okay." He began, "(1) Artificially provided fluids and nutrition, (2) cardiopulmonary resuscitation (CPR), (3) life-sustaining measures, (4) decision-making capacity, (5) health care representative or health care proxy, (6) terminal condition, (7) permanent unconsciousness, (8) persistent vegetative state, (9) incurable and irreversible chronic diseases, (10) whole brain death, and (11) the name of the attending physician."

"Do you have a clue as to what most of that means?" Tara asked smiling.

He answered, "Well, I did take an estates and trusts course in college, and the terms are familiar from my nursing classes. Right now, I'm thinking that I must have been figuratively, if not literally, absent the day we learned most of those terms."

Tara answered, "Well, many college courses don't have time to review in detail the vocabulary related to advance directives for health care. So it's settled. You'll learn it right now. Let's see. Numbers 2, 4, 5, and 10 are fairly self-explanatory. Number 1 concerns the giving of fluids and nutrition through tubes in a patient's arm or directly into the stomach. I usually think of Number 3 as including any action that will extend life. A terminal condition is one where the patient has no hope of recovery. Only one or more of the patient's physicians can determine Numbers 7, 8, and 9. Pretty easy, eh?"

(continues)

ELDER LAW PRACTICE *(continued)*

"Yeah , right," Luke mumbled, "If you've been doing this for years."

"Oh, it's not that bad," Tara remarked good-naturedly. "Anything worth doing and understanding is going to take some effort."

EXHIBIT 3–3   HEALTH CARE POWER OF ATTORNEY

This Health Care Power of Attorney is made this 10th day of May, 2007.

I. DESIGNATION AND AUTHORITY OF REPRESENTATIVE

I, JULIANA JAMESON, being of sound mind, do hereby willfully and voluntarily nominate, constitute and appoint my AGENT, REINA STEM, as my lawful health care representative. If, for any reason, my said AGENT is unable or unwilling to serve as my health care representative at the time that a health care decision must be made, I nominate, constitute and appoint MARY STEVENS, SUBSTITUTE AGENT, as my health care representative, whose affidavit shall be accepted by third parties as conclusive and binding.

Health Care Power of Attorney

1. To consent, refuse to consent, withdraw consent to any care, treatment, service or procedure to maintain, diagnose or treat my physical or mental condition.

2. To inspect and disclose any information relating to my physical and mental health or condition.

3. To sign documents, waivers, and releases, including documents titled or purporting to be a "Refusal to Permit Treatment" and "Leaving the Hospital or Refusing Treatment Against Medical Advice" and to execute any waiver or release from liability required by a hospital, medical institution or physician.

4. I DECLARE that this Power of Attorney, in its entirety, and its validity or operation thereof, shall not be affected by my subsequent disability, incompetence or incapacity as recognized under the applicable state laws and that the authority granted herein shall continue and remain in full force and effect in the event that I become, and during any period while I am disabled, incompetent or incapacitated, unless sooner revoke or terminated by me in writing.

5. The foregoing power and authority granted herein are herewith granted without, in any way, limiting the said appointed Agent, generally to do, execute and perform any other act, deed, matter or thing whatsoever that ought to be done, executed and performed in and about my premises, financial affairs, medical treatment, or health care of every nature and kind whatsoever consistent with my directives as fully effectual as I could do if personally present.

(continues)

EXHIBIT 3–3 HEALTH CARE POWER OF ATTORNEY *(continued)*

6. And I do hereby ratify and confirm all things whatsoever that my said attorney-in-fact or his substitute or substitutes, shall do, or cause to be done, in or about the premises, and my affairs, by virtue of this power of attorney.

7. This instrument may not be changed orally.

8. If the first person I named above is unavailable to act as the agent or attorney-in-fact in my behalf, I hereby authorize MARY STEVENS as the substitute agent(s) or attorney-in-fact with the same powers, authority and responsibilities.

_____

JULIANA JAMESON

IN WITNESS WHEREOF, I have hereunto set my hand and seal the _____ day of _____ 2007.

_____

Notary

Acknowledgment

State of New Jersey

County of Morris

On the _____ day of _____ 2007, before me personally came Mr./Mrs./Ms. _____ to me known or made known to me to be the individual described in, the foregoing Power of Attorney, and who, upon first being duly sworn executed the said Power of Attorney, and thereupon acknowledged to me under oath the he/she executed the same.

LIVING WILLS TRACED TO *QUINLAN* CASE

Karen Ann Quinlan is a well-known name in the personal right-to-die national debate. Quinlan was only 21 years old when she suffered irreversible brain damage and her parents' fight to have her removed from a respirator sparked a national debate. Quinlan's case has been described as "the icon of the right to die movement."[12] It certainly changed the way many people look at life and death. In large part, the living will concept can be traced back to the 1975 *Quinlan* case.

The Quinlan family lost their privacy in what became a media farce when one reporter dressed as a nun to gain access to the comatose Quinlan's room. The family met with hospital officials and Karen Quinlan's doctors. An open discussion was conducted, the Quinlans expressed their wishes to have their daughter disconnected from her respirator and returned to her natural state. Hospital officials asked the Quinlans to sign an authorization for the hospital to disconnect, and they did. The next day the hospital reneged, according to Julia Quinlan, Karen Ann's mother. The Quinlans eventually took their case to the New Jersey Supreme Court. New Jersey's highest court sided with the Quinlans, and Karen Ann Quinlan's respirator was removed. Surprising the experts, Karen Ann continued to breathe on her own while in what was described as a vegetative state. Karen Ann Quinlan died in 1985.

The *Quinlan* decision also is considered to have led to the current requirement that all hospitals, nursing homes, and hospices must have ethics committees available to discuss medical care issues. Virtually every court in the country dealing with a right-to-die issue has looked to the *Quinlan* case for guidance. The Quinlan family was influential in the opening of the Karen Ann Quinlan Hospice in Newton, New Jersey. It is designed to help terminally ill patients and their families.[13]

National attention was focused for years on the more recent case of Floridian Terry Schiavo, also severely brain-damaged.[14] The *Schiavo* case very publicly asked questions answered privately every day in hospitals and nursing homes across the country. The Schiavo case has been called an aberration because of the bitter conflict between Terry's parents and her husband. The argument centered on whether the decision should be made to withdraw nutrition and water from Terry Schiavo following her 15 years in a vegetative state. The husband's position was that Terry would not have wanted to continue to be kept alive in such a vegetative state. He claimed that Terry had made such a statement prior to lapsing into her vegetative state. Terry's parents believed she had a hope at recovery and should be kept alive at all costs.

It is doubtful the *Schiavo* case would have reached the national news if Terry Schiavo's wishes had been clearly known prior to her lapse. Nor would the Schiavo family have suffered the public anguish that resulted from the conflict.[15] The media followed efforts by Florida lawmakers and Governor Jeb Bush to pass legislation that allowed the state court to reverse an earlier order, keeping Terry Schiavo fed and hydrated until the U.S. Supreme Court could hear her case. Congress followed by allowing her parents to take the unusual step of taking the case to federal court, but the Supreme Court finally declined to hear their appeal. The result was that her nutrition and hydration tubes were removed and Terry died in 2005.

Private Questions Answered Publicly in Court

The U.S. Supreme Court ruled in 1990 on the well-publicized case of Nancy Cruzan, a Missouri woman in her twenties who was severely injured in a 1983 car accident. Cruzan was in a comatose state, like Karen Quinlan and Terry Schiavo, after being deprived of oxygen for over 20 minutes at the time of her accident. (Brain damage can occur after only six minutes of oxygen deprivation.) It was the first case where the Supreme Court was presented with the issue of whether the U.S. Constitution provided a right-to-die.

In the Cruzan case, state officials (who got involved because Nancy was in a state-supported rehabilitation hospital) refused attempts made by Nancy's parents to have their daughter's life support treatment shut down. Joyce and Lester Cruzan, Nancy's parents, asked the hospital caring for Nancy for the *cessation of all nutrition and hydration tubes*. The hospital refused to do so without a court order. The Cruzans subsequently requested a Missouri trial court to issue a declaratory judgment. The Missouri court appointed a **guardian ad litem** for Nancy. A *guardian ad litem* is a person (often a lawyer) who is appointed by a court to take care of the interests of a person who cannot legally take care of himself in a lawsuit involving him. Subsequently, the court ordered the hospital to remove Nancy's nutrition and hydration tubes. The hospital appealed, and the Supreme Court ultimately ruled that Nancy's life support could be withheld. She died a short time later. The following case brief of the Supreme Court's opinion explains its decision.

■ **guardian ad litem**

A person who is appointed by a court to take care of the interests of a person who cannot legally take care of himself in a lawsuit involving him.

CASE LAW *Cruzan v. Director, Missouri Department of Health, et al.*

497 U.S. 261, 110 S. Ct. 2841, 111 L.Ed. 2d 224 (1990)

Facts: Petitioner Nancy Beth Cruzan was rendered incompetent as a result of severe injuries sustained during an automobile accident. Co-petitioners Lester and Joyce Cruzan, Nancy's parents and co-guardians, sought a court order directing the withdrawal of their daughter's artificial feeding and hydration equipment after it became apparent that she had virtually no chance of recovering her cognitive faculties. The Supreme Court of Missouri held that because there was no clear and convincing evidence of Nancy's desire to have life-sustaining treatment withdrawn under any circumstances, her parents lacked authority to effectuate such a request. The U. S. Supreme Court granted *certiorari*. (i.e., the Court agreed to review the case and to hear an appeal).

Missouri's Supreme Court, adopting much of the trial court's findings, described Nancy Cruzan's medical condition as follows: (1) Her respiration and circulation are not artificially maintained and are within the normal limits of a 30 year old female; (2) she is oblivious to her environment except for reflexive responses to sound and perhaps painful stimuli; (3) she suffered anoxia of the brain resulting in a massive enlargement of the ventricles filling with cerebrospinal fluid in the area where the brain has degenerated and her cerebral cortical atrophy is irreversible, permanent, progressive and ongoing; (4) her highest cognitive brain function is exhibited by her grimacing perhaps in recognition of ordinarily painful stimuli, indicating the experience of pain and apparent response to sound; (5) she is a spastic quadriplegic; (6) her four extremities are contracted with irreversible muscular and tendon damage to all extremities; and (7) she has no cognitive or reflexive ability to swallow food or water to maintain her daily essential needs and she will never recover her ability to swallow sufficient [*sic*] to satisfy her needs.

In summary, *Nancy is diagnosed as in a persistent vegetative state. She is not dead. She is not terminally ill.*

Medical experts testified that she could live another thirty years. After it had become apparent that Nancy Cruzan had virtually no chance of regaining her mental faculties, her parents asked hospital employees to terminate the artificial nutrition and hydration procedures. All agreed that such a removal would cause her death. The employees refused to honor the request without court approval. The parents then sought

(continues)

CASE LAW *Cruzan v. Director, Missouri Department of Health, et al.* *(continued)*

and received authorization from the state trial court for termination. The court also found that Nancy's expressed thoughts at age twenty-five in a somewhat serious conversation with a housemate suggested that given her present condition she would not wish to continue on with her nutrition and hydration.

The Supreme Court of Missouri reversed by a divided vote. The Missouri Supreme Court found that Cruzan's statements to her roommate regarding her desire to live or die under certain conditions were unreliable for the purpose of determining her intent.

Issue: Whether the Due Process Clause will permit the state of Missouri to require that absent a patient's prior, expressed choice, a clear and convincing standard of proof is necessary to determine if a patient in an irreversible persistent vegetative state should remain on life support.

Court
Reasoning: In the *Quinlan* case, young Karen Quinlan suffered severe brain damage as the result of anoxia and entered a persistent vegetative state. Karen's father sought judicial approval to disconnect his daughter's respirator. The New Jersey Supreme Court granted the relief, holding that Karen had a right of privacy grounded in the Federal Constitution to terminate treatment. However, after *Quinlan,* most courts have based a right to refuse treatment either solely on the common-law right to informed consent or on both the common-law right and a constitutional privacy right. Despite its pitfalls and inevitable uncertainties, the inquiry must always be narrowed to the patient's expressed intent, with every effort made to minimize the opportunity for error.

The common-law doctrine of informed consent is viewed as generally encompassing the right of a competent individual to refuse medical treatment. Beyond that, many state cases demonstrate both similarity and diversity in their approaches to deciding what all agree is a perplexing question with unusually strong moral and ethical overtones. State courts have available to them for decision a number of sources—state constitutions, statutes, and common law which are not available to us. In this Court, the question is simply and starkly whether the United States Constitution prohibits Missouri from choosing the rule of decision which it did. This is the first case in which we have been squarely presented with the issue whether the United States Constitution grants what is in common parlance referred to as a *right to die.* We follow the judicious counsel of our decision in *Twin City Bank v. Nebeker,* 167 U.S. 196, 202, 17 S. Ct. 766, 769,42 L. Ed. 134 (1997), where we said that in deciding "a question of such magnitude and importance it is the better part of wisdom not to attempt, by any general statement, to cover every possible phase of the subject."

The Fourteenth Amendment provides that no State shall "deprive any person of life, liberty, or property, without due process of law." The principle that a competent person has a constitutionally protected liberty interest in refusing unwanted medical treatment may be inferred from our prior decisions. But determining that a person has a "liberty interest" under the Due Process Clause does not end the inquiry. Whether respondent's constitutional rights have been violated must be determined by balancing his liberty interests against the relevant state interest.

In the context presented here, a State has more particular interests at stake. The choice between life and death is a deeply personal decision of obvious and overwhelming finality. We believe Missouri may legitimately seek to safeguard the personal element of this choice through the imposition of heightened evidentiary requirements.

(continues)

CASE LAW *Cruzan v. Director, Missouri Department of Health, et al.* *(continued)*

Since Cruzan was a patient at a state hospital when this litigation commenced, the State has been involved as an adversary from the beginning. However, it can be expected that many disputes of this type will arise in private institutions, where a *guardian ad litem* or similar party will have been appointed as the sole representative of the incompetent individual in the litigation. In such cases, a guardian may act in good faith, and yet not maintain a position truly adversarial to that of the family. Indeed, as noted by the court below, "the *guardian ad litem* in this case finds himself in the predicament of believing that it is in Nancy's best interest to have the tube feeding discontinued, but feeling that an appeal should be made because our responsibility to her as attorneys and *guardians ad litem* was to pursue this matter to the highest court in the state in view of the fact that this is a case of first impression in the State of Missouri."

Cruzan's *guardian ad litem* has also filed a brief in this Court urging reversal of the Missouri Supreme Court's decision. In review, Missouri has permissibly sought to advance these interests through the adoption of a clear and convincing standard of proof to govern such proceedings. This level of proof, or an even higher one, has traditionally been imposed in cases involving allegations of civil fraud, and in a variety of other kinds of civil cases involving such issues as lost wills, oral contracts to make bequests, and the like. It is self-evident that the interests at stake in the instant proceedings are more substantial, both on an individual and societal level, than those involved in a run-of-the-mill civil dispute. An erroneous decision not to terminate results in maintenance of the status quo and an erroneous decision to withdraw life-sustaining treatment, however, is not susceptible to correction.

At common law and by statute in most states, the parole evidence rule prevents the variations of the terms of a written contract by oral testimony. The Statute of Frauds makes unenforceable oral contracts to leave property by will, and statutes regulating the making of wills universally require that those instruments be in writing.

In summary, we conclude that a state may apply a clear and convincing evidence standard in proceedings where a guardian seeks to discontinue nutrition and hydration of a person diagnosed to be in a persistent vegetative state. We note that many courts which have adopted some sort of substituted judgment procedure in situations like this, whether they limit consideration of evidence to the prior expressed wishes of the individual's decision would have been, require a clear and convincing standard of proof for such evidence.

The Supreme Court of Missouri held that in this case the testimony presented at trial did not amount to clear and convincing proof of the patient's desire to have hydration and nutrition withdrawn. The testimony presented at trial consisted primarily of Nancy Cruzan's statements made to a housemate about a year before her accident that she would not want to live should she face life as a "vegetable" and other observations to the same effect.

Holding: The judgment of the Supreme Court of Missouri is affirmed.

Justice Brennen, with whom Justice Marshall and Justice Blackmun joined, dissented.

Dissent: A grown woman at the time of the accident, Nancy had previously expressed her wish to forgo continuing medical care under circumstances such as these. Her family and her friends are convinced that this is what she would want. A *guardian ad litem* appointed by the trial court is also convinced that this is what Nancy would want. Yet the Missouri Supreme Court, alone among state courts deciding such a question, has determined that an irreversibly vegetative patient will remain a passive prisoner of medical technology—for Nancy, perhaps for the next 30 years.

(continues)

Today the Court, while tentatively accepting that there is some degree of constitutionally protected liberty interest in avoiding unwanted medical treatment, including life-sustaining medical treatment such as artificial nutrition and hydration, affirms the decision of the Missouri Supreme Court. Because I believe that Nancy Cruzan has a fundamental right to be free of unwanted artificial nutrition and hydration, which right is not outweighed by any interests of the State, and because I find that the improperly biased procedural obstacles imposed by the Missouri Supreme Court impermissibly burden that right, I respectfully dissent. Nancy Cruzan is entitled to choose to die with dignity.

The starting point for our legal analysis must be whether a competent person has a constitutional right to avoid unwanted medical care. Today, the Court concedes that our prior decisions "support the recognition of a general liberty interest in refusing medical treatment." But if a competent person has a liberty interest to be free of unwanted medical treatment, as both the majority and Justice O'Connor concede, it must be fundamental. We are dealing here with a decision which involves one of the basic civil rights of man.

Case
Discussion:

Do you think Nancy Cruzan's headstone is a reflection of the legal trauma suffered after her brain injury? The headstone reads as follows:

Born July 20, 1957
Departed Jan. 11, 1983
At peace December 26, 1990

The Legacy of Public Tragedies

Each of the very public tragedies of the *Quinlan, Schiavo,* and *Cruzan* cases have spurred new court battles, new laws, and new attitudes in society regarding the way the right-to-die issue is viewed. Every state in the country now recognizes a person's legal right to define how far that person wants medical treatment to go and where treating limits should be set. As noted previously, the *Cruzan* case inspired a 1991 federal law called the Patient Self-Determination Act. The Act requires hospitals and other care providers to inform patients of their state's laws about end-of-life care and advance directives.[16] Specifically, the Act addresses the right to autonomous patient decision-making. The Act also made each state responsible for developing written guidelines of its laws concerning advance directives for health care.

IS PHYSICIAN-ASSISTED SUICIDE A VIABLE END-OF-LIFE OPTION?

End-of-life issues for patients concentrate on three questions according to a recent national study spearheaded by the nation's attorney generals:

1. Will my pain be managed?

2. Will my wishes be known and honored?

3. Will I receive competent care?[17]

Lack of satisfaction with the established end-of-life practices proffered by medical and insurance fields led to a renewed interest by many groups in the late twentieth century to redefine how a patient's life is ended. One example of this interest was the attempts to legalize **physician-assisted suicide**. Physician-assisted suicide occurs when a physician knowingly assists in fulfilling a patient's desire to die. The term *assisted suicide* can be used when a non-physician assists in fulfilling an individual's desire to die.

A majority of Americans want to die at home, free of pain and surrounded by friends and family according to a Robert Woods Foundation report entitled, Study to Understand Prognosis and Preferences for Outcomes and Risks of Treatment. Interestingly, New Jersey's legislature has required that the state's version of the *Patient Bill of Rights* include the monitoring of a patient's pain level as a fifth vital sign that medical personnel are to check as part of their regular monitoring routine.

The Study noted that while patients might sign an advance directive for health care before a life-threatening illness strikes, those directives might not be included in their medical records or may be unknown to family and medical personnel. Another problem is that some health care providers knowingly disregard a dying patient's advance directives for health care.

Wrestling with Right-to-Die Issues

Many nations have wrestled with the right–to-die issue. The subject of physician-assisted suicide has been debated for years in Europe and Australia. Australia became the first country in the world to legalize **euthanasia**, but it overturned that ruling less than a year later in 1997. Euthanasia is the act of painlessly putting to death a person suffering from an incurable or painful disease without the final decision being made by the suffering person (often because the person is not conscious, capable, and communicative), but rather by the person's physician. Euthanasia sometimes is described as a *mercy killing*. During the *Schiavo* case, the Vatican weighed in with its official condemnation of the removal of Terry Schiavo's life support in particular and physician-assisted suicide and euthanasia in principal. The Netherlands was the first country in Europe to legalize physician-assisted suicide. Belgium followed in 2002 and became the second European nation to decriminalize euthanasia. *Euthanasia* is the term used in the Netherlands and Belgium for physician-assisted suicide.[18]

In the United States, Oregon's legislature enacted Oregon's Death with Dignity Act over a decade ago amidst opponent's cries that the slippery slope would end with a veritable onslaught of physician-assisted suicides. Quite a few states, including Vermont and California, have had active discussions regarding the enactment of legislation that would permit physician-assisted suicide.

physician-assisted suicide

The voluntary ending of a patient's life when a physician knowingly assists in fulfilling the patient's desire to die.

euthanasia

The act of painlessly putting to death a person suffering from an incurable or painful disease without the final decision being made by the suffering person, but rather by the person's physician; sometimes described as a mercy killing.

However, the closest vote occurred in Hawaii in 2002 when that state's senate defeated such a bill. Voters in California failed to approve assisted suicide legislation in 1992 by a vote of 54 percent to 46 percent. Oregon's Death with Dignity Act provides the right to die only to competent adults who have been diagnosed with a terminal illness; in addition, two doctors must confirm that the person is competent and has only six months to live. The patient must then write a written request for a lethal dose, but the patient must administer the dose himself.

According to Oregon state records, hundreds of people have gone through the preliminary requirements but only 171 have ingested a prescribed lethal dose since the 1994 law was enacted. This number is compared to the total 53,544 Oregon residents who died during the same period with the same diseases as the 171. Surveys by the Oregon Department of Health Services suggest that patients mainly want an option to end their life as they see fit.[19]

Former U.S. Attorney General John Ashcroft disagreed with Oregon's Death with Dignity Act and attempted to sink the legislation by urging that any physician prescribing a lethal dosage should have his medical licenses removed. Lawsuits resulted, culminating in the U.S. Court of Appeals for the Ninth Circuit upholding Oregon's law and ruling that then-Attorney General Ashcroft had overstepped his authority and doctors in Oregon should not be punished. The following case was one such lawsuit involving physicians practicing in the state of Washington. It was decided by the U.S. Supreme Court.

CASE LAW *Washington, v. Glucksberg*

117 S. Ct. 2258, 138 L.Ed.2d 772 (1997)

Facts:
Petitioners in this case were the State of Washington and its Attorney General. Respondents were Harold Glucksberg, M.D., Abigail Halperin, M.D., Thomas A. Preston, M.D., and Peter Shalit, M.D., who were physicians practicing in Washington. These doctors occasionally treated terminally ill, suffering patients, and declared that they would assist these patients in ending their lives if not for Washington's assisted-suicide ban. The Respondents in January 1994, along with three gravely ill, pseudonymous plaintiffs who have since died and Compassion in Dying, a nonprofit organization that counsels people considering physician-assisted suicide, sued in the United States District court, seeking a declaration that Wash. Rev. Code § 9A.36.060 (1) (1994) was unconstitutional.

The plaintiffs asserted "the existence of a liberty interest protected by the Fourteenth Amendment which extends to a personal choice by a mentally competent, terminally ill adult to commit physician assisted suicide." The District Court agreed, because it "places an undue burden on the exercise of that constitutionally protected liberty interest." The District Court also decided that the Washington statute violated the Equal Protection Clause's requirement that "all persons similarly situated be treated alike."

(continues)

CASE LAW *Washington, v. Glucksberg* (continued)

It has always been a crime to assist a suicide in the State of Washington. In 1854, Washington's first Territorial Legislature outlawed "assisting another in the commission of self-murder." Today, Washington law provides: "A person is guilty of promoting a suicide attempt when he knowingly causes or aids another person to attempt suicide."

A panel of the Court of Appeals for the Ninth Circuit reversed the District Court emphasizing that "in the two hundred and five years of our existence no constitutional right to aid in killing oneself has ever been asserted and upheld by a court of final jurisdiction." The Ninth Circuit reheard the case en banc, reversed the panel's decision, and affirmed the District Court. The court also discussed what it described as "historical" and "current societal attitudes" toward suicide and assisted suicide and concluded that "the Constitution encompasses a due process liberty interest in controlling the time and manner of one's death that there is, in short, a constitutionally recognized right to die." After "weighing and balancing" this interest against Washington's various interests, the court held that the State's assisted suicide ban was unconstitutional "as applied to terminally ill competent adults who wish to hasten their deaths with medication prescribed by their physicians."

Issue:	Whether Washington's prohibition against causing or aiding a suicide offends the Fourteenth Amendment to the U.S. Constitution.
Court's Reasoning:	In all due process cases, the court begins by examining our Nation's history, legal traditions, and practices. The majority of states in this country have laws imposing criminal penalties on one who assists another to commit suicide. More specifically, for over 700 years, the Anglo-American common-law tradition has punished or otherwise disapproved of both suicide and assisting suicide. In the 13th century, Henry de Bracton, one of the first legal treatise writers, observed that "just as a man may commit felony by slaying another so may he do so by slaying himself."

The earliest American statute to explicitly outlaw assisting suicide was enacted in New York in 1828, and many of the new states and territories followed New York's example. Though deeply rooted, the States' assisted suicide bans have in recent years been reexamined and generally, reaffirmed. Because of advances in medicine and technology, Americans today are increasingly likely to die in institutions, from chronic illnesses. Public concern and democratic action are therefore sharply focused on how best to protect dignity and independence at the end of life, with the result that there have been many significant changes in state laws and in the attitudes these laws reflect. States now permit "living wills" and surrogate health care decision-making. However, voters and legislators continue for the most part to reaffirm their states' prohibitions on assisting suicides. The Washington statute at issue in this case, Wash. Rev. Code § 9A. 36. 060 (1994), was enacted in 1975 as part of a revision of that State's criminal code. Four years, later, Washington passed its Natural Death Act, which specifically stated that the "withholding or withdrawal of life-sustaining treatment shall not, for a purpose, constitute a suicide" and that "nothing in this chapter shall be construed to condone, authorize, or approve mercy killing." In 1991, Washington voters rejected a ballot initiative which, had it passed, would have permitted a form of physician-assisted suicide. Washington then added a provision to the Natural Death Act expressly excluding physician-assisted suicide.

Holding:	The U.S. Supreme Court reversed.
Case Discussion:	This case made great strides by reaching the U.S. Supreme Court. The case is important because the court held that patients should have more to say in how their end-of life-issues are determined. However, the court stopped short of providing a constitutional right to physician-assisted suicide when it reversed the lower court.

Court Says No to Euthanasia

The court in the following case stated that it was very much aware of the intense emotions and competing moral philosophies that characterized the debate surrounding suicide in general and assisted suicide in particular. The infamous defendant in the case "pushed the envelope" with his admitted actions so that the issue would ultimately be heard by the U.S. Supreme Court.

CASE LAW *People of the State of Michigan v. Jack Kevorkian*

639 N.2d 291 (Mich.App.2001)

Facts: A jury convicted defendant, Dr. Jack Kevorkian, of second-degree murder and delivering a controlled substance. The trial court sentenced him to concurrent prison terms of ten to twenty-five years for the murder conviction and seven years for the controlled substance conviction. The defendant appealed.

On September 15, 1998, at 9:55 p.m., defendant went to Youk's home to discuss Youk's condition. As the videotape of this discussion revealed, defendant stated that he was recording their interaction in "connection with a request from Thomas Youk for help in ending his suffering." Youk stated that, at the time, he could not do anything for himself, that he had discussed "his wishes" with his mother, brother, and wife, and "They understand why. It's my decision." Defendant then told Youk that he needed to sign a form indicating that he was consenting to a "direct injection instead of using the device, the machine." Defendant then read the consent form, which stated in part:

"I, Thomas Youk, the undersigned, entirely voluntarily, without any reservation, external persuasion, pressure, or duress, and after prolonged and thorough deliberation, hereby consent to the following active euthanasia, to be administered by a competent medical professional, in order to end with certainty my intolerable and hopelessly incurable suffering." The meeting ended at 10:15 p.m.

On September 16, 1998, at 9:49 p.m., defendant again videotaped himself and Youk at Youk's home. Youk stated that he "wanted to go through with this" and signed the consent form. Defendant remarked that he would inject Youk in the vein because "it's quicker," and stated, "Now I'm going to put on a cardiogram so we know when your heart is stopped, okay." Defendant established a connection between Youk and the electrocardiogram. Defendant injected Youk with Anectine and Seconal before injecting Youk with potassium chloride. During this time, defendant provided a commentary on what was occurring: "Sleepy Tom? Tom are you asleep? And now we'll inject the Anectine. You asleep Tom? Tom? You asleep? He's asleep. Now the Potassium Chloride. This machine is recording for some reason so I'm pulling it by hand until the heart stops. It's been, it's been about two minutes since I injected the, ah, seconal, and one minute since I injected the—. Now we're getting agonal complexes and that's about the, the Potassium Chloride will stop the heart, so. Now there's a straight line. A straight line and the cardiogram will be turned off. His heart is stopped."

The police were dispatched to Youk's house on September 17, 1998, at 1:30 a.m. They found Youk lying on his bed, dead. The police also found a Federal Express receipt with defendant's name at the scene. The medical examiner listed the manner of death as homicide and the cause of death as intravenous injection of substances. During the autopsy, the medical examiner found two "fresh" needle marks on Youk's left and right wrists that had been covered with makeup.

(continues)

CASE LAW *People of the State of Michigan v. Jack Kevorkian* (continued)

News correspondent Mike Wallace interviewed defendant for *60 Minutes.* In the first clip from the interview shown to the jury, Wallace stated at the outset, "You killed him." Defendant responded: "I did, but it could be Manslaughter not Murder. It's not necessarily murder. But it doesn't bother me what you call it. I know what it is. This could never be a crime in any society which deems itself enlightened." Defendant then told Wallace, "Either they go or I go." Apparently meaning that he would be acquitted for killing Youk or, if convicted, he would starve to death in prison. As defendant put it: "I've got to force them to act. They must charge me. Because if they do not, that means they don't think it's a crime. Because they don't need any more evidence do they? Do you have to dust for fingerprints on this?" Defendant then returned to one of his main themes, saying: "If you don't have liberty and self-determination, you got nothing. That's what this country's built on and this is the ultimate self-determination to determine when and how you're gonna die when you're suffering."

Defendant gave his own closing argument to the jury on March 25, 1999.

Issue: Whether the right of privacy should be expanded to include a right to euthanasia.

Court's
Reasoning: In this appeal, defendant has given almost no attention to his claim that this homicide had a legal justification or excuse. Indeed, exactly seven of the fifty pages in his brief to this Court address euthanasia. Even during oral arguments, defendant's appellate counsel made not a single reference to this issue. Nevertheless, euthanasia is at the core of this case. But for defendant's self-described zealotry, Thomas Youk's death would, in all probability, not have been the subject of national attention, much less a murder trial. Defendant, in what is now apparently something of an afterthought, asks us to conclude that euthanasia is legal and, therefore, to reverse his conviction on constitutional grounds. We refuse. Such a holding would be the first step down a very steep and very slippery slope. To paraphrase the United States Supreme Court in *Washington v. Glucksberg,* it would expand the right to privacy to include a right to commit euthanasia and thus place the issue outside the arenas of public debate and legislative action.

On appeal, defendant makes two related, but separate, constitutional arguments. First, he argues that the unenumerated rights protected by the Ninth Amendment and its Michigan constitutional counterpart include a patient's right to be free from unbearable pain and suffering. Second, he maintains that the Fourteenth Amendment and its Michigan constitutional counterpart also include this right by proscribing state deprivation of liberty without due process of law either under constitutional privacy concepts or as a "necessary and direct corollary of this position and that a person should not be forced to suffer unbearably."

The Ninth Amendment of the United States Constitution states that "the enumeration in the Constitution, of certain rights, shall not be construed to deny or disparage others retained by the people." The counterpart provision in the Michigan Constitution states that "the enumeration in this constitution of certain rights shall not be construed to deny or disparage others retained by the people."

The Fourteenth Amendment of the United States Constitution states, in relevant part, that no state shall "deprive any person of life, liberty, or property, without due process of law." The counterpart provision in the Michigan Constitution states, in relevant part, that "no person shall be deprived of life, liberty or property, without due process of law."

At the outset, within the nature of the defendant's arguments, it is important to understand the nature of defendant's constitutional claims. The best way to do this is to state clearly the constitutional arguments that defendant does not raise. First, defendant does not ask us to hold that he acted properly in furtherance of the right to refuse life-sustaining medical treatment. In *Cruzan v. Director, Missouri Department of Health,*

(continues)

the United States Supreme Court "assumed that the United States Constitution would grant a competent person a constitutionally protected right to refuse lifesaving hydration and nutrition," under the Fourteenth Amendment due process liberty interest analysis.

More recently, in *Glucksberg,* the court strengthened the constitutional basis for the *Cruzan* decision, interpreting *Cruzan* as holding that "the right to refuse unwanted medical treatment was so rooted in our history, tradition, and practice as to require special protection under the Fourteenth Amendment." Here, the defendant does not, and could not, rely on *Cruzan;* factually, this case does not involve removing life support. Further, though not resting their decisions precisely on the Fourteenth Amendment, Michigan courts have arrived at the same conclusion regarding a patient's right to refuse life-sustaining medical care. The limited scope of these cases does not establish a right to be free from unbearable pain and suffering that would make euthanasia legal. There is, of course a substantial factual distinction between refusing care, even if doing so hastens death, and purposefully ending a life.

The defendant makes no attempt to assert that he was engaged in assisted suicide when he injected Youk with potassium chloride causing his death. Rather, he asserts that if the Ninth Amendment "is to have any substantive meaning," the right to be free from inexorable pain and suffering must be among the unenumerated rights protected by that amendment and its Michigan counterpart. Defendant then contends that he cannot be prosecuted for "aiding in Thomas Youk's assertion of his constitutional right to be free from intolerable pain and suffering." Although defendant's appellate counsel has carefully avoided using the words, as we have already noted, the record indicates that defendant was quite specific when describing his actions; he said he was engaged in "active euthanasia" and the consent form that Youk signed directly refers to such active euthanasia. In summary, defendant does not, nor could he, ask us to hold that his actions were legally justifiable because he simply helped Youk exercise his right to refuse medical care. Defendant does not, nor could he ask us to hold that his actions constituted a legal form of assisted suicide. In a nutshell, and using his own terminology, defendant asks us to legalize euthanasia.

Third, we observe that by expanding the right of privacy to include a right to commit euthanasia in order to end intolerable and irremediable suffering we would inevitably involve the judiciary in deciding questions that are simply beyond its capacity. Rather, the role of the courts is to apply the rule of law. As Chief Justice Burger once eloquently explained:

It is often observed that hard cases make bad law. I suspect there is some truth to that adage, for the "hard" cases always tempt judges to exceed the limits of their authority . . . to reach a "desirable" result. Cardozo no doubt had this type of case in mind when he wrote:

"The judge, even when he is free, is still not wholly free. He is not to innovate at pleasure. He is not a knight-errant, roaming at will in pursuit of his own ideal of beauty or of goodness. He is to draw his inspiration from consecrated principles. He is not to yield to spasmodic sentiment, to vague and unregulated benevolence. He is to exercise a discretion informed by tradition, methodized by analogy, disciplined by system, and subordinated to 'the primordial necessity of order in the social life.' Wide enough in all conscience is the field of discretion that remains." What Cardozo tells us is beware the "good result," achieved by judicially unauthorized or intellectually dishonest means on the appealing notion that the desirable ends justify the improper judicial means. For there is always the danger that the seeds of precedent sown by good men for the best of motives will yield a rich harvest of unprincipled acts of others also aiming at "good ends."

(continues)

CASE LAW   *People of the State of Michigan v. Jack Kevorkian* (continued)

There is no authority whatsoever for the proposition that there is a right to be free from intolerable and irremediable suffering. There may be little distinction between the intent of a terminally ill patient who decides to remove her life support and one who seeks the assistance of a doctor in ending her life; in both situations, the patient is seeking to hasten a certain, impending death.

We conclude by noting that the jury, no doubt influenced by the gritty realism of the videotapes defendant made as well as his flat statement of culpability in the 60 *Minutes* interview, convicted defendant of second-degree murder as well as delivery of a controlled substance. Defendant has on the record before us compared himself to Margaret Sanger, Susan B. Anthony, and Dr. Martin Luther King, Jr., all of whom risked imprisonment for their beliefs. How history will view defendant is a matter this court can neither predict nor decide. Perhaps in the brave new world of defendant's "enlightened" society, acts such as the one he committed in this case will be excused. Still, we find it difficult to hypothesize a rule of law under which this might be so. We deal here, however, with this application of the law as it currently exists to the facts of this case. While defendant has carefully skirted the label of murder in his past actions he cannot do so now. Here, defendant in essence convicted himself of a murder he surely committed. We will not now reverse that conviction on due process grounds. The trial court did not abuse its discretion in refusing to dismiss the charges.

Holding:	Affirmed.
Case Discussion:	Does the use of medical assistance perverse the natural progression of dying? Whatever the answer may be, the Supreme Court in the *Kevorkian* case leaves America's citizens to deal with policy questions surrounding physician-assisted suicide through ballot initiative or through their elected representatives. Interestingly, The American Hospital Association has estimated that 75 percent of hospital deaths are somehow negotiated.[20]

Status of Physician-Assisted Suicide

There are criminal prohibitions against physician-assisted suicide and heavy state criminal penalties levied upon those who participate in it. The U.S. Supreme Court has failed to find such penalties a violation of the Fourteenth Amendment's Due Process Clause in any of the state laws against physician-assisted suicide. In fact, in 1997, the Supreme Court unanimously upheld New York and Washington state court decisions that criminalized physician-assisted suicide. The Supreme Court clearly found that there was no constitutional right to die, but left it to the individual states to determine whether physician-assisted suicide would be permitted in their state. The majority of states have outright prohibited physician-assisted suicide through state statutes, and several states without statutes prohibit such assistance through common law. The American Medical Association (AMA) is very clear in its position on physician-assisted suicide. The AMA does not support it.

Oregon is currently the only state that has legalized physician-assisted suicide. The only federal law that has dealt with the concept of assisted suicide has been the Assisted Suicide Funding Restriction Act. It prohibits any federal funding to be used to support physician-assisted suicide.

PALLIATIVE CARE

■ **palliative care**

Care that treats the
symptoms of an incurable
disease to make them
easier to bear. Hospice
care.

Studies have shown that American patients near the end of their lives often spend more time in intensive care wards of hospitals than they do being treated for their incurable illnesses with **palliative care** and community-based hospice care.[21] Palliative care is the comprehensive management of the physical, psychological, social, spiritual, and existential needs of patients. Refer to Exhibit 3–4 to read the World Health Organization's definition of palliative care. This care is especially suited to individuals who have incurable progressive illnesses. Palliative care is a broad term used to define the many types of non-medically intrusive care offered to patients with incurable diseases. It concentrates mainly on keeping a patient comfortable by dealing with his pain and is most often provided in a hospice setting. Admission to a hospice is sometimes hindered by Medicare and other insurance companies requiring that a patient's physician certify that the patient is in his last six months of life. These same studies stated that a patient's end-of-life treatment may not be designed around the patient's needs, but is based on Medicare and insurance coverage. The reality is that the majority of Americans die in hospitals or nursing homes without their health care wishes known and often in intense pain.[22]

In addition, physicians historically have not been trained to deal with the palliative care of patients, but to concentrate on curing patient illnesses. All of these factors combine with the economic need to fill hospital beds.

Florida's statutes provide a thorough description of what its palliative care must consist of.[23] According to Florida's statutory authority, palliative care must include the following:

1. An opportunity to discuss and plan for end-of-life care

2. Assurance that physical and mental suffering will be carefully attended to

3. Assurance that preferences for withholding and withdrawing life-sustaining interventions will be honored

4. Assurance that the personal goals of the dying person will be addressed

5. Assurance that the dignity of the dying person will be a priority

6. Assurance that health care providers will not abandon the dying person

7. Assurance that the burden to family and others will be addressed

8. Assurance that any advance directive for care will be respected regardless of the location of care

9. Assurance that an organizational mechanism is in place to evaluate the availability and quality of end-of-life, palliative, and hospice care service, including the evaluation of administrative regulatory barriers

10. Assurance that necessary health care services will be provided and that relevant reimbursement policies are available

11. Assurance that the goals expressed in subparagraphs one through 10 will be accomplished in a culturally appropriate manner.

EXHIBIT 3–4 WORLD HEALTH ORGANIZATION'S DEFINITION OF PALLIATIVE CARE

Palliative care is an approach that improves the quality of life of patients and their families facing the problems associated with life-threatening illness, through the prevention and relief of suffering by means of early identification and impeccable assessment and treatment of pain and other problems, physical, psychosocial, and spiritual. Palliative care:

- provides relief from pain and other distressing symptoms;

- affirms life and regards dying as a normal process;

- intends neither to hasten or postpone death;

- integrates the psychological and spiritual aspects of patient care;

- offers a support system to help patients live as actively as possible until death;

- offers a support system to help the family cope during the patient's illness and in their own bereavement;

- uses a team approach to address the needs of patients and their families, including bereavement counseling, if indicated;

- will enhance quality of life, and may also positively influence the course of illness;

- is applicable early in the course of illness, in conjunction with other therapies that are intended to prolong life, such as chemotherapy or radiation therapy, and includes those investigations needed to better understand and manage distressing clinical complications.

Source: < http://www.who.int/cancer/palliative/definition/en>

SUMMARY

All 50 states allow for some kind of advance directive for health care and have statutes that provide the procedural and substantive drafting requirements. There is no "right" way to create an advance directive for health care. Most states have one or two types of advance directive documents. A living will is self-directed and should describe an individual's wishes regarding medical treatments the person would want if he was unable to share his wishes with health care providers. The second type of document is a medical power of attorney. It allows an individual to appoint a trusted person to make health care choices when the individual is not able to share his choices with health care providers. If a client wanted to create both types of powers of attorney, he would not have to make the same person the agent of both documents. All three types of powers of attorney (health care, special, and general) can be made a permanent part of a client's life planning file by being created as durable powers of attorney. A durable power of attorney remains in effect even if the creator becomes incompetent. The determination of incapacity is typically decided by an individual's primary physician and usually needs to be seconded by another physician.

The U.S. Supreme Court has failed to find a violation of the Fourteenth Amendment's Due Process Clause in any of the state laws against physician-assisted suicide. The Supreme Court has found that there is no constitutional right to die, but leaves it to the individual states to determine whether physician-assisted suicide will be permitted in their state. The majority of states have outright prohibited physician-assisted suicide through state statutes, and several states without statutes prohibit such assistance through common law. Oregon is the only state that permits physician-assisted suicide under specific conditions.

▓ KEY TERMS

advance directives for health care	guardian ad litem	medical power of attorney
agent	health care power of attorney	palliative care
attorney-in-fact	(HCPOA)	physician-assisted suicide
durable power of attorney	health care proxy	principal
durable power of attorney for	health care representative	special power of attorney
health care	health insurance portability and	springing durable power of attorney
euthanasia	accountability act (HIPPA)	
general power of attorney	living will	

▓ REVIEW QUESTIONS

1. Advance directives for health care are known by a variety of names. What are those names?

2. What are the differences between a living will and a medical power of attorney?

3. What needs to be done for a client to make a power of attorney a permanent part of his planning file?

4. What is the name of the document that is created only upon the occurrence of a certain event?

5. What responsibilities does a health care proxy's job usually entail?

6. When and with whom should a living will's creator discuss the directives of the living will?

7. Where should an advance directive for health care be stored?

8. What was the state of Washington's position on physician-assisted suicide in the *Washington v. Glucksberg* case?

9. What is the American Medical Association's position on physician-assisted suicide?

10. What is the philosophy behind palliative care?

▪ ETHICS ALERT

Humming with the sounds of telephones ringing, computer keys being struck at a furious pace, and copiers spewing out documents, it was a typical day at the law office of Tara Jensen. As usual, Tara planned to see clients all day. Unfortunately, Rena, Luke, and Tara had gotten their signals crossed. Luke had scheduled clients to come in to review and sign their wills, advance directives for health care, and durable powers of attorney at the same time Tara was scheduled to see clients across town. Feeling more confident every day, Luke told Tara that he thought he was ready to supervise the client's review and signing of the documents in the office; otherwise, they would have to cancel the appointment, disappointing their clients.

Some states frown on certain tasks being delegated to paralegals. Would Luke's suggestion that he supervise the client's executions of their wills, advance directives for health care, and durable powers of attorney be a problem if Tara's office was located in your home state? What tasks does the *ABA Model Guidelines for the Utilization of Paralegal Services* clearly state that an attorney may not delegate to paralegals? Refer to "Helpful Web Sites" at the end of the chapter for the ABA's Web site. There you will find the *Model Guidelines for the Utilization of Paralegal Services.*

▪ HELPFUL WEB SITES

AMERICAN BAR ASSOCIATION <HTTP://WWW.ABANET.ORG/LEGALSERVICES/PARALEGALS/ DOWNLOADS/MODELGUIDELINES.PDF>   This link provides the *ABA Model Guidelines for the Utilization of Paralegal Services.*

COMPASSION IN DYING® <HTTP://WWW.COMPASSIONINDYING.ORG>   This Web site is maintained by the organization Compassion & Choices, formerly known as Compassion in Dying Federation. It maintains the mission of improving care and choices at the end of one's life.

U.S. LIVING WILL REGISTRY® <HTTP://WWW.USLIVINGWILLREGISTRY.COM/FORMS.SHTM>   This site provides links to all state forms for advance directives.

AMERICAN BAR ASSOCIATION <HTTP://WWW.ABANET.ORG/AGING/TOOLKIT/HOME.HTML>   The ABA Commission on Law & Aging provides a *Consumer's Tool Kit for Health Care Advance Planning.*

AMERICAN MEDICAL ASSOCIATION <HTTP://WWW.AMA-ASSN.ORG>   The American Medical Association provides information on advance directives.

FINDING OUR WAY <HTTP://WWW.FINDINGOURWAY.NET>   This organization offers a course on death and dying in America.

AGING WITH DIGNITY <HTTP://WWW.AGINGWITHDIGNITY.ORG>   This site lists five wishes that a person should consider including in a living will. Read the Five Wishes document in the Elder Law Online Supplement.

STATE OF FLORIDA AGENCY FOR HEALTH CARE ADMINISTRATION <HTTP://WWW.FLORIDA-HEALTHFINDER.GOV>   This Web site provides information about the Florida health care system.

CARING CONNECTIONS <HTTP://WWW.CARINGINFO.ORG>   This is the Web site of the National Hospice and Palliative Care Organization. It provides free information and state-specific advance directive forms with instructions on how to fill them out.

■ ENDNOTES

[1] Written by Justice Cardozo in the *Schloendorff v. The Society of the New York Hospital*, 211 N.Y. 125, 105 N.E. 92 (1914) opinion while he was sitting on the New York Superior Court bench.

[2] Miller, Jim, "Schiavo Case Shows Living Wills Importance," *Time of Your Life*, April 23, 2005, page 2.

[3] "Incapacitated and Alone: Health Care Decision-Making for the Unbefriended Elderly," *ABA Commission on Aging*, March 2005 <http://www.abanet.org/aging>

[4] Scott, Charity, *The Atlanta Journal*, March 19, 2005.

[5] Pearson, Janet, "Pivotal Role for States in Reforming End of Life Care," *The Record*, August 24, 2003, page 4.

[6] Artificially provided fluids and nutrition—"Artificial feeding is not feeding in the sense that we normally use the word. Instead, it's a way of getting calories and nutrients into the body when a person can't eat naturally. It may involve the use of a tube inserted into the stomach through the nose, or inserted surgically through the skin and stomach wall. The tube can deliver nutrition, water and medications. Fluid and medications can also be delivered through an intravenous (IV) line. Artificially provided nutrition and water (hydration) serve different but related purposes, and are often discussed as a single topic." <http://www.commtechlab.msu.edu/SITES/COMPLETINGALIFE/audioon/tc/adv_life_feeding.html>

Cardiopulmonary Resuscitation (CPR)—"Cardiopulmonary resuscitation (CPR) is a combination of rescue breathing and chest compressions delivered to victims thought to be in cardiac arrest. When cardiac arrest occurs, the heart stops pumping blood. CPR can support a small amount of blood flow to the heart and brain to "buy time" until normal heart function is restored." <http://www.americanheart.org/presenter.jhtml?identifier=4479>

Life-sustaining measures—"These are measures used to sustain or prolong life artificially, and include:

- cardiopulmonary resuscitation or other emergency treatment to keep your heart beating

- a machine to keep you breathing because your lungs have stopped working (assisted ventilation)

- artificial feeding and artificial hydration (administered through a tube into the stomach called a PEG)." <http://www.justice.qld.gov.au/guardian/poa/ahd.htm#6>

Decision-making capacity—"Consists of three basic elements: (1) the possession of a set of values and goals necessary for evaluating different options; (2) the ability to communicate and understand information; and (3) the ability to reason and to deliberate about one's choices. There are four levels of capacity: (1) the ability to communicate a choice; (2) the ability to understand information; (3) the ability to appreciate one's personal situation; (4) the ability to weigh information in a rationally defensible way. A medical determination of *incapacity* should not be confused with the legal determination of competency

Sources: President's Commission for the Study of Ethical Problems in Medicine and Biomedical and Behavioral Research, *Making Healthcare Decisions: A Report on the Ethical and Legal Implications of Informed Consent in the Patient-Practitioner Relationship* (Washington, D.C.: U.S. Government Printing Office, 1982). Applebaum, P. S., and Grisso, T., "Assessing Patients' Capacities to Consent to Treatment," New *England Journal of Medicine* 319, 1988, p. 1635.<http://www.ascensionhealth.org/ethics/public/issues/decision.asp>

Terminal condition—"*Terminal Condition* means a condition caused by injury, disease, or illness from which there is no reasonable medical probability of recovery and which, without treatment, can be expected to cause death." <http://www.lawdepot.com/contracts/living-will/terminalcond_popup.htm>

Permanent unconsciousness—It also defines "permanently unconscious" as a "medical condition that has been diagnosed in accordance with currently accepted medical standards and with reasonable medical certainty as total and irreversible loss of consciousness and capacity for interaction with the environment." The term includes, without limitations, a persistent vegetative state or irreversible coma." <http://www.psea.org/voice/article.cfm?artid=1655>

Persistent vegetative state—"irreversible coma." <http://www.psea.org/voice/article.cfm?artid=1655>

Incurable and irreversible chronic diseases—"Chronic diseases are diseases of long duration and generally slow progression. Chronic diseases, such as heart disease, stroke, cancer, chronic respiratory diseases and diabetes, are by far the leading cause of mortality in the world, representing 60% of all deaths. Out of the 35 million people who died from chronic disease in 2005, half were under 70 and half were women." <http://www.who.int/topics/chronic_diseases/en>

[7] Kornblum, Janet, "Living Wills Not Always Followed to the Letter," *USA Today*, March 16, 2005.

[8] "Living Wills: A Matter of Life and Death," *AARP* Magazine, December 2003.

[9] Weaver, Peter, *Veterans of Foreign Wars* Magazine, Vol. 92, Issue 6, page 28.

[10] AARP's Legal Counsel for the Elderly.

[11] *McConnell v. Beverly Enterprises-Connecticut, Inc.*, 209 Conn. 692, 553 A.2nd 596 (1989).

[12] The Sparta Independent.

[13] The author is a professor at Sussex County Community College in Newton, New Jersey, and is personally aware of the wide community support and good work done at the Karen Ann Quinlan Hospice.

[14] Column Debate, *USA Today*, March 25, 2005, page A-12.

[15] "Planning for Worse Than Taxes," *Los Angeles Times*, California Metro, Part B, March 22, 2005, page B10.

[16] Patient Self-Determination Act 1991.,

[17] Last Acts Report, Robert Wood Johnson Foundation, New Brunswick, New Jersey, as reported by *The Bergen Record*, August 24, 2003.

[18] Tanner, Robert, "Right to Die Cases Change View of Death," *Associated Press*, March 24, 2005.

[19] Schwartz, John, and Estrin, James, "In Oregon, Choosing Death Over Suffering," *The New York Times*, June 1, 2004.

[20] 19 Koehler, Tamara, "Last Rights," *Scripps Howard News Service* <http://www.lastrights.com>

[21] Last Acts Report, Robert Wood Johnson Foundation, New Brunswick, New Jersey, as reported by *The Bergen Record*, August 24, 2003.

[22] Weaver, Peter, *Veterans of Foreign Wars Magazine*, Vol. 92, Issue 6, page 28.

[23] Florida Statutes Title XLIV Civil Rights Chapter 765 Health Care Advance Directives 765.102 (5)a, (2004). IN 765.102 5(B) 1-11.

Online Companion™
For additional resources, please go to
http://www.paralegal.delmar.cengage.com

4

The Guardianship and Conservatorship Process

■ OBJECTIVES_____

After completing this chapter, you will be able to

- Explain the purpose of creating a guardianship or conservatorship.
- Explain the differences between a guardianship and a conservatorship.
- Explain how the least restrictive alternative principle can be applied.
- Describe the procedural process of a guardianship or conservatorship petition and list the documentation that should be attached to a guardianship or conservatorship petition.
- List the duties of a guardian or conservator.
- Explain how a guardianship or conservatorship can be terminated.
- Explain how the appointment of a guardian can be challenged.

"The moral test of government is how it treats those who are in the dawn of life, the children; those who are in the twilight of life, the aged; and those who are in the shadow of life, the sick, the needy and the handicapped."

HUBERT HUMPHREY

INTRODUCTION

A **guardianship** is a legal management tool put in place by state law to protect and aid individuals who have different abilities to care for themselves. All 50 states and the District of Columbia have enacted guardianship statutes. Generally, there are more similarities than differences among the states. Some states have adopted the Uniform Probate Code (UPC) in their guardianship legislation; others have guardianship statutes of their own design or have modified the UPC. Nationally, many states have made changes to their guardianship statutes in the last few years as a response to changing population demographics. It may be taken for granted that a guardianship is created when a minor child's parents die or are unable to care for her; but when a guardianship involves an adult, its process intersects where law and mental health meet.[1]

Approximately 1.5 million adults are under public or private guardianship in the United States. This means that there is one alleged incompetency for every 1,750 people in the United States.[2]

Unlike a child, each adult citizen is considered to be able to make competent personal and financial decisions. It is when this presumption is questioned and found to be incorrect that a guardianship may be created for an adult person. The person found to be incompetent may then have another person, called a **guardian**, appointed by a court to make personal and financial decisions for the person adjudged incompetent. It should never be assumed that a caregiver automatically is or will become the guardian of the person for whom she is caring.

The major difference between a guardianship and a conservatorship is that a **conservatorship** is a voluntary undertaking requested by a **conservatee** that requires the **conservator** to handle some personal and financial decisions for the conservatee. A conservatee is a person who the court has determined requires a conservator to handle personal and financial decisions. The conservator is the person appointed by a court to be responsible for some of the conservatee's personal and financial decisions. The conservator must have the continuing permission of the conservatee. On the other hand, a guardianship is a completely *involuntary* proceeding with a legal declaration that a person is legally incompetent and becomes the guardian's **ward**. Some states use the term **decisional incapacity** rather than *incompetence*. Louisiana uses the term *interdiction* instead of *guardianship*. Another important difference is that a conservatorship allows management only of a person's property, while a guardianship typically permits *complete* management of a ward's property and person.

Guardianship proceedings usually are necessary only when an individual has failed to plan for her possible incapacity. In the event of incapacity, an individual can still have some say in how she wishes her life to be directed *if the person has declared her wishes in the appropriate legal documents while still competent*. These documents include advance directives for health care and durable powers of attorney. These documents are still necessary if an individual is married or has children because such relationships do not automatically give a spouse or a child the legal right to control another individual's assets or medical decisions, even in the case of incapacity. It is the lack of planning that leads to the necessity of judicial intervention. Such judicial intervention may lead to different types of guardianships being established. The establishment of a conservatorship is an example of an individual planning ahead to maintain some degree of decision-making capacity and control.

decisional incapacity
A term that some states use rather than incompetence.

THE ORIGINS OF GUARDIANSHIPS AND CONSERVATORSHIPS

The original legal concept of society and its courts protecting the incapacitated individual and her property stems from the ancient Roman concept of **Parens Patriae**. Essentially, *Parens Patriae* means that society as a whole should protect citizens who cannot protect themselves.

parens patriae
An ancient Roman concept meaning that society as a whole should protect citizens who cannot protect themselves.

The American version of guardianship law originates (like much of American law) from English common law and one fourteenth-century English statute in particular that held that the king was responsible for the property of a person if that person's *wit and memory failed*. Such a finding had to have been made before a jury of 12 men (at that time, no woman was allowed to be on a jury) following an investigation into the facts concerning an individual's *lunacy*. Lunacy was the fourteenth-century version of today's term *mental capacity*. Because the original fourteenth-century English courts were more concerned with the continued paying of taxes into the king's coffers, the property ownership aspects were deemed more important than an individual's well-being. Today a variety of legal options are available to protect citizens who cannot or will not protect themselves, and that variety is due in part to an influential 1980s newspaper exposé.

Guardianship Exposé Led to Change

The greatest changes in guardianship law may stem from two newspaper exposés that investigated the damaging effect of guardianships on elderly wards. Reporters from the national news syndicate The Associated Press and the newspaper the *St. Petersburg Times* examined over 2,200 guardianship case files from each of the 50 states. The results undeniably showed the abject failure of the then-applicable state guardianship laws to provide even *minimal* constitutional safeguards to citizens (mostly elderly) facing guardianship proceedings. The reporters found that only 44 percent of guardianship respondents were represented by counsel, many hearings lasted less than five minutes, and experts of questionable authority were allowed to testify.[3]

The exposé led to the ABA's Commission on Legal Problems of the Elderly formulating a recommendation for national improvement in guardianship law. These improvements included a more rigorous legal process, leading to an order for guardianship and support for the *least restrictive alternative* being considered.

Following the ABA Commission's recommendations, the National Conference of Commissioners on Uniform State Law (NCCUSL) approved the Uniform Guardianship and Protective Proceedings Act (UGPPA) in 1997. This was followed by the *revised* UGPPA being presented to the ABA's House of Delegates at its 1998 meeting. Massachusetts, Louisiana, and New Jersey were among the first states to draft new guardianship legislation based on the revised UGPPA. The majority of states have followed. Other states, such as Florida, had already begun reform of their guardianship legislation.

A strong element in the revised UGPPA is the insistence that limited guardianship or limited conservatorship should be tried first whenever the facts dictate and that all guardians and conservators should consult with their wards whenever possible before making a decision regarding their wards. Limited guardianship and limited conservatorship prescribe the least restrictive standard being applied to a guardianship or conservatorship. Another important change in the act was an increase in the standard of proof to *clear and convincing evidence* of the alleged respondent's incapacity.[4]

The revised UGPPA included the new concept of **parental or spousal appointments** generally called **standby guardianships** in state legislation. For example, a standby guardianship is to be used when a guardian is needed immediately. Standby guardianship can be used in any of these situations: death of an appointed parent or spouse, adjudication of incapacity of the appointed parent or spouse, or written affirmation by a physician that the appointed parent or spouse can no longer adequately care for the child or adult ward.

Applying the Least Restrictive Alternative

Alternatives to traditional cookie-cutter guardianships are in keeping with what is known as the **least restrictive alternative (LRA) principle.** Students of American constitutional law may recall that the LRA principle is in tune with the Fourteenth Amendment's due process personal liberty protections. Adult citizens who become wards of public or private guardians lose a panoply of rights including the right to vote, drive, marry, transfer real or personal property, handle financial transactions, travel, live where they choose, or even make their own health care decisions. Such wards become examples of the most powerless and disenfranchised citizens in the United States. It is not surprising that this disenfranchisement may lead to insufficient protections for essentially silenced citizens. Obviously, constitutional safeguards are necessary before instituting any level of guardianship.

---

parental or spousal appointments

Also known as standby guardianship, these are used in situations when a guardian is needed immediately and should be put in place without the need to go for court approval first.

standby guardianships

Guardianships used when a guardian is needed immediately. It should be put in place without the need to go for court approval first.

least restrictive alternative (LRA) principle

Alternatives to traditional cookie-cutter guardianships that stay in tune with the Constitution's Fourteenth Amendment for due process personal liberty protections.

Many state courts benefit from receiving guidance from statutes advising the following of the least restrictive approach. Usually a court-appointed counsel's report will provide a plan in the client's best interests. Any court-appointed counsel represents the alleged incapacitated person, not that person's family or the court system. A court-appointed counsel may believe the wishes of the client to be harmful to her and may ask the court to appoint a *guardian ad litem* who can advocate for the client and her best interests.

WHEN TO SEEK A GUARDIANSHIP

Previously discussed in Chapter 2 was the legal document the durable power of attorney. Whether a person has a durable power of attorney in effect can impact the decision of when a guardianship should be sought. A durable power of attorney is a written legal document in which the creator, called the principal, appoints another person or institution, called the attorney-in-fact or the agent, to act on the principal's behalf. Importantly, a durable power of attorney continues to be effective even *after* the principal becomes incapacitated. The big difference between a *durable* power of attorney and a non-durable power of attorney is that the latter, because it is not been made durable, will no longer be effective after the incapacity of the principal.

Only a principal who has capacity at the time of signing can sign a durable power of attorney. However, the durable power of attorney does not suffice in every situation and does not permit an agent to compel a principal to do anything against her wishes.

For example, imagine the scenario of a beloved relative who signed a durable power of attorney naming an adult child as her agent and then later refused to allow the adult child agent to provide the care the principal was too incapacitated to provide for herself. A typical example may involve an adult child who believes that a parent needs full-time care in a nursing home or an assisted living facility and the elderly parent refuses to leave home. A nursing home or an assisted living facility is not likely to allow a patient to move in when the patient refuses (even with a valid durable power of attorney) unless a court-ordered guardianship is in place. All care facilities should ask to see letters of guardianship, which are issued by the appropriate court and name a guardian.

How Should Competency Be Judged?

Does the refusal to enter a nursing home or an assisted living facility automatically make a person incompetent and in need of a guardian? Obviously not. It is the rare individual who wants to leave the comfort of home to enter such an establishment. What does make a person legally competent or incompetent? Some states use the term capacity, as in does a person have capacity to make her own decisions?

Typically, most states have a two-part criteria for determining competence. First, the person whose competence is questioned usually must fall within a specific category. This category may include an individual with mental health issues or advanced age. Second, the individual must be unable to care for her physical well-being or property. This second requirement should help ensure that advanced age or developmental disabilities alone do not initiate a guardianship proceeding.

TYPES OF GUARDIANSHIPS

Traditionally, the creation of a guardianship equated to the *complete* removal of the ward's decision-making rights and total power being given to the guardian. Where the ward would live, control over the ward's finances, medical treatments, and even menu choices could be decided by the guardian. However, a trend began in the late twentieth century post-exposé period that a more individualized case-by-case approach to guardianship should be the norm. Thus, concepts such as **limited**, **partial**, or **temporary guardianships** have become more acceptable. For example, in New Jersey, permission of the court is required before a guardian can consent or refuse medical treatment for her ward. Massachusetts requires the court to approve the placement of a ward in a nursing home. These more individualized guardianship concepts join the traditional guardianship available.

Private Guardianship

When a private individual is named a guardian, a **private guardianship** is created. The private individual could be a family member, friend, or attorney who is prepared to undertake the serious responsibility of being a guardian.

Public Guardianship

Since the early 1900s, the U.S. government has been called on to act as a surrogate decision maker through the **public guardianship** concept. The states with an Office of the **Public Guardian** seek to protect their most frail and vulnerable older adults. The public guardianship concept exists under a variety of models in approximately 42 states. The public guardianship may also be limited, partial, or temporary in nature.

---

limited, partial, or **temporary guardianships**

Guardianships that are more individualized on a case-by-case situation.

private guardianship

When a private individual is named as another's guardian.

public guardianship

A guardianship of last resort when there are no willing and appropriate family members or friends who can serve. The government is then called on to act as a surrogate decision maker.

public guardian

Government-provided guardianship or conservatorship services when there are no willing and appropriate family members or friends who can serve.

The result of a veritable wave of people age 65 and older will likely result in an escalated demand for public guardianships. The main purpose behind the Office of the Public Guardian is to provide guardianship or conservatorship services of *last resort* when there are no willing and appropriate family members or friends who can serve. The number of people needing the services of a public guardian is expected to rise at a disarmingly fast pace not only because of the expected increase in the older population but also because of the lack of available family members living close to their elderly relatives.[5]

Special Medical Guardianships

Sometimes a guardianship appointment is made so that a medical procedure can be performed. This typically occurs when life-threatening treatment is needed. A judge may appoint an attorney or a hospital representative for that sole and limited purpose. A petitioner seeking the **special medical guardianship** must file a complaint with accompanying documentation (physicians' affidavits) and present evidence in court as to why an order should be issued granting the guardianship. A special medical guardian will receive exclusive consent to have the medical treatment performed.

special medical guardianship

A guardianship appointment made so that a medical procedure can be performed.

Temporary Guardianships

There is also a need for temporary guardianships on occasion. For example, Wilma is a hospital patient who no longer needs hospital services and therefore is no longer eligible for Medicare benefits. However, Wilma does need the long-term care of a nursing home. Furthermore, Wilma does not have the funds to pay for the nursing home care and she does not have any family or friends who can apply for Medicaid benefits on her behalf. What can the hospital do? The hospital can petition for a temporary guardianship to apply for Medicaid benefits on Wilma's behalf to pay for Wilma's future nursing home care. The hospital will then be able to discharge and transfer Wilma to a nursing home for the long-term care she needs, and the nursing home can be assured that Wilma will pay for her care.

Another situation where a temporary guardianship is appropriate is when there is a report of an alleged vulnerable adult. The police or protective services personnel usually investigate such a complaint. The investigation is followed by a determination of whether the allegations are true and whether a temporary *protective order* is appropriate. This can result in protective services personnel escorting the alleged incapacitated person to the hospital for an evaluation. Based on the hospital report, a temporary guardianship order may then mushroom into a full-fledged capacity hearing. The capacity hearing should determine whether the abuse is self-inflicted or whether another person is inflicting physical, mental, and/or financial abuse. Once incapacity is partially or totally found, a protective order specifies what rights will be removed from or retained by the individual in question and who should be appointed the individual's guardian.

UNDERTAKING THE GUARDIANSHIP PROCESS

All 50 states have state-specific and comprehensive guardianship statutes. For example, Florida is in the minority by requiring a mandatory course in guardianship basics that a person must complete within one year of being named a guardian. Another example of state differences involves domicile issues. Some states do not require a guardianship petitioner to be a resident. For example, Texas and Florida allow a nonresident petitioner to start a guardianship action. It should be noted that an individual needs to have mental capacity to change her domicile.

Typically, an attorney is retained to commence a guardianship action. The attorney begins by drafting a guardianship complaint (also called a guardianship petition in some states) and an order to show cause. The petition should provide the name and address of the *alleged* incapacitated person. The allegation of incapacity is only that—an allegation—until it is proved and declared so by a judge or hearing officer. Detailed requirements for what must be alleged in the petition and how the order to show cause should be drafted are specified in each of the state's court rules. Refer to Exhibit 4–1 for a list of the guardianship legislation for the 50 states. Refer to Exhibit 4–2 to read a portion of a guardianship statute from New York State.

Generally, a guardianship petition must have documentation listing the type and value of the estate in question. The listing usually must be in affidavit form. If a petitioner is unable to complete such a listing, the petition should state the reasons. For example, the alleged incapacitated person may not be and probably is not willing or able to cooperate with the petitioner. The complete listing of all assets assists the court in determining exactly how large a bond the guardian should have to post. Generally, the bond reflects the total amount of the assets the guardian could liquidate. Refer to Exhibit 4–3 to read a sample guardianship petition.

Courts typically prefer an allegedly incapacitated respondent to appear in court unless the respondent is so mentally and/or physically infirmed that she cannot. The appearance or lack thereof is a critical due process issue that the courts and counsels should not take lightly. If the alleged incapacitated person can appear but is unable to communicate, every effort should be made to utilize whatever communication methodology is at the court's disposal (e.g., translators, electronic speech boards, and sign language). The best-case scenario has the alleged incapacitated respondent appearing in person.

Whether the alleged incapacitated person has a last will and testament, powers of attorney, and/or an advanced directive for health care should be determined. If the alleged incapacitated person does have such documents, the attorneys-in-fact of the powers of attorney should receive notice of the capacity hearing. The court generally makes the decision as to whether those documents should be validly continued. The attorney who prepared the last will and testament is likely to be called to appear and testify. The attorneys can ask the court to seal the records to guard the privacy of the alleged incapacitated person.

Typically, any interested third party can bring an action for appointment as a guardian. However, the court may not find that an individual qualifies to be a guardian. Courts have hearings to *show cause* as to why a guardian should be appointed. Each state determines the preparation that new guardians get for their job, and a great deal of variety exists between states. Some states have a monitoring system, and some do not. If counsel was court-appointed, she usually is discharged at the final hearing. Typically, there is no need for a detailed *financial report* when there are few assets. Some states have requirements for how often a guardian should visit her ward; other states do not and leave it up to the guardian to decide.

Necessary questions that a proposed guardian's attorney should ask are whether the proposed guardian has ever been convicted of a felony or filed for bankruptcy. The proposed guardian's attorney should ask these questions prior to the guardianship hearing because the judge is likely to ask them.

Of great importance is the documentation establishing probable cause and detailed specificity in the pleadings as to why the court should declare a guardianship. Refer to Exhibit 4–4 to read a sample of a physician's report that includes such specificity.

The Guardianship Proceeding

A guardianship petition filed with the county court system will be heard in court and must follow court rules. The court's name differs by state; but the more usual names are probate court, Surrogate's Court, county court, and circuit court. Essentially, a court hearing a guardianship petition must make a two-part determination:

1. Is a guardian required?

2. Who should be appointed guardian?

The individual subject of the petition has the right to be notified and a right to be present at the court hearing. The ward may nominate her choice of guardian; however, the court must determine who will promote the best interests of the ward. Many questions should be asked at the hearing. Is the respondent able to receive and process information? Are the needs of the respondent being met? Who should be appointed guardian? What are the duties of the guardian regarding a particular ward? How long should the guardianship last? Should a review date be established? Does the respondent understand why she is in court?

Of course, if the alleged incapacitated person is legitimately unable to appear in court, the proceeding are still allowed to continue without the named individual. Occasionally, under appropriate situations, the hearings are held in a nursing home or a hospital to accommodate the named party. Depending on a state's statutory requirements, an attorney, a *guardian ad litem,* or a court evaluator may appear in court for the named party. These professionals should testify as to their evaluation of the situation and state whether they recommend that the court appoint a guardian. Generally, the person hearing a guardianship case is called a judge; but in a small number of states another judicial officer serves in the role of the judge. This judicial officer at a guardianship hearing may be called a **hearing officer, referee, commissioner,** or **magistrate.** Sometimes the judge prepares the orders at the conclusion of the hearing, or the orders may be mailed later. Often the prevailing party will be asked to prepare an order conforming to the judge's **final order.** It is this order that will be produced and shown to all interested parties who need to know the outcome of the guardianship petition. Appeals from guardianship orders are collected in books called the *Mental Health Reporter.*

Physician Input Needed

Very important are medical affidavits from at least one physician, and most states usually require affidavits from two physicians who have examined the alleged incapacitated person within a short time prior to the guardianship petition being filed. The medical affidavit should be complete. For example, the state of New Jersey is typical in the extensive details that it requires. Refer to Exhibit 4–5 to read a sample of one state's version of medical affidavit requirements. Some states also require that at least one physician who provided the medical affidavit give in-person testimony. Other states only require the physician to be available by telephone conference call. Some states allow the physician's affidavit to be admitted without the physician testifying. Each law office should have its own office checklist and form for the doctors to fill out. Refer to Exhibit 4–5 to review a sample list of medical affidavit requirements.

Making Guardians Accountable

All guardianships should be monitored after they are granted. The vast majority of states require *periodic financial reports* and *personal well-being reporting* to the court that granted the guardianship. States differ in how thorough the

▓ **hearing officer, referee, commissioner,** or **magistrate**

A judicial officer who serves in the role of a judge during a judicial hearing.

▓ **final order**

A document determining the outcome of a guardianship hearing.

▓ *Mental Health Reporter*

A book in which appeals from guardianship orders are collected.

reports must be. A minority of states including Florida, Okahoma, Michigan, and New Mexico ask that the reasons for continuing the guardianship be enumerated.

Both private and public guardians are expected to be accountable for the decisions they make regarding their wards. Accountability standards vary greatly from state to state. Depending on the state, a public guardian may have different methods of accountability, including submitting written reports to the court. However, in some states, funding may not be adequate to evaluate the reports and do follow-up. Public guardians may come from a variety of professional backgrounds, including law and social work. An important job for all guardians is to monitor any services the ward should be receiving. Services may include providing assistance with medical and dental treatment, nutritional aid, and physical upkeep. Guardians may not have financial options that would allow the least restrictive type of decision. For example, a guardian may want to place a ward in an assisted living facility that is not covered by Medicaid; thus, the guardian must place the ward in a nursing home. Nursing homes may be paid for by Medicaid. Due to the fiduciary relationship between the ward and her guardian, strict accountability and even stricter sanctions are expected.

Any guardian's report should include the mental and physical state of the ward. The report should summarize the visits the guardian has made to the ward and the activities in which the ward has participated since the last report. Especially important in this era of wards participating as much as possible in their care is the decision making the ward has been involved in during the period the report covers. A description of the current care received and the suggested future care needed should be described in a guardian's report. Refer to Exhibit 4–6 to read a sample of a form used for an Annual Report of a Guardian.

National guardianship standards also have been drafted by the **National Guardianship Association**. Its Web address is listed under "Helpful Web Sites" at the end of the chapter.

National Guardianship Association

An organization that drafted a model code of ethics for guardians.

Terminating a Guardianship

Guardianships can be terminated for a variety of reasons. A ward may terminate for the following reasons:

1. The incapacitated person dies.

2. The incapacitated person is adjudicated capable.

3. The guardianship is adjudicated unnecessary.

4. A timed guardianship of a certain period has expired.

A guardianship also may be terminated because the guardian has died, has resigned, or will be replaced. A petition to discharge the guardian from further responsibility for her ward should be filed. Typically, a court hearing is held where a final report and accounting should be reviewed for accuracy. If the hearing officer believes the guardian has faithfully completed her duties, the final report and accounting is approved, the guardian is discharged, and the guardianship is closed. If the guardian had to submit a bond at the beginning of the guardianship, the approval of the final accounting is necessary to release the bond. Refer to Exhibit 4–7 to review a Petition for Termination of Guardianship and Discharge of Guardian and an Order of Termination and Discharge from Minnesota.

EXHIBIT 4–1   LIST OF STATE GUARDIANSHIP STATUTES

Alabama	Kentucky	Ohio
Ala. Code 1975, § 26-2A 102	K.R.S. § 387-065	R.C. § 2111.021
Alaska	Louisiana	Oregon
AK ST § 13.26.090	LSA-C.C. Art. 389	O.R.S. § 125.300
Arizona	Maryland	Pennsylvania
A.R.S. § 14-5101	MD EST & TRUSTS § 13.101	20 PA. Cons. Stat. Ann. § 5501
Arkansas	Massachusetts	Rhode Island
A.C.A. § 28-65-101	M.G.L.A. 201 § 6	RI ST § 33-15-1
California	Michigan	South Carolina
CA Probate § 1800	M.C.L.A. 700-5303	S.C. ST § 62.5-101
Colorado	Minnesota	South Dakota
C.R.S.A. § 15-14-101	Minn. Stat. § 529.539	SDCL § 29A-5-101
Connecticut	Mississippi	Tennessee
C.G.S.A. § 45a-644	Miss. Code Ann. § 93-13-121	T.C.A. § 34-1-101
Delaware	Missouri	Texas
12 Del.C. § 3901	V.A.M. § 475-060	TX Probate § 602
District of Columbia	Montana	Utah
D.C. Code Ann. § 21-1001	MT ST 72-5-302	U.C.A. 1953, §75-5301
Florida	Nebraska	Vermont
F.S.A. § 744.1012	Neb. U.P.C. § 30-2619	VT. Stat. Ann. Tit. 14, § 3060
Georgia	Nevada	Virginia
Ga. Code Ann., § 29-5-1	N.R.S. § 159.013	VA Code Ann. § 37.2-100
Hawaii	New Hampshire	Washington
HI ST § 560:5-304	N.H. Rev. Stat. § 464-A:1	West's RCWA § 11.92.010
Idaho	New Jersey	West Virginia
I.C.S. § 15-5-104	N.J.S.A. 3B:12-25	W.VA. Code § 44A-1-1
Illinois	New Mexico	Wisconsin
755 ILCS 5/11A-3	N.M.S.A. 1978, § 45-5-301	Wis. Stat. § 880.01
ndiana	New York	Wyoming
IC 29-3-2-1	NY Ment. Hyg. § 81.01	WY ST § 3-1-101
Iowa	North Carolina	
I.C.A. § 633-551	N.C.G.S.A. § 35A-1101	
Kansas	North Dakota	
K.S.A. 59-3001	N.D. Century Code, Art. V § 30.1 U.P.C.	

EXHIBIT 4–2   SAMPLE NEW YORK GUARDIANSHIP STATUTE

§ 81.01 Legislative findings and purpose

The legislature hereby finds that the needs of persons with incapacities are as diverse and complex as they are unique to the individual. The current system of conservatorship and committee does not provide the necessary flexibility to meet these needs. Conservatorship which traditionally compromises a person's rights only with respect to property frequently is insufficient to provide necessary relief. On the other hand, a committee, with its judicial finding of incompetence and the accompanying stigma and loss of civil rights, traditionally involves a deprivation that is often excessive and unnecessary. Moreover, certain persons require some form of assistance in meeting their personal and property management needs but do not require either of these drastic remedies. The legislature finds that it is desirable for and beneficial to persons with incapacities to make available to them the least restrictive form of intervention which assists them in meeting their needs but, at the same time, permits them to exercise the independence and self-determination of which they are capable. The legislature declares that it is the purpose of this act to promote the public welfare by establishing a guardianship system which is appropriate to satisfy either personal or property management needs of an incapacitated person in a manner tailored to the individual needs of that person, which takes in account the personal wishes, preferences and desires of the person, and which affords the person the greatest amount of independence and self-determination and participation in all the decisions affecting such person's life.

N.Y.S. Section700.5303. Petition for finding of incapacity and appointment of guardian; contents; hearing; court-ordered guardian ad litem

Sec. 5303. (1) An individual in his or her own behalf, or any person interested in the individual's welfare, may petition for a finding of incapacity and appointment of a guardian. The petition shall contain specific facts about the individual's condition and specific examples of the individual's recent conduct that demonstrate the need for a guardian's appointment.

(2) Before a petition is filed under this section, the court shall provide the person intending to file the petition with written information that sets forth alternatives to appointment of a full guardian, including, but not limited to, a limited guardian, conservator, patient advocate designation, do-not-resuscitate declaration, or durable power of attorney with or without limitations on purpose, authority, or time period, and an explanation of each alternative.

(3) Upon the filing of a petition under subsection (1), the court shall set a date for hearing on the issue of incapacity. Unless the allegedly incapacitated individual has legal counsel of his or her own choice, the court shall appoint a guardian ad litem to represent the person in the proceeding.

ELDER LAW PRACTICE

Rena is a paralegal in attorney Tara Jensen's elder law practice. An experienced paralegal, Rena had not personally experienced any elder law issues until recently. Rena has been her Aunt Jane's caregiver for years and is her aunt's closest relative. Aunt Jane has been diagnosed with what is believed to be early Alzheimer's disease. Rena has no formal caregiving arrangements. Recently, Aunt Jane has begun to refuse her medications, does not pay her bills on time, and seldom eats the

(continues)

ELDER LAW PRACTICE *(continued)*

meals Rena prepares each day. Aunt Jane has refused Rena's suggestion that Aunt Jane move out of her own home to an assisted living facility. Rena is feeling the pressure and has begun to question whether a guardianship may be appropriate for her aunt. Rena decided to confer with Tara to learn what her responsibility would be if she was named Aunt Jane's guardian.

Tara explained that guardianship responsibilities often depend on the ward's abilities. Tara added, "After everything you've told me this last year, I think in your aunt's case, the court would see that you are the likely choice to be named guardian and that she can't be left to make decisions about where to live or how to manage her finances or about her own medical treatment." How would Rena begin the guardianship process?

The guardianship process can be begun by asking Aunt Jane's doctors to write affidavits to attach to Rena's guardianship petition. A complete inventory of Aunt Jane's assets will be needed as well. Refer to Exhibit 4–3 to read the Guardianship Petition and Exhibit 4–5 to read the Medical Affidavit prepared for Aunt Jane's case.

EXHIBIT 4–3 GUARDIANSHIP PETITION

Tara Jensen, Esq.
56 Main Street
Flanders, New Jersey 12345
Attorney for Rena Vander May

_____

	:	SUPERIOR COURT OF NEW JERSEY
	:	CHANCERY DIVISION
	:	PROBATE PART
	:	SUSSEX COUNTY
IN THE MATTER OF	:	DOCKET NO: FV-214-00
	:	CIVIL ACTION
Jane Vander May	:	
	:	VERIFIED COMPLAINT
	:	

_____

Petitioner, Rena Vander May, presently residing at 64 House Road, Newton, New Jersey 07860 says that:

1. Petitioner, Rena Vander May, 50 years of age, is the niece of Jane Vander May.

(continues)

EXHIBIT 4–3   GUARDIANSHIP PETITION *(continued)*

2. Jane Vander May, the alleged incapacitated person, was born on May 5, 1920, and is presently 86 years of age. Petitioner's interest in this action is the health and welfare of her aunt, Jane Vander May.

3. Jane Vander May, the alleged incapacitated person, presently resides at 125 Sparrow Street, Newton, New Jersey. She has resided there since June 20, 1974.

GUARDIANSHIP

4. The physical health and care needs of Jane Vander May, as appears from the Certifications of Dr. Richard Owens, annexed hereto as Exhibit A, are such that she requires 24-hour care in a skilled nursing facility and can no longer care for herself or her property.

5. By way of background, Jane Vander May resided for many years in the marital home with her husband Emmett Vander May, who died on or about June 14, 1995. After the death of her husband, Emmett, the alleged incapacitated person began to deteriorate mentally and physically.

6. Jane Vander May has difficultly understanding financial matters or the impact of financial matters on her health and welfare. Her niece, Rena Vander May, has taken a strong role in ensuring bills are paid on time. Jane Vander May must be constantly urged to sign her checks to pay her debts even though there are sufficient assets in her checking account. For example, Jane has failed to endorse insurance reimbursement checks from Blue Cross/Blue Shield or to allow another to deposit on her behalf those funds in her account. She had never executed a Durable General Power of Attorney, and there is no power of attorney authorization card on file at any institution that holds her funds.

7. Jane and Emmett had no children.

8. It is now in the best interest of Jane Vander May that her niece, Rena Vander May, serve as her Guardian. On the information and belief, the Surrogate of Sussex County will provide Rena Vander May with a copy of the Judgment of Incompetency for Jane Vander May with the original docket number. If Rena Vander May is found to be mentally incapacitated, Tara Jensen may be substituted as Guardian of the Person and Property of Jane Vander May.

9. Jane Vander May is mentally incompetent, being unfit and unable to govern herself and to manage her affairs and property, as verified by the certifications of Dr. Richard Owens, M.D., dated August 29, 2006, attached hereto as Exhibit A and prepared upon a personal examination of Jane Vander May not more than 30 days prior to the filing of this complaint.

10. The names, relationship and addresses of the nearest of kin and all parties in interest to be served with notice of this action are:

Name	Relationship	Address
Bill Vander May	Nephew	342 Hill Street, Omaha, NE 48756

The above-named person is of full age and competent.

(continues)

EXHIBIT 4–3   GUARDIANSHIP PETITION *(continued)*

11. Petitioner, Rena Vander May, who is a paralegal, seeks to be appointed as Guardian of the Person and Property of her aunt, Jane Vander May.

INCOME AND ASSETS

12. Jane Vander May has not appointed an attorney-in-fact to act on her behalf. Accordingly, Petitioner is unable to determine the extent of her aunt's income and assets with precision.

13. Jane Vander May receives the following monthly income:
  (a) Social Security benefits of $1,500.00.
  All income received by Jane Vander May is automatically deposited by Social
  Security in a checking account at the National Bank.Newton, New Jersey 07860

14. Jane Vander May, the alleged incapacitated person, is the owner of the following bank account:

Account	Bank	Value
12768-908	National Bank	$2,500.00

15. Based upon statements or certificates located by the Petitioner, Rena Vander May, the alleged incapacitated person, owns or may own the following investment:
  (a) Jane Vander May owns a property located at 124 Sparrow Street, Newton, New Jersey 07860. The estimated value of The property is approximately $200,000.00.

16. Jane Vander May owns nominal personal property not exceeding $20,000.00 in value.

WHEREFORE, Petitioner respectfully requests that Judgment be entered as follows:

A. Adjudicating Jane Vander May to be an incapacitated person and unable to govern herself and manage her affairs;

B. Granting to Rena Vander May permanent letters of Guardianship of the Person;

C. Such other and different relief as the Court may deem proper.

By:_____

Tara Jensen, Esq.

Dated:_____, 2007

EXHIBIT 4–4   SAMPLE OF AFFIDAVIT REQUIREMENTS

The allegations of the complaint shall be verified as prescribed by R. 1:4-7 and shall have annexed thereto:

  (a) An affidavit stating the nature, location and fair market value (1) of all real estate in which the alleged mentally incapacitated person has or may have a present or future interest, stating the interest, describing the real estate fully or by metes and bounds, and stating the assessed valuation thereof; and (2) of all the personal estate which he or she is, will or may in all probability become entitled to, including the nature and total or annual amount of any compensation, pension,

(continues)

EXHIBIT 4–4   SAMPLE OF AFFIDAVIT REQUIREMENTS *(continued)*

insurance, or income which may be payable to the alleged mentally incapacitated person. If the plaintiff cannot secure such information, the complaint shall so state and give the reasons therefore, and the affidavit submitted shall in that case contain as much information as can be secured in the exercise of reasonable diligence;

   (b) Affidavits of two physicians, having qualifications set forth in *N.J.S.A.* 30:4-27.2 or the affidavit of one such physician and one licensed practicing psychologist as defined in *N.J.S.A.* 45:14B-2. If an alleged mentally incapacitated person has been committed to a public institution and is confined therein, one of the affidavits shall be that of the chief executive officer, the medical director, or the chief of service providing that person is also the physician with overall responsibility for the professional program of care and treatment in the administrative unit of the institution. However, where an alleged mentally incapacitated person is domiciled within this State but resident elsewhere, the affidavits required by this rule may be those of persons who are residents of the state or jurisdiction of the alleged mentally incapacitated person's residence. Each affiant shall have made a personal examination of the alleged mentally incapacitated person not more than 30 days prior to the filing of the complaint, but said time period may be relaxed by the court on an ex parte showing of good cause. To support the complaint, each affiant shall state: (1) the date and place of the examination; (2) whether the affiant has treated or merely examined the alleged mentally incapacitated individual; (3) whether the affiant is disqualified under *R.* 4:86-3; (4) the diagnosis and prognosis and factual basis therefor; (5) for purposes of ensuring that the alleged mentally incapacitated person is the same individual who was examined, a physical description of the person examined, including but not limited to sex, age and weight; and (6) the affiant's opinion that the alleged mentally incapacitated person is unfit and unable to govern himself or herself and to manage his or her affairs and shall set forth with particularity the circumstances and conduct of the alleged mentally incapacitated person upon which this opinion is based, including a history of the alleged mentally incapacitated person's condition. The affidavit should also include an opinion whether the alleged mentally incapacitated person is capable of attending the hearing and if not, the reasons for the individual's inability.

   (c) In lieu of the affidavits provided for in paragraph (b), an affidavit of one affiant having the qualifications as required therein, stating that he or she has endeavored to make a personal examination of the alleged mentally incapacitated person not more than 30 days prior to the filing of the complaint but that the alleged mentally incapacitated person or those in charge of him or her have refused or are unwilling to have the affiant make such an examination. The time period herein prescribed may be relaxed by the court on an ex parte showing of good cause.

EXHIBIT 4–5   SAMPLE MEDICAL AFFIDAVIT

EXHIBIT A

Tara Jensen, Esq.
56 Main Street
Flanders, New Jersey 12345
Attorney for Rena Vander May

(continues)

EXHIBIT 4–5   SAMPLE MEDICAL AFFIDAVIT *(continued)*

_____

	:	
	:	
	:	SUPERIOR COURT OF NEW JERSEY
	:	CHANCERY DIVISION
IN THE MATTER OF	:	PROBATE PART
	:	SUSSEX COUNTY
Jane Vander May	:	DOCKET NO: FV-214-00
	:	CIVIL ACTION
	:	
	:	PHYSICIAN'S AFFIDAVIT

_____

Dr. Richard Owens, M.D. being duly sworn says:

1. I am a resident of and physician licensed to practice medicine in the State of New Jersey. I currently maintain an office at Mercy Hospital, Division of Geriatric Medicine, Senior Health Network, Sparta Office, Sparta, New Jersey.

2. I was born on March 29, 1957.

3. I received my Bachelor of Science degree from Wales College in Pre-Med.

4. I was given a degree of Doctor of Medicine from Morris University in May 1983.

5. I completed my residency in 1985 and my fellowship in Geriatrics in June 1986.

6. I received my license to practice medicine in the State of New Jersey in 1986.

7. I am Board Certified in Internal Medicine with added qualifications in Geriatric Medicine.

8. I am not a relative of Jane Vander May, the alleged incapacitated person, either through blood or by marriage.

9. I am not a proprietor, director or chief executive of any institution for the care and treatment of the mentally disabled or incapacitated in which Jane Vander May is living or in which it is proposed to place her, nor am I employed as a resident physician with any such institution; nor am I financially interested therein.

10. I examined Jane Vander May for the purposes of the guardianship proceeding on August 24, 2006, at her home at 125 Sparrow Street, Newton, New Jersey. I am not her treating physician.

11. Jane Vander May is an 86-year-old Caucasian female, approximately five feet four inches tall, and weighs approximately 105 pounds. She has gray hair and blue eyes.

(continues)

EXHIBIT 4–5   SAMPLE MEDICAL AFFIDAVIT *(continued)*

12. Jane Vander May was alert at the time of the examination. She is diagnosed with Alzheimer's disease and is currently taking Aricept, 10 mg per day, and Paxil, 10 mg per day.

13. Her niece, Rena Vander May, reports that Jane Vander May appears to suffer from delusions. Jane has stated that her aunt believes people are stealing from her.

14. She has short-term memory loss. She did very poorly on the short-term memory test. She could not remember my name after several attempts. She is orientated to her name only. Jane thought that the date was October 19, 1978. She could not tell me her home address. She could not recall George W. Bush was president, nor could she give me the name of any past president. She could not recall the details of any recent news events. She did not know that name of her regular treating physician. She did not know she was taking any medication. She did know the name of her niece, who provides her with care. She was able to give answers to simple judgment questions, and she was able to do simple calculation.

15. Jane Vander May suffers from Alzheimer's disease and displays significant short-term memory loss. She has limited insight into her condition and is unable to formulate plans for her personal care and financial affairs. In my professional opinion, she will continue to deteriorate and she is now and will continue to remain unfit and unable to care for herself and manage her affairs. She is also at risk of being taken advantage of by others.

16. Jane Vander May is not bed bound and could attend the hearing. In my opinion, she would not comprehend the proceedings.

17. The statements made herein are true. I am aware that if any of the statements made by me herein are willfully false, I am subject to punishment.

_____

Dr. Richard Owens

Sworn and Subscribed to
Before me this _____ day
of _____, 2007

EXHIBIT 4–6   SAMPLE ANNUAL REPORT OF A GUARDIAN

ANNUAL REPORT OF GUARDIAN

Superior Court of
Chancery Division, Probate Part
38
County

In the Matter of the Annual Report of

(continues)

EXHIBIT 4–6   SAMPLE ANNUAL REPORT OF A GUARDIAN *(continued)*

Docket No.

As Guardian for,

An Incapacitated Person.

    This report must be filed by every Guardian once per year unless the Judge otherwise specifies, on the anniversary date of your appointment, which is _____.

The original must be filed with the Surrogate and a copy must also be sent to court-appointed counsel for the ward at the following address:

Surrogate: Court-Appointed Counsel:

1. Date of Report:
2. Guardian: Please Check:
   Name: __ guardian of person only
   Address (include mailing address, if different):   __ guardian of property only
                                                            __ both

   Telephone No.
   (Day)
   (Evening)
3. Incapacitated Person:
   Name:
   Address: (If the person lives in a residential facility, include name of the Director or person responsible for care):

   Telephone No.

4. Bond:
   Bonding company name:
   Bonding company address:
   Value of bond (If the bonding requirement was waived, so state):

5. Guardian's Relationship to Ward:

   1_____ spouse   2_____ parent of ward   3_____ child of ward

   4_____ other relative   5_____ friend   6_____ private attorney

   7_____ public guardian or agency   8_____ other

(continues)

EXHIBIT 4–6 SAMPLE ANNUAL REPORT OF A GUARDIAN *(continued)*

6. Does the ward live with you? __ Yes __ No If not, how many times do you or your designee visit the ward on an average each month? _____ On average, how long is the visit (in minutes)?

7. What does the guardian do for the ward? Check all that apply.

_____Manage financial affairs   _____Provide necessities

_____Provide housekeeping   _____Take on outings

_____Provide transportation   _____Bathe

_____Feed   _____Provide continuous care

    List any others:
    IF YOU ARE A GUARDIAN OF THE PERSON, PLEASE COMPLETE THE FOLLOWING QUESTIONS. IF YOU ARE A GUARDIAN OF THE PROPERTY ONLY, PLEASE GO TO QUESTION 20.

8. What is the guardian's view of the ward's overall situation, including any significant changes in physical health, intellectual functioning, emotional health and living situation that have occurred over the past year?

9. Does the guardian feel that the guardianship should continue? __ Yes __ No
Why?

10. Has there been any substantial change in the incapacitated person's medication?
__ Yes __ No If yes, please explain:

11. Examination:
Please state the date and place the incapacitated person was last examined or otherwise seen by a physician and the purpose of such visit.

Date   Physician   Purpose

Please attach a statement by a physician, psychologist, nurse clinician or social worker, or other person who has evaluated or examined the incapacitated person within three (3) months prior to the filing of this report, regarding an evaluation of the incapacitated person's condition and current functional level.

12. Residential Setting:
Is the current residential setting suitable to the needs of the incapacitated person?
__ Yes __ No If no, please explain:

(continues)

EXHIBIT 4–6   SAMPLE ANNUAL REPORT OF A GUARDIAN *(continued)*

13. Treatment:

What professional medical treatment, if any, has been given to the incapacitated person during the preceding year?

<u>Date</u>   <u>Treatment</u>

14. Treatment Plan:

Describe the treatment plan for the coming year for the incapacitated person regarding:
   (a) Medical treatment
   (b) Dental treatment
   (c) Mental health treatment
   (d) Additional related services

15. Social Skills:

Please provide information concerning the condition of the incapacitated person's social skills and needs and the social and personal services used by the incapacitated person.

16. Any changes needed in the guardianship?

17. Has eligibility for such programs as Social Security, Medicare, Medicaid, SSI or Food Stamps ever been checked?
__ Yes __No

18. Does the guardian need assistance, whether from the court or from a community agency? Please specify.

19. Guardian's current assessment of ward's: (check a rating box for each category)

	Excellent 1	Satisfactory 2	Fair 3	Poor 4	Don't know 5
Physical health					
Emotional health					
Intellectual functioning					
Living situation					

PROPERTY MANAGEMENT

   If you have been granted powers regarding the property management of the incapacitated person, please provide the following information, consistent with your order of appointment, pertaining to your fulfillment of your responsibilities to the incapacitated person to provide for property management.

(continues)

EXHIBIT 4–6 SAMPLE ANNUAL REPORT OF A GUARDIAN *(continued)*

20. Have you identified, traced and collected assets of the incapacitated person since your appointment?
__ Yes __ No If no, please explain:

21. Have all of the incapacitated person's past and current income tax returns and payments been brought up to date?
__Yes __ No If no, please explain:

22. Please complete the following schedules and summary. If you have nothing to list on a schedule, state "NONE."

SCHEDULE A
Assets on Hand at the Beginning of the Accounting Period

Please list all assets of the incapacitated person over which you had sole control as guardian as of the beginning of the accounting period. Do not include in this schedule trust principal in which the incapacitated person has an income interest, property under joint control of any court, or real property not transferred to the guardian.

1. BANK ACCOUNTS AND CASH—Please list the name and address of institutions, account numbers and balance deposited in banks or other financial institutions. Please also list any cash on hand not in bank accounts.

2. CORPORATE AND GOVERNMENT SECURITIES (e.g., CORPORATE STOCKS AND BONDS; FEDERAL, STATE OR MUNICIPAL BONDS AND NOTES)

3. PRESENT OR FUTURE INTERESTS (e.g., INTERESTS IN PARTNERSHIPS, TRUSTS, LITIGATION SETTLEMENT FUNDS OR PENSIONS)—Please list the estimated values of all present and future interests the incapacitated person has in property that has not been transferred to your control.

4. OTHER PERSONAL PROPERTY (e.g., FURNITURE, JEWELRY, ARTWORK)—Please list and describe other personal property and indicate estimated value.

5. REAL PROPERTY—Please describe location and type of real property, type of interest and market value.

SCHEDULE B
Assets Received During Accounting Period

Please list all principal assets received during the period of this report (show date received, source and amount or value).

SCHEDULE C
Income Received During Accounting Period

Please list all income received during the period from property interests listed in Schedules A and B (show date received, source and amount).

SCHEDULE D
Losses Incurred During Accounting Period

Please list all realized losses incurred on principal assets, whether due to sale or liquidation, indicating the asset involved, the date and amount of loss.

(continues)

EXHIBIT 4–6   SAMPLE ANNUAL REPORT OF A GUARDIAN *(continued)*

SCHEDULE E

Moneys Paid Out During Accounting Period

Please list all disbursements, excluding investments, during the period, including date of payment, payee and amount.

SCHEDULE F

Assets on Hand at End of the Accounting Period

Please list assets of the type listed in Schedule A on hand at the end of the period and value thereof (see Schedule A for further instructions)

1. BANK ACCOUNTS AND CASH
2. CORPORATION AND GOVERNMENT SECURITIES
3. PRESENT OR FUTURE INTERESTS
4. OTHER PERSONAL PROPERTY
5. REAL PROPERTY

CERTIFICATION

(Your name), certifies that I am the Guardian of the within named incapacitated person and that the attached annual report (and schedule(s)) (is) (are), to the best of my personal knowledge, a complete and true statement of my activities as such Guardian. I am aware that if any of the foregoing are willfully false, I am subject to punishment.

_____   _____

Date   Guardian

EXHIBIT 4–7   PETITION FOR TERMINATION OF GUARDIANSHIP AND DISCHARGE OF GUARDIAN AND
ORDER OF TERMINATION AND DISCHARGE

State of Minnesota   **District Court**
County of   **Probate Division**
                                                                                             Judicial District:
                                                                                             Court File No.

In Re: Guardianship of   **Petition for Termination of**

                                                                             Guardianship and Discharge of

, Ward   **Guardian**

_____

TO THE HONORABLE JUDGE OF THE DISTRICT COURT:

1.   Petitioner,   , is interested in this matter as   .

2.   A guardian was appointed by order of this court dated   .

(continues)

EXHIBIT 4–7 PETITION FOR TERMINATION OF GUARDIANSHIP AND DISCHARGE OF GUARDIAN AND
ORDER OF TERMINATION AND DISCHARGE *(continued)*

3. The guardianship is terminated because _____ the ward died on _____ (a copy of the death certificate is
attached to this petition as exhibit A), _____ the ward attained the age of majority on _____ , or _____ the
ward was restored to capacity by order dated _____ .

4. The guardian has performed its duties and responsibilities under law.

5. The guardian seeks discharge from its office as guardian.

WHEREFORE, your petitioner respectfully requests an order of this court, without a hearing, confirming the
termination of the guardianship and discharging the guardian.

FURTHER, under penalties for perjury for deliberate falsification therein, I declare or affirm that I have read the
foregoing petition and to the best of my knowledge or information, its representations are true, correct and complete.

Dated: _____

_____
Petitioner

Name of Petitioner's Attorney:
Name: _____
License No.:   _____
Address: _____
               _____
City/State/Zip: _____

State of Minnesota **County of**	**District Court** **Probate Division** **Judicial District:**

Court File No. _____

Case Type: 14, Guardianship

In Re: Guardianship of **, Ward**	**Order Confirming Termination of** **Guardianship and Discharging Guardian**

This matter came before the district court on a petition seeking restoration to capacity of the Ward named above. The
matter, having been considered by the Court, and the Court being duly advised in the premises now makes the following:

6. The guardianship has terminated because the above-named ward   ;   attained the age of majority
on   ;   was restored to capacity by order dated   ; or   died on   .

7. The guardian has performed its duties and responsibilities under law.

8. The guardian should be discharged from its duties.

NOW, THEREFORE, IT IS ORDERED:

(continues)

EXHIBIT 4–7   PETITION FOR TERMINATION OF GUARDIANSHIP AND DISCHARGE OF GUARDIAN AND ORDER OF TERMINATION AND DISCHARGE *(continued)*

9.   The termination of the above-named guardianship is confirmed.

10.   The guardian,   , is hereby discharged from its office as guardian.

Order Recommended by:

_____   _____

Referee of District Court   Date   Judge of the District Court   Date

CHALLENGING A GUARDIANSHIP APPOINTMENT

Trial courts are vested with broad discretion in appointing guardians. Generally, the standard of review for such matters is to determine whether the trial court abused its discretion in reaching its judgment. Absent a clear abuse of that discretion, the appellate courts infrequently reverse a lower court's decision. Abuse of discretion would be evident through proof of the trial court acting in an unreasonable, arbitrary, or unconscionable manner. The following case, *In the matter of: The Guardianship of Jessie K. Simmons,* offers a twist on the guardian appointment process. The parties in the case stipulated that the respondent, suffering from Alzheimer's disease, was incompetent.

CASE LAW   *In the Matter of: The Guardianship of Jessie K. Simmons*

Facts: Jack Simmons, a son of Jessie K. Simmons, petitioned the court to establish a guardianship for his mother, Jessie. Another son, Donald Simmons, was already handling Jessie's financial and health care needs through the use of durable powers of attorney. Jessie's daughter supported Jack's appointment as guardian. Jack claimed Donald, an attorney, misused his durable power of attorney; and Jack filed a motion to compel Donald to produce Jessie's financial records to prove his claim. Jack and Jane testified to the following:

Donald abused his powers.

Donald misused Jessie's funds.

Donald refused a financial accounting due to his claim that the accounts were confidential.

Donald refused to inform them of their mother's medical condition.

Donald scheduled the sale of the family home without notifying his siblings and taking into consideration they may have wanted to obtain family mementos from the home.

Donald failed to answer their telephone calls or e-mails.

(continues)

CASE LAW *In the Matter of: The Guardianship of Jessie K. Simmons* (continued)

Jack testified that Donald used one of Jessie's certificates of deposit as collateral for a personal loan, but Donald denied any wrongdoing. Jack testified that Donald failed to respond to his siblings request for information because Donald claimed he was bound by the confidentiality rules. The trial court failed to find an abuse of power by Donald, denied Jack's request to become his mother's guardian, and appointed Donald as Jessie's guardian without Donald making an application himself to be so named. Jack appealed.

Issue: Whether the guardianship appointment of the son holding the durable power of attorney was done according to statutory requirements.

Court's Reasoning: In our view, when family members cannot cooperate the better approach is to consider appointing a disinterested third party who will relay information and work together with all interested parties. Therefore, in light of the court's recognition of the obvious ill-will between the siblings and because of Donald's own acknowledged unresponsiveness to his brother and sister's concerns, we conclude that the trial court abused its discretion in appointing Donald as guardian. Secondly, as Jesse's attorney in fact, Donald was not prohibited from disclosing her financial information to his siblings because the financial information was not protected by the attorney client privilege.

Donald's roles involving his mother covered a wide variety of areas: attorney, attorney-in-fact, donee, executor, and heir. They overlapped and could not be fulfilled without an obvious conflict of interest. The failure of the trial court in allowing Jack full discovery of Jessie's financial records unfairly prejudiced Jack's investigation of the entire circumstances surrounding the potential for abuse of the power of attorney by Donald. Thirdly, Jack claims that the probate court, in appointing a guardian on its own motion, failed to follow the requirements of R.C. 2111.02C. A court may appoint a guardian on its own motion, as it deems necessary. Nonetheless, certain procedures must be followed to comply with the remaining statutory requirements. R.C.2111.02 C 1 provides that prior to the appointment of a guardian or limited guardian under division (A) (B) (1) of this section, the court shall conduct a hearing on the matter of the appointment. While the court had the authority to appoint a guardian on its own, in order to comply with the statutory notice requirements, the court should have first given notice of the proposed guardian to the other siblings, required Donald to file his application with the inventory of the estate and then scheduled a hearing.

Holding: The judgment of the Wood County Court of Common Pleas, Probate Division, was reversed and remanded for proceedings consistent with the appellate division's reasoning.

Case Discussion: This case illustrated that compliance with statutory notice provisions assures that those affected by the proposed guardianship are given the opportunity to be heard and afforded their right to due process.

CAREGIVING ISSUES

Caregiving has become an important issue for more and more baby boomers who find themselves serving as caregivers to aging relatives. In fact, 41 percent of baby boomers with a living parent are helping to care for them.[6] While historically families have cared for their loved ones when they became ill or as they aged, caregiving has changed over the years. Today families are providing care for longer periods of time for loved ones who are more ill, aged, or disabled than in the past. Caregiving for another usually occurs to varying degrees before a guardianship or conservatorship is considered necessary.

The Administration on Aging defines a family caregiver as anyone who provides care without pay and who has personal ties to the care recipient. A person with personal ties can include a family member, a friend, or a neighbor. Care may be provided on a part-time or full-time basis, and the care recipient may or may not live with the caregiver. Today some 44.4 million adult caregivers —or 21 percent of the country's adult population—provide unpaid care to seniors or adults with disabilities. On average, those caregivers are providing 21 hours of care per week; and the average length of time spent providing care is 4.3 years. Sixty-one percent of those caregivers are women; and of those women 41 percent are working full-time outside the home. This unpaid caregiving was estimated in 2006 to be worth $350 billion dollars per year. America's businesses lose an estimated $11–$29 billion dollars each year because of caregivers needing to take time off work to care for loved ones over 50 years old.[7]

Defining Caregiving

In addition to managing social, financial, and cultural activities, caregiving tasks may include doing household chores and arranging for outside services. Caregivers may assist in varying degrees with the activities of daily living including bathing, toileting, eating, and providing transportation.

The family caregiver's job description has ballooned in response to changes in medical care. Patients, who a generation ago would have stayed in a hospital longer to heal, are more frequently being sent home to be cared for. Family caregivers may perform such tasks as regulating the intravenous flow of medication, monitoring vital signs, changing feeding tubes and catheters, suctioning spinal cord injuries, administering injections, and cleaning and dressing serious wounds.[8]

Caregiver Stress

Caregiving can add a great deal of stress to a caregiver's life and may result in caregiver burnout. Particularly difficult is the task of caring for a person with dementia. For example, handling the caregiving needs of a person with AD (which may involve wandering, physical aggression, and incontinence) is different from handling the caregiving needs of a person who is mentally competent and cooperative, but physically limited in some way. Caregiver burnout may lead to physical and mental illness for the caregiver. In the case of the elderly, burnout has been found to lead to incidences of caregiver abuse of the elderly person being cared for.[9]

A National Family Caregivers Association survey reported that 61 percent of family caregivers reported depression; 51 percent, sleeplessness; and 41 percent, back problems. The survey found that elderly spousal caregivers with a history of a chronic illness experienced a 63 percent higher mortality rate than those with similar chronic illnesses but no caregiving burdens.

Can Caregivers Be Paid?

Caregiving can be an expensive, uncompensated undertaking. Caregivers spend an average of $2,400 per year to assist the person they are caring for. Caregivers devoting at least 40 hours per week on caregiving spend even more, an average of $3,888 uncompensated dollars per year. In 2006, Vermont's Department of Disabilities, Aging and Independent Living spearheaded a successful program called Choices for Care that pays family members or friends $10 an hour to care for Medicaid-eligible older adults who want to remain at home. The Choices for Care program was viewed as a cost-cutting measure because such in-home care is much less expensive than the alternative of a person being placed in a Medicaid-funded institution. More states are expected to join Vermont in making an effort to curb the $38 billion spent by Medicaid on institutional care nationwide.[10] A pilot program called Cash & Counseling was started a decade ago in Arkansas, Florida, and New Jersey. It allows elderly Medicaid recipients to receive special grants to pay for and manage their own care. The Cash & Counseling program was deemed successful and was expanded to 12 more states in 2007.[11] Another option for eligible caregivers is to take the dependent care tax credit for a relative a caregiver is caring for in the caregiver's home.

Another concept in compensating caregivers is the caregiver contract, also called personal-service or personal-care agreements. The caregiver contract should specify what care a caregiver will provide and what the compensation will be. The contract should state the way the payments will be made to the caregiver and the fact that income tax, Social Security, and payroll taxes may have to be paid. Of course, the parties to the contract must have the requisite mental capacity to sign it. A caregiver contract may provide the following benefits:

1. Help prevent family disputes between paid family caregivers and other family members

2. Reduce the estate assets of the person being cared for and thus possibly increase the chances of long-term care Medicaid coverage for that person. However, Medicaid may disqualify the assets transferred to a caregiver unless the payments being made are reasonable for the care being provided.[12]

Paralegals may assist with interviewing the parties to caregiver contracts as well as draft caregiver contracts under the direction of their supervising attorney. Medicaid eligibility criteria are discussed further in Chapter 7.

ELDER LAW PRACTICE

Tara Jensen, Esq., was recently contacted by client Ann Nicholls and was told that Ann's brother, Fred, was going to court to accuse her of "misconduct" in her role as guardian of their mother, Connie Nicholls.

Tara immediately ascertained the details. Apparently, Ann had placed her mother in a secure Alzheimer's unit of a nursing home after transferring her from a *locked-down* mental health facility. Ann had transferred Connie on the advice of Connie's physician, and Ann was not allowing her brother to see their mother until Connie was stabilized in her new environment. Ann believes Connie becomes upset and distraught by any visits with Fred, and she has told this to Fred repeatedly. Apparently, the brother and sister have long-standing problems with each other and neither thinks the other knows what is best for Connie. Applicable state law allows for a guardian to be removed only for misconduct, failure to discharge a statutory duty, or inability to perform duties. Ann is concerned that her decision to keep Fred away from their mother is stepping over the line ethically in what she can do as a guardian. Does Ann have cause for concern?

Tara advises Ann that she should take her brother's complaints seriously. However, in her role as a court-appointed guardian, she has been given the responsibility to make the tough decisions. Tara tells Ann that the court probably would find her decision reasonable based on Fred's visitation having a documented effect on their mother and the fact that Ann informed Fred of the reasons for the non-visitation order. Most importantly, Connie's physician confirmed Ann's decision and Fred has been informed that it is only until their mother is stabilized in her new environment.[13]

SUMMARY

Guardianships and conservatorships are legal management tools that are put in place by state law to protect and aid individuals who have different abilities to care for themselves. The major difference between a guardianship and a conservatorship is that a conservatorship is a voluntary undertaking that requires the continuing permission of the conservatee. A guardianship, on the other hand, is a completely involuntary proceeding with a legal declaration that a person is legally incompetent and becomes the guardian's ward. Some states use the term *decisional incapacity* rather than *incompetence*, and Louisiana uses the term *interdiction* instead of *guardianship*. An additional difference is that a conservatorship allows management only of a person's property while a guardianship typically permits *complete* management of a ward's property and person. Alternatives to traditional cookie-cutter guardianships are in keeping with what is known as the least restrictive alternative principle.

KEY TERMS

conservatee

conservator

conservatorship

decisional incapacity

final order

guardian

guardianship

hearing officer, referee,
   commissioner, or magistrate

least restrictive alternative (LRA)
   principle

limited, partial, or temporary
   guardianships

Mental Health Reporter

National Guardianship Association

parens patriae

parental or spousal appointments

private guardianship

public guardian

public guardianship

special medical guardianship

standby guardianships

ward

REVIEW QUESTIONS

1. What are the differences between the concepts of guardianship and conservatorship?

2. When should a standby guardianship be used?

3. What is the role of a public guardian?

4. How is a public guardianship different from a private guardianship?

5. When would a medical guardianship be appropriate?

6. How does application of the least restrictive alternative principle in guardianship law help provide some of the constitutional protections of the Fourteenth Amendment?

7. When would a durable power of attorney not suffice and a guardianship probably be needed?

8. What are some specific requirements of your state that a guardian may need to fulfill once a guardianship has been ordered?

9. Refer to Exhibit 4–6 and research a guardian's requirements in your state.

10. What documents should generally be attached to a guardianship petition? Again, you may refer to your state's requirements.

ETHICS ALERT

Missy Mayweather was busy every day caring for her cantankerous and incontinent 93-year-old grandmother, Mamie Mayweather. Johnny Justice, Esq., the senior Mayweather's longtime attorney, was recently named guardian of Mamie. Johnny has aided the family often. Johnny also represented Mamie's son, Marshall, in his divorce. Most recently, Johnny applied to the probate court for authority to release estate funds to Marshall so that he could pay off a lease on a truck as an obligation to his former spouse in a divorce. Johnny's first act as guardian was to refuse a second $4,000 payment to Missy for caring for her grandmother. Is Missy acting ethically by requesting payment for caring for her grandmother? Does Johnny's behavior appear to be in the best interests of Mamie?

The court found Johnny's behavior not to be in the best interests of his ward. Johnny's representation of Marshall and Johnny's duties as guardian were found to be a conflict of interest, and the court removed him as guardian. The court also found that the 24-hour service that Missy provided to Mamie (including cleaning, cooking, providing a home, and bathing) equaled $1.39 per hour and was reasonable compensation for the care that Missy provided to Mamie.[14]

■ HELPFUL WEB SITES

NATIONAL GUARDIANSHIP ASSOCIATION, INC. <//WWW.GUARDIANSHIP.ORG>   This Web site states its purpose is to provide educational training and networking opportunities for guardians and about guardianship.

ILLINOIS GUARDIANSHIP & ADVOCACY COMMISSION <//GAC.STATE.IL.US/LEGAL.HTML>   This is a site for a state agency created to safeguard the rights of person with disabilities.

NATIONAL ADULT PROTECTIVE SERVICES ASSOCIATION (NAPSA) <//WWW.APSNETWORK.ORG>   This is a Web site for a non-profit association whose purpose is to share information and improve the quality of service to victims of elder abuse.

THE GERONTOLOGICAL SOCIETY OF AMERICA <//WWW.GERON.ORG>   This Society is a non-profit professional organization for its members working in the field of aging.

NATIONAL ALLIANCE FOR CAREGIVING <//WWW.CAREGIVING.ORG>   The site is dedicated to daily support for family caregivers.

NATIONAL FAMILY CAREGIVERS ASSOCIATION <//WWW.NFCACARES.ORG>   The site states its organization's goal is to educate, support, and empower caregivers.

■ ENDNOTES

[1] Zinny, George H., and Grossberg, George T., *Guardianship of the Elderly: Psychiatric and Judicial Aspects*, New York: Springer Publishing, 1998.

[2] Schmidt, 1996.

[3] Barnes, Alison, "The Liberty and Property of Elders: Guardianship and Will Contests as the Same Claim," *The Elder Law Journal*, 11 Elder L.J. 1 (2003).

[4] English, David M., and Morgan, Rebecca C., "The Uniform Guardianship and Protective Proceedings Act of 1997," *Journal of Elder Law and Policy*

[5] Teaster, Pamela B., "When the State Takes Over a Life: The Public Guardian as Public Administrator," *Public Administration Review*, Jul/Aug. 2003, Vol. 63, Issue 4, page 396.

[6] USA Today/ABC News/Gallup Poll, 2006.

[7] "Empowering Family Caregivers," *Drug Store News*, Fall 2003, page 55.

[8] "Promoting Self-Care for Family Caregivers," *Drug Store News*, Fall 2003, page 47.

[9] Neergaard, Lauran, "Caregiver Training Helps Keep People with Dementia at Home," *The Star-Ledger*, August 13, 2007, page 5.

[10] Basler, Barbara, "Vermont Program Spells Success for Aging in Place," AARP Bulletin, December 2006, page 6.

[11] Fetterman, Mindy, "Proposed Legislation Would Help Caregivers," *Daily Record*, July 24, 2007, page 10.

[12] Silverman, Rachel Emma, "Who Will Mind Mom? Check Her Contract," *The Wall Street Journal*, September 7, 2006.

[13] *In re Estate of Kelton*, Missouri Appellate Court WL 139564 (Mo. App. S.D. 2004).

[14] Based on the unpublished opinion of *In re Guardianship of Walther*, WL 1454464 (Ohio App. 2 Dist.) (2004).

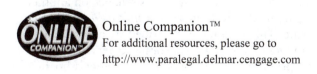

Estate Planning: Trusts

> "Old age has a great sense of calm and freedom. When the passions have relaxed their hold, you have escaped not from one master, but from many."

PLATO, *THE REPUBLIC*

■ **trust**

A legal mechanism by which one or more persons hold legal title to money or property for the benefit of another who holds equitable title.

■ **OBJECTIVES**_____

After completing this chapter, you will be able to:

• Explain the fundamental reasons for trust creation.

• Define terms related to basic trust.

• Identify various types of trusts.

• List the advantages and disadvantages of various types of trusts.

• Explain the reasons for trust termination.

INTRODUCTION

Previous chapters have suggested that a person's estate plan should provide for an orderly transfer of the individual's assets to his chosen beneficiaries. Creating a legal mechanism called a **trust** can help with that transfer. Different types of trusts also have other benefits, including some that help produce significant tax savings. Although Webster's describes the word *trust* as reliance on another,[1] a trust can also be defined as a thing, as in a *trust document* that was drafted for a client. This document described as a trust may be defined as "an arrangement by which one or more persons hold *legal title* to money or property for the benefit of another who holds *equitable title.*" The topic of trusts is often taught along with the topic of wills in an estates and trusts course, but no review of elder law would be complete without an explanation of how trusts can be a particularly powerful estate planning tool for elder law practitioners and their clients.

Essentially, a trust is a legal mechanism that lets the creator of the trust decide in writing how property put into the human-made creation called a trust is distributed and when. The trust creator may have reasons for not wanting to bequeath assets outright to certain individuals in a will or to gift those assets outright during the creator's lifetime. For example, a cautious mother may sign over her stock portfolio to a bank to manage for her fun-loving college freshman daughter. The mother's instructions may be that the income from the trust is to be used for tuition and books while the daughter is in school, but is to be given outright to her more mature daughter upon her 30th birthday. The mother in this example could be called a **creator or trustor**. A trustor transferring *personal* property is more specifically called a **settlor**. If the creator is transferring *real* property, he is called a **grantor**. The mother in the example is transferring a stock portfolio, which is considered personal property. The bank is called the **trustee** and as such holds *legal title*. A trustee is the person to whom the property has been transferred for the benefit of another and who is responsible for the trust's administration. The daughter is called the **beneficiary** and as such holds *equitable title* and is entitled to the benefit of the trust. Any document in which the trust creator creates a trust is called the **trust instrument**. A trust instrument may be created in a variety of documents including a *will, trust agreement, declaration of trust,* and *revocable or irrevocable trust.* The mother's trust is considered **express trust** because her purpose to benefit her daughter is very specific. The opposite of an express trust is an **implied trust**. An implied trust is often created by the courts to prevent an inequity. In such a case, the implied trust is called a **constructive trust**. Another type of trust, the **charitable trust**, is created for the purpose of creating a benefit for society. The mother in the fact pattern created a *private express trust.* If the mother had given the stock to a charity, the trust would have been described as an express charitable trust.

While the majority of states have adopted their own state probate codes (often based in large part on the Uniform Probate Code (UPC)), few states have adopted a uniform trust code. Generally, most state courts look to their state statutes, case precedent, and the *Restatement of Trusts* published by the American Law Institute.

Historically, trusts were used by the wealthy to preserve their wealth for their descendants. This preservation of wealth via a trust may continue for several generations. A creator also may use a trust to control the behavior of beneficiaries after the creator's death. Trusts have continued to gain acceptance by the increasingly well-to-do baby boomers.[2] As in the preceding example, parents of adult children who believe that their children are not ready to deal maturely with the outright inheritance of the family business or other assets may, in particular, appreciate the benefits of a trust. With a trust, adult children can still inherit their parent's estate, but within the protective mechanism of the trust.

creator or trustor
The individual who creates a trust.

settlor
A trustor who transfers personal property.

grantor
A creator who transfers real estate.

trustee
The person to whom property has been transferred for the benefit of another and who is responsible for the trust's administration.

beneficiary
A person who inherits property through a will.

trust instrument
Any document in which the trust creator creates a trust.

express trust
Such a trust has a specific intent with a clearly stated purpose.

implied trust
Such a trust is often created by the courts to prevent inequity.

constructive trust

A remedy employed by a court to convert the legal title of property into a trust held by a trustee for the benefit of a third party who in good conscience should have reaped the benefits of the possession of the property put into the constructive trust.

charitable trust

A trust created with the express intent and purpose to benefit a charity.

intervivos gift

A gift given while the grantor is still living.

testamentary trust

A trust included in a will that is designed to take effect after a testator's death.

intervivos trust

A trust written and enacted by a creator while he is still alive.

principal

Any cash or property placed in a trust.

In addition, if there are other issues involving beneficiaries who are mentally or physically challenged, a trust can be drafted to protect such beneficiaries and can be designed to take effect after a creator is no longer alive to protect the beneficiaries.

Trusts are also used to avoid probate. The costs and complexity of probate can vary from state to state; and in some states, the probate process is often lengthy and expensive.[3] Another good reason to create a trust and to avoid probate is when an estate involves a business or a heavy stock market position and the beneficiaries need to act quickly to preserve the estate's value. An extended probate process could result in devaluation or even loss of assets. A last will and testament should still be drafted by a trust's creator so that any item not covered by a trust will be adequately dealt with.

TRUST ESSENTIALS

The key ingredient needed to make a valid trust is the splitting of the legal and equitable interests in the property in question. If the same person is the sole beneficiary of the trust and the sole trustee of the trust, the trust will fail.

The advantages and disadvantages of using a trust, along with the subjects already tackled in the previous chapters (i.e., wills, advance directives for health care, and powers of attorney) should be included as part of the analysis of each client's life and estate planning. (These topics are in addition to information provided in upcoming chapters.) However, the subject of trusts is a complicated topic that can involve issues of tax law. Many attorneys who want to specialize in estate planning continue their education after law school by studying for a master's degree in estate planning. Many others continually fine-tune their knowledge by attending seminars offered, for example, by state bar associations. Other estate planning attorneys may have undergraduate or graduate degrees in accounting, tax, and finance.

A paralegal should never be asked to decide whether a client's situation calls for a trust. If a law firm's paralegals are making those decisions, the question of ethics comes into play. However, paralegals may interview clients in preparation for the creation of a trust and may draft a trust under the direct supervision and review of an attorney.

As you know, property left to another through a will is called a testamentary gift. A gift given while the grantor is still living is called an ***intervivos* gift**. A trust included in a will that is designed to take effect after a testator's death is called a **testamentary trust**. The testamentary trust, like any part of a person's will, can be removed or changed at any time because the creation of a trust is a *gratuitous transfer*. A trust written and enacted by a creator while he is still alive is called an ***intervivos* trust**. A distinction may be made between a trust's **principal** and a trust's *income*. This distinction is particularly important when the trust is designed to entitle the trust's income to one beneficiary and the trust's principal to another beneficiary. The trust's creator empowers the trust's trustee with certain enumerated powers within the original trust instrument.

The purpose of a trust and the other legal relationships presented so far (e. g., guardianships, conservatorships, personal representative or executor of an estate, and agency dealings) should not be confused with what a trust does. None of the other legal relationships mentioned create a *new legal title* to property along with the splitting of that title with the *benefits of ownership in another* (or at least the splitting of the beneficiary status). An intended trust beneficiary does not have a right to sue a trust's creator because the creator decided to remove the beneficiary from the trust or because the trust was altered any other way.

Strict requirements must be followed when any type of trust is created. A trust must have a *legal purpose* (e.g., a trust designed to provide for the medical care or educational needs of a child). Failure of a trust to have such legal purpose invalidates a trust. Generally, in that case, the trust property reverts back to the creator (if it was originally an *intervivos* trust and the creator is still living) or to the creator's heirs according to a deceased creator's will or to a creator's beneficiaries according to the applicable intestacy statutes if no will was written.

One of the most important requirements of creating a trust that is sometimes forgotten is the **funding of the trust**. For example, if Fred's Barbershop Building is to be transferred from Barber Fred to a new trust to benefit Fred's grandson, conveying Fred's Barbershop Building to the Fred's Barbershop Building Trust must be done via a deed, and the deed must be recorded. Failure to transfer title through the deed would mean that the trust was not effective. In other words, the trust would simply be paper and good intentions. Some states also require that the **rule against perpetuities** not be breached.[4] The short story on the rule against perpetuities is that it places a limitation on the length of time the trust can be in effect. Both irrevocable trusts and revocable trusts may be created. The creator can legally change a revocable trust during his lifetime, unlike an irrevocable trust. Once a creator dies, the revocable aspect of the trust changes and the trust can become irrevocable.

The Role of the Trust's Creator

Just as all states require a testator to have the required legal capacity to create a valid will, a trust's creator also must have legal capacity to meet the criteria for conveying property via a trust. Depending on the creator's domicile state, capacity may be evaluated by a higher standard when property is conveyed than in other areas of the law. All states require a trust's creator to have legal capacity or face the trust being found void by the courts.

A trust's creator also must have a transferable interest in the property in question and show a *clear intention* to create a trust that splits equitable and legal title in the property. Most trusts must be in a *written format* to comply with each

funding of the trust
One of the most important trust creation requirements in transferring title to property, through deed or otherwise, into the name of the trust.

rule against perpetuities
A rule that places a limitation on the length of time a trust can be in effect.

state's version of the Statute of Frauds. The Statute of Frauds is generally defined as any of the various state laws (modeled after an old English law) that require certain documents (such as contracts for the sale of real estate or goods over a certain value) to be signed and to be in writing if they are to be enforceable in court. No particular words must be used in the trust instrument as long as the trust's purpose and intention is clear. There are limited exceptions, but the majority of states require some kind of written document generally known as a trust instrument to provide proof of the trust's creation. The precise requirements for creating the written documentation vary, but the strictest state requirements follow those for writing a valid will (e.g., signature formalities and witnesses). In general, the requirements for creating a trust are less strict. Some states allow oral evidence of a trust's creation. The best practice for a legal professional is to err on the side of caution and have the trust's creator sign a trust instrument and to have that instrument notarized. Failure to meet the requirements of creating a trust will likely cause the trust to fail as a voidable instrument. As with wills, any attempts at creating a trust found to involve fraud, duress, or undue influence will cause the trust instrument to be voided. The creator's role ceases after the trust creation is complete unless the creator appoints himself a trustee or beneficiary.

The Role of the Beneficiaries

Any person or legal entity can be a trust beneficiary. A key point in the discussion of beneficiaries is that the trust must name the beneficiaries clearly. Failure to do so will cause the trust to fail. The best-case scenario is to include the specifically named persons or entities. Alternatively, a class of persons or entities usually suffices. For example, if a creator is transferring his home to a class of persons, a trust will provide that the creator's home is to be transferred to his children (i.e., a class of persons). Beneficiaries must accept the benefits of a trust along with any restrictions the creator places on the trust.

One possible problem with multiple beneficiaries sharing interest in trust property is that all of them may not reach unanimous agreement on issues that arise. A trust's termination may still allow for any remains of the trust corpus to be given to a beneficiary not named as an original beneficiary. This second-tier or subsequent interest is called a remainder. The beneficiary who receives the remainder interest is called a **remainderman**.

remainderman

The beneficiary who receives the remainder interest in a trust.

The Role of the Trustee

For a trust to work as it was designed, the trustee must understand and accept the obligations of holding legal title to property that will benefit another. The trustee must understand his role as a fiduciary. A fiduciary is a person who holds a position of trust, responsibility, and duty to another. For example, attorneys and accountants fulfill fiduciary roles to their clients. The fiduciary role of a trustee holds him to a very high standard of honesty and loyalty.

If a trustee dies, wants to resign, or becomes incapacitated, a **successor trustee** already should have been chosen and named in the trust. This person will be available to fill the role of the original trustee. Failure to name a successor trustee may mean that any state statutes that deal with the issue will apply or, failing that, that the court system must appoint a trustee. Either way, the disruption is unlikely to affect the trust or its beneficiaries positively. The named trustee must have specific duties enumerated in the trust; otherwise, he should could be considered just a caretaker for the property, thereby making the trust passive and ineffective.

Usually it is best to have one trustee named at one time. The problem with multiple trustees is the same difficulty that three people may have deciding where to go for dinner when two diners want Mexican food and the third diner wants Chinese food. The resulting decision probably will not meet everyone's expectations. Historically, in regard to trusts, all trustees had to agree or, to follow the analogy, nobody ate dinner. This made it difficult to run a trust, and disputes often landed in court. In response, many states now tend to allow the majority to rule. It becomes more problematic when there are only two trustees with clearly divergent views. That situation may lead to battling trustees asking a judge to oust one or the other so that the purpose of the trust can be fulfilled. It should be noted that co-trustees are jointly and severally liable for the actions of other cotrustees. Who wants to watch another trustee's every move?

Responsibilities often involve the financial management of a trust's **corpus** and its profits. A trust's corpus is the money or property put into the trust, as opposed to the trust's interest or profits. Failure to develop and increase assets may lead to claims of breach of trust. While failure is common, trustees are not easily excused for mismanaging investments and may be sued by the trust's disappointed and very likely angry beneficiaries. If a trustee is sued for his conduct involving investments, in some states, the courts will review the trustee's behavior under what is known as a **prudent person standard**. Other states follow the UPC standard which asks whether a *reasonable person* would have acted as the trustee did when dealing with another's property.[5] If the trustee is an investment counselor by profession, he usually will be judged by a higher level of expertise in that profession. States may have a statutory list of investments that a trustee can utilize, which helps the trustee avoid accusations of financial mismanagement. However, even with the use of an investment list, questions may still arise if a trustee invests only in the list's investments and profits are unreasonably low.[6] A trustee also can be sued for specific performance by a beneficiary who alleges the trustee is not fulfilling his obligations. Specific performance is defined as being required to do exactly what was agreed. In addition, a beneficiary can seek an injunction to stop a trustee from performing in a negligent or unusual manner.

successor trustee
An alternate trustee named in a trust to fill the role of the original trustee should the original trustee die, resign, or become incapacitated or unable to serve.

corpus
The money or property put into a trust.

prudent person standard
The standard by which courts may review a trustee's behavior. It asks whether a reasonable person would have acted as the trustee did when dealing with another person's property.

The trust's creator can include an **exculpatory clause** to lessen the burden on a trustee. An exculpatory clause is a provision in a trust instrument by which the trustee is relieved of responsibility for things that go wrong or for financial losses as long as the trustee acted in good faith. This clause is often included when a family member has been asked to be a trustee and is serving without taking a fee. No court will protect a trustee from willfully irresponsible or illegal behavior. While some professional trustees are paid, family or friends of the creator who are named as trustees often waive their fee. Another drain on a trust corpus can be a *bond* that is often required by statute unless waived by the creator. A bond is a document that promises to pay money if a particular future event happens or a sum of money that is put up and will be lost if the event happens.

Who Can Be a Trustee?

No one can be forced to be a trustee, and the position should not be taken lightly. An individual or a legal entity such as a bank or another type of corporation may fill the role of trustee. Most states have statutes detailing who or what may serve as a trustee. For example, municipal governments usually can be named a trustee only of a charitable trust. The federal government cannot be named a trustee of any type of trust. Some states require that a trustee take an oath of office. Trustees should have the expertise to handle property and financial issues because trustees negligent in handling such issues can be sued for malpractice.

The Trust Administration Process

The creator may have been the "star of the show" when deciding to create a trust, but "the show won't go on" without a trustee who appreciates the role of administering a trust. A creator can name himself as a trust's trustee, but remember that a creator cannot also be the trust's beneficiary. Once the trustee accepts his role, the list of duties and responsibilities starts growing. Some states require a trustee to register the trust with the court that has jurisdiction over the trust. An attorney representing a trustee should make sure that documents such as deeds and securities are drafted and recorded, necessary insurance is purchased, and upkeep on any trust property continues. The trustee usually is empowered by the trust to hire out any work that needs to be done to maintain the trust property. Valuable property needs continued safekeeping. Trustees should *never* commingle a trustee's personal property and a trust's property. To do so invites charges of impropriety.

The attorney who prepares a trust should keep records so that beneficiaries can be located. Remember, a trust may not take effect for years into the future following a creator's death. Any lawsuit against a trust should be as zealously defended by the trustee as if the lawsuit was against him personally.

What Type of Property Can Be Put into a Trust?

Any kind of property can be put into a trust as long as it can be legally transferred. The property can be **tangible** or **intangible**. Tangible property is defined as property that is capable of being touched; that is, it is real. Intangible property is defined as property that is a right rather than a physical object (e.g., bank accounts, stocks, and copyrights).

The property that makes up the trust may be called different names, but they all mean essentially the same thing. The property held in the trust may be called *trust property,* a *trust fund,* the *trust corpus,* the *trust* **res***,* the *trust principal,* or the *trust estate.* Cash placed in a trust is usually called the principal. Although the term **corpus estate** may be used for any property placed in trust, real property placed in a trust is usually called the *corpus.* Personal property (other than cash) that is placed in a trust is usually called the *res.*

A client may consider transferring his business into a **grantor-retained annuity trust**. A grantor-retained annuity trust allows the grantor to pass on his company to a chosen beneficiary during the grantor's lifetime, while simultaneously giving the grantor an income from the business for a designated period. This type of trust is popular because it allows the grantor to retain control and give his heirs the property relatively free of estate and gift taxes.

TAX SAVINGS WITH TRUST CREATION?

Clients with estates large enough to pay estate taxes usually want their attorneys and accountants to go to great lengths to ensure that they can avoid paying those estate taxes legally. It can be argued that seeking a reduction in estate taxes is a worthy cause. After all, each tax dollar avoided is a dollar that can be left to provide for a client's family, friends, pets, and charities.

Taxes are a big issue with estate planning, and trusts can help provide tax savings. However, the important beginning step for most elder law attorneys is analyzing a client's immediate needs. For example, are there capacity issues or health problems?

Reviewing a client's situation includes analyzing what a client's net worth will be at his death. A client's assets while he is alive do not include life insurance or the proceeds of any death benefits from pension plans. Whether a client owns any property jointly with anyone else must be determined. The final count of how much a client's estate is worth at his death figures prominently in how much federal and state estate tax the client's estate may ultimately owe—and the importance of tax planning for the client. Both federal and state governments may require an estate to pay taxes based on its value. Federal estate taxes are due from all estates with a value over a certain amount. See Exhibit 5–1 to review the *federal* estate tax chart. *State* estate taxes are calculated as a percentage of the entire taxable estate *if* the deceased person lived in a state with estate taxes. Not

tangible

Property that is capable of being touched; that is, it is real.

intangible

Refers to property that is a right rather than a physical object (e.g., bank accounts, stocks, and copyrights).

res

Any personal property, other than cash, placed in a trust.

corpus estate

A name for real property placed in a trust.

grantor-retained annuity trust

A trust that allows a grantor to pass on his business or company to a chosen beneficiary while the grantor is still alive and gives the grantor an income for a designated period.

all states have state estate taxes, and those states without that tax burden are especially popular with older citizens. See Exhibit 5–2 to review a list of states with no state estate tax.

Another way to reduce the amount of taxable estate is for the owner to begin gifting his money before he dies. Of course, this is possible only when the owner does not need the assets for his support. In 2007, the federal government allowed an individual to give away up to $12,000 and a married couple to give up to $24,000 per year. This gifting is technically known as the **annual gift tax exclusion**. There is no limit on how many different people can receive such gifts.

Federal tax savings may not be an issue for all law firm clients. The federal government assessed a federal estate tax on any estate worth over $2 million in 2008. The amount hits $3.5 million in 2009, and the federal estate tax will be completely repealed in 2010. Congress then can decide to reinstitute the tax (at any threshold) in 2011. Each state with an estate tax has different thresholds for initiating the tax, and some states assess estate taxes for estates with assets as small as $50,000. Federal estate taxes are due within nine months of a person's death. Depending on the size of a client's estate, the federal estate tax in 2006 began at 18 percent and hit a top tax rate of 45 percent. Chapter 7 discusses taxes further.

The assets of a properly created trust are not included in the creator's taxable estate. Unless a trust is included in a will, probate also is avoided when a trust is involved. No probate administration to wade through also means no public scrutiny and a smoother transition of property from one person to another. Also, there is no need to worry about intestate succession.

annual gift tax exclusion

The amount an individual or couple is permitted by federal tax law to gift each year.

EXHIBIT 5–1   FEDERAL ESTATE TAX CHART

2004 and 2005: $1.5 million

2006, 2007, and 2008: $2 million

2009: $3.5 million

2010: Temporary repeal

2011: Exemption reverts to $1 million unless Congress enacts new legislation

Gift tax exclusion is indexed for inflation.

Trusts, Marriage, and Tax Savings

There is an exception to Ben Franklin's statement that the only guarantees in life are dying and paying taxes. The exception is that an individual may inherit an unlimited amount of assets from his spouse tax free. The good news for married couples is that in 1981, Congress changed federal estate tax law and gave married couples an unlimited marital tax deduction that permits spouses to leave their entire estates (no matter the amount) to their spouses completely tax free.

EXHIBIT 5–2   STATES WITH NO ESTATE TAXES

Alabama	Alaska
Arizona	Arkansas
California	Colorado
Connecticut	Delaware
Florida	Georgia
Hawaii	Idaho
Indiana	Iowa
Kentucky	Louisiana
Michigan	Mississippi
Missouri	Montana
Nevada	New Hampshire
New Mexico	North Dakota
Pennsylvania	South Carolina
South Dakota	Tennessee
Texas	Utah
Washington	West Virginia
Wyoming	

Each individual also has a personal exemption. In 2006, the personal exemption began at $1 million. This $1 million exemption may be lessened by gifts made to anyone, including children or grandchildren. The bad news is that if an individual dies and leaves everything to his spouse, the deceased person's $1 million exemption does not transfer to the spouse with the rest of the assets. This means that when a second spouse dies, he has only a $1 million exemption and all of his assets over the $1 million exemption are taxed according to the tax rate applicable to the size of his entire estate. That is why attorneys usually plan for the creation of a trust for each spouse. A sample irrevocable trust is available for review in the Elder Law Online Supplement.

TYPES OF TRUSTS

Many clients who create trusts have been protecting and providing for loved ones (humans and animals) most of their lives. These clients often view the creation of a trust as one more way to continue to provide and protect their loved ones. Attorneys must know how to create trusts that are designed to offer this protection. Four basic kinds of trusts are designed to allow the creator of a trust to protect another individual:

1. Spendthrift trust

2. Discretionary trust

3. Support trust, also called a special needs trust

4. Irrevocable life insurance trust

In addition, a charitable trust can be used to benefit the trust creator's favorite charity. A charity can be the recipient of a trust after the primary beneficiary of a trust has died.

A marital trust may be created to continue to provide for a surviving spouse and any designated remaining beneficiaries following a surviving spouse's death. A pet owner also can ensure the continued care of a beloved pet by utilizing a pet trust document.

Spendthrift Trust

spendthrift trust
A trust that directs a trustee that a specific sum may be disbursed at specified intervals or that states how monies from the trust can be spent to keep an inheritance from being spent unwisely.

Even a loving grandfather might think that a grown grandson who is left a lump-sum inheritance would sooner spend it on wine, women, and a BMW than a college education. That being said, the colorfully descriptive spendthrift trust could be just what a wise grandfather needs. A **spendthrift trust** allows one person to give money or property to another person without fear that it will be squandered by the recipient or totally accessible to creditors. If a trust's creator believes that a loved one, whatever age, is susceptible to outside influences, this trust can be designed to keep an inheritance from filling unintended pockets or being spent unwisely. A spendthrift trust directs the trustee to disburse a specific sum at specified intervals or states how monies from the trust can be spent and disbursed at the trustee's discretion.

Discretionary Trust

discretionary trust
A trust that allows a trustee to distribute the trust's assets at his own discretion, giving the trustee a degree of personal choice in how the trust assets are distributed; also called a sprinkling or spray trust.

A **discretionary trust** allows the trustee some leeway in carrying out its terms. It allows a trustee to distribute the trust's assets at his discretion. This means that the trust's creator has provided in the trust instrument that the trustee should have a degree of personal choice in how and when the trust assets are distributed. A discretionary trust also is called a sprinkling or spray trust.

Support Trust

Because minor children lack the legal capacity to handle their own finances, a **support trust or special needs trust** fits the needs of minor children very well. This trust also is used for adult children who are unable to meet their own needs. Failure to place a minor child's inheritance in a trust with a named trustee results in the courts being forced to hold the minor's assets in trust until the minor reaches maturity. This seldom leads to the best investment of a minor's assets. The problem with an adult child with disabilities receiving monies outright from an inheritance (instead of through a special needs trust) is that the adult child likely will become ineligible to continue receiving disability and medical benefits. The special needs trust allows the trustee to provide items not available through what are often very limited disability payments. For example, special needs paid for may include transportation costs, travel, furniture, housing, and household assistance. Refer to Exhibit 5–4 to review a sample will with a special needs trust.

support trust or special needs trust

A trust established for the support of minor children or an adult child with disabilities.

Irrevocable Life Insurance Trust

Proceeds of a life insurance policy payable upon the death of a decedent become part of the decedent's estate unless a life insurance trust has been created prior to his death or the policy was owned by another person. Thus, an **irrevocable life insurance trust** may be created to guard the decedent's estate from increasing in value and subsequently having to pay taxes on life insurance proceeds. Beneficiaries are not responsible for taxes on insurance proceeds.

The life insurance trust should be drafted so that it owns the policy with no control by the insured. This is so none of the proceeds are considered part of the decedent's taxable estate. The best-case scenario is for the life insurance trust to buy the policy through the trustee. Generally, if an insured trustee transfers his current policy to the newly drafted life insurance trust, the insured will have to survive at least three years to make sure any insurance proceeds are considered out of his estate. If the insurance trust is taxable because the insured trustee is not meeting the three-year rule, the life insurance trust may turn into a *marital trust*. The life insurance trust can be funded or unfunded depending on the circumstances. A tax identification number is needed for the insurance trust; but because no income usually is generated, there should be no need to file a tax return. The key thing to remember with an irrevocable life insurance trust is that it is designed to provide tax benefits. This can make a huge difference in a very large estate. Insurance policy proceeds often help pay estate taxes due on the decedent's estate.

irrevocable life insurance trust

A trust created to guard the decedent's estate from increasing in value and subsequently having to pay taxes on life insurance proceeds.

Charitable Remainder Trusts

Another option is creating a **charitable remainder trust (CRT)**. The CRT permits the creator to transfer his assets into a lifetime income without incurring capital gains or estate taxes. The creator selects a charity to benefit from a charitable donation upon his death.

Marital Trusts

One typical purpose for the creation of a marital trust is for one spouse to provide for the other spouse. Marital trusts may be called by a variety of names in different states. Such a trust may be called a **qualified terminable interest property (QTIP) trust**. In some states, it is called a **marital trust**, **credit shelter trust**, an A and B trust, a husband and wife trust, or a **bypass trust**.

The beneficiary spouse will receive income generated by a marital trust's *corpus* tax free because the beneficiary spouse had no ownership interest. The trust is designed with one person named as both the grantor and trustee and his spouse as the secondary trustee who will benefit from the trust once the grantor dies. When such a trust is created while both spouses are living, the spouses can utilize tax-saving strategies and ultimately preserve estate assets for their designated beneficiaries. The typical marital trust designates the creator's children as beneficiaries but allows the widowed spouse to withdraw adequate income or even dip into the trust's principal for support during his lifetime. Any children are usually named **residuary beneficiaries**, which means that they receive the *corpus* of the trust after the income beneficiary dies.

Married couples applying an estate tax exemption amount to their estate through a marital type trust are reducing the estate's tax exposure when the first spouse dies. Then when the surviving spouse dies, his exemption amount is applied to the remaining estate.

The type of trust generally known as a QTIP trust protects money from the creator's creditors and keeps assets separate from a new spouse. It also may be used to ensure that any children from the creator's current or prior marriages are protected. The QTIP trust can place strong restrictions on how the trust's assets can be spent to support a surviving spouse. Restrictions go so far as to prevent the surviving spouse from designating to whom the trust's remaining assets should be given after the surviving spouse's death. This potential problem can be circumvented by making the surviving spouse one of the trustees of the QTIP trust. The surviving spouse can be given as much control as the creating spouse chooses.

For example, if Mary and John are married, have $5 million in real property-type assets, and want to pay as little estate taxes as legally possible, a marital trust may be the solution. Mary and John could each create a credit shelter trust. Mary's Trust A would be funded with $2.5 million of their assets, and John's Trust

B would be funded with $2.5 million of their assets. The assets would have to be transferred to the trusts in writing and by deed. If John and Mary had owned the property as tenants in the entirety or as joint tenants, they would have had to change title to the real property into individual ownership. Property owned in the entirety or as joint tenants passes outside the probate process.

Alternatively, the couple can create a marital type trust in their wills. This is done by funding a testamentary trust with solely owned assets owned by each testator at his or her death.

The most popular benefit of the marital type trust is that it utilizes the tax savings of transferring up to $3 million tax free (as of 2007) to any subsequent designated beneficiary after the last spouse's death. An unlimited marital deduction that is allowed by federal estate tax law permits the tax-free transfer to a surviving spouse only if the surviving spouse is a U.S. citizen.

The Life Estate Option

Another option is available for elderly clients who want to continue to live in their home but do not want sole responsibility for its maintenance and cost and want the benefit of not being alone in their home. The option is the creation of a trust called a **life estate**. A life estate is a property interest that lasts until a named person or persons die. For example, Lillian is a widow who wants to continue to live in her longtime home, but she is lonely and is having difficulty maintaining it as she ages. Lillian's son, Hugo, is willing to move in with his mother and take over maintaining the house and paying the taxes. Lillian can transfer the property to her son but retain a life estate interest in the property. There also can be tax advantages (explained in Chapter 7) to creating a life estate. The owner of property also can use a life estate to provide a place for another person to live for his lifetime.

Pet Trusts

A **pet trust** is now a viable possibility in most states. Historically, pet owners could not do this, but man's best friends have not been forgotten by most state legislatures. Essentially, the purpose of a trust created for the benefit of a beloved pet is to provide the funds necessary for a trustee to maintain a pet's lifestyle even after the pet's owner has died or has become incapacitated. Refer to Exhibit 5–3 to read a sample pet trust statute.[7]

credit shelter trust
A trust designed with one person named as both grantor and trustee and his spouse as secondary trustee who will benefit from the trust once the grantor dies. It utilizes the tax savings of transferring up to $3 million tax free to any designated beneficiary.

bypass trust
A trust that designates the creator's children as beneficiaries but allows the widowed spouse to withdraw adequate income or dip into the trust's principal for support during his lifetime.

residuary beneficiaries
Those individuals who receive the remainder interest in a trust or will.

life estate
An ownership interest in property that lasts until a named person(s) dies.

pet trust
A trust created for the benefit of a beloved pet in order to provide funds for a trustee to maintain a pet's lifestyle even after the pet owner has died or has become incapacitated.

EXHIBIT 5–3   SAMPLE PET TRUST STATUTE

a. A trust for the care of a domesticated animal is valid. The intended use of the principal or income may be enforced by a person designated for that purpose in the trust instrument, a person appointed by the court, or a trustee. The trust shall terminate when no living animal is covered by the trust, or at the end of 21 years, whichever occurs earlier.

b. Except as expressly provided otherwise in the trust instrument, no portion of the trust's principal or income may be converted to the use of the trustee or to any use other than for the benefit of the animal designated in the trust.

c. Upon termination of the trust, the trustee shall transfer the unexpended trust property as directed in the trust instrument. If no directions for such transfer exist, the property shall pass to the estate of the creator of the trust.

d. The court may reduce the amount of the property transferred if it determines that the amount substantially exceeds the amount required for the intended use. The amount of any reduction shall be transferred as directed in the trust instrument or, if no such directions are contained in the trust instrument, to the estate of the creator of the trust.

e. If no trustee is designated or if no designated trustee is willing or able to serve, a court shall appoint a trustee and may make such other orders and determinations as are advisable to carry out the intent of the creator of the trust and the purpose of this act.

ELDER LAW PRACTICE

At their first meeting, Mr. Albert asked Attorney Tara Jensen to provide him with a list of options for leaving his apple farm to his family in an equitable way. Apparently, Mr. Albert's two sons are not interested in working on the farm; but his granddaughter, Lainie, has been working with her grandfather for years.

During a subsequent meeting, Tara explained that one solution would be to give legal title of the orchard to Mr. Albert's granddaughter, but with the provision that Mr. Albert's two sons be given equitable title to the property. This setup would require Lainie, Mr. Albert's granddaughter, to provide a particularly designated percentage of the profits, the specific amount provided by Mr. Albert, from the orchard to his sons and other grandchildren if he wished.

One of the firm's paralegals, Luke, joined Tara during the meeting to take notes and learn while watching Tara's interview style. During the meeting, Tara explained, "The problem with your younger disabled son receiving disability payments is that an inheritance like yours would quickly leave him ineligible to receive his disability and medical benefits until his inheritance was depleted."

Mr. Albert asked, "What can be done about that?"

Tara explained, "A special needs trust is designed to provide special assistance for your younger son, but still allow him to receive his benefits, especially his very important medical benefits."

(continues)

ELDER LAW PRACTICE *(continued)*

Mr. Albert listened intently and Tara continued, "Alternatively, you could transfer legal title to your two sons with equitable title going to your granddaughter. This second way would provide that your children couldn't sell the farm but could benefit from the profits from the operation of the farm. Either of these two scenarios could occur prior to or after your death (sorry for the bluntness), but it would probably occur after since most people aren't too keen on giving up their property before they have to."

Mr. Albert commented, "These suggestions might tick off my eldest son; but if Lainie is going to put her blood, sweat, and tears into the business, I think she should get title—but pay off my eldest boy and her two brothers so there's no bad blood. The special needs trust sounds right for my younger son."

Tara concluded with the suggestion that Mr. Albert think about his decision and that if he wanted to move forward, he should sign a retainer agreement and make a down payment on the work. Tara added that Mr. Albert also should think about his decisions regarding his will, any advance directives for health care, and a durable power of attorney.

Analysis: Mr. Albert's actions can be described as Mr. Albert having the *express intent* to give *legal title* of the farm to his granddaughter, Lainie, with *equitable title* of the farm to his elder son; to create a *special needs trust* for his younger son; and to leave *cash gifts* to his other grandchildren through his will. The trust created for Mr. Albert's purpose is an *express private trust*. Refer to Exhibit 5–4 to review an example of a will with a special needs trust. The example provides an outline that an attorney or a paralegal can use, but it should be personalized to each client's special needs.

EXHIBIT 5–4   SAMPLE WILL WITH SPECIAL NEEDS TRUST

LAST WILL OF
   [Name of Client]

I, [Name of Client], a resident of [Address of Client], do make and publish and declare this, my LAST WILL AND TESTAMENT, hereby revoking all Wills and Codicils heretofore made by me.

SECTION 1. IDENTIFICATION

1.1. Spouse—My spouse's name is [Name of Spouse]. All references in this Will to my "spouse" are to said spouse.

1.2. Children—I have [number in words] ([number in numerals]) children, [Names of Children]. All references in this Will to my "children" are to said named children.

SECTION 2. FUNERAL AND ADMINISTRATION EXPENSES

The expenses of my last illness and funeral, including a suitable marker for my grave, and all expenses relating to the administration of my estate shall be paid out of my residuary estate.

(continues)

EXHIBIT 5–4   SAMPLE WILL WITH SPECIAL NEEDS TRUST *(continued)*

SECTION 3. DISPOSITIVE PROVISIONS

3.1. Specific Gifts—I give certain tangible, nonbusiness, personal property in accordance with a written statement or list, prepared pursuant to [cite to state statute], in my handwriting or signed by me, that describes the items and the devisees with reasonable certainty. I give all of my remaining tangible, nonbusiness, personal property, including any automobiles, together with all insurance on such property, to my spouse. If my spouse fails to survive me, I give such property to my children as survive both my spouse and me, to be divided among them as they shall agree. Should there be no agreement, such property shall be divided among them as my Executor, in my Executor's sole discretion, shall determine. All costs of safekeeping, insuring, and shipping shall be deemed to be a general estate administration expense.

3.2. Residue. I give, devise, and bequeath the entire residue of my estate to my Trustee hereinafter named, to be administered as follows:

3.2.1. Beneficiary. My trustee shall hold the Trust Estate, IN TRUST, for the benefit of my spouse ("Beneficiary") on the following conditions.

3.2.1.1. Income. My Trustee shall pay to or apply for the benefit of my Beneficiary all of the net income, in quarterly or other convenient installments.

3.2.1.2. Principal. My Trustee shall pay to or apply for the benefit of my Beneficiary such amounts of Trust principal, or all thereof, in such proportions at such time and in such manner as my Trustee, in my Trustee's sole and absolute discretion, may decide is appropriate for the satisfaction of my Beneficiary's special nonsupport needs, if any. As used in this instrument, "special nonsupport needs" refers to the requisites for maintaining my Beneficiary's good health, safety, and welfare when, in the discretion of the Trustee, such requisites are not being provided by any public agency, office, or department of the state where my Beneficiary lives, or of the United States, or are not otherwise being provided by other sources of income available to my Beneficiary. Special nonsupport needs shall include, but not be limited to, the list of suggested nonsupport items set out in this Section.

3.2.1.3. Death of Beneficiary. On the death of my Beneficiary or on termination as provided in this Section, my Trustee shall distribute the remaining principal equally among my children, or if any of my children fails to survive me, then to such child's descendants on a per stirpes basis.

3.2.1.4. Liberal Construction. My Trustee shall be liberal in authorizing expenditures to meet those needs of Beneficiary that cannot be met through any government and private programs. Such expenditures will be very important to Beneficiary and will enrich Beneficiary's life.

3.2.1.5. Intention. My Trustee may, in my Trustee's discretion, use funds from this Trust for the Beneficiary's supplementary needs, such as sophisticated medical and diagnostic work and treatment for which there are not funds otherwise available, including plastic surgery or other medical procedures not deemed to be medically necessary; dental care; recreation and transportation; the differential in the cost between housing and shelter for shared and private rooms; supplemental nursing care; and similar care that assistance programs may not otherwise provide. Distribution may be made for such things as a telephone, television service, an electrical wheelchair, mechanical bed, companions for travel, cultural experiences, periodic outings, and payments to third parties to accompany the Beneficiary. These are illustrations of the supplemental benefits that my Trustee may wish to consider in deciding to make funds available to or for the benefit of the Beneficiary. The examples are not inclusive.

(continues)

EXHIBIT 5–4 SAMPLE WILL WITH SPECIAL NEEDS TRUST *(continued)*

3.2.1.6. Residence. My Trustee may, in its sole, absolute, and uncontrolled discretion, permit my Beneficiary and [her/his] caregiver to occupy any residence constituting a part of the trust assets upon such terms as my Trustee may deem advisable and to pay the real estate taxes thereon, expenses of maintaining the residence in suitable repair and condition and hazard insurance premiums on the residence.

3.2.1.7. Trust Amendment.

A. If, in the opinion of my Trustee, this trust disqualifies my Beneficiary for any public assistance benefits, including Medicaid and SSI, to which [she/he] would otherwise be entitled, the Trustee is authorized, by written instrument filed, to amend this trust to preserve my Beneficiary's eligibility for such public assistance benefits and to protect the trust.

B. The Trustee may also amend this trust in writing from time to time to expressly state any such additional power or authority, and also to limit or grant powers, as are deemed reasonably necessary to obtain or preserve favorable tax treatment; to address new laws or regulations which affect the beneficiary; or as the Trustee determines, in its sole and absolute discretion, is in the best interest of my wife.

C. In exercising these powers, the Trustee shall observe the general fiduciary duties of loyalty, good faith, fairness, and due care.

D. The Trustee may exercise this power from time to time, and may release this power in whole or in part.

E. Any expense, including attorney's fees, incurred by my Trustee in connection with these mattes shall be paid from the Trust.

3.2.1.8. Public or Private Assistance Programs. My Trustee should resist any request for payments or reimbursement from this Trust for services or benefits that any public or private agency or program, including Medicaid and SSI, has the obligation to provide my Beneficiary. My Trustee may not be familiar with the federal, state, and local programs and agencies that have been created to financially assist disabled persons. If this is the case, my Trustee should seek assistance of an attorney in identifying public and private programs that are or may be available to my Beneficiary so that my Trustee may better serve my Beneficiary. My Trustee may take whatever legal action may be necessary to initiate or continue my Beneficiary's eligibility for public assistance programs for which my Beneficiary is or may be eligible. My Trustee may bring an action in any court or regulatory agency to secure a ruling or order that the Trust is not available to my Beneficiary for any purpose. Any expense, including attorney's fees, incurred by my Trustee in connection with these matters shall be paid from the Trust.

3.2.2. Predecease. If my Beneficiary fails to survive me, I give, devise, and bequeath the entire residue of my estate to be distributed pursuant to Section 3.2.1.3.

3.2.3. Expenses. On the death of Beneficiary, the Trustee, in the Trustee's sole discretion, may pay any inheritance, estate, or other death taxes that may be due by reason of Beneficiary's death, and all expenses of such Beneficiary's last illness and funeral and expenses related to administration and distribution of the trust estate (including fees of the Trustee, his or her attorney, and other agents) if, in the Trustee's sole discretion, other satisfactory provisions have not been made for the payment of such expenses.

3.2.4. Interest Nonassignable. No beneficiary shall, voluntarily or involuntarily, have any right to anticipate, sell, assign, mortgage, pledge, or otherwise dispose of or encumber all or any part of my trust estate, nor shall any part of my trust estate, including income, be liable for the debts or obligations, including alimony, of any beneficiary or be subject to attachment, garnishment, execution, creditor's bill, or other legal or equitable process.

(continues)

EXHIBIT 5–4 SAMPLE WILL WITH SPECIAL NEEDS TRUST *(continued)*

3.3. Age Requirement—If any person less than [age in words] ([age in numerals]) years of age is entitled to receive an inheritance under this Will (Beneficiary), my Executor shall pay such inheritance to my Trustee, hereinafter named or, if no Trustee is named, to the surviving parent of such person as Trustee, to be administered as follows:

3.3.1. Until Age [age in words] ([age in numerals])—Until my Beneficiary attains the age of [age in words] ([age in numerals]) years, my Trustee shall pay or apply the income and principal for the health, maintenance, support, and education of my Beneficiary, such payments or applications of income and principal shall be in such amounts that, in the sole discretion of my Trustee, are proper. My Trustee may use principal for my Beneficiary's education or to assist him or her in buying a home or starting a business. Undistributed income may be accumulated and may from time to time be added to principal.

3.3.2. At Age [age in words] ([age in numerals])—On my Beneficiary's attaining the age of [age in words] ([age in numerals]) years:

3.3.2.1. Income—My Trustee shall pay to or for the benefit of my Beneficiary all the net income, in quarterly or other convenient installments; and

3.3.2.2. Principal—My Trustee may, in my Trustee's sole discretion, distribute as much of the principal of my Beneficiary's share, as my Trustee may deem proper for my Beneficiary's health, maintenance, support, and education. My Trustee may use principal to assist my Beneficiary in buying a home or starting a business; and

3.3.2.3. Withdrawal Rights—My Beneficiary shall have the right to withdraw principal from his or her trust, one-half of the remaining principal balance on attaining the age of [age in words] ([age in numerals]) years, and the entire remaining principal balance on attaining the age of [age in words] ([age in numerals]) years. The balance of the trust shall be determined by my Trustee at the end of each calendar year (or such approximate date on which my Trustee appraises the Trust).

SECTION 4. FIDUCIARY PROVISIONS

4.1. Appointment of Executor—I appoint [Name of Executor 1] as Executor of my Will. If [Name of Executor 1] fails to qualify or ceases to serve for any reason, then I appoint [Name of Executor 2] as Successor Executor. Neither of my Executors shall be required to give bond or furnish sureties in any jurisdiction.

4.2. Appointment of Trustee—I appoint [Name of Trustee 1] as Trustee of any Trust under my Will. If [Name of Trustee 1] fails to qualify or ceases to serve for any reason, then I appoint [Name of Trustee 2] as Successor Trustee. Neither of my Trustees shall be required to give bond or furnish sureties in any jurisdiction.

4.3. Resignation of Trustee

4.3.1. Right of Trustee to Resign—My Trustee and any Successor Trustee shall have the right to resign, by duly acknowledged written instrument delivered to the remaining Trustee or, if there is no remaining Trustee then serving, to the adult income beneficiaries and the adults who would be entitled to share in the principal of the trust if it were then to terminate.

4.3.2. Power of Successor Trustee—Any Successor Trustee shall have the rights, powers, privileges, discretions, and duties conferred on or vested in my Trustee by the provisions of this Agreement.

4.3.3. Nomination of Successor Trustee—If a vacancy occurs in the office of Trustee and there is no Successor Trustee able to serve, the law firm of [name of law firm], or any successor law firm, shall have the right, power, and authority to designate a Successor Trustee.

(continues)

EXHIBIT 5–4   SAMPLE WILL WITH SPECIAL NEEDS TRUST *(continued)*

4.4. Compensation of Fiduciary—My individual Executor and Trustee shall be entitled to receive reasonable compensation for services rendered and to reimbursement for all reasonable expenses.

4.5. Powers of Fiduciary—In addition to the powers above provided for and those given by law, my Executor and Trustee, without any order of court and in their sole discretion, may:

4.5.1. Make Investments—Retain any property and invest and reinvest in any property, including by way of illustration and not by way of limitation, common stocks up to 100 percent of my estate, any common or diversified trust funds maintained by any bank or savings institution, and any form of life insurance, annuity, or endowment policies. In so doing, my Fiduciary may act without restriction to so-called legal investments and without responsibility for diversification.

4.5.2. Purchase Investments—Purchase investments at premiums and charge premiums to income or principal or partly to each.

4.5.3. Stocks and Bonds—Subscribe for stocks, bonds, or other investments; exercise any stock option or similar right; join in any plan of lease, mortgage, merger, consolidation, reorganization, foreclosure, or voting trust and deposit securities thereunder; and generally exercise all the rights of security holders of any corporation.

4.5.4. Registration—In the sole discretion of the Fiduciary, register securities in the name of his or her nominee or hold them unregistered so that title may pass by delivery.

4.5.5. Voting—Vote, in person or by proxy, securities held by my Fiduciary and, in such connection, delegate discretionary powers.

4.5.6. Repair—Repair, alter, improve, or lease, for any period of time, any property, and give options for leases.

4.5.7. Sell—Sell property at public or private sale, for cash or credit, with or without security; exchange or partition property; and give options for sales or exchanges.

4.5.8. Real Estate—Sell any real estate, at public or private sale, on such terms as my Fiduciary shall deem appropriate.

4.5.9. Borrow—Borrow money from any person, including any Fiduciary, and mortgage or pledge any property.

4.5.10. Compromise—Compromise claims, including any questions relating to any policy of life insurance. However, my Fiduciary need not institute litigation to collect any policy unless my Fiduciary is reasonably indemnified for costs, counsel fees, and other expenses of such litigation.

4.5.11. Distributions—Make distribution of both income and principal in cash or in kind or partly in each.

4.5.12. Employment of Agents—Employ such agents as my Fiduciary may deem advisable in the administration of my estate or any trust preowned hereunder, and pay them such compensation as my Fiduciary may deem proper out of income or principal or out of both.

4.5.13. Mutual Funds—Invest in mutual funds.

4.5.14. Trust Additions—Add to the principal of any trust created hereunder any property received from any person by Deed, Will, or in any other manner.

4.5.15. Posttermination—Exercise all power, authority, and discretion given by this trust, after termination of any trust created herein, until the same is fully distributed.

4.5.16. Limitations—Notwithstanding any of the powers conferred on my Fiduciary, no individual, acting as Fiduciary hereunder, shall exercise or join in the exercise of discretionary powers over income, principal, or termination of any Trust (1) for his or her own benefit or (2) to discharge his or her legal obligation to support any Beneficiary.

(continues)

EXHIBIT 5–4   SAMPLE WILL WITH SPECIAL NEEDS TRUST *(continued)*

SECTION 5. TAX AND ADMINISTRATIVE PROVISIONS

5.1. Death-Tax Clause—All estate, inheritance, and other death taxes, including any interest and penalties with respect to those taxes not caused by negligent delay, payable to any federal, state, or foreign taxing authority, imposed with respect to all property comprising my gross estate, whether or not such property passes under this Will, shall be paid out of the principal of my residuary estate.

5.2. Income and Gift-Tax Clause—My Executor may join with my spouse, or the personal representative of my spouse or spouse's estate, in a joint income tax return covering any period of time prior to my death or in a gift-tax return for gifts made by my spouse prior to my death and, in connection therewith, to determine what taxes, interest, and penalties are proper and to pay same, even though not attributable in whole or in part to income or gifts from my property, not requiring my spouse or the personal representative of my spouse or spouse's estate to indemnify my estate against liability to it for tax attributable to my spouse.

5.3. Protective Provision—All principal and income shall, until actual distribution to the beneficiary, be free of debts, contracts, alienations, and anticipations of any beneficiary, and the same shall not be liable to any levy, attachment, execution, or sequestration while in the possession of my Executor or Trustee.

5.4. Nonaccrual of Income—Income shall not be apportioned between successive beneficiaries. All income not actually paid to a beneficiary before termination of his or her interest shall be treated as though it had accrued and become payable thereafter; and no credit or accrual shall be made for taxes, commissions, or other charges theretofore made against income.

5.5. Optional Termination of Trust—Notwithstanding any other provisions hereof, my Trustee may, in my Trustee's sole discretion and at any time, terminate any or all of the trust shares under this Trust if the amount thereof does not warrant the cost of continuing said trust or if its administration would be otherwise impractical. On such termination, my Trustee shall pay the principal and any accumulated or undistributed income of such trust share to the person or persons entitled at that time to the income therefrom in the proportions to which they were then entitled to receive the income, and on such termination, the rights of all other persons who might otherwise have an interest as succeeding life tenants or in remainder shall cease. If any such person be then a minor or, in the opinion of my Trustee, mentally or physically incapacitated, my Trustee may pay the share of such fund to which such person would otherwise be entitled, to the parent or guardian of the estate or of the person of such income beneficiary or to the person caring for such beneficiary. In the case of a minor, my Trustee may deposit such fund in a savings account in a savings institution of my Trustee's choosing for the benefit of such minor.

5.6. Disability Provision—Unless otherwise provided for herein, any income or principal payable to any beneficiary who, in the opinion of my Trustee, is mentally or physically disabled shall be held in a separate trust by my Trustee during such disability, unless the trust share is sooner terminated, as otherwise provided herein. Income may be accumulated, and income and principal may be expended for the health, maintenance, support, and education of such beneficiary as my Trustee, in my Trustee's sole discretion, may determine. My Trustee may apply the same directly, without the intervention of a guardian, or pay the same to any person having the care or control of said beneficiary or with whom the beneficiary

(continues)

EXHIBIT 5–4   SAMPLE WILL WITH SPECIAL NEEDS TRUST *(continued)*

resides, without duty on the part of my Trustee to supervise or inquire into the application of such funds. The balance of such income and principal shall be paid to such beneficiary when the disability ceases or to such beneficiary's estate in the event of death prior thereto.

5.7. Rule Against Perpetuities—Notwithstanding anything herein to the contrary, no Trust hereunder shall extend beyond twenty-one (21) years after the death of the last survivor of myself and my descendants living at the date of my death. At the expiration of that period, my Trustee shall distribute the remaining portion of any Trust property in my Trustee's hands to the beneficiaries entitled to the income at that time.

5.8. Accountings

5.8.1. Estate Accounting—My Executor shall render an account of the administration of my estate to the beneficiaries of my estate on the conclusion of such administration or, if such administration shall continue for a period longer than eighteen (18) months after my death, then on the request of any of the beneficiaries of my estate. The approval of the accounting by the adult beneficiaries of my estate shall be conclusively binding on all my beneficiaries. The adult beneficiaries shall be conclusively presumed to have approved each such account unless he, she, or they file written exceptions thereto with my Executor within thirty (30) days after the receipt of each account. Nothing herein shall limit the right of my Executor to file an accounting in a court of competent jurisdiction at the appropriate times. The records of the Trust shall be opened at all reasonable times to the inspection of the beneficiaries of the Trust and their appointed representatives.

5.8.2. Trustee's Accountings—My Trustee shall render an account of the administration of the trust to the then-living adult income beneficiaries and adult remainderman on request by any adult income beneficiary or adult remainderman, and the approval thereof by the living adult beneficiaries and living adult remainderman shall be conclusively binding on all parties in interest under this Agreement. The aforementioned adult beneficiaries or adult remainderman, as the case may be, shall be conclusively presumed to have approved each such account unless he, she, or they file written exceptions thereto with my Trustee within thirty (30) days after the receipt of each account. Nothing herein shall limit the right of my Trustee to file an accounting in a court of competent jurisdiction at appropriate times.

5.9. Definitions

5.9.1. *Per Stirpes* Distributions—Unless otherwise specifically provided, all distributions are to be made to a person's descendants, *per stirpes*:

The distributable assets are to be divided into as many shares as there are then-living children of such deceased person and deceased children of such deceased person who left then-living descendants.

Each then-living child shall receive one (1) share, and the share of each deceased child shall be divided among such child's then-living descendants in the same manner.

5.9.2. Descendants—The "descendants of a person" means all of that person's lineal descendants of all generations. The relationship of parent and child at each generation shall be determined by the definition of parent and child contained under [name of state] law as of the date of my death.

A descendant in gestation who is later born alive shall be considered a descendant in being throughout the period of gestation.

An adopted person, and all persons who are the descendants by blood or by legal adoption, shall be considered descendants of the adopting parents as well as descendents of the adopting parent's ancestors.

(continues)

EXHIBIT 5–4 SAMPLE WILL WITH SPECIAL NEEDS TRUST *(continued)*

5.9.3. Disability—A beneficiary under this Will is disabled or under a disability when he or she is under the age of eighteen (18) years and not emancipated; or if, in the judgment of my fiduciary, the beneficiary is unable to manage his or her property and affairs for reasons such as mental illness, mental deficiency, physical illness or disability, chronic use of drugs, chronic intoxication, confinement, detention by a foreign power, or disappearance. If any court of competent jurisdiction has declared a beneficiary to be disabled or under a disability, my fiduciary shall be bound by that determination as long as that determination is in effect.

5.9.4. Executor—Any reference to my "Executor" shall include the singular or plural and the masculine, feminine, or neuter and is intended to refer to such person or persons serving as my Executor, including my original Executor or any successor Executor, whether such Executor shall be an individual or a corporation.

5.9.5. Fiduciary—For purposes of this Will, the term "Fiduciary" shall include an Executor, Executrix, Administrator, Personal Representative, Guardian, Custodian, Conservator, Trustee, or any other form of fiduciary.

As used throughout this Will, the term "Personal Representative" and "Trustee" shall refer to the original Personal Representative and Trustee as well as any single, additional, or successor Personal Representative and Trustee. It shall also refer to any individual, corporation, or other entity acting as a replacement, substitute, or added Personal Representative and Trustee.

5.9.6. Spouse—Reference in this Will to my "spouse" means the person who answers to such description on the assumption that all decrees of divorce rendered by a Court of record, wherever located, are valid. If my marriage to my spouse shall be dissolved at any time, my spouse shall cease to be a beneficiary under this Will and shall be treated, for purposes of interpreting this Will, as though my spouse predeceased me.

5.9.7. Other Definitions—Except as otherwise provided in this Will, terms shall be as defined in the [name of state probate code] [cite to state statute], as amended after the date of this Will and after my death.

5.10. Contest Clause—If any beneficiary shall in any manner, directly or indirectly, attempt to contest or oppose the validity of this Will, including any codicils thereto, or commence or prosecute any legal proceedings to set aside this Will, then in such event such beneficiary shall forfeit his or her share and cease to have any right or interest in the estate property. Such beneficiary's share shall be distributed as if the contesting beneficiary predeceased me without any living descendants.

My Executor is authorized to defend, at the expense of the estate property, any contest or other attack of any nature on this Will or any of its provisions.

5.11. Applicable State Law—The validity of this Will shall be determined by reference to the laws of the [name of state].

Any question with regard to the construction and administration of the various trusts contained in this Will shall be determined by reference to the laws of the state in which the trust is then currently being administered.

IN WITNESS WHEREOF, I subscribe my name this [date] day of [year].

———————————————————
[Name of Client]

(continues)

EXHIBIT 5–4   SAMPLE WILL WITH SPECIAL NEEDS TRUST *(continued)*

The foregoing instrument was signed, published, and declared by [Name of Client], the [Testator/Testatrix], to be the [Testator/Testatrix]'s Last Will and Testament in the presence of each of us, present at the same time, and we, at the [Testator/Testatrix]'s request and in the [Testator/Testatrix]'s presence, and in the presence of each other, have hereunto subscribed our names as witnesses this [date] day of [year].

_____

_____

WE, the [Testator/Testatrix] and [names of witnesses], the witnesses, respectively, whose names are signed to the attached or foregoing instrument, being first duly sworn, do hereby declare to the undersigned authority that the [Testator/Testatrix] signed and executed the instrument as [his/her] Last Will and that [he/she] signed willingly and that [he/she] executed it as [his/her] free and voluntary act for the purposes therein expressed, and that each of the witnesses, in the presence and hearing of the [Testator/Testatrix], signed the Will as witness and that to the best of the witnesses' knowledge the [Testator/Testatrix] was, at the time, eighteen years of age or older, of sound mind, and under no constraint or undue influence.

_____

[Name of Client], [Testator/Testatrix]

_____

Witness

_____

Witness

STATE OF:

COUNTY OF:

Subscribed, sworn to, and acknowledged before me by [Name of Client], the [Testator/Testatrix], and subscribed and sworn to before me by [Names of Witnesses], the witnesses, this [date] day of [month, year].

SUMMARY

Trusts created during a creator's lifetime are not part of the creator's probate estate. Thus, probate is avoided with regard to the trust's principal—no intestate succession, no probate administration, no publicity, and a smooth transition of property from one person to another. This means that there is no interruption in assets being allocated to the beneficiaries of the trust, as there is if the assets must go through a sometimes time-consuming process before being distributed. A trust's creator can retain the responsibilities of running the trust and thereby utilize any investment expertise he may have to increase the value of the trust. Finally, tax savings can be significant depending on the size of the estate that was transferred to a trust. A trust created in a will is known as a testamentary trust, and the last will and testament must be probated. A testamentary trust is revocable until the creator's death, at which point it becomes irrevocable. An intended trust beneficiary does not have a right to sue a trust's creator because the beneficiary was removed from the trust or the trust was altered in any way.

An estate includes all of an individual's assets, including life insurance proceeds not held in a trust, minus any debts. An individual does not have to be wealthy to benefit from an up-to-date estate plan. An up-to-date estate plan helps ensure that an individual's personal decisions regarding his health, finance, and personal wishes will be carried out. In addition, individuals of high financial worth should be able to minimize estate taxes paid and thus ensure that their beneficiaries receive a larger inheritance. An estate plan may include a will, a durable power of attorney, an advance directive (commonly called a living will), some type or types of trusts, and possibly a marital property settlement agreement. An individual should not confuse the purpose of a trust with other legal relationships such as guardianship, custodianship, personal representative or executor of an estate, or agency. None of the other legal relationships create new legal title to property along with the splitting of the beneficiary status.

■ KEY TERMS

irrevocable life insurance trust	funding of the trust	remainderman
annual gift tax exclusion	grantor	res
beneficiary	grantor-retained annuity trust	residuary beneficiaries
bypass trust	implied trust	rule against perpetuities
charitable remainder trust (CRT)	intangible	settlor
charitable trust	*intervivos* gift	spendthrift trust
constructive trust	*intervivos* trust	successor trustee
corpus	life estate	support trust or special needs trust
corpus estate	marital trust	tangible
creator or trustor	pet trust	testamentary trust
credit shelter trust	principal	trust
discretionary trust	prudent person standard	trust instrument
exculpatory clause	qualified terminable interest property (QTIP) trust	trustee
express trust		

▓ REVIEW QUESTIONS_____

1. List the reasons for the creation of a trust.
2. Define the fundamental elements of trust creation.
3. Why should elderly clients in particular appreciate the creation of a trust?
4. What is the role of a trust's creator?
5. What is the role of a trustee?
6. What is the role of a beneficiary?
7. What are the advantages and disadvantages of a revocable versus an irrevocable trust?
8. When should a spendthrift or sprinkling trust be used?
9. Why should a will still be necessary if a trust is drafted?
10. What are the differences between a public and private trust?
11. What are differences between an *intervivos* trust and a testamentary trust?
12. When should a constructive trust be considered?

▓ ETHICS ALERT_____

Rena had worked as a paralegal in the county for many years. She knew the supporting staff at area law firms and many of the attorneys. Several times in her long and varied career, attorneys from other firms had attempted to hire her because they knew she was an outstanding worker. She had been tempted, but Rena had moved on to another firm only when the circumstances were right.

However, she had to admit that her most recent offer had been quite interesting. Attorney Walter Wonka wanted to know if Rena would be interested in being *set up* in a law office in a nearby town directly across the street from the largest retirement community in the state. Attorney Wonka said that the office would be a cash cow and that an experienced elder law paralegal like Rena would be able to handle it on her own because she related well to seniors and had years of experience. Obviously, there are ethical issues with Wonka's suggestions. What are those issues? Could Wonka hire Rena, open his satellite law office in the next town, and still develop the firm into the descriptively termed *cash cow* while following legal and ethical guidelines?

▓ HELPFUL WEB SITES_____

NORTH DAKOTA STATE UNIVERSITY <HTTP://WWW.NDSU.NODAK.EDU>   This site states that its goal is to inform and educate by providing introductory explanations of legal concepts.

STATE BAR OF CALIFORNIA <HTTP://WWW.CALBAR.CA.GOV>   California is the state with the most seniors, and the site emphasizes legal concepts and protections especially designed for seniors.

NORTH AMERICA MILITARY FINANCIAL EDUCATION CENTER <HTTP://MILITARYFINANCE.UMUC.EDU>   This site provides helpful information including estate planning.

ENDNOTES

[1] *Webster's New Twentieth Century Dictionary of the English Language,* Unabridged, Second Edition, William Collins and World Publishing, 1975.

[2] Cowan, Lynn, "Trust Funds Not Needed for Many Estates," *Daily Record,* June 28, 2003, page 10.

[3] "Strategy for Creating an Estate Plan," *Fidelity Newsletter,* Spring 2003, page 7.

[4] The word *perpetuity* means "forever." If there is any attempt to control the disposition of your property for longer than the life of a person alive (or at least conceived by then) when you die plus 21 years, the rule against perpetuities will be used by most states to prevent such control in perpetuity.

[5] Uniform Probate Code Section 7-302 (2004).

[6] The Trustee Act of 2000 introduced a statutory duty of care when trustees exercise their prowers of investment.

[7] N.J.S.A. 3B:11-38 (2006).

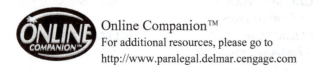

Online Companion™
For additional resources, please go to
http://www.paralegal.delmar.cengage.com

6

Cohabitation, Marriage, and Divorce

OBJECTIVES

After completing this chapter, you will be able to:

- Describe the legal ramifications of unmarried cohabitation on older cohabitants.

- Explain the development and ramifications of domestic partnerships and civil unions.

- List the benefits and responsibilities of marriage.

- Explain the protective measures that can be taken by older couples planning to marry.

- Explain the legal and psychological effects that marriage between older spouses may have on their children from previous relationships.

- Describe the possible legal ramifications of divorce on older spouses.

"Love is lovelier,
the second time
around . . ."

SAMMY CAHN[1]

INTRODUCTION

Older Americans seeking new love relationships is a growing trend. Whether they marry, become unmarried life partners, or become serial monogamists, older Americans seem to be taking to heart the lyrics of Sammy Cahn's vintage song quoted above.

Unfortunately, the American divorce rate for first-time marriages hovers at just over 50 percent and the percentage of marriages ending in divorce is even higher for those who marry twice or more. Maybe that is why one of the largest segments of society consists of *unmarried* partners sharing a household. In fact, more than three in seven adults are not currently married, but share their home with a partner.[2] Also, a significant number of unmarried partners sharing a household are gay and are not legally permitted to marry in the majority of states even if they wanted to. However, a small minority of states are now allowing unmarried heterosexual partners and homosexual partners to register their partnership or proceed with limited civil unions in order to activate some marriage-like rights.[3]

On the other hand, marriage brings with it a wealth of over 1,000 rights and obligations to spouses. Studies also have shown that marriage promotes a healthier lifestyle and a longer life. Married men and women are more likely to eat breakfast, wear a seat belt, engage in physical activity, have their blood pressure checked, and not smoke.[4]

COHABITATION AND THE ELDER LAW PERSPECTIVE

Senior citizens are a huge part of the cohabitating population. According to the U.S. Census Bureau, unmarried cohabitating opposite-sex couples aged 65 and older rose 73 percent from 1990 to 1999.[5]

Why is this trend of cohabitation occurring? Some older cohabiting partners may live together to avoid the possibility of divorce or to keep alimony from a previous marriage. Another reason for cohabitation may be that disabled citizens receiving public assistance may lose financial benefits if they marry; so some of them remain in unmarried partnerships.

In addition, senior citizens receiving financial benefits because of their marriage to a spouse who is now deceased may lose those benefits upon remarriage. For example, if a widowed spouse remarries before turning 60, Social Security benefits stemming from the previous marriage are forfeited. Remarriage after 60 has no effect on Social Security eligibility.[6] Another reason for living together is that hospitals and Medicaid cannot look to a cohabiting (but unregistered) partner to pay the other partner's medical bills, but spouses can be required to pay each other's medical bills. Actually, an individual may be held responsible for *any* of her spouse's unpaid bills.

Legal Protections for Cohabitating Partners

Being an unmarried partner sharing a household can create far-reaching emotional and financial ramifications. Clients should be steered away from relationship pitfalls. Instead, a client who creates legal protections may find that love can indeed be lovelier the next time around.

The increasing numbers of cohabiting partners, along with society's increasing acceptance of cohabitation without marriage, has made these partners (both heterosexual and homosexual) a force to be reckoned with. Some countries—such as Canada, France, and Sweden—have taken the lead in protecting partners in unmarried cohabiting relationships. Unmarried but cohabiting citizens of those three countries are allowed to register and gain marital-type rights as domestic partners. The term **domestic partner** usually refers to a person who has been designated as another's life partner outside marriage and who, because of such designation, may receive benefits of some kind. While the focus of domestic partner legislation has been primarily on same-sex couples, some cities and states in the United States allow homosexual residents to register as domestic partners or **reciprocal beneficiaries**. Refer to Exhibit 6–1 for a list of some states and cities that offer such registration.

Elder law practitioners should be prepared for a discussion of domestic partnerships or reciprocal beneficiaries. Certain states permit heterosexual couples to enter into domestic partnerships only if they are above a certain age. For example, Washington, a recent addition to the list of states creating domestic partnership status, joins California and New Jersey's Domestic Partnership Acts by permitting unmarried heterosexual seniors 62 years old and above to register as domestic partners. Couples usually must register their domestic partnership, reciprocal beneficiary status, or civil union for any of their new rights and obligations to be initiated. Termination of such rights and obligations usually can occur by filing for termination with the applicable court (usually a family court in the county where the couple is domiciled). Domestic partnership legislation may provide designated seniors with health care decision rights, visitation rights to their partner in a hospital or other health care settings, limited taxation relief, and health care. Of course, a registered partnership usually will result in the partners becoming responsible for each other's basic living expenses. Registered partners usually are not jointly liable for each other's individual debt contracted before or during the partnership, unlike married couples. No domestic partnership-type legislation is recognized under federal law, which is limited by the *Defense of Marriage Act*. This means that no federal entitlements (e.g., Social Security, federal taxes, and immigration issues) are provided as a result of a domestic partnership, reciprocal beneficiary status, or civil union.

domestic partner

A person who has been designated as another's life partner outside marriage and who may receive benefits of some kind.

reciprocal beneficiaries

People who have registered and been designated as life partners outside marriage and who may receive benefits of some kind.

EXHIBIT 6–1   SAMPLE OF STATES AND CITIES OFFERING DOMESTIC PARTNER REGISTRATION

States	Cities
California	New York, NY
District of Columbia	San Francisco, CA
Hawaii	Toledo, OH
Maine	
New Jersey	
Oregon	
Washington	

Landmark Cohabitation Case: *Palimony* Added to Dictionary

One of the best-known cases concerning a cohabiting and unmarried couple involved the late actor Lee Marvin and his live-in partner Michelle Triola Marvin. The plaintiff, Michelle Triola Marvin, was initially awarded the property and support historically received only by a divorcing spouse, not a former live-in lover. That decision did not last long once Lee Marvin appealed the trial court's decision.

The California case of *Marvin v. Marvin*, 122 Cal. App.3d 871, 176 Cal. Rptr. 555 (1981), added the word *palimony* to the English language. The case also added new legal ramifications for unmarried couples living together. **Palimony** is defined as financial support paid between persons who are not and never were married.

Michelle claimed that she gave up her career as a singer and actress to be Lee's companion and that except for benefit of clergy and an $8 marriage license, they lived together as man and wife in every way. Ms. Marvin, who legally changed her surname to Marvin shortly before their relationship ended, alleged in her suit that they had a verbal agreement to share any property they acquired during their relationship and, therefore, that she was entitled to half of Mr. Marvin's earnings during the six years they lived together as a "married" couple. She sought $100,000 for sacrificing her career and half of the $3.6 million he earned while they lived together.

Originally, the trial court dismissed Ms. Marvin's complaint without hearing any arguments on the grounds that enforcing such a contract between unmarried persons was tantamount to promoting prostitution and was, therefore, illegal. This decision was upheld on appeal. However, in 1976, the

■ **palimony**

Financial support paid between persons who are not and never were married.

California Supreme Court overruled the two lower courts. It remanded the case back to trial court, stating that the plaintiff had provided a suitable basis for her breach-of-promise suit for which the trial court could give damages and, furthermore, that her complaint could be amended to state a cause of action for breach of **implied contract**. An implied contract is a legal concept that the courts use to explain the existence of a contract with its terms determined by the *actions* of the persons involved, not by their words. In explaining its decision, the court declared that society no longer viewed cohabitation as morally reprehensible and that enforcing judicial rules based on moral considerations now ignored by most of society would not be just.

The sensational 11-week trial attracted international attention not only because Mr. Marvin was a major movie star who was supported by many of his equally famous colleagues but also because it was the first legal test of palimony, or the property rights of unmarried couples. On April 18, 1979, the Superior Court of California again rejected Ms. Marvin's claims, saying they found no legal basis for her claim that she had either an **express contract** or an implied contract with the actor to share his assets. An express contract is a contract with terms stated in oral or written words. However, under the legal principle of **equitable remedy**, the judge awarded Ms. Marvin the sum of $104,000 to be used primarily for her economic rehabilitation. An equitable remedy is defined as a solution that is just, fair, and right for a particular situation. The $104,000 was equivalent to $1,000 a week for two years, which was based on the highest salary Ms. Marvin earned in her career as a singer.

Lee Marvin appealed the rehabilitative award, while Michelle Triola Marvin challenged the amount of the award. The Court of Appeals for the Second District of California affirmed the lower court's decision that Ms. Marvin was not entitled to any of Mr. Marvin's earnings. The court stated that she had benefited economically and socially from their relationship, while Mr. Marvin had never acquired anything of value from Ms. Marvin, was not unjustly enriched by their relationship because of any wrongful act, and was under no obligation to pay a reasonable sum for her support. The court also reversed the $104,000 rehabilitative award on the basis that it was not within the issues framed by the pleadings. Ms. Marvin appealed to the state supreme court to have the $104,000 rehabilitative award reinstated, but she was denied a hearing.

Marvin Case Has Long-Term Effect

The decision in *Marvin* likely inspired scores of live-in lovers to think seriously about the financial ramifications of falling out of love. Although Michelle Triola Marvin lost the rehabilitative award and any share in the property or assets of her cohabitant, the precedent was established that unmarried couples could sue each other based on alleged contractual obligations and the word *palimony* was added to the English vocabulary.

implied contract
A contract with existence and terms determined by the *actions* of the persons involved, not by their words.

express contract
A contract with terms stated in oral or written words.

equitable remedy
A solution that is just, fair, and right for a particular situation.

The famous and the unknown have been inspired by the contractual issues and palimony concepts of the *Marvin* case. For example, the former maid and mother of three of the late senior citizen Marlon Brando's children sued the actor for $100 million in damages. Her April 2003 complaint claimed: *Brando expressed to Plaintiff at the commencement of, and throughout the course of, the parties' relationship that she and Brando were in fact equal partners together in their mutual endeavors, and that she would always be financially compensated and secured for the rest of her life and the lives of their children.*

Furthermore, she claimed: *Brando agreed that in the event of the dissolution of their relationship by death, separation or otherwise, that all of Defendant Brando's property, including that acquired during the time of the parties' relationship, would be divided equally for the benefit of Plaintiff and the parties' children.*[7] The parties confidentially resolved issues of custody, support, and palimony before Brando's death.

Palimony after Death?

The palimony concept continues to be expanded, as evidenced by a recent New Jersey Supreme Court case that allowed palimony claims to be made against a deceased cohabitant's estate.[8] The case, *In the Matter of the Estate of Arthur J. Roccamonte, Sr.,* 174 N.J. 381; 808 A.2d; (2002), involved a 30-year relationship that ended with the death of one of the elderly partners. The deceased partner had failed to draft a will or otherwise provide for his surviving partner. The surviving partner was left practically destitute while the deceased partner's estate was left to his children and the long-estranged wife with whom he had not lived for over 25 years. The court explained that if one of the partners is lured into cohabitation by a promise of support given by the other, as alleged by the plaintiff, that promise should be enforced regardless of the fact that the deceased partner was married to another. This is clearly an example of implied contract principles and an equitable remedy being applied. According to the court, the deceased partner had made a promise, *clearly implied, if not expressed, that he would see to it that she was adequately provided for during her lifetime.* The decision ordered the apportionment of the estate between the partner, wife, and children of the deceased.

Cohabiting Couples Must Create Their Own Legal Protections

The first point that an unmarried but cohabiting couple should realize is that married couples take vows that give them access to an extensive legal arsenal. Each of the 50 states has statutes and well-established case law pertaining to just about every marriage scenario imaginable. Unmarried and cohabiting couples are largely on their own in crafting legal protections that fit their particular partnership.

Other protections come from some state courts, such as New Jersey, that are now using *equitable remedies* to prevent a formerly cohabiting but unmarried partner from facing financial hardship after the arrangement of living together ends. The courts use equitable remedies to apply fairness in a particular situation. A court has the power to do justice where specific laws do not cover the situation. The unclear legal ramifications of living together without marriage continue to make the creation of a written and notarized cohabitation agreement a good idea. The alternative to having created a valid cohabitation agreement may mean that an impersonal court system will be deciding the outcome of a dispute.

Creating the Optimum Cohabitation Agreement

When unmarried couples decide to create a cohabitation agreement, both parties should be aware of the agreement's ramifications. Such an agreement should not be negotiated over glasses of wine and signed on a whim to make one of the parties happy.

The parties to the agreement may come to an attorney's office together. If so, the attorney should be hired by only one party. The other party should have the agreement negotiated and/or reviewed by her own attorney. Each party should have separate legal representation, particularly when there is unequal wealth between the parties. No one should have to face a disgruntled former partner who claims that she was not properly advised by her own legal counsel. A paralegal's role in the creation of a cohabitation agreement can begin the minute a client enters a law office. A paralegal may be involved in the interviewing process and may be given the responsibility of creating the agreement with the oversight of an attorney.

Both parties should clearly state their intentions to each other to ensure that there is mutual understanding as to the content of the agreement. The parties should then memorialize their intentions in a written agreement that is *signed* and *witnessed*. There are legal guidelines for creating a cohabitation agreement, but they are not as stringent as those covering prenuptial or postnuptial agreements drafted between spouses prior or subsequent to their marriage. For example, the parties to a cohabitation agreement are not required to give each other a complete listing of their assets and liabilities unlike parties to a prenuptial or postnuptial agreement. The only significant legal restriction is that no state court will enforce any portion of a cohabitation agreement that involves the exchange of sexual favors.

When a couple contemplates the creation of a cohabitation agreement, they should ask themselves *why* they want to create such an agreement. In most cases, the couples are attempting to circumvent any hard feelings they may feel toward each other if they break up. Truthfully, it is doubtful that a legal document will prevent such hard feelings from occurring; but what a cohabitation agreement can do is clearly define the property that each person is bringing or will bring into the partners' mutual home. A cohabitation agreement also can be the vehicle through which a couple defines its expectations. A cohabitation agreement does not guarantee that a lawsuit will not be filed by one party against the other. However, if a lawsuit is filed, the court can use the cohabitation agreement as evidence to determine the intentions of the parties when they became cohabitants. If a court finds the cohabitation agreement to be a valid contract, the court is not likely to ignore it. The agreement will be used as a guideline in determining the parties' mutual expectations.

On a technical note, when any type of agreement is created, each paragraph of the agreement should be delineated by a letter or a number. This allows readers to locate easily any paragraph that is being discussed.

MARRIAGE AND THE ELDER LAW PERSPECTIVE

Women are far more likely than men to be widowed, but elderly men are twice as likely to remarry following a divorce or death of a spouse. In 1990, only four out of 1,000 divorced elderly women remarried compared with 19 out of 1,000 elderly men.[9] Despite these facts, marriage among the elderly is rising.

Each state has attempted to define marriage. The definition of California's *Family Code* is typical. It defines **marriage** as a *personal relationship arising out of a civil contract between a man and a woman, to whom the consent of the parties capable of making that contract is necessary. Consent alone does not constitute marriage. Consent must be followed by the issuance of a license and solemnization.*[10] A **civil marriage** is defined as a government-sanctioned union that is created when a government employee officiates at a marriage ceremony, after which the participants are declared husband and wife. In some countries, it is essential to the validity of the union that the couple first complete a civil marriage even if a religious ceremony is planned. In the United States, a civil marriage ceremony is merely another way that a marriage may be conducted.

Another type of marriage is a common law marriage. Common law spouses live together as man and wife but do so without the licensing and solemnization that is required for an officiated civil marriage. The minority of states that recognize common law marriage usually require that the couple has a mutual intent to be married, must continue cohabitation, and must publicly hold themselves out to the world as husband and wife. However, once one state recognizes common law spouses as being legally married, they enjoy all of the same rights, privileges, and responsibilities of a traditional marriage and their marriage should be recognized in all other states. A disadvantage of common law marriage is that the hurdle of receiving official recognition must be dealt with.

marriage

A personal relationship arising out of a civil contract between a man and a woman, to whom the consent of the parties capable of making that contract is necessary.

civil marriage

A government-sanctioned union that is created when a government employee officiates at a marriage ceremony, after which the participants are declared husband and wife.

This can be particularly onerous after one spouse dies and proof is needed to establish that a common law marriage existed in order for the surviving spouse to receive benefits based on marital status.

A deterrent against marriage is the fear of financial obligations for a new spouse's debt becoming the responsibility of each spouse. A good way to avoid mutual responsibility of spousal debt is to maintain separate ownership of all assets under separate names and avoid commingling of assets. However, certain states impose financial obligations on spouses for all expenses. A surviving spouse who is receiving pension benefits based on a deceased spouse's work history can lose those benefits if the survivor spouse remarries. In addition, inheritance issues play a role in remarriage. For example, how much a second spouse should inherit and what issues adult children from previous relationships may have.

The American concept of marriage has changed with the times and has evolved to become a union defined by love with a legal arsenal of over 1,000 laws pertaining to it.[11] For example, an individual is financially protected if an illness forces her spouse into a nursing home. The spouse still at home cannot be forced to sell the marital home or be forced to completely spend down a shared bank account to pay for the nursing home care. In addition, each state sets aside a certain percentage of a couple's income to pay for the spouse at home. Another important benefit of marriage is that spouses may inherit property from their spouse tax free.

A key issue for elder law attorneys and their engaged-to-be-married client usually is the preservation of the client's premarital assets. Refer to Exhibit 6–2 to review marriage statistics provided by the U.S. Census. These statistics highlight selected years between 1970 and 2000.

EXHIBIT 6–2   MARRIAGE IN THE UNITED STATES

Table A1. Marital Status of People 15 Years and Over, by Age, Sex, Personal Earnings, Race, 2006
(Numbers in thousands, except for percentages.)

All Races	Total	Married Spouse Present	Married Spouse Absent	Widowed	Divorced	Separated	Never Married	Total	Married Spouse Present	Married Spouse Absent	Widowed	Divorced	Separated	Never Married
	Number	Number	Number	Number	Number	Number	Number	Percent	Percent	Percent	Percent	Percent	Percent	Percent
BOTH SEXES														
Total 15+	233,039	119,055	3,785	13,914	22,806	4,963	68,515	100.0	51.1	1.6	6.0	9.8	2.1	29.4
15-17 years	13,340	40	17	7	48	53	13,176	100.0	0.3	0.1	0.1	0.4	0.4	98.8
18-19 years	7,561	197	24	6	14	44	7,275	100.0	2.6	0.3	0.1	0.2	0.6	96.2
20-24 years	20,380	3,163	215	30	232	220	16,521	100.0	15.5	1.1	0.1	1.1	1.1	81.1
25-29 years	20,138	8,317	351	51	838	449	10,132	100.0	41.3	1.7	0.3	4.2	2.2	50.3
30-34 years	19,338	11,464	404	64	1,333	524	5,550	100.0	59.3	2.1	0.3	6.9	2.7	28.7
35-39 years	20,754	13,154	412	135	2,307	609	4,137	100.0	63.4	2.0	0.6	11.1	2.9	19.9

(continues)

EXHIBIT 6–2   MARRIAGE IN THE UNITED STATES *(continued)*

Table A1. Marital Status of People 15 Years and Over, by Age, Sex, Personal Earnings, Race, 2006
(Numbers in thousands, except for percentages.)

All Races	Total	Married Spouse Present	Married Spouse Absent	Widowed	Divorced	Separated	Never Married	Total	Married Spouse Present	Married Spouse Absent	Widowed	Divorced	Separated	Never Married
	Number	Number	Number	Number	Number	Number	Number	Percent	Percent	Percent	Percent	Percent	Percent	Percent
40-44 years	22,335	14,309	415	263	3,120	707	3,521	100.0	64.1	1.9	1.2	14.0	3.2	15.8
45-49 years	22,505	14,738	407	365	3,472	693	2,829	100.0	65.5	1.8	1.6	15.4	3.1	12.6
50-54 years	20,270	13,278	365	533	3,483	600	2,011	100.0	65.5	1.8	2.6	17.2	3.0	9.9
55-64 years	30,956	20,978	517	1,864	4,873	653	2,071	100.0	67.8	1.7	6.0	15.7	2.1	6.7
65-74 years	18,540	11,842	310	3,252	2,101	293	741	100.0	63.9	1.7	17.5	11.3	1.6	4.0
75-84 years	12,959	6,408	245	4,925	855	102	424	100.0	49.4	1.9	38.0	6.6	0.8	3.3
85+ years	3,962	1,166	102	2,419	130	17	128	100.0	29.4	2.6	61.1	3.3	0.4	3.2
15-17 years	13,340	40	17	7	48	53	13,176	100.0	0.3	0.1	0.1	0.4	0.4	98.8
18+ years	219,699	119,016	3,768	13,907	22,758	4,911	55,340	100.0	54.2	1.7	6.3	10.4	2.2	25.2
15-64 years	197,577	99,640	3,128	3,318	19,720	4,550	67,222	100.0	50.4	1.6	1.7	10.0	2.3	34.0
65+ years	35,462	19,416	658	10,596	3,086	413	1,293	100.0	54.8	1.9	29.9	8.7	1.2	3.6

Marriage and Gay Couples

■ **civil union**

A legal designation given to homosexual partners that confers certain marriage-like rights.

Older gay couples must face many issues despite a small minority of states initiating civil unions. A **civil union** is a legal designation given to homosexual partners that confers certain marriage-like rights. On October 1, 2005, Connecticut was the first state to pass a civil union law conferring the same legal rights to gay partners as to heterosexual spouses. As of the date of publishing, Vermont and New Jersey are other states that allow civil unions. Massachusetts is the only state that allows same-sex marriage. Older gay couples, whether they have entered civil unions or not, still face significant financial issues since they do not have the same protections as heterosexual married couples. For example, same-sex couples do not automatically inherit property from each other tax free nor is a gay couple's home protected for one partner in the event the other partner must enter a nursing home.

PRENUPTIAL AGREEMENTS

Americans love the white lace and promises of a wedding. In fact, the majority of Americans marry in their lifetimes. Another fact of American life is that those marriages are not lasting.[12]

This is where the **prenuptial agreement** concept comes in handy. A prenuptial agreement, also known as an **antenuptial agreement**, is a contract that two individuals make *before* their marriage to each other. However, the contract does not take effect until *after* the individuals are married to each other. Just as a life insurance policy defines the financial payout prior to an insured person's death, both parties to a prenuptial agree to the details of any post-divorce financial settlement *prior* to a divorce occurring. Married couples who have separated, but then decide to remain married may wish to have a *postnuptial agreement* drafted. The legal guidelines for postnuptial agreements are generally the same as for prenuptial agreements.

When an engaged couple makes the decision to create a prenuptial agreement, they often seek legal advice. Frequently, the couple will see one attorney together to have the agreement written. Before signing it, one party should go separately to another attorney to have the agreement reviewed by her counsel. While the attorneys are responsible for explaining the legal ramifications of signing a prenuptial agreement, a paralegal may handle the prenuptial agreement interview and draft the agreement under the supervision of an attorney.

Parties who create their own prenuptial agreements are defining their own rights and responsibilities to their future spouses and turning their backs on one-size-fits-all state laws that list the statutorily imposed rights and duties of spouses. Because the parties are stepping outside specific statutory requirements, they must comply with other requirements in order for the prenuptial agreement to be considered binding and valid.[13]

Historically, many states frowned on prenuptial agreements because they were thought to promote divorce. In the past, judges in such states declared the agreements void and against public policy and would not enforce them. Interestingly, even in the most stridently anti-prenuptial states, most courts upheld those portions of prenuptial agreements that dealt with the rights given to each spouse in the event of either spouse's death.

Today each state's requirements for creating a valid prenuptial agreement can be different based on whether the state has enacted the **Uniform Premarital Agreement Act (UPAA)**. At least 25 states and the District of Columbia have enacted the act. The remaining 25 states have legislation and case law applicable to their individual states. However, the general requirements for all states include the following:

1. A written agreement

2. Contractual capacity of the parties

3. Voluntary agreement free of *fraud,* *duress,* and *undue influence*

4. The fact that agreement must not be unconscionable

5. **Full disclosure of assets**

---

prenuptial agreement

A contract that two individuals make *before* their marriage to each other, which does not take effect until *after* the individuals are married to each other.

antenuptial agreement

Another name for prenuptial agreement.

Uniform Premarital Agreement Act (UPAA)

Legislation enacted that sets forth the requirements for creating a valid prenuptial

full disclosure of assets

A complete listing of all real and personal property in which the parties have ownership interest.

Fraud is any kind of trickery used to cheat another person of money or property. Unconscionable behavior is defined as acting in a manner that is grossly unfair. As noted earlier in the text, duress is any pressure that takes away a person's free will to make decisions. Full disclosure of assets is a complete listing of all real and personal property in which the parties have ownership interest. Refer to Exhibit 6–3 to review a listing of states that have enacted the UPAA or a state-specific combination of case and statutory law.

EXHIBIT 6–3   GUIDE TO UNIFORM PREMARITAL AGREEMENT ACT

What States Follow the Uniform Premarital Agreement Act?

State	Valid in State	State	Valid in State
Alabama	No	Montana	Yes
Alaska	No	Nebraska	No
Arizona	Yes	Nevada	Yes
Arkansas	Yes	New Hampshire	No
California	No	New Jersey	Yes
Colorado	Yes	New Mexico	No
Connecticut	No	New York	No
Delaware	No	North Carolina	Yes
District of Columbia	No	North Dakota	Yes
Florida	No	Ohio	No
Georgia	No	Oklahoma	No
Hawaii	Yes	Oregon	Yes
Idaho	Yes	Pennsylvania	No
Illinois	Yes	Rhode Island	Yes
Indiana	Yes	South Carolina	No
Iowa	Yes	South Dakota	Yes
Kansas	Yes	Tennessee	No
Kentucky	No	Texas	Yes

(continues)

EXHIBIT 6–3 GUIDE TO UNIFORM PREMARITAL AGREEMENT ACT *(continued)*			
What States Follow the Uniform Premarital Agreement Act?			
State	**Valid in State**	**State**	**Valid in State**
Louisiana	No	Utah	Yes
Maine	Yes	Vermont	No
Maryland	No	Virginia	Yes
Massachusetts	No	Washington	No
Michigan	No	West Virginia	No
Minnesota	Yes	Wisconsin	No
Mississippi	No	Wyoming	No
Missouri	No		

What Should Be Included in a Prenuptial Agreement?

Whatever the factual scenario, all prenuptial agreements should clearly state what each individual understands she is to receive or give to the other spouse if the marriage fails. Creators of a prenuptial agreement should review basic concepts of contract law to ensure that they understand the necessary elements of the agreement.

A **contract** is defined as an agreement or a covenant between two or more persons in which each party binds herself to do or not to do an act and in which each acquires a right to what the other promises. When broken down, the definition of a *contract* includes these basic elements: an *offer, an acceptance, mental intent to make a contract,* and *consideration.* An **offer** is defined as the act of making a proposal and presenting it for acceptance or rejection. An **acceptance** is defined as an agreeing to an offer. **Consideration** is the promise to do or to forbear from doing (that means *not do*) something that a party otherwise would have the right to do, such as sue for a larger share of marital property. In a prenuptial agreement, the consideration is often the promise of Party A not to sue and ask for a larger or different property settlement from Party B; in return, Party B promises to give a clearly defined amount to Party A in the event of a divorce between Party A and Party B.

In the American legal system, courts hesitate to push aside a contract. A fundamental principle of contract law is that judges will look at the *four corners of the contract.* This means that in the case of a dispute, a judge first will read the actual contract to determine what the parties to the contract intended when they

▓ **contract**

An agreement or a covenant between two or more persons in which each party binds herself to do or not to do an act and in which each acquires a right to what the other promises.

▓ **offer**

The act of making a proposal and presenting it for acceptance or rejection.

▓ **acceptance**

An agreeing to an offer.

▓ **consideration**

The promise to do or to forbear from doing something that a party otherwise would have the right to do.

created the contract. Typically, judges do not like to go outside the agreement to hear testimony explaining what the parties meant when they wrote the contract. Such testimony is known as **parole evidence**; and with a few exceptions, it is usually frowned upon by the courts. Occasionally, in an effort to keep the contract in effect, the courts will hear testimony to bring some clarity to an ambiguous contract. Another reason a judge may hear parole evidence is if the evidence will prevent an inequity.

■ **parole evidence**
Testimony explaining what the parties meant when they wrote a contract.

Creating a prenuptial agreement is the responsibility of the attorneys representing the parties *and* the parties representing themselves since they must comply with the agreement. Judges are hesitant to rewrite contracts that have turned out unsatisfactorily for one or both parties. However, if the parties to the contract mutually agree to a rewriting, the legal term by which that rewriting is known is **rescission**. Also, an unhappy party may go to court to set aside a prenuptial agreement if she can prove that all of the legal requirements for preparing such an agreement have not been met. As previously discussed, not all state requirements are the same. Therefore, state-specific research must be done.

■ **rescission**
The legal term used for the rewriting of a contract.

Although an individual may reside in a state that does not require full disclosure of assets, she still should be completely honest when listing assets and liabilities. A complete listing is necessary so that both parties to a prenuptial agreement are aware of the other's financial position *before* they sign the agreement. It also is a good idea to list liabilities. The complete listing is necessary because each person who is married in any of the 50 states has certain rights that are given only upon marriage; and if a person signs a contract giving up those rights, that signer must be aware of what she is giving up. For example, in California, a **community property** state, a person has a right under community property laws to 50 percent of all of her spouse's earnings from the day the couple is married. The opposite of that situation is that a spouse in a community property state can be held 50 percent responsible for all of her spouse's debts from the first day of marriage. A prenuptial agreement circumvents that state's law as long as both the bride and groom (or less romantically stated, both parties to the contract) are put on notice of all of the facts.

■ **community property**
A person has a right to 50 percent of all of her spouse's assets from the day the couple is married and can be held liable for 50 percent of all of her spouse's debts as well.

No Two Prenuptial Agreements Are Alike

Each prenuptial agreement is different from the next because each agreement is negotiated by the parties involved. Typically, most prenuptial agreements include an introductory paragraph that describes *why* the couple is entering into the agreement. This paragraph allows the couple to make their intentions clear and supports the validity of the prenuptial agreement if one of the parties to the agreement attempts to have a court declare the agreement invalid. For example, a couple with children from previous marriages could state that their intent is to protect assets earned during prior marriages for the children of those marriages.

Usually, a prenuptial agreement describes the rights that each party has to property or spousal support in the event the marriage ends in divorce. For example, a prenuptial agreement may include a clause that designates a certain amount of property or spousal support to which a divorcing spouse would be entitled after a certain number of years of marriage. Many divorce settlements are tied to the number of years of marriage. A spouse who is entitled to a certain lump-sum settlement after two years of marriage may be entitled to an increase in the monetary amount of the lump-sum settlement after each succeeding year of marriage. Perhaps a certain yearly monetary sum of spousal support is tied to the marriage lasting at least five years.

Some prenuptial agreements include warnings that proof of adultery by the payee spouse will lead to a reduction in the financial settlement for the payee spouse and proof of adultery by the payor spouse will lead to a larger financial settlement for the payee spouse. This is not permitted by most states. Some states consider such contingencies against *public policy,* in which case those clauses pertaining to the contingency (or perhaps the entire agreement) can be found void. The **payee spouse** is the spouse receiving the money, and the **payor spouse** is the spouse paying the money. Certain key items should be included in the agreement:

1. A list of all assets, liabilities, income, and expectations of gifts and inheritances

2. A description of how premarital debts will be paid

3. A description of what happens to each party's premarital property in reference to appreciation, gains, income, rental, dividends, and proceeds of such property in the event of death or divorce

4. A decision about who will own the marital or secondary homes in the event of death or divorce

5. A specification of the status of gifts inheritances and trusts that either spouse receives or benefits from whether before or after the marriage

6. Clarification of what will happen to each type of property, such as real estate, artwork, furniture, and jewelry

7. A decision on the amount allocated for alimony, maintenance, or spousal support or a provision for a waiver or property settlement instead of support

8. Details of death benefits stating what each party will provide for the other

9. A decision about medical, disability, life, and long-term care insurance[14]

A prenuptial agreement can be as specific as the parties' desire. For example, the agreement might designate the household duties that each party will undertake once the couple is married. (Party A will take the trash out on even-numbered days, and Party B will take the trash out on odd-numbered days.) A relatively recent prenuptial phenomenon is the very specific *no-children clause.*

payee spouse

The spouse who receives money.

payor spouse

The spouse who pays money.

The choice not to have children may arise when an older man who already has adult children marries a woman still in her child-bearing years. For example, *The New York Times* quoted one Manhattan couple's no-children clause as follows:

> *The parties have discussed their future plans and desires relating to having or adopting children once they are married. Both parties hereby acknowledge that after careful deliberation they agree that they shall not have or adopt children once married. This decision is not made out of a limitation of commitment to the other, but rather this provision is based upon an analysis of the parties' present and anticipated family structure, financial situation, and the lifestyle the parties anticipate having upon and during their marriage.*[15]

It is doubtful that a court would use a no-children clause to reduce or eliminate paternal responsibility.

ELDER LAW PRACTICE

Prenuptial scenarios involving older couples often involve adult children from previous relationships as well. While such a couple may not be wealthy, they usually want to protect what they do have for their children's futures. This is the case with Bridget and Robert, both divorced senior citizens. Although their love for each other makes them feel young again, Bridget has a son, John, in his thirties and Robert does not have any children. Neither Bridget nor Robert, not to mention Bridget's son, wants John to be forgotten financially.

Bridget and Robert have turned to Tara Jensen, Esq., and her staff to help them protect John's interests and start their married life looking toward the future.

Tara and her paralegal, Luke, met with the couple. Luke was introduced to the couple and was on hand to take notes. Bridget, who had done some reading on second marriages and adult children, wanted to share the information with Tara and Luke. Bridget stated that some family therapists think there are four steps that adult children must take in dealing with a parent's remarriage.

Interested, Tara asked, "What did the therapists in your research report?"

Bridget answered, "Adult children need to recognize a parent's right to happiness, remember that they have a unique relationship with their parent, seek help, and deal with money issues. We can't personally do the first three steps for my son, but we did come to you to deal with our money issues."[16]

Robert smiled and then explained the situation knowledgeably, "We're here because we know there are two possible scenarios that can happen to us unless we're careful. First, our marriage can end in divorce, and any financial position we've resurrected after our first marriages will be ruined. Second, even if this marriage turns out to be the success I know it's going to be, one of us could die. Then without a prenuptial agreement or a will, instead of individual assets going to each of our chosen beneficiaries, the inheritance would go to the surviving spouse and, in Bridget's case, eventually, the surviving spouse's offspring."

Bridget added, "We don't want John to be overlooked. My only son and I have talked for years about his sweat equity in my house having a twofold purpose. He's helping his mom and working on a house that he'll inherit one day. Robert understands that."

What solution can Tara recommend to Bridget's and Robert's concerns?

(continues)

ELDER LAW PRACTICE *(continued)*

Analysis: Tara can recommend that a prenuptial agreement be drafted along with a coordinating and up to date will (and durable powers of attorney and advance healthcare directives) following a thorough review of Bridget's and Robert's assets. Tara also should recommend that either Bridget or Robert hire a separate attorney to review the completed prenuptial agreement.

Summary of Bridget and Robert's Interview

Following her interview with Bridget and Robert, Tara asked Luke to write a summary of the information he gathered during the interview and to prepare a file. Tara also asked Luke to prepare a draft of the couple's prenuptial agreement for her review.

The previous marriages of Bridget and Robert ended in acrimonious divorces. Bridget is 57 years old and has returned to work as a real estate agent. Due to fluctuations in the real estate market, her income the last three years has ranged from $23,000 to $37,000 annually. Robert is 61 years old; and for the last 21 years, he has been employed as an administrator for a pharmaceutical company. He is now earning $64,000 annually. Although Bridget's income is not as large as Robert's, she is the proud owner of a home she purchased seven years ago with the lump-sum settlement from her divorce. Bridget purchased the tired fixer-upper for $120,000; but after spending seven years working on the house (with help from her only son), Bridget thinks she could sell it for $220,000. There is a small mortgage on the home in the amount of $25,000. Bridget also inherited from her aunt, Helen Goodanty, an annual annuity in the amount of $10,000.

Robert rents a glamorous and expensive apartment overlooking the ninth hole of the local country club's golf course. Robert's previous marriage (or rather his divorce) was so nasty and expensive that the home Robert and his first wife owned was sold to pay for their attorneys' fees. His first wife did not work outside the home and, therefore, could not afford to pay for her own attorney. The profit remaining after their legal fees were paid was left to his wife, instead of her taking a share of Robert's pension. Robert's only asset is $100,000 in his pension account. Robert also is paying annual alimony of $22,000 to his ex-wife. Robert does not have children.

A sample of typical questions that should be asked during a prenuptial agreement interview is provided in Exhibit 6–4. Robert and Bridget's completed prenuptial agreement is shown in Exhibit 6–5.

EXHIBIT 6–4   QUESTIONS FOR THE PRENUPTIAL AGREEMENT INTERVIEW

1. What is the full name of the bride?

2. What is the address of the bride?

3. What is the age of the bride?

4. What is the Social Security number of the bride?

5. What is the full name of the groom?

6. What is the address of the groom?

7. What is the Social Security number of the groom?

8. What are the names and addresses of the bride's children?

9. What are the names and addresses of the groom's children?

10. Is this the first marriage for the bride?

11. If not, how many times has the bride been married?

12. What are the names of previous husbands of the bride?

13. Is this the first marriage for the groom?

14. If not, how many times has the groom been married?

15. What are the names of previous wives of the groom?

16. Where is the bride employed?

17. What is the bride's job title?

18. What is the bride's yearly salary?

19. Does the bride have a pension and/or investment plan at her place of employment?

20. If so, what is the value of the pension or investment plan?

21. Where is the groom employed?

22. What is the groom's job title?

23. What is the groom's yearly salary?

24. Does the groom have a pension and/or investment plan at his place of employment?

25. If so, what is the value of the pension or investment plan?

26. What real property is owned solely or otherwise by the bride?

27. What is the assessed value and purchase price of any real property listed?

28. What real property is owned solely or otherwise by the groom?

(continues)

EXHIBIT 6–4   QUESTIONS FOR THE PRENUPTIAL AGREEMENT INTERVIEW *(continued)*

29. What is the assessed value and purchase price of any real property listed?

30. What personal property valued over $100 is owned by the bride?

31. What is the assessed value and purchase price of any such personal property valued over $100?

32. What personal property valued over $100 is owned by the groom?

33. What is the assessed value and purchase price of any such personal property valued over $100?

EXHIBIT 6–5   SAMPLE PRENUPTIAL AGREEMENT

Prenuptial Agreement of Bridget Beaumont and Robert Smith

A. This is a Prenuptial Agreement between Bridget Beaumont, to be known as Party A, and Robert Smith, to be known as Party B. The intention of the parties is to maintain their respective estates for the benefit of children born of prior marriages.

B. Party A and Party B enter this Agreement with full knowledge of the approximate value of each other's estate and of all the rights and privileges to each other's estate that would be conferred by marriage if this Agreement had not been entered into; and

C. Upon separate legal advice, both parties have agreed to waive any rights to each other's estate upon death of either or both parties, or in the event of the separation or dissolution of their marriage; and

D. Both Parties, by virtue of this Agreement, desire to determine, fix and establish the rights that will accrue to each of them in the property and estate of the other upon the death of either or both of them, or in the event of separation or dissolution of their marriage; and

E. The Parties do hereby acknowledge that Party A is the sole owner of the property located at 25 Forever Young Drive, Soultown, Bliss, U.S.A., with such property acquired by her prior to marriage to Party B and without any contribution from party B, and Party B acknowledges that he has no rights to said property nor any future rights that may occur by marriage to Party A, or any rights in the event of death of Party A, or separation or dissolution of marriage to Party A.

F. The Parties do hereby acknowledge that Party B has exclusive right to his retirement pension account with Drugs R Us Pharmaceuticals and Party A acknowledges that she does not own any right in said pension upon marriage to Party B, or any rights incurred upon the death of Party B, or upon separation or dissolution of their marriage; and

G. Party B acknowledges that party A is the sole owner of the annual annuity from Helen Goodanty and hereby waives any rights to said Annuity in event of the death of Party A, or upon separation or dissolution of their marriage; and

H. The Parties acknowledge that whatever debts they incurred prior to their marriage are their sole responsibility and they shall indemnify and hold harmless the other party for any such indebtedness, to wit Party A acknowledges sole responsibility for the $25,000 equity mortgage on her home, and Party B acknowledges sole responsibility for the $22,000 yearly alimony to his ex-wife.

(continues)

EXHIBIT 6–5 SAMPLE PRENUPTIAL AGREEMENT *(continued)*

I. The Parties acknowledge that they each received independent legal counsel in the preparation of this Agreement and are satisfied as to its content.

J. Any property, real, personal, or mixed, which shall now or hereafter be held in the joint names of the parties shall be owned in accordance with the title of joint ownership and barring any other designation, shall be presumed to be held equally by the parties with survivorship rights, if any, as may be specifically designated by the title ownership.

K. Nothing in this agreement shall prevent or limit either party from making provisions for the other by Last Will and Testament,

In which case provisions of the Last Will and Testament shall prevail.

L. The Financial Statements and List of Assets of both parties are attached in an Addendum.

M. In the event of a divorce, dissolution, or annulment of the marriage between the parties, Robert Smith will vacate the home owned by Bridget Beaumont. In the event of Bridget Beaumont's death, Robert Smith will vacate the home within six months of Bridget's death. All expenses of maintaining the marital home during this period of occupancy by Robert shall be his sole obligation.

N. This agreement has been executed and delivered in the State of Bliss and the provisions shall be construed and enforced in accordance with the laws of Bliss, regardless of either party's change of domiciliary.

O. The fact that this agreement was prepared by counsel for one of the parties shall create no presumptions and specifically shall not cause any ambiguities to be construed against that party.

On this _____ day of 2008, before me personally came Bridget Beaumont and Robert Smith, known to me as the individuals described in and who executed this instrument.

Witness _____

DATED: _____

Bridget Beaumont _____

DATED: _____

Robert Smith _____

DATED: _____

Prenuptial Agreement Leads to Constructive Trust Created for Widower

The case of *Martin v. Farber* (see case that follows) placed the court in the role of protector of Mr. Farber. Apparently, he was a loving husband to Nettie Sue Farber for over 40 years. The court created a constructive trust upon Mrs. Farber's estate to financially provide for Mr. Farber following Mrs. Farber's death. A constructive trust is defined as a remedy employed by a court to convert the legal title of property into a trust held by a trustee for the benefit of a third party who in good conscience should have reaped the benefits of the possession of the property put into the constructive trust.

CASE LAW *Martin v. Farber*

68 Md. App. 137, 510 A.2d 608 (1986)

Facts:

Three days prior to their marriage on June 22, 1939, Nettie Sue Farber, then Nettie Sue Goldberg, and Morris W. Farber entered into a prenuptial agreement. The agreement provided, in essence, that Mrs. Farber would retain sole control of the property she acquired either prior to or during the marriage. Mr. Farber relinquished all rights in the property and the estate of Mrs. Farber.

At the time of the execution of the agreement, Mrs. Farber was 39 years old, a widow, and the mother of two boys. Her first husband, Dr. Chester Goldberg, died in 1936. Mrs. Farber inherited property from him, which included real estate located in Baltimore City. She also received more than $20,000 from insurance proceeds.

Mr. Farber, although steadily employed as an electrician, had no accumulated wealth at the time of his marriage to Mrs. Farber. However, he did continue to work until his retirement in 1967. During his 44-year marriage to Mrs. Farber, Mr. Farber turned his paychecks over to his wife. Mrs. Farber, meanwhile, remained at home and managed the couple's household and financial affairs.

When Mrs. Farber died intestate in August 1983, she had accumulated, in her own name, assets valued at approximately $275,000. The Baltimore County Court appointed Mr. Farber as personal representative of his deceased wife's estate. Mrs. Farber's grandchildren filed a petition in the Circuit Court for Baltimore County to remove Mr. Farber from that position. They asserted that he had signed a valid prenuptial agreement in which he renounced any claim to Mrs. Farber's estate. In response, Mr. Farber filed a petition for relief alleging that the prenuptial agreement was invalid and that, under Maryland's intestacy laws, he was entitled to his share of the estate.

Following a trial, the judge concluded: *It is true that many, many years ago Morris released any claim that he might have to Nettie's property or estate. After some forty-four years of seemingly happy marriage, in which Morris turned everything he owned over to Nettie without question, and also upon her assurances that she would take care of Morris, it would not only be unjust, but unconscionable for the court to enforce the agreement.*

The trial judge determined that a constructive trust should be imposed upon Mrs. Farber's estate for the benefit of Mr. Farber during his life, with the remainder to be distributed equally to Mrs. Farber's heirs. Dissatisfied with the decision of the trial court, both sides appealed.

Issue:

(1) Whether the prenuptial agreement entered into by Morris W. Farber and Nettie Sue Farber in 1939 was still valid and enforceable 44 years after it was signed? (2) Whether the imposition of a constructive trust on the estate of Nettie Sue Farber was proper?

Court's
Reasoning:

The grandchildren claimed that the prenuptial agreement was valid and enforceable and that Mr. Farber was precluded from obtaining any interest in Mrs. Farber's estate. Mr. Farber contended that since the agreement was not to be enforced, the proper action of the lower court should have been to order that the intestacy law would determine the distribution of assets of the estate. Proceeding from the premise, Mr. Farber further asserted that he was entitled to the first $15,000 plus half the residual of his wife's estate.

The trial judge erred in ruling that the agreement was unconscionable. It was not. The trial judge was particularly concerned by the fact that Mr. Farber turned everything he earned over to Mrs. Farber, and that she repeatedly assured her husband that she would take care of him. No matter how disturbing those facts may be, they do not afford an adequate basis for the court's ruling. Yet to be determined is whether, under the circumstances of the case, a constructive trust was properly imposed. Ordinarily, before a constructive trust can

(continues)

CASE LAW *Martin v. Farber* (continued)

be imposed by a court, there must be clear and convincing evidence of wrongdoing, coupled with circumstances that render it inequitable for the holder of legal title to retain the beneficial interest. When a confidential relationship exists, different rules are applicable.

In order to establish the existence of a confidential relationship, it must be shown that one party is under the domination of another or that the circumstances are such that one party is justified in assuming that the other will not act in a manner inconsistent with the party's welfare. Once it is demonstrated that a confidential relationship exists, a presumption arises that a confidence was placed in the dominant party, and the presumption shifts the burden to the dominant party to show, by clear and convincing evidence, that the transaction entered into was fair and reasonable.

The record before us revealed that throughout the Farber's 44 year marriage, Mrs. Farber stayed home attending to the domestic chores and the couple's financial matters. Mr. Farber continued to work outside the home. He regularly earned wages, which he diligently turned over to his wife. Those facts, when viewed in light of Mrs. Farber's repeated assurances to her husband that she would take care of him, lead us to the conclusion that a confidential relationship existed between the Farbers, and that Mrs. Farber was the dominant of the two.

Based on the evidence presented to support Mr. Farber's assertion that his wife abused that confidential relationship by using his earnings to acquire assets that she titled, or placed, solely in her own name, we agree that the imposition of constructive trust was proper. We think, however, that the trust should only be imposed to the extent that Mr. Farber's funds were used to acquire assets that were not a part of, or attributable to, the assets in Mrs. Farber's estate prior to the marriage of the couple. In limiting the scope of the constructive trust, we are mindful that a primary purpose of that form of trust is to prevent unjust enrichment. Therefore, the constructive trust should be limited to the extent that Mr. Farber is able to trace his funds into his wife's estate. The imposition by the trial court of a constructive trust over the *entire* estate, without regard to the amounts actually contributed by Mr. Farber was in error.

Holding: Judgment affirmed in part and reversed in part. Case remanded for further proceedings in accordance with this opinion. Costs to be divided between the parties.

Case   The appellate court's decision put Mr. Farber in the position of proving how much he contributed to the
Discussion: acquisition of property by Mrs. Farber. Do you think Mrs. Farber intended the prenuptial agreement to be used
             by her *grandchildren* after a 44-year marriage to Mr. Farber?

Deceased Spouse's Honesty Is Questioned

With regard to prenuptial agreements, most states require the prospective spouses entering into the agreement to be completely honest about their financial positions. Alternatively, some states look only to whether the prenuptial agreement is essentially fair in how it treats the less economically secure spouse in the event the marriage fails. This difference between states is important because if one spouse fails to be completely candid in a state that requires candid admissions, the prenuptial agreement may be considered invalid. A finding of such invalidity would necessitate the application of that particular state's laws on the division of property and spousal support.

The case of *In re Estate of LeRoy A. Hillegass* (refer to case that follows) concerns an attempt by a widowed spouse to have a prenuptial agreement found invalid because of her spouse's alleged lack of truthfulness about the state of his financial resources at the time of their marriage. The court described the legally permitted option of the widow taking an *election* against her late husband's estate. The law permits the spouse of a deceased person to elect to take a statutorily provided percentage of a deceased spouse's estate if the amount bequeathed in a will is less than the amount provided for by statute or if there is no will.

CASE LAW   *In re Estate of LeRoy A. Hillegass*

431 Pa. 144, 244 A.2d 672 (1968)

Facts:

LeRoy A. Hillegass died at the age of 76, leaving an estate inventoried at $265,876. He was survived by his widow, Esther V. Hillegass, who was 60 years old, to whom he had been married for five years before his death. He was also survived by David Hillegass, his son by a former marriage; Bradford LeRoy Hillegass, a grandson; and Alda M. Holtzman, his sister. Mr. Hillegass left a will dated March 19, 1964, and a codicil dated April 15, 1965. In his will, which was executed over a year before his marriage to Esther, he bequeathed a legacy to his son and to his sister conditioned upon their surviving him. He also created a trust of $40,000 for the benefit of his grandson. Finally, he gave his residuary estate in trust to pay the net income to his son for life, with the remainder to certain charities. Thirteen days after his marriage on April 15, 1965, Mr. Hillegass executed a codicil bequeathing Esther property valued at approximately $30,000.

LeRoy A. Hillegass and Esther V. Cassel, his intended wife, had entered into a prenuptial agreement. The Hillegass prenuptial agreement stated: *Whereas, it is the purpose of this agreement to give each of the parties hereto the free and absolute control and disposal of his or her separate property or estate; and Whereas, it is the intention of the intended wife to waive, relinquish and bar all her inchoate interest and other rights or interests, either as wife or widow of the First Party, in and to any property now owned or hereafter acquired by the First Party, including her right of election to take against the Will of the First party.*

Now, Therefore, in consideration of the said marriage and the covenants of the Second Party, The First Party agrees to pay the Second Party, the sum of Ten Thousand Dollars ($10,000.00) immediately after April 1, 1965; and in consideration of the said marriage and covenants of the First Party, the Second Party agrees to pay the First Party the Sum of One Dollar ($1.00) immediately after April 1, 1965. She hereby releases unto the First Party, his heirs, personal representatives and assigns forever all of her interests, rights and claims in and to the said property of every nature and kind.

LeRoy A. Hillegass released all his rights in and to the property of his intended wife in provisions identical with those provisions for the wife hereinabove quoted.

Issue:

Whether the wife presented clear and convincing evidence of material misrepresentations or nondisclosure prior to her signing the prenuptial agreement.

Court's Reasoning:

In compliance with the prenuptial agreement, Hillegass paid Esther the sum of $10,000 on April 15, 1965, which was 13 days after they were married. Moreover, he gave Esther gifts that totaled approximately $30,000.

(continues)

In spite of the prenuptial agreement, Esther filed an election to take against her husband's will. The executor of the will, David Hillegass, joined in by other heirs, filed a petition to set aside Esther's election. The lower court granted the petition and set aside Esther's election to take against her husband's will. A prenuptial agreement calls for the highest degree of good faith and a reasonable provision for the surviving spouse or, in the absence of such a provision, a full and fair disclosure of all pertinent facts and circumstances.

Reasonableness will depend upon the totality of all the facts and circumstances at the time of the Agreement, including: (a) the financial worth of the intended husband; (b) the financial status of the intended wife; (c) the age of the two parties; (d) the number of children of each; (e) the intelligence of the parties; (f) whether the survivor aided in the accumulation of the wealth of the deceased spouse; and (g) the standard of living the survivor had before marriage and could reasonably expect to have during marriage. Full and fair disclosure *does not* require one to disclose the exact dollar amount of one's property.

We shall now consider the facts in the light of the aforesaid principles. In this case, there was no clear and convincing evidence by the wife of material misrepresentations or nondisclosure, and consequently we need not consider whether the provision for the intended wife was, or was not, reasonable.

Holding: Decree affirmed, appellant to pay the costs.

Case
Discussion: If Mrs. Hillegass could have proved by clear and convincing evidence that Mr. Hillegass had misrepresented his estate, could the amount provided for Mrs. Hillegass in the prenuptial have been considered unreasonable by the court?

THE RIGHTS OF SURVIVING SPOUSES

All of the separate property states (except Georgia) provide for surviving spouses via an *elective share.* The elective share (sometimes called a *forced share)* provides that a spouse may take the option of accepting a devise from her deceased spouse's will or may renounce the devise and take a legislatively designated share of the estate. The specific amount of the share differs from state to state, but it generally provides at least a statutorily mandated one-third share of the decedent's estate after the decedent's debts are paid. The elective share usually is made up of equal deductions taken from all other devisees. Surprisingly, in most states, a person who abandons her spouse may still be awarded an elective share.[17] An elective share is permitted to be taken in Hawaii by persons who register as each other's reciprocal beneficiaries. This unusual Hawaiian variation (the reciprocal beneficiaries can be same-sex partners) of the elective share concept stems from a decision in the *Baehr v. Lewin* 852 P.2d 44 (Haw. 1993) case.

Surviving spouses also may have a right to their deceased spouse's Social Security benefits, as well as any benefits from applicable retirement plans. This is an especially important benefit when a surviving spouse has not worked outside the home or has not worked long enough to qualify for Social Security benefits. A surviving spouse is not entitled to both his deceased spouse's Social Security benefits and her own; instead, the surviving spouse will receive any additional difference between the benefit amounts. Refer to Chapter 7 for more information on Social Security benefits.

Homestead Exemption Designed to Protect Families

Homestead laws were originally designed to ensure that a decedent's spouse and children would be able to stay in the family home after the decedent's death. Exempting the family residence from creditors ensured this. Some states require the filing of a homestead exemption form prior to a spouse's death; otherwise, the opportunity is lost. Some states have very small monetary exemptions, and other states exempt the home regardless of value.

DIVORCE AND THE ELDER LAW PERSPECTIVE

The legal costs of divorce in the United States amount to more than $30 billion per year. In fact, each year more than 1.8 million people divorce.[18]

Elder law clients marrying later in life usually have two pragmatic concerns before walking down the aisle. First, what type of asset protection can be instituted prior to the nuptials? For example, how can I make sure the children from my first marriage do not lose out because I remarried? Second, if one of the spouses dies, the issue of financial protections for the surviving spouse becomes important. For example, a widow may question whether her husband's death will result in her not being able to afford or even inherit the house she has been living in for years.

A well-drafted prenuptial agreement and an estate plan (e.g., at least a will and perhaps some kind of trust) can take care of these concerns. Of course, not every couple believes in drafting a prenuptial agreement or is aware of how such an agreement can protect them from post-marriage events.

Problems usually occur when planning has not. Statistically speaking, divorce should be a concern for those marrying for a second or subsequent time (the probability of divorce increases with each marriage) and it should be a *major* concern for those without planning documents in place. Divorces also have been increasing for older couples married only once for a significant number of years. Historically, the courts have dealt differently with older couples who are seeking divorces after longtime marriages.

Family law courses typically cover the legal precedent and procedures in place across the country for couples seeking divorce. Issues of family law and elder law often overlap. For example, family issues such as custody, child support, alternative dispute resolution, domestic violence, adoption, paternity, and tax ramifications of divorce may still affect elderly clients to differing degrees. For example, some elder law clients may have young families with much younger spouses.

The next section will deal with a general overview of divorce law and the way it applies to the mature client.

Deciding to End a Marriage

A husband and wife who want to end their marriage typically have two choices. The spouses may be able to meet the criteria to be granted an *annulment,* or they may seek an *absolute and full divorce* from each other. However, at times, divorce may not be the answer for some couples; instead, they may choose to live apart from each other. Some states allow spouses to legally formalize this intention of "marriage limbo." The common legal term used to describe a separation from one's spouse is **judicial separation,** although some states use other names, including *legal separation, limited divorce, divorce mensa et thoro, separation from bed and board,* and *divorce from bed and board.* Essentially, whatever it is called, a court judgment provides that a husband and wife have decided to live apart by agreement instead of seeking a full and absolute divorce. The judgment usually makes the same provisions for spousal and child support, visitation, and property division that a divorce judgment would make. *Separate maintenance* is another term similar to *judicial separation.* Separate maintenance is spousal support paid by one married person to the other if they are no longer living as husband and wife. The main purpose of the separate maintenance action is to seek a court order for spousal support without getting involved with the distribution of marital property. Instead, property distribution usually is dealt with in a separate judicial separation or divorce claim.

A particular court's legal duty to hear a case depends on whether that court has subject matter (also known as *in rem*) jurisdiction over the subject matter in the legal dispute. It is equally important to determine the jurisdiction of the court over the persons involved in the case. Jurisdiction over a person is known as *in personam* jurisdiction. A person's domicile determines which court has *in personam* jurisdiction.

The inclusion in the **divorce complaint** (also called the *divorce petition* or *dissolution petition* in some states) of the reason the plaintiff is seeking a divorce is important legally. Most states demand that only statutory *causes of action* (i.e., the legal reason) be included in the divorce complaint. Depending on the state, the available causes of action may include adultery, alcoholism, imprisonment, and impotence. In addition, each of the 50 states now has a **no-fault divorce statute** available for spouses who want to divorce without levying blame. The creation of no-fault causes of action opened a new world in divorce litigation. The discord was lessened and the negative connotation of fault was eclipsed by no-fault statutes that included the new legal terms *irreconcilable differences, irremediable breakdown,* and

---

■ judicial separation

The common legal term used to describe a separation from one's spouse.

■ divorce complaint

The pleading citing the legal cause of action for the requested divorce.

■ no-fault divorce statute

A cause of action that permits a spouse filing for divorce not to levy blame within the complaint.

incompatibility. The specific term used as a no-fault cause of action for divorce is determined by individual state statutes. Many states have replaced the negative-sounding term *divorce* with the milder term *dissolution.* A no-fault cousin to the causes of action of irreconcilable differences and irremediable breakdown is the cause of action that requires the spouses to live apart for a certain period of time. Many states have *living apart causes of action* that require the spouses to have lived apart for a statutorily mandated amount of time before they file a complaint.

When a petition or complaint is filed by one spouse, the other spouse must respond to the complaint by filing an answer, a response, or a waiver. Providing an answer to the complaint within a certain number of statutorily required days is necessary to avoid the plaintiff being granted a *default judgment.* A default judgment occurs when a party has failed to take a required step in a lawsuit. Each state has its own requirements, but the *responsive pleading* usually must be filed with the court within 20 to 35 days.

All 50 states have a requirement that a divorcing couple's finances and budget be detailed and submitted to the court. A defendant also may include a counterclaim in the answer. An important step is ensuring that the pleadings have been properly served upon the parties.

Temporary Support

Temporary support, also known as *pendente lite* support, is a legal solution to the financial difficulties that can occur during divorce proceedings. Literally translated, *pendente lite* means "during the pending litigation." For a court to grant an order for temporary support, the parties usually must appear before a judge (or in some states, a commission) at a hearing to argue why such support is needed. Support paid by one spouse for the other spouse's temporary support is usually granted unless both spouses are self-supporting. If one spouse has temporary custody of minor children, the other spouse usually is ordered to pay temporary child support as well. Also filed with the *pendente lite* application is a *financial accounting* of the couple's finances, often called a *case information statement,* although it may be called by a different name depending on the state. All 50 states require that a financial accounting for the couple be filed with the court when temporary support is requested. The temporary support request is made in a motion to the court and should be accompanied by an order for *pendente lite* relief along with a plaintiff's certification.

How Property Is Owned

In general, the two concepts of property ownership applicable to marriage are community property and **separate property**. Eight states are known as community property states: Arizona, California, Idaho, Louisiana, Nevada, New

separate property
A type of property ownership that permits individual ownership of property by a married couple except for property clearly designated as jointly owned.

Mexico, Texas, and Washington. Alaska allows a married couple to choose which type of concept they want to apply. Wisconsin has a differently named system, but it is similar to community property. The rest of the states (with some individual variation) use the separate property type of ownership between spouses.

Community property states call most property acquired during a marriage the property of both partners no matter whose name the property is in. In essence, the separate property concept permits individual ownership of property by a married couple except for property clearly designated as jointly owned. Each spouse is the owner of an undivided one-half interest in jointly owned property. Property acquired before marriage or through a gift or an inheritance can be owned individually and not be subject to property division—even in community property states.

A big question, especially regarding separate property states, is the economic protection that a spouse should have. There is a fear (unfortunately often proven true) that the property-owning spouse can disinherit the surviving spouse and leave her without the proverbial roof over the head and in need of public assistance.

However, in the United States, most homes purchased by a husband and wife describe on the deed that the legal ownership is a *tenancy by the entirety* or a *joint tenancy*. Either type of ownership states that the death of one of the spouses provides for the legal ownership of the home to pass solely to the survivor spouse.

How Property is Divided between Divorcing Spouses

■ **equitable distribution**

A legal concept some states use to determine a fair division of marital assets based on a couples' particular set of facts.

The majority of states apply property division laws that utilize the legal concept known as **equitable distribution**. States using equitable division also look at the earnings and losses of both spouses during the marriage, but the allocation of the marital assets and debts usually is based on the facts of the individual marriage. Equitable distribution does not mean that the assets of the married couple will be cut down the middle so that each spouse receives an equal part of the assets. Rather, the emphasis is on the court's interpretation of a fair division of the marital assets for a particular couple under a particular set of factors. Each state using an equitable distribution standard has a state statute listing the factors to consider in determining how a couple's assets can be allocated. Examples of these factors include need and ability to pay, duration of the marriage, age of the parties, physical and mental health of the parties, standard of living during the marriage and likelihood that each party can maintain a reasonably comparable standard of living, earning capacities, educational level, employability of the parties, parental responsibilities for children, history of the financial and non-financial contributions to the marriage, personal assets of each party, and property distribution to each party.

The minority of states apply the community property concept. Basically, states using community property statutes look at all of the earnings and losses that both spouses incurred during the marriage and split them between the parties.

Issues Involving Death, Divorce, and Beneficiaries

The majority of states provide that if a person dies without drafting a will and without children, her spouse will inherit all of the deceased spouse's assets. The majority of states also provide that the spouse of a married person with children who dies without drafting a will usually splits the deceased person's assets with those children. Clients who are planning to divorce or are separated should not permit soon-to-be ex-spouses access to important documents such as a will. The beneficiary designation on any assets (such as stocks, bank accounts, IRAs, life insurance, and employment benefits) should be changed. The soon–to-be ex-spouse may have to sign a beneficiary waiver prior to any divorce judgment.

The Divorce Discovery Process

Paralegals often take the lead in preparing the discovery needed in a divorce case. Emotions run high during a divorce, and paralegals should be aware of how emotionally draining a divorce can be for a client. This is especially true when the divorce involves elderly spouses who may have been married for a long period of time.

Creating and answering interrogatories and depositions and sending and receiving notices to produce documents are part of the discovery process in a typical divorce case. Each party's divorce attorney usually sends *interrogatories* to the other side. The interrogatories usually ask extensively about a couple's finances and any other issues that may be in dispute. The answers to all interrogatories should aid attorneys in preparing a case for depositions and possibly for trial. Experts and appraisers may be hired to accurately determine the value of marital property.

A contentious divorce may ultimately lead to a trial, but trials occur in a very small percentage of cases. Across the nation, courts encourage spouses to settle their cases without going to trial. Many courts foster the settlement of divorces by making mandatory settlement conferences a standard practice. When the divorcing spouses agree on a negotiated property settlement, the matters agreed to are memorialized on paper in a **property settlement agreement**. Courts usually schedule a hearing to have the parties publicly attest to the claims they made in the complaint and incorporate the property settlement agreement into the final judgment of divorce.

Alimony

Alimony is defined as an allowance from one spouse to another that usually continues until the recipient spouses remarries, dies, or perhaps begins cohabitating with another partner. Alimony is called *spousal maintenance* or *spouse support* in some states. Historically, alimony was viewed as a male-only

---

property settlement agreement

Divorcing spouses who agree on negotiated matters concerning marital property, support and/or custody arrangements memorialize those agreed decisions on paper in a property settlement agreement.

alimony

An allowance from one spouse to another that usually continues until the recipient's spouse remarries, dies, or perhaps begins co-habitating with another partner. Alimony is called *spousal maintenance* or *spouse support* in some states.

responsibility. It was usually linked to spousal conduct during the marriage. This often necessitated an extensive he-said, she-said confrontation for the courts to untangle. No-fault divorce reforms inspired the courts to look upon divorce as a fresh start for both spouses. Courts across the nation began to look upon permanent alimony awards as the levying of an unfair and lifelong burden on the payor-spouse. The new no-fault thinking began to foster a fresh-start approach by granting alimony awards with a definite cutoff date. Most courts told spouses claiming a need for alimony (the majority being women) that they should retrain themselves to become self-supporting.

The problem with attempting to retrain every divorcing spouse with a disparate financial position from that of the ex-spouse is that many spouses are never able to regain the economic status enjoyed before their divorce. For example, the long-term housewife who maintained the home so that her husband could be free of household worries and pursue his career is seldom able to financially recoup all of those years spent at home.

The judicial pendulum has swung to a middle ground in the weighing of the economic consequence of divorce. Today courts will award permanent alimony where the factual circumstances include one spouse's long-term household contributions (even if they are nonmonetary). Considering one of the spouse's unequal post-divorce earning capacity, failure to award permanent alimony in such situations is usually looked upon as unjust. Courts often award permanent alimony when the age or health of the dependent spouse precludes her from becoming self-supporting.

So how do courts determine how much alimony is reasonable and fair? They ask a five-part question: When, why, how, how much, and for how long should alimony be paid? The considerations in determining the needs of an economic-ally dependent spouse typically include the individual dependent spouse's needs, that spouse's ability to contribute to the fulfillment of those needs, and the supporting spouse's ability to pay and maintain the dependent spouse at the former living standard enjoyed during the couple's marriage.

The hunt for the answer to that question is complicated by the types of alimony generally used across the country. For example, different types available in most but not all states include alimony *pendente lite,* rehabilitative alimony (or transitional support), lump-sum alimony (or alimony in gross), limited duration (or term) alimony, reimbursement alimony, and permanent alimony. Alimony *pendente lite* is temporary monetary support payments that one spouse makes to the other spouse while they are waiting for their divorce to be finalized. Rehabilitative alimony, sometimes called transitional support, is payable for a specific period of time and ceases when the supported spouse is self-supporting. For example, a spouse seeking rehabilitative alimony may want to return to college to train for a career. Lump-sum alimony, also called alimony in gross, entails a monetary payout of the total alimony amount that has been ordered. However, receiving lump-sum alimony does not preclude periodic alimony payments. Limited duration alimony, also known as term alimony, is often utilized where rehabilitation of the dependent spouse is not necessary or the marriage was of a short duration. Reimbursement alimony is typically awarded in cases in which one party supported the other party's pursuit of an advanced education.

The facts in the following case supported the award of permanent alimony because the circumstances indicated that the dependent spouse was a woman in her fifties who was unlikely to be rehabilitated to a level that would allow her to reach the standard of living she enjoyed during her lengthy marriage.

CASE LAW	***In re Marriage of Donna J. Robinson v. Robinson***

184 Ill.App.3D 235, 539 N.E.2D 1365, 132 Ill. Dec. 559 (1989)

Facts:	On May 26, 1983, the petitioner, Donna Robinson, filed a petition for dissolution of marriage. The Court entered a memorandum on June 18, 1985 regarding property division. That decision awarded the wife maintenance, which was to be used to rehabilitate herself through education or job training to obtain gainful employment. The husband was ordered to pay $1,500.00 per month, beginning July 1, 1985 for 24 months; and $750.00 per month, beginning July 1, 1987, for the next 36 months.
	On July 12, 1985, the Court's final judgment amended the previous memorandum to state the payments beginning July 1, 1987 for $750.00 were to be paid for a total of 35 months instead of 37 months. This decision barred any further maintenance from the Defendant. In addition, the Court also awarded a cash payment to the wife from the husband totaling $175,000 to be paid as follows: $10,000 by August 1, 1985; $15,000 by October 1, 1985; and $150,000 to be paid in ten annual principal installments of $15,000 each, plus annual interest payments at a rate of 10% payable from July 1, 1985 on the remaining balance and payable on the first of July of each year starting on July 1, 1986. The Court placed a lien on the 400-acre farm to secure these payments.
	On October 1, 1987, the husband, respondent, filed a petition to modify maintenance payments, stating a substantial reduction in income since the decree of dissolution. The Court found that the maintenance could not be modified since it was maintenance in gross, and thus non-modifiable. The respondent appealed further.
	Respondent argued that Section 510 of the Illinois Marriage and Dissolution of Marriage Act (the Act) does not distinguish between maintenance and maintenance in gross. Alleging further that all maintenance is modifiable under certain circumstances, Petitioner responded that the maintenance was rehabilitative maintenance in gross.
	The Court found that the respondent did not correctly cite the law. It stated that the goal of the Act was to help and encourage a spouse seeking maintenance to regain dormant employment skills or to develop new ones. A specific termination date should not be set unless evidence supported that the dependent spouse would be able to support his or herself at a specific time period.
Issue:	Whether the trial Court erred in determining that the original maintenance order was for maintenance in gross and as such non-modifiable.
Court's Reasoning:	Circumstances reveal that it was not maintenance in gross that was ordered, but rehabilitative maintenance. The petitioner was married for 34 years. The petitioner was never employed outside of the home, nor did she ever receive her high school diploma because she married when she was 16 years old. Therefore, as a woman in her 50s, and solely dependent on her husband, rehabilitative maintenance was an incorrect decision and one

(continues)

which the statute was designed to recognize. This Court finds that the maintenance is modifiable upon showing a change of circumstances. Furthermore, we hold that the petitioner, upon remand, may seek to have the Court modify the automatic termination date.

Holding: Judgment reversed and remanded for further proceedings.

Case Discussion: This case is a good example of what can happen when you stir up a pot but you are not sure what is on the bottom. Following your reading of the case, you should understand that Mr. Robinson went to court to modify his ex-wife's alimony payment downward. The alimony was described by the original court as rehabilitative alimony. Mr. Robinson lost his first motion for modification; but not satisfied, he appealed that loss. The court in this case looked to the Illinois Marriage and Dissolution of Marriage Act and determined that Mrs. Robinson could return to court to *extend* the previously ordered payments because in her situation as an older woman dependent on her spouse, she would have very little likelihood of rehabilitation.

Modification of the Alimony Obligation

In discussions about alimony, the bottom line is that a judge's order to pay alimony is subject to the court's review and modification at a later time. The spouse's return to court to seek an increase, a decrease, or an ending of alimony has the burden of proving that *changed circumstances* warrant such modification. What is considered a changed circumstance? Examples include a change in income, a change in employment status, cohabitation with an adult sexual partner by the payee spouse, and changes in a medical condition, to name a few.

Termination of the Alimony Obligation

Numerous factors come into play as to when a spouse should receive alimony, and numerous factors can lead to a court terminating an alimony obligation. The four main reasons that most courts terminate alimony include remarriage of the payee spouse, death of the payee or the payor spouse, cohabitation by the payee spouse, and disability of the payor spouse.

SUMMARY

Senior citizens are part of a growing trend in cohabitation. According to the U.S. Census Bureau, cohabitation of unmarried opposite-sex couples aged 65 and older rose 73 percent from 1990 to 1999. Some older cohabiting partners may live together to avoid the possibility of divorce and to keep alimony from a previous marriage. Another reason for cohabitation is that disabled citizens receiving public assistance may lose financial benefits if they marry. Also, a significant number of unmarried partners sharing a household are gay and are not legally permitted to marry even if they wanted to. A small minority of states now allow unmarried heterosexual and homosexual partners to register their partnership or proceed with a limited civil union in order to activate some marriage-like rights. Senior citizens receiving financial benefits from a deceased spouse may lose those benefits upon remarriage. If a surviving spouse remarries before turning 60, any Social Security benefits from the previous marriage are forfeited. Remarriage after 60 has no effect on Social Security ineligibility. Medical care providers and Medicaid cannot look to a cohabiting but unregistered partner to pay the other partner's medical bills, but a spouse can be required to pay a spouse's medical and other bills. The term *domestic partner* usually refers to a person who has been designated as another's life partner outside marriage and who, because of such designation, may receive benefits of some kind.

Being an unmarried partner sharing a household can create far-reaching emotional and financial ramifications. Unmarried and cohabiting couples are largely on their own in crafting legal protection that fits their particular partnership. A prenuptial agreement, also known as an antenuptial agreement, is a contract that two individuals make *before* their marriage to each other. However, such a contract does not take effect until *after* the individuals are married to each other. Certain key items should be included in a prenuptial agreement:

1. A list of all assets, liabilities, income, and expectations of gifts and inheritances

2. A description of how premarital debts will be paid

3. A description of what happens to each party's premarital property in reference to appreciation, gains, income, rental, dividends, and proceeds of such property in the event of death or divorce

4. A decision about who will own the marital or secondary homes in the event of death or divorce

5. A specification of the status of gifts, inheritances, and trusts that either spouse receives or benefits from whether before or after the marriage

6. Clarification of what will happen to each type of property, such as real estate, artwork, furniture, and jewelry

7. A decision on the amount allocated for alimony, maintenance, or spousal support or a provision for a waiver or property settlement instead of support

8. Details of death benefits stating what each party will provide for the other

9. A decision about medical, disability, life, and long-term care insurance

The divorce pleading that begins the divorce lawsuit is called the complaint (also called the petition in some states), and it is filed by the plaintiff (also called the petitioner in some states). The complaint should describe why the court has jurisdiction to hear the complaint, what the cause of action (the legal reason the plaintiff is seeking a divorce) is, and what the plaintiff wants in the way of a financial and property settlement. If children are involved, the complaint also should detail the plaintiff's wishes pertaining to custody, support, and visitation. All 50 states have a requirement that a divorcing couple's finances and budget be detailed and submitted to the court. The defendant (also called the respondent in some states) should file either an answer or a waiver of service. If the defendant fails to respond to the complaint, the court will issue a default judgment. A defendant also may include a counterclaim in the answer. An important step is ensuring that the pleadings have been properly served upon the parties. Among all of the states, the courts analyze a variety of factors to determine whether alimony should be ordered in a particular case. The types of alimony (depending on the state) include rehabilitative, lump-sum, maintenance in gross, limited duration or term, reimbursement, and permanent. In the case of changed circumstances, alimony is subject to the court's review and modification. The majority of states apply the concept of equitable distribution to determine the financial settlement of divorcing spouses. A minority of states use the community property model. Today courts award permanent alimony where the factual circumstances include one spouse's long-term household contributions (even if they are nonmonetary).

■ KEY TERMS

acceptance	equitable distribution	parole evidence
alimony	equitable remedy	payee spouse
antenuptial agreement	express contract	payor spouse
civil marriage	full disclosure of assets	prenuptial agreement
civil union	implied contract	property settlement agreement
community property	judicial separation	reciprocal beneficiaries
consideration	marriage	rescission
contract	no-fault divorce statute	separate property
divorce complaint	offer	Uniform Premarital Agreement Act
domestic partner	palimony	(UPAA)

REVIEW QUESTIONS_____

1. Explain why the elderly are a part of the growing cohabitation trend?

2. Explain the development during the late twentieth and early twenty-first century of new legal protections for cohabitating partners.

3. In the *Marvin* case, did the court take on the role of protector of the institution of marriage, follow basic contract law, or combine those two elements? Does expanding the rights of an unmarried cohabitant to include some or all of the rights of a spouse result in an appropriate expansion of individual rights?

4. How have contract and/or equitable remedies been applied to the scenario of being unmarried but cohabitating?

5. What are typical state requirements for drafting a valid prenuptial agreement?

6. What four steps should adult children consider when dealing with a parent's remarriage?

7. What topics should be discussed and decided upon when elderly clients consider the drafting of a prenuptial agreement?

8. How was a constructive trust applied in the *Martin v. Farber* case?

9. What is the first step in determining a court's jurisdiction over a person?

10. How many states have no-fault divorce statutes?

11. Find and read your state's divorce statutes. What did you find to be most interesting?

12. What is a judicial separation?

13. What is a separate maintenance action?

14. What are the differences between a property distribution that is determined using community property statutes versus one that is determined using equitable property division statutes?

15. What assets are usually immune from distributions?

16. What types of alimony are available in some but not all states?

17. Why would a court be more likely to grant permanent alimony after a long-term marriage?

18. When is an alimony obligation typically terminated?

ETHICS ALERT_____

Paralegal Luke had known Bridget and Robert for years before Luke's boss, Tara Jensen, agreed to draft the couple's prenuptial agreement. In fact, Bridget is Luke's longtime neighbor. Should Luke have any ethical concerns regarding Bridget being a neighbor and now a client of the law firm where he works? Robert also wants to save some money and, instead of hiring his own attorney, have Tara represent him and Bridget as a couple. After all, Robert and Bridget are in love, want to save up for a honeymoon, and have already agreed to the terms they want in the prenuptial agreement. Should Tara help Robert and Bridget save some legal fees? Why or why not?

▧ HELPFUL WEB SITES

US MARRIAGE LAWS <HTTP://WWW.USMARRIAGELAWS.COM>   This Web site provides marriage requirements and laws in the United States and selected countries.

GO4MARRIAGE.COM <HTTP://WWW.GO4MARRIAGE.COM>   This matchmaking site provides informative descriptions of Hindu, Muslim, and Christian marriage laws.

▧ ENDNOTES

[1] Lyric from song lyricist Sammy Cahn's Oscar-nominated film *High Time* (1961).

[2] United States Census Bureau, Population Survey 2002.

[3] States that permit civil unions include Vermont, Massachusetts, New Jersey, and California.

[4] Schone, Barbara, PhD, and Weinick, Robin, PhD, "Health-Related Behaviors and Benefits of Marriage for Elderly Persons," *The Gerontologist*, October 1998, page 618.

[5] United States Census Bureau Population Survey, 2000.

[6] Social Security Administration

[7] Gallo, Nancy R., *Introduction to Family Law*, Delmar, Cengage Learning (2004).

[8] Booth, Michael, "Palimony After Death Do Us Part," *New Jersey Law Journal*, October 28, 2002, page 14.

[9] Solot, Dorian, "No Ring to It: Considering a Less Married Future," *Jewish Public Forum Archive*, August 25, 2002, pages 1, 9.

[10] CAL. FAM. CODE ANN Section 4100 (1) (2003).

[11] Podell, Peggy L., "Before Your Client Says I Do," *American Bar Association Journal*, August 1999, page 80.

[12] "Premarital Agreement," *Family Advocate*, 1995, page 8.

[13] Weidel, Cecile C., "Love on the Dotted Line," *American Bar Association Journal*, May 2000, page 25.

[14] Grama, Joanna Lyn, "The New Newlyweds: Marriage Among the Elderly, Suggestions to the Elder Law Practitioner," *The Elder Law Journal*, Vol. 7, January 11, 2000, page 379.

[15] Paul, Pamela, "Mom's in Love Again," *Time* Bonus Section: Connections, April 2003, page 5.

[16] Baskie, Jeffrey A., "Time to Change Your Will," *Family Advocate*, 1996, page 18.

[17] Schramm, David, *What Could Divorce Be Costing Your State?* Utah State University, June 25, 2003.

[18] Division of Vital Statistics, National Center for Health Statistics, CDC

Online Companion™
For additional resources, please go to
http://www.paralegal.delmar.cengage.com

CHAPTER 7

Financial Planning

OBJECTIVES

After completing this chapter, you will be able to:

- List the sources of retirement income.
- Explain the differences between Social Security, SSI, and OASDI benefits.
- Explain the eligibility requirements for different types of Social Security Administration benefits.
- Describe the Social Security Administration appeals process.
- Describe the objectives of the Medicare and Medicaid programs.
- Explain the ramification of taxes on income and inheritance.
- List the financing options of long-term care.
- Explain the benefits and negatives of reverse mortgages.
- Explain the use of viatical agreements.

"Every citizen will be able, in his productive years when he is earning, to insure himself against the ravages of illness in his old age."

**LYNDON JOHNSON
AT THE SIGNING OF THE
MEDICARE ACT ON
JULY 21, 1965**

INTRODUCTION

Paraphrasing *Of Mice and Men*, by novelist John Steinbeck, the best-laid financial plans of men and women often go awry. This is particularly true when discussing the subject of long-range financial and retirement planning.

A significant number of baby boomers are reportedly planning to deal with their long-range financial needs (and possible lack of saving) by working longer than their fathers and mothers did, but such plans may not be realistic.[1] For example, although over half of all baby boomers expect to work past their 65th birthdays, only 13 percent of all current retirees actually did so. In fact, as of 2005, just 60 percent of 60-year-olds, 32 percent of 65-year-olds, and 19 percent of 70-year-olds were still employed.[2] So while many workers plan to keep working, life events sometimes interrupt those plans. For example, unexpected illness, unemployment, and age bias have been blamed for forcing full-time employees into retirement. At the same time, life expectancies have increased and it has been reported that there is a 50 percent chance of one member of a married couple living past 90 years of age.[3] Obviously, this increases the need for longer projections with regard to retirement planning and makes the topic of finances more important for elder law clients.

If most of the American population will not be working past 65 years of age, from where will their source of income derive? Some retirees can look to their savings. Fortunately for some, median net worth of households headed by people over 65 years old was close to $200,000 in 2004, according to the Federal Reserve. However, the Federal Reserve has also reported that one in seven households headed by individuals 65 to 74 years old are worth $10,000 or less. Current retirees report that 58 percent look to the Social Security Administration's (SSA's) benefits as a major source of income. In fact, the Social Security trust fund paid out $454 billion to 46 million beneficiaries in 2002.[4] Some baby boomers will not be eligible to receive full Social Security benefits until they reach 66 years of age or older. Traditional pension plans have been cited as a major source of income for 43 percent of current retirees. However, traditional pension plans are dwindling in private sector employment and are becoming outnumbered by employee-funded private investment plans. Thirty-two percent of current retirees have cited personal investments as a major source of income as well.[5]

Saving for retirement is a challenging goal for America's women. The median income for America's retired women was $12,080 in 2004 compared to $21,102 for retired men. Historically, women have spent less time working outside the home and have earned less than men. This means that women have less to contribute to retirement savings accounts and receive smaller pensions and Social Security benefits. In fact, Social Security benefits are the only source of retirement income for 25 percent of unmarried women and fewer than 20 percent of women 65 years and older received private pension income in 2000.[6]

Whether they are current retirees or baby boomers who are still working, a typical concern for elder law clients is whether they will be able to preserve their assets to make sure they have enough to last throughout their lives. In this regard, elder law attorneys can offer financial and retirement planning strategies to benefit clients. Paralegals can be of assistance in drafting the documents needed to carry out an attorney's recommendations.

SOCIAL SECURITY BENEFITS

Social Security benefits are a major factor in the financial solvency of many Americans. These benefits have been called a *lifeline* for the 20 percent of Americans that depend *solely* on Social Security benefits, particularly the widowed, divorced, orphaned, and disabled.[7] The majority of Americans over 65 years old depend on Social Security benefits for at least 58 percent of their annual income. The average benefit paid in 2007 was $963 per month. The maximum Social Security benefit available at full retirement age in 2007 was $2,116 per month. How are benefits determined? According to the SSA, if a man was born January 2, 1942, he would have reached full retirement age in November 2007 (age 65 years and 10 months). If he paid the maximum in Social Security taxes for most of his working years, he would have been eligible to begin receiving an annual Social Security benefit of $24,544. This represents about 30 percent of the person's average Social Security taxable income based on his 35 highest earning years from age 22 until retirement.[8]

Benefits are not so generous that the typical elder law client can or should depend on Social Security benefits payments as his sole source of retirement income. The national dependency on Social Security benefits explains why any tinkering with the Social Security system fosters strong feelings across the country. Even a casual observer of the news media knows that the solvency of the Social Security benefits programs has been a hot news item and election issue for years.

Elder law attorneys and their staff must understand the importance of those benefits to most of their clients and, more importantly, understand how the Social Security system works and is integrated into the life and financial plans of those clients. In addition, elder law attorneys and their staff must be prepared to appeal any improper denials of Social Security benefits and navigate the administrative intricacies of the SSA. The SSA's internal operations manual is the Program Operations Manual System (POMS). The POMS is helpful, but it does not carry the status of agency regulation. The POMS is no longer published in paper form and can be accessed by CD or read online. Refer to "Helpful Web Sites" at the end of this chapter for the SSA's online address.

Fortunately, many Americans plan early in their working lives to use their Social Security benefits as a *supplement* to pensions and employ other investment strategies designed to support their post-working lives. These investment strategies may include 401k and 403B plans, IRAs, real estate and business ownership, and the bond and stock markets.

Social Security: Where It Began

Otto von Bismarck, then the prime minister of Germany, introduced the first pension system in Germany in 1890. Bismarck's philosophy of government-mandated protections being put into place for retiring workers is fundamentally similar to the SSA system developed in the United States.

The original concept of providing benefits to America's retired workforce is attributed to President Franklin D. Roosevelt's New Deal legislation of the 1930s Depression era. In particular, the Social Security Act set into motion a legislative snowball of entitlement legislation that gained momentum. The Old Age Survivors & Disability Insurance (OASDI) is the official name for U.S. Social Security benefits, the federal program that gives money raised from a payroll tax to retired and disabled citizens. The amendments to the original 1930s Social Security Act are plentiful, but standing out among the many are the **Medicare** and **Medicaid** amendments.

The Differences between OASDI and Supplemental Security Income (SSI)

The OASDI benefits should not be confused (although they often are) with **Supplemental Security Income (SSI)** benefits. OASDI benefits are funded by contributions made to a *general revenues fund;* SSI benefits are not. Those individuals who are eligible to receive SSI benefits are physically or mentally disabled in ways that are statutorily described and whose incomes are within extremely low limits. SSI is not age-restricted, but approximately 2 million SSI recipients were 65 years of age and older in 2007. SSI recipients do not have to be eligible to receive Social Security or OASDI benefits in order to be eligible for SSI benefits.

SSI benefits are not based on the same insurance concept as Social Security retirement benefits. It is not necessary for SSI recipients to have made contributions into a fund or to have worked for a certain period of time to be an SSI recipient. SSI is a means-tested program. It is a state supplement to Social Security benefits if an individual meets certain criteria. All SSI recipients also are categorically eligible for Medicaid funding.

medicare

A government program that provides health insurance to U.S. residents age 65 and older regardless of income. Coverage for younger individuals with disabilities is also available.

medicaid

A federally funded and state-administered health insurance program providing all types of medical care to individuals who cannot afford to pay for some or all of their medical bills.

supplemental security income (SSI)

Benefits for citizens who are physically or mentally disabled and whose incomes are within extremely low limits.

How to Become Eligible for OASDI Benefits

The Social Security Act usually covers any person working in the United States full-time. A covered full-time worker and his employer each contribute a certain percentage of the worker's salary. (In 2007, it was 6.2 percent each.) This dual contribution is commonly known as the FICA tax because it was created from the Federal Insurance Contribution Act. A self-employed worker has the unenviable task of sending 12.4 percent (the 2007 figure) to the FICA coffers. If a worker is lucky enough to have unearned income or income in excess of $97,500 (the 2007 amount), he does not have to remit any FICA tax on income earned over $97,500. Full-time employees of the federal government hired before 1984 and railroad workers are not covered and do not receive benefits under the Social Security Act; instead, they receive a federal pension. The federal government and railroad employees can still qualify for Medicare coverage.

Will Benefits Be Available in the Future?

A cursory review of the current assets of the Social Security benefits system would appear to lead one to conclude that the system is solvent. After all, the trust funds held by the **Social Security Administration** had assets of $1.378 trillion in 2002. This amount was $165 billion higher than in 2001. However, the pundits who study this type of thing predict that the graying of the large number of baby boomers will mean a smaller number of employed workers and more retired baby boomers seeking benefits. And therein lies the chief problem with the funding formula of the Social Security benefit system. The FICA tax of current workers is supposed to be funding the Social Security benefits of the retired workers. Trustees of the Social Security and Medicare programs, the nation's two largest benefit programs, have announced that the benefits for 78 million baby boomers expected to retire will not be available by 2019 and 2041, respectively, unless the federal government can fund the programs differently.[9]

social security administration
The federal agency that provides retired individuals with income.

Who Is Entitled to Receive Benefits?

The original legislation was designed with a retirement age of 65 years, but solvency concerns and the longer life spans of Americans has led to some changes. The retirement age has been increased to 67 years old for anyone born after 1960. Social Security benefits also may be paid to the survivors of a deceased eligible worker including a spouse, ex-spouses, children, and other family members. Refer to Exhibit 7–1 to review the age requirements for Social Security eligibility.

The Individual Worker

First, to qualify for benefits for himself, a worker must be fully insured. The fully insured status is determined by counting the number of years a worker has been employed. If a worker has at least 10 years of total employment and FICA contributions, he is considered fully insured. If a nondisabled worker retires after he turns 62 but before the eligible retirement age, his Social Security check will be reduced by five-ninths of one percent for the first 36 months of retirement before his eligible retirement age and five-twelfths of one percent for any additional months of early retirement.

EXHIBIT 7–1   SOCIAL SECURITY ELIGIBILITY

You can retire anytime between age 62 and full retirement age. However, if you start benefits early, they are reduced a fraction of a percent for each month before your full retirement age.

The following chart lists age 62 reduction amounts and includes examples based on an estimated monthly benefit of $1,000 at full retirement age. If you go to the Social Security Eligibility web page the site will ask you to **click on your year of birth** to find out how much your benefit will be reduced if you retire between age 62 and full retirement age.

Note: If your birthday is on January 1, your benefit is figured as if your birthday was the previous year.

Full Retirement and Age 62 Benefit by Year of Birth						
Year of Birth	Full (Normal) Retirement Age	Months between Age 62 and Full Retirement Age	At Age 62			
			Amount a $1,000 Retirement Benefit Is Reduced To	Amount a Retirement Benefit Is Reduced By	Amount a $500 Spouse's Benefit Is Reduced To	Amount a Spouse's Benefit Is Reduced By
1937 or earlier	65	36	$800	20.00%	$375	25.00%
1938	65 and 2 months	38	$791	20.83%	$370	25.83%
1939	65 and 4 months	40	$783	21.67%	$366	26.67%
1940	65 and 6 months	42	$775	22.50%	$362	27.50%
1941	65 and 8 months	44	$766	23.33%	$358	28.33%

(continues)

EXHIBIT 7–1   SOCIAL SECURITY ELIGIBILITY *(continued)*

Full Retirement and Age 62 Benefit by Year of Birth						
Year of Birth	Full (Normal) Retirement Age	Months between Age 62 and Full Retirement Age	At Age 62			
			Amount a $1,000 Retirement Benefit Is Reduced To	Amount a Retirement Benefit Is Reduced By	Amount a $500 Spouse's Benefit Is Reduced To	Amount a Spouse's Benefit Is Reduced By
1942	65 and 10 months	46	$758	24.17%	$354	29.17%
1943–1954	66	48	$750	25.00%	$350	30.00%
1955	66 and 2 months	50	$741	25.83%	$345	30.83%
1956	66 and 4 months	52	$733	26.67%	$341	31.67%
1957	66 and 6 months	54	$725	27.50%	$337	32.50%
1958	66 and 8 months	56	$716	28.33%	$333	33.33%
1959	66 and 10 months	58	$708	29.17%	$329	34.17%
1960 and later	67	60	$700	30.00%	$325	35.00%

1. If you were born on January 1, you should refer to the previous year.

2. If you were born on the first of the month, the benefit is figured as if your birthday was the previous month. You must be at least 62 for the entire month to receive benefits.

3. Percentages are approximate due to rounding.

4. The maximum benefit for the spouse is 50 percent of the benefit the worker would receive at full retirement age. The percent of reduction for the spouse should be applied after the automatic 50 percent reduction. Percentages are approximate due to rounding.

If an individual is eligible for Social Security benefits, the question of when to retire and begin collecting those benefits is important. Younger retirement means more checks but at a reduced rate. However, a worker who delays retirement past his eligible age will receive an increased benefit. Waiting to collect means larger checks but collecting them for a shorter period. Retiring later has no negative effect on Medicare benefits received or Medicare eligibility. A Social Security penalty is applied to any income earned by a worker between 62 years old and the SSA's designation of the worker's eligible retirement age. In 2006, workers who were eligible for benefits lost $1 of Social Security benefits for every $2 earned over $12,480. A different earning limit is applied for each year until a worker reaches eligible retirement age. Laws stemming from the Senior Citizens' Right to Work Act now allow workers who have reached their eligible retirement age to continue to work and earn at a lesser rate of earnings' forfeiture. For example, in 2007, every $3 in excess earnings over an individual's Social Security benefits payment resulted in a reduced $1 forfeiture. In addition, beginning in 2007, the SSA did not begin forfeiture until a worker earned $34,440 above his Social Security payment.

Derivative Beneficiaries

Survivors of eligible workers are known as derivative beneficiaries. Any benefits paid to a derivative beneficiary are based on the deceased worker's earnings history. Survivors include the deceased worker's spouse, minor children, adult children disabled before age 22, and perhaps other dependent family members. The survivors must file a benefits claim by contacting their closest Social Security office. When filing a benefits claim form, the survivor must have the following documents:

1. Original birth and death certificates of the decedent
2. Marriage certificate if applicable
3. All applicable Social Security numbers
4. Copies of the decedent's most recent federal income tax return

There are two types of survivor benefits: a one-time **lump sum death benefit** of $255 (the 2007 figure) to be used toward burial expenses and the **survivor income benefits**. Benefits paid to derivative beneficiaries are limited to a certain amount per family. The maximum family benefit amount depends on what the deceased worker was earning. Derivative beneficiaries do not automatically receive survivor benefits. They first must past a series of eligibility thresholds. These thresholds are listed in Exhibit 7–2.

The same derivative spouse benefits based on the deceased worker's benefits are available for any divorced spouse or a surviving spouse. Multiple recipients do not affect the monetary amount to which a recipient is entitled. To be eligible, a divorced spouse must have been married to an eligible worker for at least 10 years. The benefit eligibility begins at the divorced spouse's retirement age even

lump sum death benefit

A one-time lump sum payment made by the Social Security Administration ($255) to be used toward burial expenses.

survivor income benefits

Benefits paid to a deceased worker's surviving spouse, minor children, or adult children disabled before the age of 22.

if the working spouse is still employed. However, the divorced recipient must be over 60 or at least 50 years old and disabled. A divorced spouse under 60 or a disabled former spouse under 50 cannot be remarried and continue SSA benefits eligibility under a former spouse. In addition, any surviving spouse applying for benefits must have been married at least nine months unless the deceased worker was on active military duty or the spouses were previously married to each other for at least nine months. An alleged common law surviving spouse is recognized by the SSA for spousal benefits only if the marriage in question was recognized as a common law marriage by a state that recognizes such marriages. Additional proof including signed statements from the common law spouses and two blood relatives also will assist in proving the veracity of a common law marriage.

EXHIBIT 7–2   SOCIAL SECURITY THRESHOLDS FOR SURVIVOR ELIGIBILITY

1. Full benefits to a surviving spouse at the surviving spouse's full retirement age.

2. Reduced benefits to a surviving spouse who opts to receive benefits at age 60.

3. Full benefits to a fully disabled surviving spouse at age 50.

4. Full benefits to a surviving spouse of any age if he or she cared for the deceased worker's children under age 16 *or* if the children are disabled and receiving Social Security benefits.

5. Full benefits to unmarried children under age 18 *or* up to age 19 if they are full-time high school students. Depending on certain circumstances, these benefits may extend to stepchildren and grandchildren.

6. Full benefits to any children who were identified as fully disabled before age 22.

7. Full benefits to any dependent parent of the deceased over the age of 62.

How to Apply for Benefits

Each person in the workforce receives notification from the SSA when he has worked long enough to fulfill the requirements to receive Social Security payments. The estimated amount of an individual's future Social Security payment is included in annual notifications from the SSA. The notifications should be scrutinized so that any errors can be brought to the attention of the SSA. An individual must apply for his benefit called the *primary insurance amount* (PIA) at the local Social Security office. Social Security payments are not automatically made to eligible recipients. All applicants and beneficiaries must file Form SSA-1696-U4 to formally designate a representative to deal with the SSA. If necessary, the SSA may appoint another person called a *representative payee* to receive benefits on behalf of a recipient. Typically, a representative payee is appointed by the agency when the original payee is unable to protect his own interests. If a guardianship or conservatorship has already been established, the agency will accept a court-appointed guardian or conservator as a representative payee.

Any worker who is unsure about his benefits may request a copy of his work credits earned, total wages earned, and Social Security taxes paid by contacting the SSA and requesting an *Earnings and Benefit Estimate Statement*.

A husband and a wife may receive their individually earned Social Security benefits based upon the number of years in the workforce. If a spouse dies, the local SSA agency office should be notified. A surviving spouse is entitled to continue to receive his individual Social Security benefits payment or may opt to receive his deceased spouse's Social Security benefits payment if the amount is higher than his own. The surviving spouse will not continue to receive both Social Security benefits payments. Social Security recipients have had mandatory direct deposit since 1998 in an effort to curb theft. Also, an automatic *cost of living adjustment* (COLA) is made to benefits.

Challenging SSA Decisions

If a worker disagrees with the SSA's annual statement regarding the worker's earnings, he may request that a correction be made to the official record. This can be done by submitting accurate financial records to the SSA. The time limit for requesting such a correction is 3 years, 3 months, and 15 days since the end of the year in which the earnings were made. There are some limited exceptions to the time limit. Double-checking one's earnings record is important to ensure that every dollar of Social Security benefits earned will be available.

If an individual has a dispute with any OASDI determination, he also may challenge it. Such a challenge goes through basically the same process as SSI appeals and is similar to procedures used to challenge determinations (or lack thereof) of Medicare coverage. An attorney may be hired to handle such appeals, but that is not required.

There are three stages to such administrative appeals:

1. The SSA's self-monitoring review process for all case claims it denies

2. A hearing to be held before an Administrative Law Judge

3. Any appeal of an Administrative Law Judge heard by the SSA Appeals Council

Such an appeal should be made within 60 days, but the 60 day period for appeals can be extended for good cause. A decision can be *affirmed, modified,* or *reversed* at any stage of the appeal process. Any closed case can be reopened by an Appeals Council within four years of the initial decision. Administrative remedies must be exhausted before an appeal can be made to the federal courts. However, if the constitutional ramifications of an SSA provision are challenged, a case can go straight to the federal courts and bypass the many administrative remedies. Published Social Security Rulings (SSRs) are binding on the SSA and administrative judges, but they do not have the force of law.[10]

MEDICARE

The maintenance and/or loss of health are of increasing concern as people age. Health issues can prevent individuals from living the lifestyle they want, interfere with their work, affect their relationships, and generally impact their quality of life. The lack of medical care and health insurance brings additional worries. Responding to the fact that a lack of health insurance had a huge impact on the medical care then available for America's senior citizens, the federal government created the Medicare program in 1965.

Medicare is health insurance provided by the federal government to seven out of eight of U.S. residents 65 years and older whether they are rich or poor. Medicare also offers medical insurance coverage for younger people with disabilities. There were approximately 41 million beneficiaries in 2005, with over 62 million beneficiaries expected by 2020. There were approximately $284 billion in Medicare expenditures in 2005, with expenditures expected to rise to $898 billion in 2020.[11]

A prominent part of the Social Security Act, Medicare is under Title XVIII and Medicaid is under Title XIX. Medicare and Medicaid legislation was enacted at 42 U.S.C. Section 1395 and 42 U.S.C. Section 1396, respectively. Medicare eligibility is tied to Social Security eligibility. The federal agency responsible for Medicare and Medicaid is the U.S. Department of Health & Human Services Centers for Medicare & Medicaid. Medicare-eligible individuals need to sign up for benefits at their local Social Security office within seven months after their 65th birthday unless they are already receiving Social Security benefits or a railroad pension. Late enrollment results in a surcharge.

The Parts of Medicare

Medicare has multiple parts. Generally, **Medicare Part A** pays hospital bills and **Medicare Part B** pays an insured person's physician bills. Medicare Part C provides different options from Parts A and B, and Medicare Part D provides prescription coverage. Part A is funded from an employment tax on all income. Employed workers pay half, and employers pay the other half of the tax. An individual can enroll in Medicare A at 65 years of age even if he is still working and not yet receiving Social Security benefits. Enrollment in Social Security

medicare part a
Pays hospital bills and is funded from an employment tax on all income.

medicare part b
Pays physicians' bills.

brings automatic enrollment in Medicare Parts A and B. An individual can decline the Part B coverage. However, because of the surcharge, there is no financial incentive to put off enrollment as there is with Social Security.

Medicare Part A is usually provided cost-free, but a premium is required to receive Part B coverage. If an individual opts not to sign up for Part B when he is eligible, there is a caveat. Failure to sign up for both Parts A and B leads to permanently higher Part B premiums if Part B is purchased at a later date. The only way around this is for an individual to sign up for Part B while still working and to be covered through work or to sign up for Part B coverage within eight months of ending any work-related group coverage. Refer to Exhibit 7–3 to review a chart detailing 2007 Medicare Premiums.

Medicare Part C arrived with the Balance Budget Act of 1997. Generally known as the Medicare Advantage Plan, the purpose of Medicare Part C is to offer options not provided in the other parts. Medicare Advantage Plans are run by private companies and are similar to health maintenance organizations (HMOs) and preferred provider organizations (PPOs).[12] Medical Advantage Plans provide all of a subscriber's Part A (hospital) and Part B (medical) coverage and must cover medically necessary services. These plans generally offer extra benefits such as dental, vision, hearing, and wellness programs; and many include Part D drug coverage. These plans usually have a network of doctors that plan members must use if their health care is to be covered. The purpose of Medicare Part C is to coordinate a subscriber's care using networks and referrals, thereby managing a subscriber's care more efficiently and less expensively. The goal is a cost savings for the subscriber. Medicare does pay a monthly fee to all Medicare Part C private companies whether or not health care services are used. Examples of Medicare Advantage Plans include Medicare PPOs, Medicare HMOs, Medicare private fee-for-service plans (PFFSs), Medicare special needs plans, and Medicare medical savings account plans (MSAs).

Medicare-eligible individuals may choose to join Medicare Part C if they live in an area serviced by a plan they want to join. Individuals who already have Part A and/or Part B may change to Part C once a year during the November 15 to December 31 enrollment period. However, costs may be higher than those under the Original Medicare Plan if a treating doctor is not in a Part C plan network. Part C subscribers also have to pay for Part B coverage. An advantage of joining Part C is that **Medigap insurance** is not necessary. Medigap insurance covers all medical treatment not covered by the primary Parts A and B Medicare coverage.

■ **medigap insurance**
Insurance coverage for all medical treatment not covered by the primary Parts A and B Medicare coverage.

Any spouse, widow, or widower who is eligible to receive Social Security benefits because of his spouse's work record also is eligible to enroll in the Medicare programs when he reaches 65 years of age. A divorce interrupts the eligibility only when former spouses were married less than 10 years. Multiple ex-spouses as well as a current spouse can be eligible for Medicare enrollment.

Traditional Medicare Parts A and B are still the choice of most eligible Americans. Medicare Part C ushered in a relatively huge change in coverage for all Medicare recipients. For example, a proactive position on medical screenings

EXHIBIT 7–3 MEDICARE PREMIUMS FOR THE FOUR PARTS OF MEDICARE (2008)

Part A (Hospital Insurance) Monthly Premium

Most people do not pay a Part A premium because they paid Medicare taxes while working. You pay up to $423 each month if you do not get premium-free Part A.*

Part B (Medical Insurance) Monthly Premium

IF YOUR YEARLY INCOME IS		YOU PAY
File Individual Tax Return	**File Joint Tax Return**	
$82,000 or below	$164,000 or below	$96.40*
$82,001–$102,000	$164,001–$204,000	$122.20
$102,001–$153,000	$204,001–$306,000	$160.90*
$153,001–$205,000	$306,001–$410,000	$199.70*
Above $205,000	Above $410,000	$238.40*

Part C (Medicare Advantage Plan) Monthly Premium

Actual plan premiums* are available at <http://www.medicare.gov> or from the plan. You also pay the Part B premium* (and Part A if you do not get it premium-free). An extra premium is charged unkextra benefits.

Part D (Medicare Prescription Drug Plan) Monthly Premium

Actual plan premiums* are available at <http://www.medicare.gov > or from the plan. You also pay the Part B premium* (and Part A if you do not get it premium-free), or an amount for your Part D coverage is added to your Part C premium.

*If you pay a late enrollment penalty, this amount is higher.

begun with Medicare Part C eventually overlapped and led to Part B covering early detection screenings. Previously, early routine screenings were not covered by Medicare, but early detection screening coverage has subsequently proved to have saved lives and health care costs.

Prescription Coverage

A new Medicare Part D was added with the passage of an approximately 800-page bill providing prescription drug coverage. Part D became available to current Medicare Part A or Part B enrollees in 2006. Medicare Prescription Drug Coverage is insurance provided by private companies. Each Part A or Part B enrollee can choose the insurance drug plan that best fits his needs. A prospective enrollee should assess the plan's total costs, including premiums, annual deductibles, and co-payments, and drugs covered by the plan. Most Part

D plans permit a coverage gap after a person has spent a certain amount on drugs. The enrollee then must pay 100 percent of the cost until another monetary threshold of out-of-pocket costs has been met, usually (as of 2007) $3,600. Catastrophic drug coverage can be purchased for those enrollees able to pay up to $3,600 of out-of-pocket costs. After that amount, the plan picks up all costs. An individual who fails to enroll in a Part D plan when he is first eligible will face an enrollment penalty fee if he decides to enroll later. The penalty increases one percent per month after the eligibility date. This penalty can have significant financial ramifications. Anyone who is currently enrolled in a non-Medicare prescription program can contact a Medicare office for assistance in comparing his current plan to a Medicare plan. The national average for Medicare Part D premiums was $32 a month or $384 a year in 2006.[13] The final version of the 2003 Part D Health and Human Services regulations can be found at 68 Fed. Reg. 69839-6927 (December 15, 2003).

What Medicare Covers

Medicare covers specific acute medical treatment. Medicare does not pay for general custodial type care of a patient. For example, the daily management care that Alzheimer's patients need is not covered. However, Medicare does cover claims for the non-custodial treatment of Alzheimer's and other degenerative diseases (e.g., the coping therapies necessary to deal with degenerative issues). Such coverage reflects the position that Medicare benefits will pay for medical services described as *reasonable and necessary in the treatment of illness, injury, or to improve the function of a malformed body member.*[14] This means that Medicare covers the following care categories: medical care received as an inpatient in a hospital, at a skilled nursing facility, at home, and at a hospice. Each care category, in turn, has its own restrictions. Refer to Exhibit 7–4 for a list of non-hospital Medicare coverage. The Medicare program in 2007 had a deductible of $992 per benefit period for Part A and a deductible of $131 per year for Part B.

EXHIBIT 7–4   NON-HOSPITAL MEDICARE COVERAGE

Abdominal Aortic Aneurysm Screening
Ambulance Services
Ambulatory Surgery Center Fees
Blood
Bone Mass Measurement
Cardiovascular Screenings
Chiropractic Services (limited)

(continues)

EXHIBIT 7–4   NON-HOSPITAL MEDICARE COVERAGE *(continued)*

Clinical Laboratory Services

Clinical Research Studies

Colorectal Cancer Screenings

Diabetes Screenings/Diabetes Self-Management Training/Diabetes Supplies

Doctor Services

Durable Medical Equipment

Emergency Room Services

Eye Exams/Eyeglasses (limited)

Flu Shots

Foot Exams and Treatment

Glaucoma Tests

Hearing and Balance Exams

Hepatitis B Shots

Home Health Services

Mammogram Screenings

Medical Nutrition Therapy Services

Mental Health Care (Outpatient)

Occupational Therapy

Outpatient Hospital Services

Outpatient Medical and Surgical Services and Supplies

Pap Tests and Pelvic Exams (includes clinical breast exam)

Physical Exam (one-time "Welcome to Medicare" exam)

Physical Therapy

Pneumococcal Shot

Practitioner Services

Prescription Drugs (limited)

Prostate Cancer Screenings

Prosthetic/Orthotic Items

Rural Health Clinic and Federally Qualified Health Center Services

Second Surgical Opinions

Smoking Cessation (counseling to stop smoking)

Speech Language Pathology Services

Surgical Dressing Services

Telemedicine

Tests

Transplants

Travel (health care needed while traveling outside the United States)

Urgently Needed Care

Once a deductible is met, Medicare has extensive coverage for practically every hospital cost. However, hospital stays over 60 days result in a coverage reduction. Medicare applies a daily deductible for Days 61 through 90 of a hospital stay. Medicare covers a small amount of nursing home coverage. For example, Medicare limits the number of days a subscriber can stay in a nursing or hospital facility. The term *spell of illness* is used for each 60-day period beginning with a patient's entrance to a skilled nursing facility up to 60 days later. A patient still may be in a medical facility, but if he is not receiving skilled care for 60 days in a row, the spell of illness will end. Each succeeding spell of illness starts up the per-day limit on treatment and any applicable deductibles. Once the Medicare coverage ends, the patient must self-pay, become Medicaid-eligible, or already have long-term care insurance in place. Costs for covered services and supplies under Part C vary due to geographic locale. However, all Medicare Advantage Plans must cover all services and supplies covered by Part A and Part B. Part D costs vary greatly depending on plan coverage.

Appealing Medicare Decisions

Every individual entitled to Medicare also is entitled to certain guaranteed rights (e.g., the right to appeal a decision concerning a health care payment). Medicare guarantees a fair appeals process for all programs under the Medicare umbrella. Each subscriber also is entitled to a detailed list of Medicare items or services that his health care providers provided to him. This list may provide evidentiary support for a subscriber undertaking the appeal of a Medicare decision.

The requirements of the Original Medicare Plan appeals process include the following:

1. The subscriber must circle the item in question on the Medicare Summary Notice and explain the coverage disagreement.

2. The subscriber must affix his signature and include a telephone number.

3. The subscriber must send the Medicare Summary Notice to the address on the Appeals Information section.

The appeal must be made within 120 days of receiving the Medicare Summary Notice. Recent changes include the requirement that all second-level appeals, also known as Medicare reconsiderations, be conducted by Qualified Independent Contractors (QICs). See Exhibit 7–5 to review Medicare rights and Exhibit 7–6 to review the Notice of Privacy Practices for the Original Medicare Plan. The other Medicare plans and the Prescription Drug Plan have similar privacy protections in place. Subscribers to the Medicare Advantage Plan or the Medicare Prescription Drug Plan follow a similar appeals process with slight differences. For example, subscribers to the Medicare Advantage Plan have the right to a *fast-track review* by the Quality Improvement Organization (QIO) in their state if they believe they have been dismissed too early from a hospital. Medicare Advantage Plan subscribers also have access to a quick QIO review when Medicare coverage of their skilled nursing facility, home health agency, or comprehensive rehabilitation facility services are about to end.

The Medicare Prescription Drug Plan has many participating insurance companies, and the coverage decisions made by a subscriber's plan can be appealed. This is done by asking a plan for a *coverage determination*. If a plan does not respond to a subscriber's request for a drug, an appeal, or an exception, the subscriber can file a grievance with the plan sponsor or by calling 1-800-MEDICARE. Appeals of the Medicare Prescription Drug Plan must be requested within 60 days of a plan's original decision and must be made in writing unless noted otherwise by the plan. Medicare must respond within seven days for a standard appeal for a request for coverage or within 72 hours for an expedited request for coverage.

Subscribers to the Original Medicare Plan may receive notices called Advance Beneficiary Notices when a health care provider offers to provide health care services that are not likely to be covered under the Medicare plan. This notice is usually followed by a request that the provider sign an agreement stating that he will pay for the non-covered health care service. Other Medicare Plans including HMOs, PPOs, and the Medicare Prescription Drug Plans have similar methods of notification.

An expedited review of Medicare-covered services may be necessary under certain circumstances. If this is the case, a *fast appeal,* also called an *immediate appeal,* may be necessary. Again, evidentiary material will be needed from a subscriber's health care providers.

Once the internal appeals process is exhausted, subscribers have the right to appeal to an Administrative Law Judge and possibly to a federal district court. Denial of medical services is considered an action undertaken by a state through a state agency; therefore, failure to promote and protect due process through an efficient appeals process is considered a failure to provide constitutional due process.

Attorneys Advocating for Medicare Beneficiaries

It is unlikely that an elder law attorney will be asked to handle Medicare appeals because many clients in such a position cannot afford an attorney's fees. The Medicare statute does provide that an attorney can file a fee petition if the fees have been approved by the client. In addition, regulations allow for the withholding of retroactive benefits for payment of attorney fees which were previously agreed upon.

EXHIBIT 7–5   MEDICARE RIGHTS

Medicare subscribers have the following rights:

- The right to appeal Medicare coverage decisions
- The right to get information
- The right to get emergency room or urgently needed care services
- The right to see doctors and specialists and to go to Medicare-certified hospitals
- The right to participate in treatment decisions
- The right to know treatment choices
- The right to get information in a culturally competent manner in certain circumstances
- The right to file complaints
- The right to nondiscrimination
- The right to have personal and health information kept confidential

EXHIBIT 7–6   NOTICE OF PRIVACY PRACTICES FOR THE ORIGINAL MEDICARE PLAN

THIS NOTICE DESCRIBES HOW MEDICAL INFORMATION ABOUT YOU MAY BE USED AND DISCLOSED AND HOW YOU CAN GET ACCESS TO THIS INFORMATION. PLEASE REVIEW IT CAREFULLY.

By law, Medicare is required to protect the privacy of your personal medical information. Medicare is also required to give you this notice to tell you how Medicare may use and give out ("disclose") your personal medical information held by Medicare.

Medicare **must** use and give out your personal medical information to provide information:

To you or someone who has the legal right to act for you (your personal representative),

To the Secretary of the Department of Health and Human Services, if necessary, to make sure your privacy is protected, and

Where required by law.

Medicare **has the right** to use and give out your personal medical information to pay for your health care and to operate the Medicare program. For example:

Medicare Carriers use your personal medical information to pay or deny your claims, to collect your premiums, to share your benefit payment with your other insurer(s), or to prepare your Medicare Summary Notice.

(continues)

EXHIBIT 7–6 NOTICE OF PRIVACY PRACTICES FOR THE ORIGINAL MEDICARE PLAN *(continued)*

Medicare may use your personal medical information to make sure you and other Medicare beneficiaries get quality health care, to provide customer services to you, to resolve any complaints you have, or to contact you about research studies.

Medicare **may** use or give out your personal medical information for the following purposes under limited circumstances:

To State and other Federal agencies that have the legal right to receive Medicare data (such as to make sure Medicare is making proper payments and to assist Federal/State Medicaid programs),

For public health activities (such as reporting disease outbreaks),

For government health care oversight activities (such as fraud and abuse investigations),

For judicial and administrative proceedings (such as in response to a court order),

For law enforcement purposes (such as providing limited information to locate a missing person),

For research studies that meet all privacy law requirements (such as research related to the prevention of disease or disability),

To avoid a serious and imminent threat to health or safety,

To contact you about new or changed benefits under Medicare, and

To create a collection of information that can no longer be traced back to you.

By law, Medicare must have your written permission (an "authorization") to use or give out your personal medical information for any purpose that isn't set out in this notice. You may take back ("revoke") your written permission at any time, except if Medicare has already acted based on your permission.

By law, you have the right to:

See and get a copy of your personal medical information held by Medicare.

Have your personal medical information amended if you believe that it is wrong or if information is missing, and Medicare agrees. If Medicare disagrees, you may have a statement of your disagreement added to your personal medical information.

Get a listing of those getting your personal medical information from Medicare. The listing won't cover your personal medical information that was given to you or your personal representative, that was given out to pay for your health care or for Medicare operations, or that was given out for law enforcement purposes.

Ask Medicare to communicate with you in a different manner or at a different place (for example, by sending materials to a P.O. Box instead of your home address).

Ask Medicare to limit how your personal medical information is used and given out to pay your claims and run the Medicare program. Please note that Medicare may not be able to agree to your request.

Get a separate paper copy of this notice.

Look at our Medicare Privacy Practices (HIPAA) FAQs for more information on:

Exercising your rights set out in this notice.

Filing a complaint, if you believe the Original Medicare Plan has violated these privacy rights.

Filing a complaint won't affect your benefits under Medicare.

(continues)

EXHIBIT 7–6   NOTICE OF PRIVACY PRACTICES FOR THE ORIGINAL MEDICARE PLAN *(continued)*

You can also call 1-800-MEDICARE (1-800-633-4227) to get this information. Ask to speak to a Customer Service Representative about Medicare's privacy notice. TTY users should call 1-877-486-2048.

You may file a complaint with the Secretary of the Department of Health and Human Services. Visit http://www.hhs.gov/ocr/hipaa or contact the Office for Civil Rights at 1-866-627-7748. TTY users should call 1-800-537-7697.

By law, Medicare is required to follow the terms in this privacy notice. Medicare has the right to change the way your personal medical information is used and given out. If Medicare makes any changes to the way your personal medical information is used and given out, you will get a new notice by mail within 60 days of the change.

The Notice of Privacy Practices for the Original Medicare Plan became effective April 14, 2003.

The Role of the Medicare Ombudsman

The role of a Medicare Ombudsman is to make certain that the Medicare program provides help to its subscribers regarding all aspects of the program's benefits. A Medicare Ombudsman should ensure that beneficiaries get assistance with Medicare questions or complaints and assistance with appeals. Beneficiaries have many ways to get information and have their problems resolved. An Ombudsman is not meant to replace those mechanisms, but to enhance them.[15] Refer to "Helpful Web Sites" at the end of the chapter for information on contacting the Medicare Ombudsman.

MEDICAID

Medicaid is a federally funded and *state-administered* health insurance program that provides all types of medical care to individuals who cannot afford to pay for some or all of their medical bills. According to federal law, states can provide medical assistance based on SSI eligibility (e.g., if a person is eligible to receive SSI benefits, he automatically is entitled to Medicaid) or states may impose stricter eligibility requirements. States imposing stricter eligibility requirements are often called *Section 209(b)* states. States also are permitted through the Medicaid program to provide nursing home coverage for the truly medically and economically needy. Federal law requires that a Medicaid applicant be a resident of the United States or a qualified alien. States are given substantial leeway to design and fine-tune Medicaid benefits and qualification requirements. Any Medicaid planning should be based on the law of the state in which the Medicaid recipient will be receiving long-term care. If a Medicaid recipient moves to another state, he must reapply there. Depending on the condition of the Medicaid recipient, he may receive Medicaid-funded care in a variety of settings, including an assisted living facility, his home, or a nursing home if the state covers the costs of such facilities, but not all states do. All Medicaid applicants must satisfy financial eligibility requirements and show the care they are requesting is medically necessary.

The Centers for Medicare & Medicaid Services (CMS) of the Department of Health & Human Services (HHS) administers Medicaid at the federal level. However, each state participates in the administration of the Medicaid program within its own borders. Policies of the HHS are found in the *Medical Assistance Manual* and *Information Memoranda*. Federal regulations governing Medicaid are located at 42 C.F.R. Parts 430-456. Each state also has statutes and regulations governing Medicaid. For example, some states known as *income cap states* bar Medicaid eligibility if the nursing home resident's income exceeds $2,000 (in 2007), unless the excess above this amount is paid into what is known as a *Miller Trust.*

Medicaid Eligibility Requirements

The Medicaid program has strict eligibility requirements. These require-ments include the following: a person's age; the fact that a person is pregnant, disabled, blind, or aged; a person's income and resources (such as bank accounts, real property, and other items that can be sold for cash); and the fact that a person is a U.S. citizen or a lawfully admitted immigrant. The rules for counting a person's income and resources vary from state to state and from group to group. There are special rules for those who live in nursing homes and for disabled children living at home. In general, a person should apply for Medicaid if his income is limited and he matches one of the descriptions of the eligibility requirements. If a person is unsure as to eligibility, he still should apply and have a qualified caseworker in the state evaluate his situation. Refer to "Helpful Web Sites" at the end of the chapter for some Web sites that can help an individual determine his eligibility. Coverage may start retroactive to any or all of the three months prior to the application date if the individual would have been eligible during the retroactive period. Coverage generally stops at the end of the month in which a person's circumstances change. Most states have additional state-only programs to provide medical assistance for specified people with limited incomes and resources who do not qualify for the Medicaid program. No federal funds are provided for state-only programs.

The federal government shares the cost with states participating in the Medicaid program, and the program's main purpose has been to serve the *truly* needy. Over a decade ago, the federal government attempted to curb Medicaid entitlement with the 1993 Omnibus Budget Reconciliation Act. Essentially, the act requires all states participating in the Medicaid program to enact **recovery provisions** in their state Medicaid programs. This means that states must attempt to recover from a recipient's assets *any* Medicaid funding provided to the recipient. Nationally, $347 million was recovered in 2003.[16] Since 1993, the

recovery provisions

Provisions in state Medicaid programs whereby the states must attempt to recover from a recipient's assets *any* Medicaid funding provided to the recipient.

federal government also has required that procedures be put in place so that an estate's beneficiaries can attempt to prove that a Medicaid recovery would be a hardship.

In some states, a Medicaid recipient's home is not considered a countable asset as long as the nursing home resident intends to return home. In other states, the nursing home resident must prove a likelihood of returning home. Some states also restrict the intent-to-return-home exemption to a stated time period; after that time, the care facility is considered the Medicaid recipient's residence. All states allow the house to be kept out of the asset qualification computation when the Medicaid applicant's spouse or dependent child lives there. Other exceptions may be allowed. Assets transferred to an *inter vivos* trust are not considered in determining Medicaid eligibility if the trust was written to include the applicable state's Medicaid program as a primary remainder beneficiary.

Using Medicaid to Finance Long-Term Care

A major concern for anyone facing the need for long-term medical care is the escalating costs of such care. Long-term care is not just a nursing home issue and does not pertain just to the elderly. In fact, 85 percent of long-term care patients are not in nursing homes. These patients are being cared for in their own homes utilizing family caregivers and home health-care agencies, as well as in assisted living facilities. Over 40 percent of those needing long-term care are working-age adults under the age of 65.[17] Elderly patients who need long-term care, typically nursing home care, may pay for it in several different ways:

1. Out-of-pocket payments with no reimbursement

2. Long-term care insurance

3. Medicare

4. Federal or state veterans benefits

5. Medicaid

Privately paying for nursing home care quickly depletes the average patient's savings. Some nursing homes take only private pay patients. Some nursing homes require a patient to self-pay a certain number of months in order to be admitted to the nursing home. Proof of a patient's financial status and his ability to pay the nursing home's fees may need to be provided to a nursing home administrator. However, once the patient's savings are depleted, most nursing homes expect the patient to become Medicaid-eligible and for Medicaid to begin paying the monthly care fees. Medicaid pays only those nursing homes that are *certified* as a *Medicaid-approved facility*.

■ **long-term care insurance**

Insurance coverage that pays nursing home costs.

The cost of long-term care can deplete a lifetime of savings. **Long-term care insurance** pays the costs of an insured person's long-term care (usually nursing home care) to enable the insured to bequeath a less depleted estate to his beneficiaries. Of course, an individual must be able to afford the insurance policy's costs and be considered insurable if long-term care insurance is to be considered a viable funding option.

Medicaid planning is one way to prevent family assets from being depleted to pay for nursing home care. Since Medicaid does provide nursing home coverage to income-eligible individuals, a large part of many elder law practices has dealt with assisting clients, within legal limitations, to become Medicaid-eligible while preserving their estate for inheritance.

Preventing Self-Imposed Impoverishment

Medicaid eligibility planning was made more difficult over the past few years by the federal and state governments. The most recent tightening of eligibility requirements came from passage of the federal **Deficit Reduction Act of 2005 (DRA).** President Bush signed the DRA on February 8, 2006. Its purpose is to prevent individuals in need of nursing home or other long-term care from transferring their assets to others and then applying for Medicaid-funded long-term care due to their *self-imposed* impoverishment.

Most states require long-term care patients to spend down to $2,000 in assets before they can qualify for Medicaid. Married couples have higher asset allowances. Long-term care residents are allowed to receive a monthly personal needs allowance of approximately $30. All other sources of income (e.g., pension and Social Security checks) must be turned over to Medicaid to pay for the long-term care.

Intentionally misrepresenting oneself on a Medicaid application or aiding in such intentional misrepresentation has always been a crime. All applicants must provide a *waiver* to the state to allow the state to verify the application statements through a credit report and the Internal Revenue Service (IRS). Medicaid rules require applicants to have *spent down* their assets, with some exceptions, before qualifying for Medicaid-funded long-term care. Exceptions include the marital home *if* it is still occupied by a spouse or child (with some caveats). An additional exception is certain prepaid funeral contracts. A new tool for dealing with Medicaid costs pertains to the Medicaid rules that now require individuals (but not married couples if a community spouse is still in the marital home) to tap any home equity in excess of $500,000 to pay for their own care. Property owners can do this by selling the property, borrowing against the equity, or using a reverse mortgage. Reverse mortgages will be discussed later in this chapter. This should be particularly applicable in areas of the country that have seen huge real estate appreciation. Another DRA change is that anyone with more than $750,000 of home equity is banned from Medicaid eligibility entirely.

The DRA now requires all states to review any transfers of assets by a Medicaid applicant within the *60 months* before application was made. This time period for investigating asset transfer is called the **look-back period**. Before the

deficit reduction act of 2005 (DRA)
An act that prevents individuals in need of nursing home or other long-term care from transferring their assets to others and then applying for Medicaid-funded long-term care due to self-imposed impoverishment.

look-back period
The time period for investigating asset transfer.

DRA's passage in early 2006, the look-back period was 36 months. At different times previously, the look-back period had been 24 months and 12 months. The DRA also requires that the states look to see whether the date of the asset transfer or the Medicaid eligibility date is later and use that later date to start the 60-month look-back period. Medicaid's five-year look-back period can lead to Medicaid ineligibility.

A person who transfers assets to another person for less than market value and then applies for Medicaid may lose eligibility for a period of time. Usually, this ineligibility period is determined by Medicaid looking to the total cumulative uncompensated value of all assets transferred from the look-back date divided by the average monthly cost of nursing home services in the transferor's state. The result is the number of months of Medicaid ineligibility.

ELDER LAW PRACTICE

How would the new DRA requirements affect the following property transfer? Aunt Mary has a home worth $90,000. Aunt Mary gratuitously transferred it to her nephew, Huey, on January 1, 2008. Huey promptly moved into his aunt's former home, and Aunt Mary moved into a nursing home. Monthly nursing home costs in Aunt Mary's state are $3,000.

Analysis: The transferred asset (the $90,000 home) divided by $3,000 (the average monthly private pay nursing home rate in Aunt Mary's state) results in a 30-month penalty period. Aunt Mary and Huey would have to self-pay for Aunt Mary's nursing home care for 30 months before Medicaid would begin to pay for it.

Exceptions to Medicaid Transfer Penalties

There are certain kinds of transfers to which penalties would not be applied. The principal exceptions include the following:

1. Transfers to a spouse or to a third party for the sole benefit of the spouse

2. Transfers by a spouse to a third party for the sole benefit of the spouse

3. Transfers to certain individuals with disabilities or to a trust established for those individuals

4. Transfers for a purpose other than to qualify for Medicaid

5. Transfers where imposing a penalty would cause undue hardship

A transfer to a blind adult or a child with disabilities or a minor child under 21 and a trust for the sole benefit of a blind adult or a disabled child are additional exceptions. Also, a trust for the sole benefit of a person with a disability (nonchild) under age 65 or a direct transfer to that person is another exception.

Exceptions apply to the transfer of a home to the following individuals without a transfer penalty being incurred:

1. The applicant's spouse

2. An applicant's child who is under age 21 or who is blind or disabled

3. A person with a disability (a nonchild under age 65 or a direct transfer to that person) (put into a trust for this person's sole benefit)

4. A sibling who has lived in the home for one year or more preceding another sibling's institutionalization provided the noninstitutionalized sibling holds an equity interest in the home

5. A caretaker child defined as a child of the applicant who is living in the house for at least two years prior to the applicant's institutionalization and who during that period provided care that allowed the applicant to avoid a nursing home stay.

Congress has created an important remedy for the transfer penalty by allowing the penalty to be cured if the transferred asset is returned in its entirety. Federal statute 42 U.S.C.S. Section 1396 c is the statute that requires all transfers of assets be considered when determinations of Medicaid benefits eligibility are made.

Avoiding Spousal Impoverishment

The costs of nursing home care can quickly outpace the savings of a lifetime for most individuals and couples. Self-paying for nursing home care for a medically needy spouse may leave the spouse still living in the community (described by Medicaid as the **community spouse**) with little income or few resources. This led Congress in 1988 to enact Medicaid's spousal protection provisions to prevent what had begun to be described as *spousal impoverishment.*

Protections for a community spouse are designed to preserve the minimum income needed to allow a community spouse to support himself and stay in the community after his spouse has entered a Medicaid-paying facility. If a Medicaid applicant is married, the assets of both spouses are totaled beginning on the date the Medicaid applicant spouse entered a hospital or another long-term care nursing facility for at least 30 days.

Generally, a community spouse may keep one-half of the couple's total countable assets up to a maximum of $101,640 (2007). This designated amount is called the **community spouse resource allowance (CSRA)**. According to the federal government, the least a state may permit a community spouse to retain is $20,328 (2007). The community spouse also does not have to pay for his spouse's nursing home costs from his own income *after* Medicaid begins paying for the institutionalized spouse. Prior to Medicaid eligibility, the unspent income of both spouses is considered available to be spent down for health care costs. An exception occurs when the institutionalized spouse is the main or only income earner and the community spouse does not have enough income to live on. The community spouse is then entitled to some or all of the monthly income of the

community spouse

The term used by Medicaid to describe a person who does not live in a nursing home, but who has a spouse that does.

community spouse resource allowance (CSRA)

A designated amount a community spouse is permitted by their state to retain from a couples' total countable asset.

■ **minimum monthly maintenance needs allowance (MMMNA)**

A designated monthly amount of the institutionalized spouses' income that the community spouse may retain for their own support.

institutionalized spouse. The amount of the entitlement is determined by the minimum monthly income level provided by the state Medicaid agency. This dollar amount is called the **minimum monthly maintenance needs allowance (MMMNA)**. The MMMNA is determined according to the community spouse's actual housing and living costs. Nationally, the MMMNA was within a low of $1,650 to a high of $2,541 range in 2007. If the community spouse's income is less than the MMMNA, the difference can be made up from the institutionalized spouse's income. A community spouse can go to court to apply for additional support beyond the applicable range. Medicaid has few exemptions, and items that would not normally be taxable income (e.g., gifts, Social Security, and tax-exempt interest) and jointly owned property are countable when Medicaid eligibility is determined.

ELDER LAW PRACTICE

Adam and Evelyn are retired with combined total countable assets of $400,000 above the value of their house. Adam suffered a stroke several years ago, but Evelyn has always cared for him in their longtime home. However, now burdened with a worsening case of arthritis, Evelyn can no longer care for Adam at home. She has made the difficult decision to move Adam to a local nursing home. Evelyn has decided to visit her attorney, Tara Jensen, for clarification about Medicaid-funded nursing home stays.

Analysis: Tara tells Evelyn that a community spouse's 50 percent interest in countable assets is capped at $101,000 in their state plus $2,000 for the applicant. Therefore, $297,000 must be spent on Adam's nursing home care before Medicaid will begin paying unless Evelyn takes some legally permitted *spending down* action.

Tara also explains that Medicaid regulation in the state allows Evelyn to spend some of her assets on prefunded funeral and burial or cremation expenses, buy goods and services, and pay down debts. In addition, converting countable resources to exempt resources can help preserve savings. For example, buying a car and paying for home improvements to a community spouse's principal residence are examples of assets that are exempt from Medicaid's countable assets. Evelyn decides to renovate her kitchen and bathroom and have a new roof installed as soon as possible. She also is going to prepay for her and Adam's funeral costs and then apply for Medicaid benefits.

Evelyn also is concerned about supporting herself in the community if Adam's income has to be used for his nursing home care. If Adam and Evelyn have a joint income of $2,000 per month (Adam's income is $1,500, and Evelyn's income is $500) and Evelyn's MMMNA is $1,500 (based on her housing costs), the question is *how much of Adam's income will Evelyn be able to retain?*

Analysis: Tara explains to Evelyn that Medicaid should allow $1,000 of Adam's income to Evelyn's support because of her MMMNA. In addition, in their state, Medicaid allows Adam to retain a $100 monthly *needs allowance*. The result is that Adam's obligation toward his nursing home costs is $400 per month ($500 - 100 = $400).

The Medicaid Appeals Process

Each state must have an administrative appeals process in place for its Medicaid program or face the loss of federal funding. An applicant who believes that he has been unfairly denied Medicaid funding and believes he is facing too long a period of Medicaid ineligibility due to an allegedly improper transfer of assets can proceed with the submission of a **hardship waiver**. The applicant has the burden of proving the alleged hardship. The hardship waiver should provide for exceptions when the period of ineligibility would leave the applicant physically endangered or deprived of food, shelter, clothing, or medical treatment.

hardship waiver
A waiver that provides for exceptions when the period of Medicaid ineligibility would leave an applicant physically endangered or deprived of food, shelter, clothing, or medical treatment.

TAXES

Elder law practitioners and their staff find one constant—clients who want to avoid the payment of taxes. Elder law practitioners should be aware that in general, any client who has taxable assets will want his attorney to pursue all measures available to avoid the paying of taxes.

Income Taxes

All income earned in the United States has been subject to federal income taxes ever since the Twentieth Amendment was passed in 1913. Federal income taxes were soon followed by state income taxes in the majority of states. Several states do not have a state income tax, making them popular with younger and older citizens alike. However, states without income taxes usually have some sort of sales tax to collect revenue for state coffers. The states that do not have a personal state income tax include Alaska, Florida, Nevada, South Dakota, Tennessee, Texas, Washington, and Wyoming. Before a person can figure the amount of federal income taxes due, he must determine the tax rate to apply. The tax rates in 2007 began at 10 percent and went as high as 35 percent. Any individual or couple who earns over a certain minimum amount must file an income tax form. In 2007, for an individual 65 and older, that amount was $10,050; for a couple both of whom are over 65, the total amount was $19,600. Extensions may be filed if the annual April 15 income tax filing date is missed, but prepayment of estimated taxes due will decrease or eliminate interest penalties. Estimated taxes can be paid quarterly. Refer to the Elder Law Online Supplement to review the IRS's filing requirements and the Federal Tax Rate Schedules (2008).

Income earned from Social Security benefits is a good thing, but it was even better prior to Congress deciding in 1983 to tax Social Security benefits. Specifically, **Section 83** of the Internal Revenue Code concerns the taxing of Social Security benefits. The amount of each recipient's tax bill is determined through a formula. For example, once a certain amount of Social Security

section 83
The IRS Code concerning the taxing of Social Security benefits.

benefits is paid, any benefits over an adjusted income amount are considered part of a beneficiary's gross income and will be taxed. The adjusted base income amount was $25,000 for single individuals and $32,000 for married couples filing jointly in 2007. There is a graduated scale for higher incomes, but the maximum amount that Social Security benefits could be taxed at in 2007 was 85 percent.

Capital Gains Taxes

capital gains

Profits made on the sale of real and personal property assets.

Capital gains are any profits made on the sale of assets, including real and personal property. Capital gain is computed by subtracting the original purchase price of the asset from the selling price minus any costs for maintaining or improving the asset.

The federal Taxpayer Relief Act of 1997 limited the amount of capital gains that can be enjoyed tax free from the sale of a personal residence. This can be important because the largest single asset owned by the majority of Americans is their personal residence. A homeowner who sells his personal residence is allowed a limited federal tax-free gain. An individual home seller during 2008 could enjoy a $250,000 federal tax-free gain and a jointly filing couple could enjoy a $500,000 federal tax-free gain. The seller must have been domiciled in the sold residence for at least two out of the last five years before the sale. An individual who sells his personal residence and purchases a more expensive home does not have to pay capital gains taxes.

The federal capital gains tax rate for properties other than a personal residence has been lowered over the last few years, but the new lower rate schedules were set to expire in 2008. Some states have their own capital gains taxes. As with the federal capital gains tax, any state capital gains taxes would be due to a state if the capital gain was for more than what a particular state permits.

gross estate

All of a decedent's assets that are added together and include all gifts made within three years of the date of the decedent's death plus all business interests, annuities, real estate of any kind, stocks, bonds, personal property, cash, and insurance.

Estate Taxes

Each estate tax dollar avoided is a dollar that can be left to provide for a client's family, friends, and charities. Interestingly, fewer than two percent of estates owed any federal estate tax in 2006.[18]

taxable estate

The gross estate minus the debts the deceased owed, which may include funeral costs, medical expenses, estate administration costs, mortgages, and credit card bills.

When a person dies, all of his assets are added together to determine the total value amount of the **gross estate**. A gross estate includes all gifts made within three years of the date of the decedent's death plus all business interests, annuities, real estate of any kind, stocks, bonds, personal property (including cash), and insurance. The gross estate *minus* the debts the decedent owed is calculated to come up with a dollar value. Debts may include the decedent's funeral costs, medical expenses, estate administration costs, mortgages, and credit card bills. This dollar value is what the decedent's estate is worth and is called the **taxable estate**. The federal government requires that any estate valued over a particular dollar amount will owe *federal* estate taxes that must be paid *before* the first dollar is disbursed to beneficiaries of the estate.

Until 2005, a federal *estate tax credit* (i.e., a tax deduction) for payment of federal estate taxes was permitted by the IRS for any *state* estate taxes paid. This estate tax deduction credit was eliminated in 2005 but is due to be reinstated in 2011. The states that do have a state estate tax (not every state does)[19] require a state estate tax to be paid if the estate is valued over a certain state-designated monetary amount. The good news is that the amounts of *federal* estate tax exemptions have increased over the last few years due to the passage of the Economic Growth and Tax Relief Reconciliation Act of 2001. The Act permits an exemption for estates with net worths as high as $3.5 million in 2009. The federal estate tax will expire in 2010. There also is a scheduled reduction in the federal gift tax from a high of 50 percent to a low of 35 percent for 2010.

The bad news is that the Tax Relief Reconciliation Act will expire in 2011 and the estate tax exemption will go back to its pre-Act tax exemption amount of $1 million *unless* Congress votes for a higher amount. Refer to Exhibit 7–7 to review the estate tax chart for the federal government.

Any state estate tax is calculated by a percentage of the *net assets* of the estate in question. Depending on the state, an estate's beneficiaries may have to pay a **state inheritance tax**. However, no state imposes an inheritance tax if the relationship of the beneficiary to the deceased was that of an immediate family. Typically, the farther removed the blood relationship, the higher the beneficiaries' rate and the higher the inheritance tax bill. None of the 50 states require a spouse to pay a state inheritance tax.

state inheritance tax

A tax paid by a beneficiary to the individual state.

EXHIBIT 7–7   FEDERAL ESTATE TAX CHART

FEDERAL ESTATE TAX RATES—OVERVIEW

The Economic Growth and Tax Relief Act of 2001 was signed into law on June 7, 2001. Under this law, the federal estate tax continues, *but* with increasing Unified Credit and decreasing top federal estate tax rates until 2010. The federal estate tax will be repealed in 2010 only. In 2011, the federal estate tax will be reimposed, the Unified Credit will return to $1,000,000 and the top tax rate will again be 55 percent.

ESTATE TAX RATES—Table I

FOR A TAXABLE ESTATE		THE FEDERAL ESTATE TAX	
From	**To**	**Is**	**of Amount Over**
$0	$10,000	18%	$0
10,001	20,000	1,800 + 20%	10,000
20,001	40,000	3,800 + 22%	20,000

(continues)

EXHIBIT 7–7   FEDERAL ESTATE TAX CHART *(continued)*

FOR A TAXABLE ESTATE		THE FEDERAL ESTATE TAX	
From	**To**	**Is**	**of Amount Over**
40,001	60,000	8,200 + 24%	40,000
60,001	80,000	13,000 + 26%	60,000
80,001	100,000	18,200 + 28%	80,000
100,001	150,000	23,800 + 30%	100,000
150,001	250,000	38,800 + 32%	150,000
250,001	500,000	70,800 + 34%	250,000
500,001	750,000	155,800 + 37%	500,000
750,001	1,000,000	248,300 + 39%	750,000
1,000,001	1,250,000	345,800 + 41%	1,000,000
1,250,001	1,500,000	448,300 + 43%	1,250,000
1,500,001	2,000,000	555,800 + 45%	1,500,000
2,000,001	& Up	780,800 + 48%	2,000,000

UNIFIED CREDIT—Table 2

If You Die During	Top Estate Tax Rate	Applicable Unified Credit	Equivalent Exemption
2003	49%	345,800	1,000,000
2004	48%	555,800	1,500,000
2005	47%	555,800	1,500,000
2006	46%	780,800	2,000,000
2007	45%	780,800	2,000,000
2008	45%	780,800	2,000,000

(continues)

EXHIBIT 7–7   FEDERAL ESTATE TAX CHART *(continued)*

If You Die During	Top Estate Tax Rate	Applicable Unified Credit	Equivalent Exemption
2009	45%	1,455,800	3,500,000
2010	Repealed for 1 year	Unlimited	Unlimited
2011	55%	345,800	1,000,000

Federal estate taxes are paid on assets that *do not* go to a surviving spouse or a trust for a spouse's benefit. To calculate, ascertain total estate value and add lifetime taxable gifts (if any). This figure is the total taxable estate. Determine the federal estate tax due from Table 1 and subtract the appropriate Unified Credit for the year of death from Table 2. This figure is the federal estate tax due.

Table provided by The Wealth Transfer Group, Inc., Altamonte Springs, Florida, January 10, 2008.

How Tax Deductions Are Created

The Internal Revenue Code provides that certain expenses will create income tax *deductions* or *credits*. For example, the interest paid as part of a homeowner's mortgage payment creates an income tax deduction. This means that the interest paid all year is added up and deducted from a homeowner's *gross income*. The income on which the income tax is based is called the **adjusted gross income**. It is the total gross income minus all allowable deductions. Additional examples of deductions include medical, drug, and dental expenses if those expenses were more than a certain percent of a taxpayer's adjusted gross income. Another way to reduce taxable income is to gift up to a certain allowable amount by making a payment to a custodial account for the benefit of a minor. Such an account involves the Uniform Transfer to Minors Act (UTMA) and the creation of a trust. Deductions are either **itemized or standard**. Itemized deductions are included on IRS Schedule A, which is attached to the annual IRS Form 1040. The IRS announces the standard deductions each year, and they are listed on the IRS Form 1040.

The Internal Revenue Code also provides that certain expenses can be deducted from the total value of a person's estate. For example, funeral and burial costs can be deducted from an estate's gross value. Exempt expenses are not the only way to lower the value of an estate with the ultimate intention of paying less estate tax. The IRS allows a certain amount of cash or other assets to be given away as gifts each year without being considered income to the recipient. The annual gifting amount allowed for a single person in 2007 was $12,000, and for a couple, $24,000. The person who gives a gift is permitted a lifetime gift tax exemption. The gifter must be legally competent to make any gifts. The IRS describes a gift as occurring when a donor transfers all right, title, and interest in

adjusted gross income

The total gross income minus all allowable deductions on which income tax is based.

itemized or standard

Two types of deductions, one of which is allowed by the IRS.

a piece of property, personal or real. The donor should report all gifts to the IRS. The donee does not have to report the gift or file a gift tax return. However, the donee should report whatever profits he earns from the gift. Depending on the state, gifts also may be subject to state taxes. Donors should keep proof of all gifts they give. Generally, a limited amount can be gifted each year, but grandparents can gift by direct payment to an educational institution an unlimited amount of tuition for a grandchild. The IRS also allows the creation of trusts as a way to avoid the owing of taxes. Trusts were discussed in Chapter 5.

Procedure for Paying Estate and Inheritance Taxes

state estate tax
A tax paid by the estate to the individual state.

The executor/personal representative or administrator of every estate must ensure that a federal estate tax return is filed with the IRS within nine months of a decedent's death. Depending on the size of the estate, an executor/personal representative or administrator probably should hire professionals to assist with this task and ensure that proof of mailing is requested (e.g., send the tax return via certified mail or by electronic filing). The tax return is not filed in the name of an individual, but in the name of the decedent's estate; and the estate gets its own *tax I.D. number*. Filing extensions up to six months are available if needed. A decedent's estate may continue to earn income after the decedent's death, and this income can be taxable. All income earned by an estate or in the name of a trust is reported on *IRS Form 1041*. Any income distributed by an estate or a trust must be reported on IRS *Schedule K-1*.

retirement plan
A plan set up by an employer to provide financially for employees after they stop full-time employment.

qualified plan
A retirement plan that meets IRS requirements for employers to deduct payments from an employee's paycheck and place them in a retirement account.

An estate pays a **state estate tax**. The recipient pays any inheritance taxes that are due. Any life insurance purchased and paid out to named beneficiaries will not result in an inheritance tax being owed by the beneficiaries. If a life insurance policy pays out to the estate instead of to specific beneficiaries, the insurance amount will be counted as part of the total assets of the decedent and federal or state taxes could be owed from the estate. Clients should be advised that the IRS can audit tax returns three years from the date they were filed. Financial records should be kept at least seven years.

FINANCIAL AND RETIREMENT PLANNING

401k plans
A retirement plan where the employer is a for-profit business.

If money is your hope for independence you will never have it. The only real security that a man will have in this world is a reserve of knowledge, experience and ability.

Henry Ford

403b plans
A retirement plan where the employer is a nonprofit entity.

A retirement plan may utilize different methods to create the plan. A plan set up by an employer to provide financially for employees after they stop full-time employment is generally called a **retirement plan**. A **qualified plan** is a plan that meets IRS requirements for employers to deduct payments from an employee's paycheck and place them in an employee's retirement account. All of the money placed in and earnings from such an account is tax free until the employee begins to withdraw cash from the plan. These qualified plans are generally known as **401k plans** (when the employer is a for-profit business) or **403b plans** (when the employer is a nonprofit entity). Although it is not a requirement for either plan, some employers provide matching funds up to a certain percentage of an employee's deductions.

The **defined benefit plan** is often used to describe a pension. A defined benefit plan has benefit distributions specified in advance, usually as a percentage of salary and related to years of service, with no individual account kept for each employee. With a **money purchase plan** (or defined contribution plan), an employer, an employee, or both has specified that a certain amount of money be contributed to a retirement fund. The money is invested (usually in mutual funds) with earnings divided proportionately among all participants in the plan. An **individual retirement account (IRA)** (there are different varieties of IRAs) is designed for an individual to self-manage and fund his own retirement account. An IRA is particularly appropriate for a self-employed individual or homemaker with no opportunity to benefit from a qualified or defined benefit plan. An IRA may be funded with a tax-deductible contribution. Another similar investment opportunity is the Roth IRA. Contributions made to a Roth IRA are not tax-deductible, but their earnings are tax-free. There are annual limits to the amount that can be invested in both the qualified plans and the different types of IRAs. The best-case scenario has an individual benefiting from the compounding of the investment by beginning any plan as early as possible in his career.

A **required minimum distribution (RMD)** is the minimum amount of money that individuals with IRAs, 401ks, or 403bs *must* withdraw by a certain age. Failing to withdraw the minimum amount can result in a hefty penalty. One exception is that anyone still working for the company where he has a retirement account can delay the first withdrawal until April 1 of the year the person finally retires. All retirement accounts allow their owners to make withdrawals without penalty after the owner is 59½ years old. Of course, if the owner's account was created with pretax income, any withdrawals will be taxed. However, if the employee is retired from employment, he should be taxed in a lower tax bracket due to the likelihood that the employee is earning a lower income. The amount of the RMD is calculated using the life expectancy of the account owner and a real or hypothetical beneficiary at least 10 years younger.

Update Beneficiary Designations

IRAs or retirement plan accounts administered by the owner's employer require that a beneficiary designation be made. These types of accounts *will pass outside the probate process.* Any changes in an owner's relationship with a designated

defined benefit plan

A pension plan in which benefits are specified in advance, usually as a percentage of salary and related to years of service, with no individual account kept for each employee.

money purchase plan

A retirement plan in which an employer, an employee, or both has specified that a certain amount of money be contributed to a retirement fund. The money is invested with earnings divided proportionately among all participants in the plan. Also called defined contribution plan.

individual retirement account (IRA)

An investment account designed for an individual to self-manage and fund his own retirement account.

required minimum distribution (RMD)

The minimum amount of money that individuals with IRAs, 401ks, or 403bs *must* withdraw by a certain age.

beneficiary may signal the need for the alteration of the designated beneficiary. For example, a divorce from or death of a designated beneficiary indicates a need for an immediate change in the beneficiary designation.

FINANCING LONG-TERM CARE

Long-term care can be defined as assistance to a person who is unable to help himself with the daily requirements of living. Such care may range from the basics of helping a person use the toilet, bathe, and dress to providing highly skilled medical care. Long-term care may be provided by a caregiver in the person's home or in a relative's home. The caregiver may be a registered nurse, a practical nurse, a physical or occupational therapist, or a housekeeper. Long-term care may be provided in a large variety of housing venues, described in Chapter 8.

The fact that Medicare does not pay for long-term custodial or in-home care is not universally known. Medicaid is the largest source of funding for long-term care; unfortunately, Medicaid coverage usually is not activated until a nursing home patient has spent down most of the assets he spent a lifetime accumulating.

It has been estimated that by 2020, 12 million older Americans will need some kind of long-term care.[20] Longer life expectancies have created a new category of caregivers (often described as the *sandwich generation*), often too busy raising their own young children and working full-time to care for their aging and increasingly infirm parents at home without some type of caregiving assistance in their home or at an outside facility.

Unfortunately, individuals and their families can incur huge financial burdens when custodial, in-home, or nursing home care is necessary. For example, today the average cost of home health care is more than $20,000 per year at $18 per hour with a visit of five hours per day five days per week.[21]

Nursing home care costs an average of $52,000 a year for a semiprivate room, and the average stay is 2.6 years. The cost of a semiprivate room in a nursing home is projected to increase to $190,000 a year by 2030.[22] Refer to Exhibit 7–8 to estimate the cost of a nursing home stay.[23]

EXHIBIT 7–8 ESTIMATING THE FUTURE COST OF NURSING HOME CARE

Use the following steps to determine the estimated cost of a nursing home stay of 2.5 years. Begin with the assumption that the care is for an 80-year-old person and that nursing home costs will rise 6 percent per year.

Subtract a person's age from 80 to determine the number of years of future planning. _____ years.

Indicate the annual rate of nursing home care in the area in which the person intends to be. _____

(Costs can vary by state. For example, in a recent year, a one-day stay in an Oklahoma nursing home averaged $69; the cost in Alaska was as high as $720 a day.)

(continues)

EXHIBIT 7–8   ESTIMATING THE FUTURE COST OF NURSING HOME CARE *(continued)*

Compound the current annual rate at a yearly rate of 6 percent for the number of years shown in the first step. This is the estimated annual rate for nursing home care when the individual is 80 years old.

Determine the estimated cost of an average nursing home stay by multiplying the answer to the third step by 2.5. This is the estimated cost of an average length of stay in a nursing home when the individual is 80 years old.

Complete the steps with information from the state where the nursing home resident will be located.

Example:

Step 1: Subtract current age from 80 (80 – 50).

The number of years of future planning is 30.

Step 2: Use the current annual nursing home rate of $60,000.

Step 3: Compound current nursing home rates by 6% for 30 years.

Year 1: $60,000 × 1.06 = $63,600

Year 2: $63,600 × 1.06 = $67,416

Year 3: $67,416 × 1.06 = $71,461

The estimated annual rate for nursing home care at age 80 is $344,609.

Step 4: Multiply the estimated annual rate for nursing home care at age 80 by 2.5 ($344,609 × 2.5).

The estimated cost of an average length of stay in a nursing home at age 80 is $861,522.

Should a Client's Plans Include Purchasing Long-Term Care Insurance?

Most individuals are familiar with fire insurance. In fact, banks usually do not approve a mortgage on property that is not covered by fire insurance. Interestingly, the risk of a home catching fire and a fire insurance claim being made is 1 in 1,200. The statistical probability of a purchaser of long-term care insurance needing long-term care is a contrastingly large 50 percent. Yet only 8 million Americans had purchased long-term care insurance as of 2001.[24] That figure leaves 82 million people over age 45 without any financial protection from the high costs of long-term care.

Elder law clients may be unaware that Medicare does not pay for long-term care. (Medicare covers short-term acute and recovery care provided by skilled medical professionals only.) Clients also may be unaware that costs for long-term care vary dramatically by state. For example, in 2004, a day's stay in an Oklahoma nursing home averaged $69 per day, while in Alaska the cost ran as high as $720 per day. When advising uninsured clients about long-range planning, elder law practitioners should ask whether insurance coverage for long-term care is needed.[25]

The answer lies in what type of policy is purchased and what that policy provides for the costs incurred. First, every insurance policy is a *contract*. The policyholder must be aware that it is the policy that dictates what benefits are provided. Each client should be warned that sales tactics, no matter how warm and gracious, are tactics to get the client to buy a policy. No oral promises that a company's salesperson makes and no promises spelled out in glossy brochures will dictate the contract's terms (i.e., the policy). All insurance companies have teams of lawyers who are responsible for writing policies that reflect more positively on the insurance company than on customers. What is promised and agreed to in the policy is the legal language the insurance company's lawyers will ask the court to look to in the event of a contract dispute. Some states sponsor long-term care insurance policies sold in their state.

Clients should be warned that the process of purchasing long-term care insurance is particularly vulnerable to fraud because it involves older individuals and the commissions that agents receive (30 to 65 percent of the first year's premium) are among the highest in the insurance industry.[26] The majority of agents may be ethical, but morally and legally dubious agents may take advantage of vulnerable seniors. The premiums increase as a policy owner ages, which may result in a person dropping the long-term care insurance before he needs it.

Long-term care insurance should not be purchased if paying the premiums will significantly compromise the purchaser's lifestyle. For example, the purchasing of basic necessities should not become a hardship when premium needs to be paid. Individuals who own significant assets they want to leave to loved ones or who want to ensure the type of long-term care available (if needed) are the best candidates for long-term care insurance. One difficulty with long-term care insurance is that industry-wide standardized policies are not provided. The old expression about not being able to compare apples and oranges holds true for long-term care policies.

Some insurance companies offer to pay a percentage of a policyholder's long-term care costs. Most companies offer a specific per-day coverage amount. Regardless *inflation coverage is essential.* Many policies cover long-term care provided only in a nursing home facility. Other polices fail to cover any long-term care provided in a policyholder's home. Rarely does a standard policy provide for homemaking services in an insured person's home or allow a family member to be paid for caring for a relative. The number of restrictions on where, how, and who can provide long-term care can fill pages.

The safest route for the insured is to understand any restrictions before purchasing a policy. The place to start is to know how much area nursing homes are charging and then make sure the policy provides for inflation. If it is important for the insured to be at home rather than in a nursing home, the policy should provide for in-home care and specify how long that care is covered. Long-term care policies can be purchased with lifetime coverage, but all policies should allow the insured to specify the length of the policy.

Many policies have elimination periods where coverage does not begin until after a specific waiting period. The majority of insurance companies offering long-term care insurance require their policyholders to pay for a specified number of days of care before they will begin paying benefits. Typically, 30 days of self-paid care is the low end of the spectrum.

An important question is who will decide whether an insured is entitled to benefits. Denial of a claim is a possibility. For example, denial of long-term care claims in California reached 1 in 4 in 2005.[27] Generally, policies are put into effect in one of three ways. The least restrictive policy allows an insured person's personal doctor to determine whether long-term care is needed. Some policies are put into effect only when the insurance company deems that an insured person's needs have reached a certain threshold (usually a fairly high one). Another way that a long-term care policy is put into effect is when an insured is unable to complete certain activities of daily living (ADL). ADL standards may change from company to company.

The bottom line is that long-term insurance is too expensive for many people; and if a person is already ill, he may not be considered insurable. The National Association of Insurance Commissioners has stated that 16 percent of all nursing home insurance buyers drop their coverage each year because they no longer can afford it.

Generally, long-term care policies are sold to customers as renewable and cannot be canceled unless an insured fails to pay the premiums or the insured lied on the policy application. However, because premiums are likely to increase, the policy should detail when such increases are allowed.

Legal action may be appropriate when a client is unhappy about his long-term care insurance contract. All courts should look to the wording of the policy and the reasonableness of the policy terms. Typically, courts do this by evaluating the policy using an **objective standard**. An objective standard is the principle that a court should resolve most contract issues by considering only the actions, writings, and other objective evidence of what the parties did rather than considering what the parties subjectively meant to do (by asking them what they were thinking).

When reading the contract, all courts usually look to the **plain meaning of the words** that the company used. Plain meaning is the principle that if a contract, a statute or another writing seems clear, the meaning of the writing should be determined from the writing itself, not from other evidence such as testimony (e.g., policy terms used to exclude or limit coverage). Exclusions and limitations on policy coverage must be clear to the reader. Questions that a person should ask when determining the legality of a long-term care contract include whether the marketing was deceptive. Was there negligent or intentional misrepresentation? Courts typically allow some *puffing* (e.g. positive statements regarding the product being sold) except when a trust relationship exists. Another important question is whether the contract is so one-sided that it may be considered unconscionable?

objective standard
The principle that a court should resolve most contract issues by considering only the actions, writings, and other objective evidence of what the parties did rather than considering what the parties subjectively meant to do.

plain meaning of the words
The principle that if a contract, a statute, or another writing seems clear, the meaning of the writing should be determined from the writing itself, not from other evidence such as testimony.

Medicaid Changes Affect the Purchasing of Policies

The federal government has issued a policy that allows state Medicaid programs to disregard any assets that a Medicaid recipient received from a private long-term care insurance policy when the state moves to recover assets from a Medicaid beneficiary's estate. The aim of this policy change is to inspire the purchase of long-term care policies. Another advantage of long-term care insurance premiums is that they are tax-deductible. Refer to Exhibit 7–9 to review the allowable tax deductions on long-term care insurance.

EXHIBIT 7–9 TAX DEDUCTIONS ON LONG-TERM CARE INSURANCE

Age at Year-End	IRS-Eligible Premium Deduction (2007)
40 or younger	$260
Ages 41–50	$490
Ages 51–60	$980
Ages 61–70	$2,600
71 and older	$3,250

VIATICAL SETTLEMENTS

■ **viatical settlements**

Involve the purchase of another person's life insurance policy by an investor in return for a cash payment that is a percentage of the policy payout.

Viatical settlements involve the purchase of another person's life insurance policy by an investor in return for a cash payment that is a percentage of the policy payout. For example, Mildred is the 80-year-old insured and owner of a life insurance policy with $1 million in coverage. If Mildred sells the policy to Fred at a discounted rate of $250,000 she will have $250,000 to enjoy immediately in her elder years. Fred has invested $250,000 with a guaranteed return (if he continues to pay the premiums) of $1 million when Mildred dies. This is an example of a viatical settlement in its simplest form. Viatical investments have become a more complicated investment strategy and big business for investors who are spending billions each year to buy life insurance policies from the elderly.[28] On a negative note, viatical fraud remains one of the country's top investment scams according to the North American Securities Administrators Association.[29]

REVERSE MORTGAGES

An appreciated housing market has left many seniors with their home as their largest asset. A **reverse mortgage** allows the older homeowner to benefit from such appreciation and to use the accrued equity in his home to mortgage the house. The mortgage is considered *reversed* because the lending institution holding the mortgage typically gives the homeowner a monthly payment based on that equity, compared to the typical mortgage where the homeowner makes monthly payments to the lending institution. This way the elderly homeowner is using the equity in his home for financial support. The reverse mortgage concept stems from the federal government's decision in 1987 to begin a federally insured program to allow older homeowners to tap into their homes' equity to finance their needs without selling.

A reverse mortgage is designed for the older homeowner who is having difficulty making ends meet, owns his home, and wants to continue living in that home until his death. The homeowner must be at least 62 years old to apply for a reverse mortgage.

Banks structure reverse mortgage loans similarly to *annuities*. Like annuities, the mortgagee relies on an estimate of how long a person is likely to live in his home to calculate how much cash a homeowner can receive and how much equity in the home must be reserved as interest. The monthly loan payment to the homeowner continues as long as the homeowner lives in the home and is not due to be paid back until the homeowner moves out, sells the home, or dies. The homeowner still must pay the usual taxes, homeowners insurance, and maintenance costs to keep up the property's condition. Failure to do so can result in the bank immediately demanding repayment. The number of federally insured reversed mortgages rose from fewer than 8,200 in 2001 to 55,659 in the first nine months of 2006 and shows no sign of slowing.[30] There are a few different types of reverse mortgages. The largest number are financed through the Department of Housing and Urban Development's Home Equity Conversion Mortgage (HECM).[31] This mortgage provides that any homeowner over age 62 may choose a *line of credit*, a *lump sum*, or a *monthly income* for as long as he lives in the home.

> **reverse mortgage**
> A mortgage that allows an older homeowner to receive a monthly payment based on his equity in the home rather than make monthly payments to a lending institution.

Balancing the Benefits and Drawbacks of Reverse Mortgages

Clients have some negatives to consider when deciding whether to apply for a reverse mortgage. When an elderly homeowner dies, the mortgaged house passes to the lending institution *unless* the estate of the deceased homeowner can pay back the money lent through the reverse mortgage. If an elderly homeowner leaves his house for 12 consecutive months, the reverse mortgage will become due in its entirety. This can lead to a sorry result if the homeowner needed the care of a nursing home for 12 or more months but had plans to return home. Closing costs on reverse mortgages are some of the highest in the mortgage industry. Such costs include legal fees, recording fees, points or mortgage origination fees, homeowners insurance, and title insurance. The mortgage company typically requires an appraisal of the subject property and a title search. Any property liens, including mortgages and taxes, must be paid off and the title found to be clear before the reverse mortgage closing will be permitted. Interestingly, all homeowners are required to attend a free counseling session before they can apply for a reverse mortgage.

A positive note is that any other assets of the borrower are untouchable by the lending institution making the reverse mortgage. The Federal Truth in Lending Act requires all lenders handling reverse mortgages to inform a potential mortgagor of the mortgage's terms and costs. A reverse mortgage may have some flexibility and be paid out with a fixed term or have an open-ended term for as long as the mortgagor is in his home. The reverse mortgage also can be used as a line of credit to be drawn upon only when necessary. Similar to regular home mortgages, the reverse mortgage borrower has a right to reconsider during a three-day right of rescission period.

Reverse mortgage loan advances are nontaxable. They also do not affect Social Security benefits.

FINANCIAL PLANNING AFTER LOSING A SPOUSE

An elder law attorney and his staff often will be faced with clients who need assistance recovering from the death of a spouse or a life companion. The emotional pain that a person suffers when a loved one dies may not be alleviated by advanced planning, but such planning can help prevent a chaotic aftermath. If necessary, clients may need to be advised on how to prepare for the continued financial support of loved ones after their death. Before a crisis, clients should be advised to organize financial documentation. These documents may include trusts, business contracts; tax returns; employee, life, medical, and life insurance benefits; and investments and bank accounts.

The important trio of a will, an advance directive for health care, and a durable power of attorney for finances should be in place. Prearranging a funeral may be recommended. A review of the designated beneficiaries on insurance policies and investment accounts should be done. Any decision regarding organ donation should be considered. Perhaps a letter of instruction is appropriate to inform a client's executor/personal representative, loved ones, and/or a designated trustee as to the client's personal wishes.

Attorneys may be asked to offer their opinion on the appropriateness of a client's investment strategy. The attorney without training in financial planning will direct clients to more appropriate advisers. However, an attorney may be in a position to protect clients who may be swayed to inappropriate investments. For example, the Securities and Exchange Commission (SEC) and the National Association of Securities Dealers (NASD) released a joint report stating that some brokers may make unsuitable investment recommendations to elderly customers and fail to disclose the steep fees and costs that accompany the recommended investments. The NASD particularly described some brokers as using *scare tactics* to sell variable annuity contracts.[32] Variable annuity contracts are a type of insurance policy with payments that depend on the income that particular investments generate.

Before hiring a financial planning expert, clients should scrutinize how the adviser gets paid. A form called an *ADV* will disclose that information. The contract between a client and a financial adviser also should state how the adviser gets paid; the client should review the contract carefully.[33]

CLAIMING FORGOTTEN MONEY

The passage of the Sarbanes-Oxley Act in 2002 mandated the tightening of corporate accounting practices and tougher rules concerning auditing. This has led to large amounts of unclaimed money being handed over to state governments. For example, clients who have forgotten about bank accounts may have those accounts transferred to their state's unclaimed property offices within three to five years of the end of their contact with the bank.

Other reasons for the huge increase in unclaimed property have been attributed to the popularity of Internet stock accounts being opened and forgotten. Also, the surge in mutual insurance companies being publicly traded and policyholders being unaware of the stock and cash to which they are entitled may be another reason.

States must hold on to unclaimed property until it is claimed. Unclaimed property is often inherited by beneficiaries of the original owner years after the owner's death. Attorneys and their staff should include as a routine inquiry whether their clients have a right to any unclaimed funds in the state treasury. (Found money always makes for happy clients.) Unclaimed funds collected by all 50 states totaled $15.8 billion in 2000 and increased 44 percent to $22.8 billion in 2003. Refer to Exhibit 7–10 for each state's address to use in finding unclaimed money.[34]

EXHIBIT 7–10   WHERE TO FIND UNCLAIMED MONEY IN STATE COFFERS

State addresses to obtain State Unclaimed Property claim forms and to mail the required state documents for Unclaimed Property claims.

Alabama	Alaska	Arizona
Office of State Treasurer	State of Alaska	Department of Revenue
Unclaimed Property Division	Tax Division	Unclaimed Property Unit
P.O. Box 302520	P.O. Box 110420	P.O. Box 29026, Site Code 604
Montgomery, AL 36130-2520	Juneau, AK 99811-0420	Phoenix, AZ 85038-9026
Phone: (334) 242-9614	Phone: (907) 465-3726	Phone: (602) 364-0380
Toll Free: 1-888-844-8400		

(continues)

EXHIBIT 7–10 WHERE TO FIND UNCLAIMED MONEY IN STATE COFFERS *(continued)*

Arkansas
Unclaimed Property Division
Auditor of State
1400 West Third Street, Suite 100
Little Rock, AR 72201-1811
Phone: (501) 682-6000
Toll Free: 1-800-252-4648
claimit@auditorjimwood.org

California
Division of Collections
Bureau of Unclaimed Property
P.O. Box 942850
Sacramento, CA 94250-5873
Phone: (916) 323-2827
CA Residents: 1-800-992-4647

Colorado
Colorado Department of the Treasury
Great Colorado Payback
1580 Logan, Suite #500
Denver, CO 80203
Phone: (303) 866-6070
Toll Free: 1-800-825-2111
Fax: (303) 866-6154

Connecticut
Office of the State Treasurer
Unclaimed Property Division
P.O. Box 5065
Hartford, CT 06102
Toll Free: 1-800-833-7318

Delaware
Department of Finance, Division of
Revenue
State Escheator
P.O. Box 8931
Wilmington, DE 19801-3509
Phone: (302) 577-8220

District of Columbia
DC Office of Finance and Treasury
Unclaimed Property Unit
810 1st Street, NE, Suite 401
Washington, DC 20002
Phone: (202) 442-8181
dcunclaimed.property@dc.gov

Florida
Florida Department of Financial Services
Unclaimed Property Bureau
200 E. Gaines Street
Tallahassee, FL 32399-0358
Phone: (850) 413-5555
Toll Free: 1-888-258-2253
Fax: (850) 413-3017
funclaim@fldfs.com

Georgia
Georgia Department of Revenue
Local Government Services—Unclaimed
Property
4245 International Parkway, Suite A
Hapeville, GA 30354-3918
Phone: (404) 968-0490
Fax: (404) 968-0772
ucpmail@dor.ga.gov

Guam
Treasurer of Guam
P.O. Box 884
Agana, GU 96910

Hawaii
Department of Budget and Finance
Unclaimed Property Program
P.O. Box 150
Honolulu, HI 96810
unclaimedproperty@hawaii.gov

Idaho
State Tax Commission
Unclaimed Property Program
P.O. Box 70012
Boise, ID 83707-0112
Phone: (208) 334-7627
Toll Free: 1-800-972-7660
lostandfound@tax.idaho.gov

Illinois
Office of State Treasurer
Unclaimed Property Division
P.O. Box 19495
Springfield, IL 62794-9495
Phone: (217) 785-6992
IL Residents: 1-866-458-7327

(continues)

EXHIBIT 7–10   WHERE TO FIND UNCLAIMED MONEY IN STATE COFFERS *(continued)*

Indiana
Office of the Attorney General
Unclaimed Property Division
P.O. Box 2504
Greenwood, IN 46142
Toll Free: 1-866-462-5246
upd@atg.state.in.us

Iowa
Great Iowa Treasure Hunt
Lucas State Office Building
321 E. 12th Street, 1st Floor
Des Moines, IA 50319
Phone: (515) 281-5367
foundit@tos.state.ia.us

Kansas
Kansas State Treasurer
Unclaimed Property Division
900 SW Jackson, Suite 201
Topeka, KS 66612-1235
Phone: (785) 296-4165
Toll Free: 1-800-432-0386
KS Residents: 1-800-432-0386
Fax: (785) 291-3172
unclaimed@treasurer.state.ks.us

Kentucky
Kentucky State Treasury
Unclaimed Property Division
1050 US Highway 127 South, Suite 100
Frankfort, KY 40601
Phone: 1-800-465-4722
Fax: (502) 564-4200
unclaimed.property@ky.gov

Louisiana
Office of the State Treasurer
Unclaimed Property Division
P.O. Box 91010
Baton Rouge, LA 70821-9010
Phone: (225) 219-9400
Toll Free: 1-888-925-4127

Maine
Office of the State Treasurer
Attn: Unclaimed Property
39 State House Station
Augusta, ME 04333
Phone: (207) 624-7470
ME Residents: (888) 283-2808
up.claimstatus@maine.gov

Maryland
Comptroller of Maryland
Unclaimed Property Unit
301 W. Preston Street
Baltimore, MD 21201-2385
Phone: (410) 767-1700
Toll Free: 1-800-782-7383
unclaim@comp.state.md.us

Massachusetts
Department of the State Treasurer
Abandoned Property Division
One Ashburton Place, 12th Floor
Boston, MA 02108-1608
Phone: (617) 367-0400
MA Residents: 1-800-647-2300

Michigan
Office of the State Treasurer
Unclaimed Property Division
Lansing, MI 48922
Phone: (517) 636-5320
Fax: (517) 636-5324

Minnesota
Minnesota Department of Commerce
Unclaimed Property Program
85 7th Place East, Suite 500
St. Paul, MN 55101-2198
Phone: (651) 296-2568
MN Residents: 1-800-925-5668

Mississippi
Mississippi Treasury
Unclaimed Property Division
P.O. Box 138
Jackson, MS 39205
Phone: (601) 359-3600

Missouri
State Treasurer's Office
Unclaimed Property Section
P.O. Box 1004
Jefferson City, MO 65102-1272
Phone: (573) 751-0840
ucp@treasurer.mo.gov

Montana
Department of Revenue
Attn: Unclaimed Property
P.O. Box 5805
Helena, MT 59604-5805
Phone: (406) 444-6900
Fax: (406) 444-0722
unclaimedproperty@mt.gov

Nebraska
Office of the State Treasurer
Unclaimed Property Division
809 P Street
Lincoln, NE 68508
Phone: (402) 471-2455

Nevada
Office of the State Treasurer
Unclaimed Property Division
555 E Washington Avenue, Suite 4200
Las Vegas, NV 89101-1070
Phone: (702) 486-4140
NV Residents: 1-800-521-0019

(continues)

EXHIBIT 7–10   WHERE TO FIND UNCLAIMED MONEY IN STATE COFFERS *(continued)*

New Hampshire
Treasury Department
Unclaimed Property Division
25 Capitol Street, Room 205
Concord, NH 03301
Phone: (603) 271-2619
NH Residents: 1-800-791-0920
aptreasury@treasury.state.nh.us

New Jersey
Office of the State Treasurer
Unclaimed Property
P.O. Box 214
Trenton, NJ 08695-0214
Phone: (609) 292-9200

New Mexico
Taxation & Revenue Department
Unclaimed Property Division
P.O. Box 25123
Santa Fe, NM 87504-5123
Phone: (505) 476-1774
uproperty@state.nm.us

New York
Office of the State Comptroller
Office of Unclaimed Funds
110 State Street, 8th Floor
Albany, NY 12236
Phone: (518) 270-2200
Toll Free: 1-800-221-9311
NY Residents: 1-800-221-9311
NYSOUF@osc.state.ny.us

North Carolina
Department of State Treasurer
Unclaimed Property Program
325 North Salisbury Street
Raleigh, NC 27603-1385
Phone: (919) 508-1000
Fax: (919) 508-5181
unclaimed.property@treasurer.state.nc.us

North Dakota
State Land Department
Unclaimed Property Division
P.O. Box 5523
Bismarck, ND 58506-5523
Phone: (701) 328-2800
llfisher@state.nd.us

Ohio
Department of Commerce
Division of Unclaimed Funds
77 South High Street, 20th floor
Columbus, OH 43215-6108
Phone: (614) 466-4433
Toll Free: 1-877-644-6823
unfdmm@com.state.oh.us

Oklahoma
Oklahoma State Treasurer
Unclaimed Property Division
4545 N. Lincoln Blvd., Suite 106
Oklahoma City, OK 73105-3413
Phone: (405) 521-4273
unclaimed@treasurer.ok.gov

Oregon
Division of State Lands
Trust Property Section
775 Summer Street NE, #100
Salem, OR 97301-1279
Phone: (503) 378-3805

Pennsylvania
Treasury Department
Bureau of Unclaimed Property
P.O. Box 1837
Harrisburg, PA 17105-1837
Toll Free: 1-800-222-2046

Puerto Rico
Office of the Commissioner
of Financial Inst.
Alfredo Padilla, Commissioner
P.O. Box 11855
San Juan, PR 00910-3855
Phone: (787) 723-3131

Rhode Island
Office of the General Treasurer
Unclaimed Property Division
P.O. Box 1435
Providence, RI 02901
Phone: (401) 222-6505
ups@treasury.state.ri.us

South Carolina
Unclaimed Property Program
State Treasurer's Office
P.O. Box 11778
Columbia, SC 29211
Phone: (803) 737-4771
Fax: (803) 734-2668
payback@sto.sc.gov

South Dakota
Office of the State Treasurer
Unclaimed Property Division
500 East Capitol Avenue, Suite 212
Pierre, SD 57501-5070
Phone: (605) 773-3379

Tennessee
Treasury Department—Unclaimed
Property Division
Andrew Jackson Bldg., 9th Floor
500 Deaderick Street
Nashville, TN 37243-0242
Phone: (615) 741-6499

(continues)

EXHIBIT 7–10 WHERE TO FIND UNCLAIMED MONEY IN STATE COFFERS *(continued)*

Texas	Utah	Vermont
Comptroller of Public Accounts	State Treasurer's Office	Vermont State Treasurer
Unclaimed Property Division	Unclaimed Property Division	Abandoned Property Division
P.O. Box 12019	341 South Main St., 5th Floor	Pavillion Building 109 State Street, 4th
Austin, TX 78711-2019	Salt Lake City, UT 84111	Floor
Toll Free: 1-800-654-FIND (3463)	Phone: (801) 320-5360	Montpelier, VT 05609-6200
unclaimed.property@cpa.state.tx.us	Toll Free: 1-888-217-1203	Phone: (802) 828-2407
		VT Residents: 1-800-642-3191
Virgin Islands	**Virginia**	**Washington**
Office of the Lieutenant Governor	Virginia Department of the Treasury	Department of Revenue
Division of Banking	Division of Unclaimed Property	Unclaimed Property Section
18 Kongens Gade	P.O. Box 2478	P.O. Box 47477
St. Thomas, VI 00802	Richmond, VA 23218-2478	Olympia, WA 98504-7477
	Phone: (804) 225-2393	Phone: (360) 705-6706
	Toll Free: 1-800-468-1088	WA Residents: 1-800-435-2429
	ucpmail@trs.virginia.gov	
West Virginia	**Wisconsin**	**Wyoming**
Office of the State Treasurer	State Treasurer's Office	Office of the State Treasurer
Unclaimed Property Division	Unclaimed Property Unit	Unclaimed Property
One Players Club Drive	P.O. Box 2114	2515 Warren Avenue, Suite 502
Charleston, WV 25311	Madison, WI 53701-2114	Cheyenne, WY 82002
Phone: (304) 558-2937	Phone: (608) 267-7977	Phone: (307) 777-5590
Toll Free: 1-800-642-8687	Toll Free: 1-877-699-9211	
	Fax: (608) 261-6799	
	unclaim@ost.state.wi.us	

RAILROAD RETIREMENT BENEFITS

A railroad employee can earn a service annuity based on his age and depending on the employee's years of creditable railroad service. The employee must file an application to receive the annuity, and full retirement age occurs when the employee has at least 30 years of service and is 67 years old (for those employees born after 1938). The amount of an employee's annuity is the total of portions that are computed separately under different formulas, called tiers. An employee may be required to take an annuity reduction if he receives other retirement benefits. For example, Social Security benefits reduce the annuity amount paid. Detailed and extensive information about railroad retirement information can be found at <http://www.rrb.gov>.

VETERANS BENEFITS

Living armed services veterans 65 years old and older make up 39 percent of the veterans population in the United States. The sheer number of elderly veterans ensures that veterans benefits will be a topic of importance for most elder law practices. Armed services veterans may be eligible for federal and state veterans benefits. The Department of Veterans Affairs (VA) pays **Dependency and Indemnity Compensation (DIC)** whenever a military member's or veteran's death is due to service-related causes. The DIC benefits also may be paid to a surviving spouse when the death is not service-related. The VA provides care in its own facilities to veterans who need skilled or intermediate nursing care. The VA maintains contracts with community nursing homes to outsource such care for veterans.

Veterans may be eligible to receive a veterans' pension, and some veterans may be eligible to receive benefits associated with a service-related disability. Veterans benefits do not reduce Social Security benefits. Detailed and extensive information about veterans benefits can be found at <http://www.va.gov>. A user-friendly VA benefits document can be downloaded from the site as well.

ELDER LAW PRACTICE

Rena could not believe that her first employer, Mr. Sussex, a partner in the six-lawyer firm Sussex and Newton, Esqs, had died. Unfortunately, Mr. Newton, a founding partner with Mr. Sussex, had died years ago. Rena had heard the sad news from an old friend who had stayed on at Mr. Sussex's office after Rena had left. It seemed the whole place was in an uproar. Nobody knew what was going to happen to the firm. Apparently, Rena learned, that as good a lawyer as Mr. Sussex was, he had not planned for his own death. There was no plan in place. Rena wondered what the firm would do now.

What planning could Mr. Sussex have done before he died?

Analysis: When a partner in a law office dies, having a *buy-sell agreement* to be funded with life insurance benefits facilitates a transitional stage for a law firm with more than one partner. In addition, an up-to-date client list and the partner's schedule can help during a difficult time for a firm. A firm with a solo practitioner, like Tara Jensen's, would have a more difficult transitional period.[35]

ELDER LAW PRACTICE

Luke, the newest paralegal at Tara Jensen's law office, was looking forward to attending a seminar entitled "Appreciating Your Clients." It was sponsored by the paralegal program from which he had recently graduated. Greeting the alumni, current students, and faculty, the speaker began by explaining her career choice.

(continues)

ELDER LAW PRACTICE *(continued)*

"Hi, I'm Judy Cousins and I'm a law office manager for MacMillan & MacMillan *and* a graduate of this college's paralegal program. I enjoyed my years as a paralegal but decided to take my career in a different direction after several years at MacMillan. I'd like to subtitle my talk "You Never Get a Second Chance to Make a First Impression.""

Seeing a few confused faces in the audience, Judy added, "I know your mothers and fathers might have told you the same thing, but I'm telling you that the old adage is especially true when it comes to clients."

"Clients are quick to pounce on anything they find the slightest bit annoying," Judy commented. "For example, don't keep clients waiting more than 5 or 10 minutes unless you absolutely cannot avoid it."

"A messy desk may signal that you are too busy for a new client or have organizational issues," Judy explained. "For example, are storage boxes stacked everywhere? Does the carpet need cleaning? Does the office need a dusting?" Judy asked.

Judy continued to discuss how she had taken her career in a new direction by serving as a consultant to law firms. She explained, "Basically, I'm 'Miss Manners' for some of the law firms in the area. I give lectures and provide practice sessions for attorneys and their staffs."[36]

Luke listened as a student interrupted Judy in midsentence and asked if Miss Manners wasn't "a bit old-fashioned for the busy and important world of the law."

Judy was not fazed by the question or the manner in which it had been asked. She answered, "Unfortunately, manners aren't as emphasized as much as they once were in many schools and homes. Most people who need help with their social skills don't even know that they need help or, even worse, that their lack of skills can harm a practice."

Thirty minutes later Judy finished her talk and read the audience members comments she had collected regarding their own law office experiences. The comments included, "I always send a letter telling clients what documents to bring to the office meeting, where to park, and where to get their parking ticket validated." And she also added, "The firm that handled my grandmother's estate provided soda in a crystal glass to me and tea in a porcelain cup to my mother. We obviously were important to them."

After the seminar, Luke better understood that manners were yet another way to enhance his client relationship skills, especially with the mature clients at Tara's firm. He was ready to share the highlights of the meeting with Rena and Tara.

SUMMARY

Current retirees report that 58 percent look to the Social Security Administration's benefits as a major source of income. Whether they are current retiree or still-working baby boomers, all elder law clients wonder whether they will be able to preserve their assets to make sure they have enough to last until they die. Fortunately, many Americans plan early in their working lives to use their Social Security benefits as a *supplement* to pensions and other investment strategies designed to support their post-working lives. These investment strategies may include 401k and 403b plans, IRAs, real estate and business ownership, and the bond and stock markets. When an individual has at least 10 years of employment and FICA contributions, he is considered fully insured by the Social Security Administration. Survivors of eligible workers are known as derivative beneficiaries. Each person in the workforce should receive notification from the Social Security Administration when they have worked long enough to fulfill the requirements to receive Social Security payments.

Medicare is health insurance provided by the federal government to seven out of eight of the country's residents who are 65 years old and older whether they are rich or poor. Medicare has multiple parts. Generally, Medicare Part A pays hospital bills and Medicare Part B pays an insured person's physician bills. The purpose of Medicare Part C is to offer options not provided in the other parts. A relatively new Medicare Part D added prescription drug coverage.

Medicaid is a federally funded and *state-administered* health insurance program that provides all types of medical care to individuals who cannot afford to pay for some or all of their medical bills. The Medicaid program has strict eligibility requirements. These may include a person's age; the fact that a person is pregnant, disabled, blind, or aged; a person's income and resources (such as bank accounts, real property, and other items that can be sold for cash); and the fact that a person is a U.S. citizen or a lawfully admitted resident alien. The rules for counting a person's income and resources vary from state to state and from group to group. The most recent tightening of eligibility requirements came from the passage of the federal DRA. The DRA requires all states to review any transfers of assets by a Medicaid applicant within the *60 months* before application was made. This time period for investigating asset transfer is called the look-back period.

Spousal protections for a community spouse are designed to preserve the minimum income needed for a community spouse to support himself and stay in the community after his spouse has entered a Medicaid-paying facility. All income earned in the United States has been subject to federal income taxes ever since the Twentieth Amendment was passed in 1913. Capital gains are profits made on the sale of assets, including real and personal property. When a person dies, all of his assets are added together to determine the amount of the gross estate. The Internal Revenue Code provides that certain expenses will create income tax deductions or credits. The federal government requires that the estate of any deceased person with a taxable estate over a particular dollar amount will pay federal estate taxes before the first dollar is disbursed to beneficiaries of the estate. Depending on the state, a state inheritance tax may have to be paid by an estate's beneficiaries; however, no state inheritance tax will be imposed if the relationship of the beneficiary to the deceased was as an immediate family member.

Long-term care is assistance to a person who is unable to help himself with the daily requirements of living. Long-term care may be provided in a variety of housing venues. Long-term care insurance may be purchased to pay for such care.

A reverse mortgage allows an older homeowner to benefit from his home's appreciation by using the accrued equity in the home to mortgage his house. A reverse mortgage is designed for the older homeowner who is having difficulty making ends meet, owns his own home, and wants to continue living in that home until his death. The homeowner must be at least 62 years old to apply for a reverse mortgage.

REVIEW QUESTIONS

1. What are different sources of income for Americans 65 years old and older?
2. What do the abbreviations SSI and OASDI mean? What is the difference between SSI and OASDI benefits?
3. What is the objective of the Medicare program? What is the objective of the Medicaid program?
4. How does an individual become eligible to receive OASDI benefits?
5. What benefits are available to derivative beneficiaries?
6. What steps are taken if an OASDI determination is challenged?
7. What do the different parts of the Medicare program provide?
8. Explain a medicare subscriber's rights.
9. What are the eligibility requirements of the Medicaid program?
10. How can Medicaid funding be used to finance a patient's long-term care?
11. What is the purpose of the DRA's current look-back period?
12. How can the DRA's transfer penalty be cured?
13. How are the taxes, if any, on Social Security benefits determined?
14. What are capital gains taxes? Why would they be important to an elder law client?

ETHICS ALERT

The American Bar Association's (ABA's) *Model Rules of Professional Conduct*[37] serves as a basis for the majority of state codes of professional conduct for lawyers. The Sarbanes-Oxley Act resulted in the the Association changing provisions in the *Model Rules of Professional Conduct.* The Sarbanes-Oxley Act is designed to limit corporate wrongdoing and allow lawyers to report any suspected wrongdoings by officers or workers of companies they represent without breaching attorney/client confidentiality rules. This change also had far-reaching effects on elder law practitioners. The ABA's revisions focused on a particularly important question and one often asked by elder law practitioners: Who is the client?

KEY TERMS

401k plans	itemized or standard	qualified plan
403b plans	long-term care insurance	recovery provisions
adjusted gross income	look-back period	required minimum distribution
capital gains	lump sum death benefit	(RMD)
community spouse	medicaid	retirement plan
community spouse resource	medicare	reverse mortgage
allowance (CSRA)	medicare part a	section 83
deficit reduction act of 2005 (DRA)	medicare part b	social security administration
defined benefit plan	medigap insurance	state estate tax
dependency and indemnity	minimum monthly maintenance	state inheritance tax
compensation (DIC)	needs allowance (MMMNA)	supplemental security income (SSI)
gross estate	money purchase plan	survivor income benefits
hardship waiver	objective standard	taxable estate
individual retirement account (IRA)	plain meaning of the words	viatical settlements

HELPFUL WEB SITES

U.S. GOVERNMENT BOOKSTORE <HTTP://BOOKSTORE.GPO.GOV> This site directs the user to the Program Operations Manual System (POMS), the internal manual of the Social Security Administration. The POMS covers the practice and procedures of the Social Security Administration; it is no longer published in a paper format.

SOCIAL SECURITY ONLINE <HTTP://WWW.SOCIALSECURITY.GOV/OACT/TR/TR03> This site directs the user to the various approaches proffered to improve the future diagnosis of Social Security benefits.

UNITED STATES DEPARTMENT OF VETERANS AFFAIRS <HTTP://WWW.VA.GOV> This is the site to go to for VA information.

INTERNAL REVENUE SERVICE <HTTP://WWW.IRS.GOV> This is the site to go to for information about the Internal Revenue Service.

ASC UNCLAIMED PROPERTY CLEARINHOUSE <HTTP://WWW.NAPPCO-NY.COM> This is the site for ACS Unclaimed Property Clearinghouse, the largest reporter of unclaimed property in the United States.

BUREAU OF THE PUBLIC DEBT <HTTP://WWW.PUBLICDEBT.TREAS.GOV> This is the United States Department of the Treasury unclaimed property site.

MEDICARE <HTTP://WWW.MEDICARE.GOV>   The helpful contacts on this Web site direct the reader to the phone numbers for the offices of SHIP (State Health Insurance Assistance Programs) for all 50 states and the U.S. territories. Consumers can call the SHIP offices for help with buying Medigap or long-term care insurance policies. In addition, consumers can use this site to submit complaints about Medicare to the Office of the Medicare Ombudsman.

NATIONAL REVERSE MORTGAGE LENDERS ASSOCIATION <HTTP://WWW.REVERSEMORTGAGE. ORG>   This national nonprofit trade association for financial services is involved in reverse mortgages in the United States and Canada.

FEDERAL TRADE COMMISSION <HTTP://WWW.FTC.GOV>   The FTC's goal is to protect consumers by preventing fraudulent, deceptive, and unfair business practices.

FINANCIAL INDUSTRY REGULATORY <HTTP://WWW.FINRA.ORG/INVESTORINFORMATION/ INVESTORPROTECTION/P005882>

This site can be used to determine whether a prospective financial adviser has a disciplinary history.

AMERICAN HEALTH CARE ASSOCIATION AND NATIONAL CENTER FOR ASSISTED LIVING <HTTP://WWW.LONGTERMCARELIVING.COM>   This site provides consumer information about long-term care and long-term care insurance, including useful links to other Web sites.

MEDICARE <HTTP://WWW.MEDICARE.GOV/NURSING/CHECKLIST.ASP>   This assists the user in comparing nursing homes.

MEDICARE <HTTP://WWW.MEDICARE.GOV/NHCOMPARE/HOME.ASP>   This site lists every nursing home that accepts Medicare and Medicaid by state, city, and ZIP Code.

NATIONAL ASSOCIATION OF INSURANCE COMMISSIONERS <HTTP://WWW.NAIC.ORG>   This is the organization of insurance regulators from 50 states, the District of Columbia, and the U.S. territories. Although insurance is regulated on a state-by-state basis, the NAIC provides a forum for the development of uniform policy when appropriate. The site include consumer resources.

A.M. BEST COMPANY <HTTP://WWW.AMBEST.COM>   A rating services company that a client may use when considering the purchase of long-term care insurance.

MOODY'S INVESTOR SERVICES <HTTP://WWW.MOODYS.COM>   Another rating services company that a client may use when considering the purchase of long-term care insurance.

■ ENDNOTES

[1] Westerberg Reyes, Karen, "Myths and Truths about Social Security," *AARP*, March/April 2005, page 32.

[2] Weston, Liz Pulliam, "7 Pitfalls Retiring Baby Boomers Must Avoid," November 2, 2006 <http://articles. moneycentral.msn.com/RetirementandWills/PlayingCatchUp/7pitfallsRetiringBabyBoomersMustAvoid. aspx >

[3] Reyes, Karen Westerberg, "Myths and Truths about Social Security," *AARP*, March/April 2005, page 32.

[4] Boroson, Warren, *Daily Record*, 2005, page D3.

[5] Boroson, Warren, *Daily Record*, 2005, page D3.

[6] Boselovic, Len, "Women Face Additional Retirement Challenges," *Daily Record*, July 17, 2007, page 10.

[7] Boselovic, Len, "Women Face Additional Retirement Challenges," *Daily Record*, July 17, 2007, page 10.

[8] Fahlund, Christine, "Invest or Delay? Strategies for Taking Social Security Benefits," *The American Association of Individual Investors,* Vol. XXVIV, No. 2, February 2007, page 5.

[9] Garden State Pharmacy Association Seminar, Teaneck, NJ, April 17, 2005.

[10] *Floress v. Massanari,* 181 F. Supp. 2d 928 (N.D. Ill.2202).

[11] Centers for Medicare & Medicaid Services Takes Steps to Improve Coverage, Federal News Service, Washington, DC, July 27, 2006.

[12] Centers for Medicare & Medicaid Services Takes Steps to Improve Coverage, Federal News Service, Washington, DC, July 27, 2006.

[13] "A Guide to Medicare Prescription Drug Coverage," *The Advisor,* April 27, 2006, page 2.

[14] 42 U.S.C. Section 1395 (a) (1) 2007. U.S. Department of Health & Human Services and Section 1924 of the Social Security Act 42 U.S.C 1396r-5 (2006).

[15] <http://www.hhs.gov>

[16] Miller, Andy, "Medicaid Will Go After Assets," *The Atlanta Journal Constitution,* March 12, 2006, page 1a.

[17] Cummings, Mary Garza, "Long-Term Care Financial Planning Helps Protect Your Independence, Retirement and Quality of Life," *The NALS Magazine for Legal Professionals,* Vol. 53, Issue 3, Winter 2004–2005, page 16.

[18] Internal Revenue Service (2006).

[19] The following states currently have an estate tax: Illinois, Kansas, Maine, Maryland, Massachusetts, Minnesota, Nebraska, New Jersey, New York, North Carolina, Ohio, Oregon, Rhode Island, Vermont, Virginia, and Wisconsin.

[20] Hogan, Paula, "What You Need to Know About Long-Term Care Insurance," *The American Association of Individual Investors,* Vol. XXVII, No. 4, May 2005.

[21] *A Shopper's Guide to Long-Term Care Insurance,* National Association of Insurance Commissioners, 2002, page 6.

[22] Guide to Long Term Healthcare, July 19 2004 <http://www.insurancepa.com/guide-to-long.htm>

[23] Cericola, Sandra, "Factors to Consider When Choosing Long-Term Insurance," *Plastic Surgical Nursing,* Fall 2000.

[24] Guide to Long Term Healthcare, July 19, 2004 <http://www.insurancepa.com/guide-to-long.htm>

[25] Adams, Jill, "A Useful Diagnosis," *Fidelity Outlook,* February 2004, page 11.

[26] "Elder Care Claims Denied," *St. Petersburg Times,* March 26, 2007, page 1.

[27] "Elder Care Claims Denied," *St. Petersburg Times,* March 26, 2007, page 1.

[28] DuHigg, Charles, "Late in Life, Finding a Bonanza in Life Insurance," *The New York Times,* 2007.

[29] Kirchheimer, Sid, "Caught in a Deathtrap," *AARP Bulletin,* June 2006, page 33.

[30] Geller, Adam, "Reverse Mortgages Let Owners Remain in Homes Have Cash," *Daily Record,* October 2, 2004, page 3.

[31] Boroson, Warren, *Daily Record,* 2005, page D3.

[32] Colgan, Mark, "Surviving a Loss: Financial Planning for Widow and Widowers," *AAII Journal,* August 2004, page 7.

[33] Colgan, Mark, "Surviving a Loss: Financial Planning for Widow and Widowers," *AAII Journal,* August 2004, page 7.

[34] Simpson, Doug, "Forgotten Money," *Daily Record,* July 24, 2005, pages 3–4.

[35] Herman, Gregg M., "Preparing the Unthinkable: Death of a Partner," *Family Advocate,* Fall 2004, Vol. 27, No. 2, page 6.

[36] Neil, Martha, "Forum For Decorum," *ABA Journal,* October 2002, page 20.

[37] Podgers, James, "Who Is the Client?" *ABA Journal,* January 2004, page 49.

Online Companion™
For additional resources, please go to
http://www.paralegal.delmar.cengage.com

CHAPTER 8

Housing Options

"Our senior citizens have given us so much, and Americans with disabilities make remarkable contributions to our society every day. Neither group should ever have to worry about being able to afford a decent place to live."

ALPHONSO JACKSON, HOUSING AND URBAN DEVELOPMENT SECRETARY[1]

■ OBJECTIVES

After completing this chapter, you will be able to:

- Explain the importance of housing and the person-environment fit.
- List the variety of housing accommodations available to senior citizens.
- List the payment options for a variety of housing accommodations.
- Explain the protections available for nursing home residents.

INTRODUCTION

Where and how people choose to live as they age is a critical factor in determining a person's level of happiness and independence. People need to be in a living environment that meshes with their physical and emotional needs. This has been called the *person-environment fit.*[2] Environments that are *too challenging* or *not challenging enough* can be equally harmful to a resident's emotional health and physical well-being.[3] An individual's choice of living arrangement is influenced by financial, health, family, and cultural factors.

THE ATTORNEY'S ROLE IN CLIENT HOUSING ISSUES

Elder law attorneys and their support staff should be aware of the various housing options available to clients in their geographical area. Clients usually need guidance on the ramifications of signing contracts involving housing or transactional real estate matters. Housing options will depend on an analysis of a client's medical and social needs.

A recently ill client who no longer needs hospitalization should be informed that a nursing home is not the only answer to her housing needs if the client needs only personal living assistance. The health services needs of a client along with the best housing option are usually measured with the assistance of the **activities of daily living (ADL)** barometer. ADL include basic tasks essential for day-to-day functioning, such as bathing, dressing, grooming, eating, moving about, and using the toilet alone.

An individual's personal needs should also be weighed to determine if **instrumental activities of daily living (IADL)** have been compromised. IADL include those activities that are less basic than the traditional ADL. IADL include activities such as shopping, paying bills, cleaning, doing the laundry, and preparing meals. Many seniors initially need more assistance with IADL (e.g., cleaning, paying bills, and driving) than with ADL. If feasible, all alternatives should be considered before the decision is made to move a senior to a nursing home. However, failure to reach an acceptable level of ability in undertaking the ADL can lead to the conclusion that a client may need the services of a nursing home.

Many seniors who require help with some activities are largely independent, requiring help with only one or two IADL. In some cases, intermittent help from a family member or friend may be all that an elderly client needs to remain in her own home. If friends or family are unavailable, informal care arrangements may not be adequate. Elderly clients who need some help with daily life may utilize the following resources:

- Home care services
- Home sharing
- Meals on Wheels
- Telephone reassurance programs
- Shopping assistance services
- Special transportation services
- Special in-home health aids

activities of daily living (ADL)

Basic tasks essential for day-to-day functioning, such as bathing, dressing, grooming, eating, moving about, and using the toilet alone.

instrumental activities of daily living (IADL)

Those activities that are less basic than the traditional activities of daily living (e.g., shopping, paying bills, cleaning, doing laundry, and preparing meals).

- Adult foster care
- Life care communities
- Home care
- Adult day care
- Assisted living facilities

Of course, an attorney alone should not determine the housing choice for a client. The client and her family, if available, along with the client's physician and perhaps a geriatric care manager, should be the primary decision makers. A geriatric care manager is a health and human services specialist who helps families care for older relatives while encouraging as much independence for the older relative as possible. However, an attorney is often an integral part of ensuring that all legal precautions and preparations are attended to and that the legal ramifications of any decisions are explained.

SENIOR HOUSING OPTIONS

America's elderly are choosing all types of living arrangements. The country's elderly are living by themselves, with their spouses, with family members, and with unrelated adults. Living options range from independent housing to subsidized and unsubsidized senior citizen communities to assisted living facilities with partial care to nursing homes with complete medical care. The newer options of lower-level care, such as adult day care and assisted living, are growing as nursing homes become a narrowly specialized service catering to those in the greatest need. For example, while just over 1.5 million people lived in U.S. nursing homes in 2006, 800,000 people lived in assisted living facilities where care may have been as minimal as the providing of prepared dinners.[4] Refer to Exhibit 8–1 to review a chart showing the living environments of Americans.

For seniors who need living assistance, the variety of options keeps growing. In the United States, all types of assisted living facilities have emerged as an important shelter and care component to accommodate the needs of frail seniors. The growth of these facilities was especially striking during the 1990s; and there are now over 27,000 assisted living facilities in the United States, with more being built each day.[5]

EXHIBIT 8–1   HOW AMERICANS LIVE

Characteristic	Number		Percent	
	Men	**Women**	**Men**	**Women**
OLDER ADULTS				
65 years old and over				
Total	13,886	18,735	100.0	100.0
Living Alone	2,355	7,427	17.0	39.6
Married Spouse Present	10,084	7,743	72.6	41.3
None of the Above	1,447	3,565	10.4	19.0
65–74 years old				
Total	8,049	9,747	100.0	100.0
Living Alone	1,108	2,983	13.8	30.6
Married Spouse Present	6,170	5,156	76.7	52.9
None of the Above	771	1,608	9.6	16.5
75 years old and over				
Total	5,837	8,988	100.0	100.0
Living Alone	1,247	4,444	21.4	49.4
Married Spouse Present	3,914	2,587	67.1	28.8
None of the Above	676	1,957	11.6	21.8
YOUNGER ADULTS				
18–34 years old				
Total	31,854	32,464	100.0	100.0
Living Alone	2,830	2,156	8.9	6.6

(continues)

EXHIBIT 8–1 HOW AMERICANS LIVE *(continued)*

Characteristic	Number		Percent	
	Men	**Women**	**Men**	**Women**
Married Spouse Present	10,603	13,298	33.3	41.0
No Married Spouse Present—				
Child of Household	9,737	6,661	30.6	20.5
None of the Above	8,684	10,349	27.3	31.9
18–24 years old				
Total	13,291	13,242	100.0	100.0
Living Alone	551	588	4.1	4.4
Married Spouse Present	1,305	2,332	9.8	17.6
No Married Spouse Present—				
Child of Household	7,497	5,629	56.4	42.5
None of the Above	3,938	4,693	29.6	35.4
25–34 years old				
Total	18,563	19,222	100.0	100.0
Living Alone	2,279	1,568	12.3	8.2
Married Spouse Present	9,298	10,966	50.1	57.0
Not Married Spouse Present—				
Child of Household	2,240	1,032	12.1	5.4
None of the Above	4,746	5,656	25.6	29.4

Source: U.S. Census Bureau, Current Population Survey, March 2000.

Staying at Home

The majority of Americans over age 50 own their own home. A post-WWII phenomenon, personal home ownership, became a way for the average American to have her slice of the American pie. U.S. homeowners typically point to their homes as their largest personal asset and loathe leaving home ownership behind as they age.[6]

Most senior citizens want to stay in the comfort of their own home. This is often referred to as **aging in place**. In fact, one poll of AARP members over 75 years old showed that more than 80 percent wanted to stay in their own home as they aged.[7] Usually, to remain at home, at the very least, a person must be able to drive (unless mass transit is readily available), go shopping, cook, and handle mundane household chores. Many areas of the United States do not accommodate individuals who are unable to drive a car. Seniors who depend on driving for their personal freedom are hesitant to admit that they are no longer able to drive. It is the exception rather than the rule that the average senior can afford to hire household help, often called *home care,* for all chores. Historically, home care meant *any* medical or nonmedical care provided in a home setting. Today the term *home care* has evolved to describe nonmedical care such as housekeeping and companionship.[8]

The stay-at-home option can more easily become a reality with careful planning. Self-sufficient seniors may be able to stay in their home if they downsize to a smaller single-family home, a townhouse, a condominium, or an apartment. The planning and preparation also may include the following:

- Home modification and repair
- Reverse mortgage
- Rural housing loan
- In-home household help
- Meals on Wheels[9]

One newer option assisting seniors in making their stay-at-home choice easier is **virtual retirement community**. This type of Web-based assistance began in Boston, Massachusetts, as a nonprofit solution for seniors who needed help at home if they wanted to stay there. Basically, the Web can be used to provide access to social services, basic living necessities (e.g., medications, groceries, and automatic bill paying), and social outreach programs.[10]

House sharing is another option for those who want to remain at home. The 1990's television situation comedy *Golden Girls* popularized house sharing among the senior set. House sharing can provide the older homeowner with revenue, maintenance around the house, added security, and companionship. According to the U.S. Census Bureau, house sharing can consist of two types of households: a family or a nonfamily household. A family household has at least two members related by blood, marriage, or adoption, one of whom is the householder (i.e.,

aging in place
The desire of seniors to stay in the comfort of their own home as they age.

virtual retirement community
Web-based assistance that can be used to provide access to social services and social outreach programs.

house sharing
An option that allows seniors to remain in their home by living with another family member or boarder.

the person who rents or owns the premises). A nonfamily household is a person living alone or a householder who shares the housing unit with nonrelatives only (e.g., boarders or roommates). The nonrelatives of the householder may be related to each other.

Subsidized Housing

Subsidies for public housing usually are funded by the federal government's Department of Housing and Urban Development (HUD) and administered by each state through local county and city agencies. The Elderly Housing Program is commonly known as Section 202. Its original mission in 1959 as part of the National Housing Act was to focus on the construction of subsidized rental housing for older adults. Over 3,500 Section 202 housing units are operating today.

There are basically two types of subsidized housing. The first type is generally described as public housing, which usually refers to the government-subsidized project-based construction of **public housing**. The second type of subsidized housing is usually called **public voucher-based**. The public voucher-type program is typically portable in nature and can be used by the recipient in any rental unit that is approved by the local Public Housing Authority (PHA). The local PHA approves project-based housing and usually manages the public housing being provided. Public housing residents typically are chosen to receive housing assistance through income eligibility. HUD-sponsored housing subsidies specifically address the needs of low-income senior citizens. Private nonprofit agencies often apply to HUD for funding to supply low-income senior citizens with affordable housing. Subsidized senior housing usually calculates a resident's monthly rental costs on a percentage of the senior citizen's income.

Assisted Living Facilities

A variety of assisted living definitions are used in state regulations. Across the country, *assisted living* is the generic term used to describe housing that provides assistance to residents with daily needs. The levels of services vary greatly among the states. Common terms for **assisted living facilities** include *residential care, personal care, adult congregate living care, board and care, domiciliary care, adult living facilities, supported care, enhanced care, community-based retirement facilities, adult foster care, adult homes, sheltered housing,* and *retirement residences*. Assisted living facilities aid residents with their daily personal needs; again, they are not nursing homes offering skilled nursing care on a 24-hour basis. Assisted living facilities should involve family and friends in providing a homelike atmosphere that maximizes a resident's personal dignity, autonomy, independence, privacy, and choice.[11]

---

public housing
Usually refers to government-subsidized project based construction

public voucher-based
Refers to subsidized housing typically portable in nature that can be used by the recipient in any rental unit that is approved by the local Public Housing Authority.

assisted living facilities
Housing options for seniors based on the level of need for assistance.

Two-thirds of assisted living facility residents pay out of pocket for their expenses. In 2003, the national average cost for assisted living facilities was $2,379 per month. Many facilities charge a base rate and offer services on an à la carte basis.[12]

Senior Communities

Senior communities (also called **congregate housing**) are designed for more active seniors who can live independently in their own residence. The emphasis is on the similarities that come with being in the same age range as other residents. Although relatively good health may be a prerequisite (unless a caregiver is residing with the resident), the physical design of senior communities usually emphasizes physical accessibility of the units. Senior communities may be available as rentals or as owner-occupied units. These communities also may be designed using mobile or modular homes.

Moving from a House to an Apartment

Not every senior citizen wants to stay in her own home, particularly when maintaining the house has become a burden. A viable alternative for some seniors is to sell their home and move to an apartment. Apartment living comes in many price ranges and accommodations. Rental types include the following:

- Rental housing offering all types of market rate units to all age ranges
- Rental housing designed for anyone 55 years and older (there are usually exceptions to the age restrictions for spouses or caregivers who are younger)
- Affordable rental housing designed for senior citizens below a certain income level
- Public housing
- Rural rental help

Elder Cottage Housing Opportunity

The better known term for **Elder Cottage Housing Opportunity (ECHO)** is **granny flat** (or mother/daughter unit). The name ECHO may sound new, but the concept harkens back to classic multigenerational living accommodations with a contemporary twist. Granny flats are small apartments built onto an adult child's home or built independently on the adult child's property. A granny flat

senior communities
Communities designed for more active seniors who can living independently in their own residence.

congregate housing
Another term for senior communities.

elder cottage housing opportunity (ECHO)
A concept of classic multigenerational living accommodations, often small apartments built onto an adult child's home or built independently on the adult child's property.

granny flat
Small apartments built onto an adult child's home or built independently on the adult child's property. Can also be a mobile home.

even may be a mobile home. The granny flat works only if local zoning regulations allow it. According to a national survey, only three percent of those asked were living with an elderly parent in a granny flat.[13]

Group Homes

Group homes are another option that are usually designed for the relatively self-sufficient senior to provide some household maintenance and companionship. Group homes are not nursing homes; and if a resident needs more than basic assistance, the group home usually asks the resident to leave.

Adult Foster Care

The term *foster care* is familiar to most people as an option for minors needing care, but **adult foster care** is also used to house elderly adults. It is more typically used for adults when they do not need continual caregiving. The average cost for an elderly foster care resident in 2007 was approximately $2,100 per month.[14]

Board and Care Homes

Board and care homes are a type of group home that offers 24-hour supervision and some personal care services. Homes may be licensed or unlicensed. They range in size from two to many more residents. They are similar to adult foster care.

Continuing Care Retirement Communities

Another housing option that covers every type of eventuality is a **continuing care retirement community (CCRC)**. These communities are sometimes called **step care** or **progressive communities**. The communities also may be called life care communities. Whatever the name, these communities are designed to care for a resident until the end of the resident's life. The resident of a life care community can (for a fee) move to a life care facility as an independent elder and be assured that any future reductions in her physical or mental abilities will still allow her to be part of this chosen life care community. This is accomplished by transferring the resident to one of the other available care level accommodations within the life care community. All CCRCs offer essentially three levels of care: *independent living, assisted living,* and *skilled nursing care.*

All CCRCs promise that once a resident has agreed to move to the facility, any medical needs the individual develops due to declining health will be provided for within the community. This often means that if a resident develops a short-term illness or an injury, she stays in the community's on-campus hospital or health center and then returns to her residence at the appropriate level. The resident should have access to all levels of care within the CCRC.

Typically, a large one-time out-of-pocket entry fee is charged; monthly fees for utilities and maintenance of the community are additional. The downside includes the fact that the initial fee (which can go as high as hundreds of thousands of dollars) is usually nonrefundable. CCRC rules are usually plentiful and can be inflexible. A typical resident is a white affluent female in her early eighties.[15]

A CCRC usually is regulated by the state in which it is located. Some states highly regulate CCRCs; others states do not. Many states have statutes that clarify resident and CCRC rights and obligations. Numerous agencies usually have jurisdiction over a CCRC. For example, any state agency that deals with licensure of nursing facilities can affect a CCRC. State housing agencies are responsible for inspections. An incorporated CCRC usually deals with a state's treasury department. A state's attorney general may be responsible for dealing with state regulation and financial disclosure requirements of CCRCs. State ombudsmen offices are usually empowered to investigate the quality of care for CCRC residents. The HHS becomes involved with CCRCs (as well as other housing options) whenever Medicare reimbursement and enforcement of the Health Insurance Portability and Accountability Act (HIPPA) is called for.

In addition, the Continuing Care Accreditation Commission, a private nonprofit organization, accredits CCRCs that complete the voluntary process of having their finances, governance administration, resident health, and life issues evaluated. Refer to Exhibit 8–2 for an example of CCRC legislation from New York.

Contractual Ramifications of a CCRC

CCRC contracts are as varied and different as the communities themselves. Generally, the contracts differ according to the types of services, housing, and amenities included. Residents may be able to opt for plans that range from traditional or modified to a more à la carte selection. Obviously, the more detailed and less ambiguous the contract, the more protected and informed the resident. Each contract should set forth all financial obligations the resident will be assuming upon signing the contract. State CCRC statutes generally require that financial solvency disclosure statements be provided to incoming residents prior to their signing of any contracts. Whether a resident can receive a refund of any portion of the entry fee should be clearly stated in the contract.

EXHIBIT 8–2   AN EXAMPLE OF CCRC STATUTORY LANGUAGE

NY Public Health Law § 4600

§ 4600. Legislative findings and purpose

The dramatic increase in the numbers of elderly people, especially those seventy-five years of age and older, coupled with the special housing and health care needs of this growing segment of the population, requires the development of new and creative approaches to help ensure the care of older people in residential settings of their own choice. If carefully planned and monitored, life care communities have the potential to provide a continuum of care for older people that will provide an attractive residential option for such persons, while meeting their long term care needs for life. To ensure that the financial, consumer, and health care interest of individuals who enroll in such communities will be protected, such communities must be effectively managed and carefully overseen.

The intent of the legislature, therefore, is to allow for the prudent development of life care communities. The legislature further intends to require that the relevant state agencies coordinate the regulation of such communities in order to ensure that there are adequate safeguards for those elderly who become residents and to assist in the orderly development of such communities. Although lead responsibility for the interagency coordination of the regulation and establishment of such communities is vested in the department of health, the legislature does not intend that such communities become or be perceived as primarily medically-oriented facilities. The legislature intends, instead, that such communities be viewed as an attractive and innovative residential alternative for older New Yorkers who are seeking to maintain, to the extent possible, an independent and active life in a community in which their long-term care needs will be met.

Nursing Homes

Admissions to nursing homes, once a typical prescription for elder care, have dropped 10 percent in the past decade even though the number of Americans over age 75 grew by 27 percent during the same time period. Nursing homes are no longer as prominent among long-term care options as they used to be as recently as the early 1990s. Downsizing has forced some nursing homes to become more narrowly specialized, catering to those individuals requiring the greatest assistance. The descriptive term **nursing home** is an umbrella term used to define a residential care facility whose purpose is to care for individuals who are no longer in need of hospitalization but are still too dependent on personal assistance to reside in their own home without that personal assistance. In 2003, the national average cost of a private room in a nursing home was $181 per day, approximately $66,000 per year.[16]

Even as expensive as that may seem, a nursing home stay is still a cost-effective alternative to hospital care.

There is no way to view a move to a nursing home other than the extreme life-altering event that it is. Typically, discussion regarding a move to a nursing home is initiated by a patient's doctor or another health care person (e.g., a

nursing home

A general term for different types of medical facilities that provides meals, skilled nursing, rehabilitation, medical services, personal care, and recreation in a supervised and protected setting.

social worker, a gerontologist, or hospital staff if the prospective resident has been hospitalized). The suggestion usually is made when there are concerns about a patient's cognitive and physical conditions worsening.

Federal law requires that the term *nursing home* be used only when a facility provides *skilled nursing care or rehabilitation services for injured, disabled, or sick persons.*[17] Most nursing homes are profit-oriented, and their owners design their businesses to provide the variety of care that the residents need. Generally, nursing homes provide professional nursing care or some lesser types of intermediate care. Many nursing homes also accept residents who do not need medical assistance, but still need some personal assistance with daily responsibilities.

A person who requires continuous supervision by skilled medical staff usually needs a nursing home. A **skilled care facility** offers nursing care 24 hours a day. The nursing care provided is usually considered **rehabilitation** or **special care nursing**. Rehabilitation nursing care emphasizes the recovery of the patient, and the usual goal is to return the patient to her home or at least to one of the assisted living alternatives described previously. Special care nursing is for patients who have specific physical or mental needs that probably will leave the patient in the care setting for the rest of her life. A big difference between a skilled care facility and other alternatives is that a resident can be admitted to a skilled care facility only with a physician's permission. Another difference is how a skilled care facility is paid for. If treatment ordered is considered medically necessary, Medicare or Medicaid may pay for it.

Choosing a Nursing Home

When choosing a nursing home is necessary, the emphasis should be on the word *home*, with an understanding that it is to be the home of a person who has difficulty caring for herself. According to AARP, a nursing home should still be considered a person's home—*just one that also provides meals, skilled nursing, rehabilitation, medical services, personal care, and recreation in a supervised and protected setting.*

The job of locating an appropriate nursing home often falls on family or a designated health care proxy (if one has been chosen). Picking a nursing home is a difficult task. Research is necessary to make sure the facility will meet the needs of the person moving there, will be an acceptable place to live, and will be affordable and within the means of those who pay the bill.

After they have established a list of available nursing homes that meet an individual's criteria, the individual (if possible) and family members (if available) should visit the home personally. Elder law practitioners can offer helpful advice. The individual and her family should be prepared to ask questions to see if the facility will meet the needs and expectations of the individual. They should read the home's state inspection report. If the home will not allow them to read the report, this should be considered a red flag. They should ask the personnel many questions: What kinds of care are provided? What are the credentials of the staff? What is the turnover of the staff? What is the patient–to-caregiver ratio? What

skilled care facility
A nursing home that offers nursing care 24 hours a day.

rehabilitation
Emphasizes the recovery of the patient and the goal of returning the patient to her home or at least to one of the assisted living alternatives.

special care nursing
Care for patients with specific physical or mental needs that probably will leave the patient in the setting for the rest of her life.

kinds of activities and continuing programs are available for the future resident and the resident's family to enjoy together? What type of accommodations are provided, and what is the cost? Can residents bring their own furnishings and other belongings? Does the facility consider resident input? Especially important to most elderly residents is the quality of the food. The family should dine at the facility so they can taste the food. Very important is the location of the facility. Is it conveniently located so that family members and friends can visit and monitor the patient's care? Does the facility have ombudsmen numbers and patient's rights displayed? Does the facility seem to be the right temperature? Does it appear clean and as odor-free as possible?[18]

Financially speaking, nursing homes may be run by a for-profit corporation or by a nonprofit corporation that is overseen by a governmental entity or charitable organization. The benefit of not-for-profit housing is that surplus funds are usually reinvested in the facility to better serve the elderly residents.

Choosing a Nursing Facility for Alzheimer's Patients

Special considerations should be investigated when choosing a housing option for a patient with AD or another type of cognitive disorder. Any of the options mentioned already, including assisted living, skilled nursing home care, and a CCRC, may be the right fit for these patients. The same questions asked at a nursing home also should be asked for the Alzheimer's patient, but with added focus on whether the special needs of Alzheimer's patients are considered. Quality programs for Alzheimer residents feature both group and individual activities that are designed to be failure-free and to build patients' confidence.[19] Some Alzheimer-focused facilities are designed with features that assist Alzheimer patients (e.g., color-coded hallways, visual cues, and secure wandering paths). Especially important when choosing an Alzheimer care facility is to ask what services are included in the basic rental agreement and if any services are extra.

How to Pay for a Nursing Home Stay

The bottom line is that a nursing home stay is expensive. The shocker is the reality of just how expensive. The average cost by 2005 rose to $69,000 per year and even 20 to 30 percent higher in some areas of the country. The costs inevitably rise each year.[20] This price tag does not include the ultimate in luxuries either, but usually middle-of-the-road amenities such as general nursing supervision and assistance with ADL. Private rooms and enjoyable activities such as hairdressing and manicures usually cost extra.

The choice of a nursing home will lead to a complete assessment of a proposed resident's finances. Does the client have the ready cash to pay for the care? If not, then the question begs to be asked, "How do you intend to pay for the nursing home?"

One way to pay for a nursing home stay is by **self-paying** if a resident has available income, has savings accumulated, has family or adult children who can pay, or uses a combination of all three. Self-pay may be the way that most residents begin their nursing home residency; but once their self-pay options are depleted, more than half of all nursing home residents have Medicaid pay for their care. In fact, the federal government paid nearly $39 billion for nursing home care in 1999.[21]

Medicare covers the cost of a nursing home stay under certain restricted circumstances. These restrictions include whether the patient requires skilled care (not custodial or personal care, but usually nursing care) and only after a stay of three or more days in a hospital for treatment of the same condition requiring nursing home care. The nursing home facility must be Medicare-approved, have a skilled nurse on duty 24 hours a day, and assign the patient to a Medicare-approved bed; in addition, there must be proof that only a nursing home can provide the care required. When all of these prerequisites are met, Medicare covers the nursing home care for up to 20 days and may co-pay up to an additional 80 days.

Preparing Legal Documents Prior to Moving to a Nursing Home

Several legal documents should be in place prior to an individual moving to a nursing home. A new nursing home resident should have the following legal documents

- A last will and testament
- Advance directives for health care
- A durable general power of attorney
- A nursing home admissions contract

Nursing home admissions contracts should detail the obligations of the nursing home and patient to each other. A nursing home admissions contract may include a clause that specifies mandatory and binding arbitration before a single arbitrator or a multiple arbitrator panel. The arbitrators are often chosen from the American Health Lawyers Association. The laws regarding the use and enforceability of arbitration clauses in nursing home contracts vary from state to state. Some states void such clauses. Federal Medicare and Medicaid law is very clear and strictly forbids such arbitration clauses involving patients with Medicare and Medicaid reimbursement.

During the admissions process, the majority of nursing homes ask what may seem like impolite questions at a time when the new resident is already nervous. These questions may include "Have you planned your funeral?" and "Do you have special funeral directions or burial directions?" This information is placed in the resident's file at the nursing home.[22]

self-paying

Paying for nursing home care with a patient's available income, a patient's accumulated savings, a family or adult children who can pay, or a combination of all three.

Nursing Home Regulation

Nursing homes are issued a governmental *license* permitting them to provide such nursing care. The licensing should involve a personal inspection of the nursing home in question and investigate the adequacy of the facility and staff as well as the reaching of caregiving goals. Along with a license, many homes want to be *certified* to accept Medicare/Medicaid-paying patients. The seeking of Medicare/Medicaid certification involves another long list of requirements that the nursing home must meet. A term often used to impress new residents is *accreditation*. Some organizations conduct a nursing home accreditation process, but such accreditation does not provide a guarantee that the home is meeting accreditation standards every day—indeed, neither does licensing or certification.

The Patient's Bill of Rights

▌ **patient's bill of rights**

A list of legal rights that are guaranteed by the federal government.

Every nursing home resident has a lengthy list of legal rights that are guaranteed by the federal government. In 1987, Congress enacted the Nursing Home Reform Law, which has since been incorporated into Medicare and Medicaid regulations. The purpose of such reform legislation is to provide nursing home residents with the legal protections necessary to ensure that residents receive the level of care needed to reach each resident's highest potential. These rights are enumerated in a federal statute commonly referred to as the **Patient's Bill of Rights**.[23] In addition, every nursing home must have written policies that incorporate the patient rights enumerated in the federal regulations. Complete listings of these rights must be openly displayed in all nursing homes. See Exhibit 8–3 to read a sample of these enumerated rights.

EXHIBIT 8–3   PATIENT'S BILL OF RIGHTS

Under federal regulations, nursing homes must have written policies covering the rights of patients. These rights must be posted where residents and visitors can easily see them. A *Patient's Bill of Rights* ensures that each person admitted to a facility will have his/her rights protected. Flagrant violations of these rights should be reported to the proper state authorities listed in the appendixes.

A Patient:

1. is fully informed as evidenced by the resident's written acknowledgment of these rights and of all rules and regulations governing the exercise of these rights.

2. is fully informed of services available in the facility and of related charges for services not covered under Medicare/Medicaid, or not covered by the facility's basic daily rate.

(continues)

EXHIBIT 8–3 PATIENT'S BILL OF RIGHTS *(continued)*

3. is fully informed of his/her medical condition unless the physician notes in the medical record that it is not in the patient's interest to be told, and is afforded the opportunity to participate in the planning of his/her medical treatment and to refuse to participate in experimental research.

4. is transferred or discharged only for medical reasons, or for his/her welfare or that of other residents, and is given reasonable advance notice to ensure orderly transfer or discharge.

5. is encouraged and assisted, through his/her period of stay to exercise his/her rights as a resident and as a free citizen. To this end he/she may voice grievances and recommend changes in policies and services to facility staff and/or outside representatives of his/her choice without fear of coercion, discrimination, or reprisal.

6. may manage his/her personal financial affairs, or is given at least a quarterly accounting of financial transactions made on his/her behalf if the facility accepts that responsibility to safeguard the funds.

7. is free from mental and physical abuse, and free from chemical and physical restraints except as authorized in writing by a physician for a specified and limited period of time or when necessary to protect patients from injury to themselves or others.

8. is assured confidential treatment of his/her personal and medical records and may approve or refuse their release to any individual outside facility.

9. is treated with consideration, respect, and full recognition of his/her dignity and individuality, including privacy in treatment and in care of his/her personal needs.

10. is not required to perform services for the facility that are not included for therapeutic purposes in this plan of care.

11. may associate and communicate privately with persons of his/her choice, and send and receive her/his personal mail unopened.

12. may meet with, and participate in activities of social, religious, and community groups at his/her discretion.

13. may retain and use his/her personal clothing and possessions as space permits, unless to do so would infringe upon rights of other patients, or constitute a hazard of safety.

14. is assured privacy for visits by his/her spouse; if both are inpatients in the facility, they are permitted to share a room.

Problem-Solving Residents' Complaints

The role of a long-term care ombudsman is clear: to help residents living in long-term care situations. Ombudsmen do this by being available to residents and their families as an information resource and a complaint investigator. If a resident or the resident's representative has a complaint regarding the long-term care facility, an ombudsman can intervene on behalf of the resident. Ombudsmen are located throughout the country, will investigate complaints, and often will mediate between a facility and a complainant. The ombudsmen are paid by the federally funded state offices on aging and are free to the public. Ombudsmen also are good sources of information for patients' families. The long-term care ombudsman program nationally investigated 20,673 complaints of abuse, gross neglect, and exploitation on behalf of nursing home and board and care residents in 2003 alone. Physical abuse was the most common type of abuse reported to ombudsman offices.[24]

Suing to Get Out

Jesse Fitchett was a 70-year-old partially paralyzed resident of the Laguna Honda Nursing Home in San Francisco, California, for over six years before a class action lawsuit led to his being released and moved to a one-bedroom apartment in an outside community. The class action lawsuit was one of the first of its kind in the country, and it claimed that the failure of San Francisco to offer alternatives to a move to a nursing home for its citizens with disabilities was discriminatory. The lawsuit was based, in large part, on a 1999 U.S. Supreme Court decision that found that if a person with a disability preferred to live in the outside community and the cost would be the same or less than living in a nursing home, then failure to offer a choice would be considered discriminatory. States such as Oregon and Washington have reformed their long-term care programs and support multiple alternatives to nursing homes. The main roadblock to such reform is that Medicaid money coming from the federal government has not been shifted to residential programs within the community and away from nursing homes.[25]

ELDER LAW PRACTICE

"I can't stand the idea of Mama all alone in there," Annie exclaimed on the verge of tears at her neighbor Rose's house.

"You can't be the only one who has doubts about your mom's nursing home," Rose offered.

"Doubts!" Annie retorted, "I have gut feelings compounded by the reality of Mama having bruises."

"I respect your feelings, but didn't your mom have bruises when she lived alone?" Rose asked. "It doesn't do you any good to think the worst. Maybe you could talk to other family members who have elderly relatives at the home and see if they have any complaints."

Nodding, Annie responded determinedly, "I did plan that at my last visit. In fact, one of my mom's friends from the senior center suggested I call our state's long-term care ombudsman to see what could be done. I didn't even know we had an ombudsman whose job it is to look after nursing home residents and investigate complaints about long-term care institutions. I didn't think it could get much worse; but now my mother's nursing home has gone to court to stop me from talking to the other residents, their families, and the staff!"

Shocked, Rose responded, "I can't believe it did that!"

(continues)

ELDER LAW PRACTICE *(continued)*

Annie answered, "The owner of the home sure did, and I think my only alternative is to call a lawyer and see if the nursing home can do this."

Within a few days, Annie spoke with families from her Families Dealing with Elderly Patients counseling group and asked for recommendations for a lawyer they thought would know how to handle the situation. Not surprisingly, Tara's name came up several times; so, Annie called her office and made an appointment. Driving to the lawyer's office the next morning, Annie gripped the steering wheel, feeling both anger and fear about her mom's situation.

Annie found the office without any trouble and hoped a solution to this ridiculous situation would be just as easy. Entering the building, Annie was met by the early morning smell of fresh coffee and the friendly greeting of Rena.

"Good morning. I'm Rena. May I help you?"

"Yes, thank you," Annie politely answered. "I'm Annie Jones. I'm here to see Tara Jensen about my mom."

"Of course, Ms. Jones. Tara is expecting you," Rena smiled. "She's just finishing up a conference call. May I get you a cup of coffee or tea while you wait?"

"Tea would be great, thanks," Annie answered.

A few minutes later Annie's relaxing interlude was interrupted by the brisk step of Tara entering the waiting room. Following introductions and offers of more tea, Annie was soon ensconced in another chair in Tara's office. Annie quickly began to explain to Tara how shocked she had been to be served with a temporary restraining order by the Ease Inn Nursing Home and how she wanted to hire Tara to help her. Tara listened patiently and took notes of Annie's story about the nursing home's claims that Annie was harassing nursing home residents, their families, and the staff and owner of the home with complaints regarding her mother's treatment.

Wound up like a spring, Annie finally took a breath and finished by asking Tara, "What do I do now?"

"If the nursing home refuses to lift the order voluntarily after I speak with the owner on your behalf, we'll get into court as soon as possible to ask the court to remove it," Tara offered.

"Let me explain. Temporary restraining orders are exactly that, temporary," Tara said. "The nursing home was able to get it without your being in court because such orders are designed for emergency situations. When only one party is in court, that's called *ex parte*. Our state's laws allow the recipient of such an order to go into court to fight the alleged claims. Restraining orders are more typically sought in cases of domestic violence or serious situations of harassment."

Tara continued, "I can honestly say that I haven't come across a situation quite like this."

"The nursing home owner must have been really aggravated by your complaints to get this aggressive and go on the offensive," Tara commented.

"I don't know if it's righteous indignation or fear that I'll uncover some illegal behavior, but I don't really care," Annie answered. "I do care about my mom; and this order restricts my visitation to certain hours, requires that I call ahead to notify the home I'm coming, and refrain from talking to anyone else at the home unless the director is present."

Tara responded, "I totally understand how you can be this upset. Let me see what I can do, and I'll get back to you as quickly as possible."

Tara concluded the meeting with Annie by reviewing the office's professional hourly fee structure and Tara's retainer agreement. Tara then asked Luke to take Annie's personal information, have her sign a retainer agreement, and set up her file.

(continues)

ELDER LAW PRACTICE *(continued)*

How could someone in Annie's position have handled the situation differently from the beginning?

Analysis: An individual with the authority to act on behalf of the nursing home resident should first talk directly to the staff caring for the resident. If that does not work, the individual should talk to a supervisor. Holding a meeting with all personnel involved with the resident's care, even on a regular basis to prevent problems, can alleviate problems before they escalate. An ombudsman can intervene. If a resident's rights are being interfered with, contacting the appropriate licensing agency may work to put pressure on the facility. Another advocate is a geriatric care manager who can intervene and speak the language of the facility. Hiring a lawyer may be necessary to clarify and assert a resident's rights. Of course, hiring an attorney may escalate the dispute. Another alternative is to move the resident, but that option requires preparation and planning.

Hospice Facility

A hospice facility is not a residential option for seniors; it is end-of-life care that should be seriously considered at the appropriate time. Most nursing homes are not designed to act as a hospice facility dealing with an individual's final days. A hospice facility provides end-of-life palliative care for individuals who are no longer receiving medical treatment. The ultimate goal of a hospice is to ensure that medical, physical, emotional, and spiritual support is given to patients and their families so that the patients live as fully and comfortably as possible. Hospice facilities provide supportive care to meet the special needs arising from the physical, psychological, spiritual, social, and economic stresses that are part of the final stage of an illness and that occur during the dying process and bereavement period. Medicare provides payment for a list of hospice services that are provided under the care of a treating physician. Hospice services are provided when all other curative treatment has ended.

Hospice services may include the following:

- Medical social services
- Nursing services
- Physical therapy, speech language pathology, and occupational therapy
- A certified home health aide
- Medical supplies, appliances, drugs, and biologicals (subject to co-payment by the recipient)
- Physicians
- Short-term inpatient care for pain control or respite for family caregivers
- Dietary counseling
- Emotional counseling

- Other appropriately prescribed items or services
- Bereavement counseling for the immediate family of the hospice patient[26]

SUMMARY

People need to be in a living environment that meshes with their physical and emotional needs. This has been called the person-environment fit. Environments that are too challenging or not challenging enough can be equally harmful to a resident's emotional health and physical well-being.

In addition to helping clients understand the ramifications of signing contracts involving housing or transactional real estate matters, elder law attorneys and their staff often are expected to know about housing options and funding those options. A client's health service needs along with the best housing option are usually measured with the assistance of the activities of daily living barometer. Instrumental activities of daily living include those activities that are less basic than the traditional activities of daily living. Most senior citizens want to stay in their homes as they age, even as their health may decline, making it more difficult to do so. This is often referred to as aging in place. The planning and preparation of staying in the home may include the following:

- Home modification and repair
- Reverse mortgage
- Rural housing loan
- In-home household help
- Meals on Wheels

Senior communities (also called congregate housing) are designed for more active seniors who can live independently in their own residence. A viable alternative for many seniors is to sell their home and move to an apartment. Group homes, another option, are usually designed for the relatively self-sufficient senior to provide some household maintenance and companionship. Board and care homes are a type of group home that offers 24-hour supervision and some personal care services.

Assisted living facilities help residents with their daily personal needs but do not provide skilled medical care. Adult foster care is more typically used for adults who do not need continual caregiving. Continuing care retirement communities are sometimes called step care or progressive communities. All continuing care retirement communities offer essentially three levels of care. A nursing home is an umbrella term used to define a residential care facility whose purpose is to care for individuals who are no longer in need of hospitalization but are still too dependent on personal assistance to reside in their own home without that personal assistance. A hospice facility provides end-of-life palliative care for individuals who are no longer receiving medical treatment.

KEY TERMS

activities of daily living (ADL)

adult foster care

aging in place

assisted living facilities

board and care homes

congregate housing

continuing care retirement
 community (CCRC)

elder cottage housing opportunity
 (ECHO)

granny flat

group homes

house sharing

instrumental activities of daily living
 (IADL)

nursing home

patient's bill of rights

public housing

public voucher-based

rehabilitation

self-paying

senior communities

skilled care facility

special care nursing

step care or progressive
 communities

virtual retirement community

REVIEW QUESTIONS

1. What is the person-environment fit?

2. How might an elder law attorney and the attorney's staff assist clients with housing issues?

3. What is the difference between ADL and IADL? Do ADL and/or IADL matter in determining an elderly person's housing options? Explain.

4. How can a virtual retirement community assist seniors who want to remain in their own home?

5. What are the two basic types of government-subsidized housing?

6. What type of senior housing would be appropriate for an individual diagnosed with dementia? What criteria should be used to choose the appropriate housing?

7. What type of senior housing would be appropriate for an individual diagnosed with arthritis and faced with limited mobility, but otherwise without any other pressing mental or physical health issues?

8. What details should be included in a CCRC contract?

9. When should a nursing home be chosen?

10. What factors should be considered in choosing a nursing home?

11. How can a patient pay for her nursing home accommodations?

12. What legal documents should be in place prior to a person's move to a nursing home?

13. What is the role of a long-term care ombudsman?

14. What type of services does a hospice provide?

15. What state agencies may be empowered to provide the overseeing and guidelines of CCRCs?

▨ ETHICS ALERT_____

Luke, the newest paralegal at Tara Jensen's law firm, was told by Tara that if he needs sample work to review, he should take advantage of the large number of legal documents that have been drafted at Tara's law firm over the last few years. Tara also suggested that for future reference, he keep a file of work samples that he has prepared. Luke wonders whether client confidentiality should be a concern and whether it is fair to charge one client for work that may be shared by another client in the future. Should he be concerned?

▨ HELPFUL WEB SITES_____

MEDICARE <HTTP://WWW.MEDICARE.GOV/NHCOMPARE/HOME.ASP>   This site lists by state every nursing home that accepts Medicare and Medicaid.

MEDICARE <HTTP://WWW.MEDICARE.GOV/NURSING/CHECKLIST.ASP>   This site contains a checklist to aid in the evaluation of nursing homes.

MEALS ON WHEELS ASSOCIATION OF AMERICA <HTTP://WWW.MOWAA.ORG>   The Meals on Wheels Association of America (MOWAA) is the oldest and largest organization in the United States representing those who provide meal services to people in need.

NATIONAL ASSOCIATION OF PROFESSIONAL GERIATRIC CARE MANAGERS <HTTP://WWW. CAREMANAGER.ORG>   This Web site offers assistance with finding a Professional Care Manager and information on the profession.

ALZHEIMER'S ASSOCIATION <HTTP://WWW.ALZ.ORG>   This site is a resource for all types of information pertaining to Alzheimer's disease.

THE JOINT COMMISSION <HTTP://WWW.JOINTCOMMISSION.ORG>   This site provides information about nursing homes and senior living facilities, as well as accreditation information for the Joint Commission on Accreditation of Healthcare Organizations.

HEALTH CARE ASSOCIATION AND NATIONAL CENTER FOR ASSISTED LIVING <HTTP://WWW. LONGTERMCARELIVING.COM>   This Web site describes itself as a guide to planning, preparing and paying for long term care for yourself or a loved one.

AMERICAN ASSOCIATION OF HOMES AND SERVICES FOR THE AGING <HTTP://WWW.AAHSA. ORG>   This organization provides a nationwide listing of facilities.

ASSISTED LIVING FEDERATION OF AMERICA <HTTP://WWW.ALFA.ORG>   The focus of this Web site is on assisted living facilities.

NATIONAL ASSOCIATION FOR HOME CARE & HOSPICE <HTTP://WWW.NAHC.COM>   This is the Web site for a trade association representing the interest and concerns of home care agencies hospices and home care aide organizations.

NATIONAL ADULT DAY SERVICES ASSOCIATION <HTTP://WWW.NADSA.ORG>   This organization's Web site states that NADSA is the voice of the adult day care services industry.

ENDNOTES

[1] <http://www.seniorjournal.com/NEWS/Housing/6-0-06-Low-incomeElderly.htm> September 11, 2006.

[2] Lawton, M. P., "Housing Elderly: Residential Quality and Residential Satisfaction," *Research on Aging 2*, 1980, pages 309–328.

[3] Teaster, Pamela, and Roberto, Karen, *Living Options for Adults Needing Assistance*, Virginia Cooperative Extension, Publication Number 350-254, August 1999.

[4] "Elderly Care Options," *The Research and Training Center on Independent Living*, Vol. 1, Issue 8, May 25, 2005.

[5] <http://www.assistedlivinginfo.com/alserve.html>

[6] United States Census Bureau, Fourth Quarter 2007 (67.8 percent homeownership).

[7] Mahar, Maggie, "A Roof Over Their Heads," *AARP* Magazine, page 65.

[8] Whitaker, Barbara, "These Days, 'Retirement Living' Can Mean Many Things," *The New York Times*, February 6, 2005, page 3.

[9] <http://www.comfortkeepers.com> May 25, 2005.

[10] Independent Housing Options & Issues for Seniors, New Jersey Institute for Continuing Legal Education 2006 Seminar, New Brunswick, NJ.

[11] "Sunset Story: The Graying of America," Public Broadcasting Service, May 25, 2005.

[12] Introduction to Adult Foster Care in Portland, *Exit/Acclaim Realty*, June 13, 2007.

[13] Golant, Stephen M., "Assisted Living: A Potential Solution to Canada's Long-Term Care Crisis," January 2001, page 3.

[14] Ernst & Young for the American Association of Homes for the Aging, Continuing Care Retirement Communities: An Industry in Action: Analysis and Developing Trends, Washington, DC, 1987.

[15] Bornstein, Robert F., and Langirand, Mary A., *When Someone You Love Needs Nursing Home Care*, New Market Press (2001).

[16] Elderly Care Options, Vol. I, Issue 8, May 25, 2005 <http://www.getriil.org/elderly.htm>

[17] 11.42 U.S.C. 1395x(dd); 42 C.F.R. 418.72 (2006).

[18] Bausell, R. Barker, Rooney, Michael A., and Inlander, Charles, *How to Evaluate and Select a Nursing Home*, Addison-Wesley, (1988).

[19] "Professional Alzheimer's Care," *Daily Record*, May, 8, 2005.

[20] MetLife Market Survey of Nursing Home & Home Care Costs, September 2005.

[21] Sheppell, Arthur, "Do Research Before Choosing a Nursing Home," *Daily Record*, June 2005, page E1.

[22] Bornstein, Robert F., and Langirand, Mary A., *When Someone You Love Needs Nursing Home Care*, New Market Press (2001).

[23] United States Administration on Aging.

[24] National Ombudsman Reporting System Data Tables, 2003, Washington, DC: United States Administration on Aging.

[25] Basler, Barbara, "Suing to Get Out in the World," *AARP Bulletin*, June 2004, page 3.

[26] The Karen Ann Quinlan Hospice brochure, 99 Sparta Avenue, Newton, NJ (2006).

Online Companion™
For additional resources, please go to
http://www.paralegal.delmar.cengage.com

9

Age Discrimination

"We cannot afford to squander our manpower through prejudice, which obscures the values of maturity, responsibility and constancy found in older workers."

PRESIDENT DWIGHT D.
EISENHOWER, 1955

"Age discrimination has oozed into every pore of the workplace."

CLAUDE PEPPER
(D-FLORIDA), 1986

■ OBJECTIVES_____

After completing this chapter, you will be able to:

- Define age bias and discrimination.
- Explain the constitutional safeguards in place against age discrimination.
- Define the purpose of the Equal Employment Opportunity Commission.
- Explain the steps taken to prove an age discrimination in employment case.
- List the remedies available in an age discrimination in employment case.
- List the available defenses in an age discrimination in employment case.

INTRODUCTION

It has been said that racial bias targets people for what they are and that age bias targets people for what they become.[1]

Historically, the subject of age discrimination in the United States failed to stir a mainly agrarian and self-employed nation of farmers. During the early years of the country, 9 out of 10 Americans lived on farms. The topic of age discrimination was not the electorate's main concern considering 45 years was the average life expectancy and the mostly self-employed farmer was unlikely to experience age prejudice.

Move forward to the early 1900s and the American economic landscape was still supported by a two-thirds agrarian population. That changed, though, with the onset of a more industrial age. Industrial growth brought many positives to American society, but with such growth came increased discrimination suffered by older workers.

In the past, the argument was made that age discrimination was only a natural by-product of the making of sound economic business decisions. This argument emphasized that with the high cost of pensions, workers' compensation, and health insurances for older workers, profits invariably would go down when older workers were hired and their employment continued. This argument has since been soundly defeated in numerous studies on the subject.[2] No less a respected entity than the *New York Times* on its editorial pages has commented that the humanitarian ideal of providing for older workers as they aged created an insurance and pension paradox for employers. Insurance and pensions may be good for the individual, but on the whole as an age group, such employment costs has made U.S. employers shy away from the older worker. In fact, even the federal government actively engaged in its own age discrimination in the early twentieth century when it imposed age limits for employment in the U.S. civil service.

Another reason for the failure of many companies to hire older workers can be traced to the policy of promoting from within. This policy usually leaves only one employment opportunity for older applicants—starting a job at beginners' wages.

Rampant age discrimination led to the 1938 formation of one group in New York called the Forty Plus Club. The club's primary purpose was to fight against employment discrimination in workers over age 40. At about the same time, the California State Department of Industrial Relations published a series of bulletins on the general subject of the older worker in industry. One bulletin announced that *the arbitrary discharge of workers because of age and regardless of their fitness, is becoming a general policy.* Another study conducted in 1930 by the New York State Commission on Old Age Security looked at data from 2,100 manufacturing firms in that state. The report declared that the older job seeker was barred from 59 percent of the then-available jobs and was discriminated against in 89 percent of them.

The economic boom brought by World War II trickled down to the over-40-year-old workforce. Employers who were losing younger workers to the four-year war effort welcomed the older workers. However, many older workers were pushed back into unemployment or underemployment by the return of millions of young soldiers eager to get back to work.

The 1950s saw the age bias problem continue and grow. A mid-twentieth-century Department of Labor study found that the primary obstacle to employment for older workers was the stigma of age and the unfounded assumptions regarding two points. First, employers believed that age brought a decline in physical and mental acuity in employees. Second, the older employee was considered overly burdensome on private pension systems. The unfairness of these unsubstantiated assumptions was cited at that time by the Department of Labor because of the lack of evidence supporting this employer bias. Little reliable evidence has been proffered since to support the claim that pension plans are unduly restrictive in terms of reducing labor mobility or hindering the hiring of older workers.

U.S. News & World Report surveyed the problem in 1955 and declared that after a man reached 45 and a woman reached 35, the problem of finding a job grew. The magazine cited a government report that stated that 60 percent of the help wanted ads and employment agency jobs in the United States in 1955 offered employment to men less than 45 years of age and to women less than 35 years of age. This was reported at a time when the 45- to 65-year-old age group had tripled in size since 1900.

The private and public studies of age bias in employment prompted legislators and pundits by the early 1960s to promote the creation of a federal age discrimination law. A joint Senate and House of Representatives Legislative Committee on Aging finally recommended that Congress adopt an anti-age discrimination law. The recommendation followed months of hearings filled with statistics proving what unemployed and frustrated older Americans searching for employment already knew.

By the mid-1960s, laws barring age discrimination in employment had already been passed in 14 states. Unfortunately, such state legislation had little impact on lessening age bias. During the same time period, Congress passed the landmark 1964 Civil Rights Act barring race, color, religion, national origin, and sex discrimination. The *1964 Act did nothing to bar age discrimination,* but President Lyndon B. Johnson did sign an executive order prohibiting age discrimination in the federal government.

FEDERAL PROTECTION AGAINST AGE DISCRIMINATION

The federally created Age Discrimination Act of 1975 prohibits discrimination on the basis of age in programs and activities receiving federal financial assistance. The 1975 act, which applies to all ages, permits the use of certain age distinctions and factors other than age that meet the act's requirements. Another federal law geared to seniors only is the Older American Act (OAA). The OAA is a federal act that provides that states must offer eligible senior assistance with everyday needs or face federal funding cuts. Different types of assistance include housing assistance; health and wellness programs; senior legal aid; employment programs; tax relief; reduced transportation fares; tuition-reduced education; and recreation, leisure and entertainment cost reductions.

This chapter will be focusing on the **Age Discrimination in Employment Act of 1967 (ADEA)**. The ADEA is a federal act that provides protection to certain applicants and employees 40 years of age and older from discrimination on the basis of age in hiring, promotion, discharge, compensation, or terms, conditions or privileges of employment. Recognizing that stereotypical preconceptions about abilities and age are the basis for age discrimination, the fundamental tenet of the ADEA legislation is that aging varies with individuals; thus, the effect of a stereotype is not only inaccurate but also morally and legally wrong.

Originally targeting the 45- to 65-year-old worker, the age limit was brought down to 40 years of age before Congress passed the act. Congress later revised the upper limit in 1986 by *eliminating forced retirement at any age with certain exceptions*. The ADEA applies to private employers with 20 or more employees, the federal government, and any local government. The U.S. Supreme Court has held that the ADEA cannot be applied to state governments. However, most states have enacted state versions of the ADEA. Other exceptions include high-level executives in policymaking positions and government officials who are appointed or elected and their non-civil service staff. If employment involves a **bona fide occupational qualification (BFOQ)**, an exception may be made to the ADEA. A BFOQ is defined as a good faith job requirement that must be fulfilled by the applicant. For example, a job opening for a lifeguard would have a BFOQ that requires lifeguard certification. Using age as a BFOQ exception is rare and places the burden of proof on the employer to show such age discrimination is a reasonable and necessary BFOQ.

Essentially, the ADEA instructs applicable employers that benefits, training, promotions, and job assignments cannot be given to younger employees but denied to older employees because of their age. The ADEA's job protections apply to job applicants and employees. The ADEA makes it unlawful to discriminate against a person because of his age with respect to any term, condition, or privilege of employment, including hiring, firing, promotion, layoff compensation, benefits, job assignments, and training. It also is unlawful to retaliate against an individual for opposing employment practices that

---

age discrimination in employment act of 1967 (ADEA)

A federal government act that provides protection to certain applicants and employees 40 years of age and older from discrimination on the basis of age in hiring, promotion, discharge, compensation, or terms, conditions, or privileges of employment.

bona fide occupational qualification (BFOQ)

An exception to the ADEA where an employer must prove that age discrimination is reasonable and necessary.

discriminate based on age or for filing an age discrimination claim, testifying, or participating in any way in an investigation, proceeding, or litigation under the ADEA.[3] The wording of the federal ADEA statute does not include a clear-cut definition of what exactly constitutes age discrimination. Instead, a variety of events shown together is how most age-related discrimination claims are proved. For example, a typical scenario would involve pink slips going only to workers over 40 years of age. Refer to Exhibit 9–1 to read an excerpt from the ADEA.

EXHIBIT 9–1   EXCERPT FROM ADEA STATUTE

It shall be unlawful for an employer to do the following:

1. to fail to hire or to discharge any individual or otherwise discriminate against any individual with respect to his compensation, terms, conditions, or privileges of employment, because of such individual age;

2. to limit, segregate, or classify its employees any way which would deprive or tend to deprive any individual of employment opportunities or otherwise adversely affect his status as an employee, because of such individual's age; or to reduce the wage rate of any employee in order to comply with this [Act].

The ADEA Today

Today there are 80 million Americans who were born during the 20 years following the end of World War II. The individuals born during this time period are called baby boomers. This baby boom generation is the largest generation ever born in the United States. The youngest baby boomers were born in 1965; the oldest that were born in 1945 will be 65 years old in 2011. They are a huge part of the American workforce with an estimated 49 percent of all workers today having been born during the baby boom.

All of the baby boomers are now old enough to be covered under the ADEA.

The number of age discrimination cases was at a 10-year low in 1999, and a 41 percent surge occurred from 14,141 to 19,921 in 2002. Yet only 14 percent of those 19,921 cases led to a settlement or positive outcome for the plaintiffs. Of all workers filing age bias charges in 2002, 64 percent were from 40 to 59 years old.[4]

The Equal Employment Opportunity Commission (EEOC) has been empowered by Congress through the ADEA statute and the earlier Civil Rights Act of 1964 to fight discrimination in employment, but the commission's allocated budget has never matched the number of cases that need investigating.

FILING AN AGE DISCRIMINATION IN EMPLOYMENT CASE

Any worker who thinks his employment rights have been violated should exhaust all available options to resolve the situation before filing a charge with the EEOC. A worker should present all of the facts of the case to a union or grievance board of the employer if one is available. After exhausting any available remedies, a worker may file an age discrimination in employment charge with the EEOC. Any other person, organization, or agency may file such a charge on behalf of a worker whose identity the filer is attempting to protect. The EEOC requires that the filer fill out an intake questionnaire, which is available online at the EEOC Web site.

The EEOC charge should include the following:

1. The complaining party's name, address, and telephone number(s)

2. The name, address, and telephone number(s) of the respondent employer, employment agency, or union that the filer is alleging discriminated against the complaining party

3. The number of respondent's employees

4. A short description of the alleged violation

5. The date of the alleged violation.

All laws enforced by the EEOC (except the Equal Pay Act) require filing a charge with the EEOC before a private lawsuit may be initiated in court.

Proving an Age Discrimination in Employment Case

Discerning what acts rise to the discriminatory level is problematic. Not every unwanted act can or should be defined as age discrimination. Identifying discriminatory treatment can be difficult. To understand how to describe an age discrimination in employment scenario, it is necessary to understand the **employment-at-will** concept first. Employment at will is employment that may continue only as long as the employer or employee wants to continue the employment relationship. When a person is employed *at will*, he may be fired or leave the job of his own volition at any time.

Generally, any worker can be fired (or leave the job) for just about any reason or for no reason at all if he is an at-will employee. Montana is an exception because it is the only state that statutorily prohibits firing without just cause.[5] Clearly, the ADEA does not permit an employee to be fired only because of age. The problem is that some employers ignore the ADEA's mandate. The EEOC has reported that between 1970 and 1989, the number of cases filed with the federal courts claiming age discrimination as per the ADEA had increased

■ employment-at-will

Refers to a mutual employer/employee relationship where a person may be fired or leave a job of his own volition at any time.

2,200 percent, while other types of discrimination cases filed (sex, race, or national origin) had risen 125 percent. Clearly, by 1990, the ADEA had become a force in the American workplace and legal system.

Claims of age discrimination continued to grow in number at the EEOC until the *Hazen Paper Co. v Biggins,* 508 U.S. 948; 113 S. Ct. 2437; 124 L. Ed. 2d 656 (1993) case was decided by the U.S. Supreme Court. The Court in the *Hazen Paper Co.* case essentially decided that if the employer can prove that an older worker was laid off as a cost-cutting measure, that action alone may not be enough to prove age bias. Subsequent to the *Hazen* decision, the 1990s saw over 90 percent of all age discrimination bias cases settled before complaints were filed with the EEOC.[6]

However, litigation in the federal courts has been brisk in the last decade. Large firms representing employers have used tactics such as inundating the plaintiff's attorney (often attorneys from smaller firms with less support staff) with discovery requests and motions (as permitted within court rules). The defense firms handling age discrimination cases know it is very important to stay away from a trial and jury due to the often sympathetic nature of juries dealing with an older litigant allegedly tossed out of his job. Thus, age discrimination cases are often heavy with **motions to dismiss** and **summary judgment** requests. A motion to dismiss is a request that the court throw the case out of court (i.e., dismiss the case). A summary judgment is a final judgment (victory) for one side in a lawsuit (or in one part of a lawsuit), without trial, when the judge finds (usually based on pleadings, depositions, affidavits, etc.) no genuine factual issue is in dispute in the lawsuit (or in one part of the lawsuit). If an issue of fact can be presented to a judge during the summary judgment motion (questions of fact should be for a jury to decide), a plaintiff usually will be permitted to continue with the case toward trial.

Prior to a trial, most cases involve the taking of depositions from the parties and their witnesses. A deposition is the process of taking a sworn out-of-court testimony from a witness. Any defense counsel worth his fee will attempt to catch the plaintiff in inconsistent deposition testimony and testimony that contrasts with the plaintiff's answers to interrogatories. Interrogatories are written questions sent from one side in a lawsuit to the other side, attempting to get written answers to factual questions or seeking an explanation of the other side's legal contentions. It is through interrogatories, depositions, and requests for production of documents that the evidence grows (or does not grow) to support a case. This evidence is gathered during the **discovery process**. For example, the plaintiff's work record, job performance reports, and any history of promotion will be reviewed by both sides during the discovery process undertaken for an age discrimination case. Age discrimination cases may be taken on a *contingency fee basis.* A contingency fee is a payment to a lawyer of a percentage of the financial settlement, if any, from a lawsuit rather than payment of an amount of money or payment according to the number of hours worked.

■ **motions to dismiss**
Requests that the court throw a case out of court, or dismiss the case.

■ **summary judgment**
A final judgment (victory) for one side in a lawsuit, without trial, when the judge finds no genuine factual issue is in dispute in the lawsuit.

■ **discovery process**
Evidence gathered prior to trial through interrogatories, depositions, and requests for production of documents to support a case.

In what can be described as a litigious age, most employers know better than to be obvious about leaving evidence of age discrimination practices. So it is left to the plaintiff's attorneys and their paralegals to ferret out proof of such discrimination. The proof of age discrimination is usually shown through **circumstantial evidence** or **indirect evidence**. Rarely is the proof of age discrimination admitted outright with the defendant's oral or written statement: "Yes, I wanted to get rid of all the old, dead wood; I got rid of John because he sure is old." Employers know to be more circumspect in their actions and statements. It is up to the credibility of the worker to tell his story truthfully and convincingly to compel a jury to identify an employer's actions as age discrimination. Statistical evidence also can be helpful in making a case for age discrimination.

Civil trials require the plaintiff to carry the burden of proving his claim against the defendant. A plaintiff's case (including age discrimination in employment cases) is judged by the legal standard described as a **preponderance of the evidence**. The preponderance of the evidence is defined as a standard used to determine civil liability. It requires that the weight of the evidence offered by the plaintiff to prove a matter is more probable than not. The U.S. Supreme Court has allowed a presumption of discrimination, even without direct evidence, if the plaintiff's legal team has eliminated all other legitimate reasons for the firing. Failure of an employer to prove legitimate reasons for a firing can lead to a finding that the reasons given by the employer were mere pretext and subterfuge. For example, claiming a worker has a deteriorating job performance may be only a ruse to hide age discrimination and a reason given after many years of quality work. In fact, the Supreme Court continues to use this reasoning and allow judges or juries to infer prejudice if all of the employer's reasons for the firing are not justified.

Another typical scenario occurs when an employee is fired because of a company downsizing. For example, a company's downsizing could entail younger workers being offered alternative job placement and an older worker being told he is overqualified for any other available positions. If there is a reduction in force, the employer must treat the age of all employees neutrally. Some courts have described the term *overqualified* as a buzzword that may indicate that age discrimination has occurred. Generally, courts will not accept *overqualified* as an excuse for not transferring or hiring an older worker. It is not the same as an employer explaining that an older worker was unqualified and thus was not hired.

Although the burden of proving discrimination is usually with the employee, the burden may shift to an employer to disprove that age discrimination occurred under certain circumstances. This occurs, for example, when an employer claims that even though age discrimination may have played a part in a worker's dismissal, there still was another legitimate business reason for letting the employee go. This is sometimes known as a **mixed motive case**.

circumstantial evidence

Evidence that is not obvious. Usually used to prove age discrimination.

indirect evidence

Evidence that is not obvious.

preponderance of the evidence

A standard used to determine civil liability. It requires that the weight of the evidence offered by the plaintiff to prove a matter is more probable than not.

mixed motive case

A case in which an employer seeks to prove that even though age discrimination may have played a part in a worker's dismissal, there still were other legitimate business reasons for letting the employee go.

disparate treatment

Occurs when one or more employees are treated differently by an employer because of their age.

Courts dealing with age discrimination claims use the terms **disparate treatment** and **disparate impact**. There are subtle differences between the two. Disparate treatment occurs when one or more employees are treated differently by an employer because of their age. Disparate impact occurs when a seemingly innocent nondiscriminatory action results in the reality that older workers suffer and young workers do not.

Remedies Available to Successful Plaintiffs

disparate impact

Occurs when a seemingly innocent nondiscriminatory action results in the reality that older workers will suffer from the action.

An age discrimination plaintiff is responsible for proving the damage incurred by him due to the claimed age discrimination.[7] The term *making the plaintiff whole* is often used in a discussion of how a plaintiff's financial damages should be calculated. Making the plaintiff financially whole in the case of an age discrimination case entails placing the plaintiff in the same financial position *as if the financial loss suffered because of the age discrimination never occurred.*

back pay

The pay the plaintiff would have earned had he never been fired.

Remedies may include claims for **back pay**, **front pay**, **liquidated damages**, injunctive relief (a nonfinancial remedy), and attorney fees. Back pay is the pay the plaintiff would have earned had he never been fired. Front pay is defined as prospective payments made to a victim of job discrimination who cannot yet be given the job to which he is entitled. These payments, made until the job comes through, make up the difference between money earned now and money that would be made if the new position were available immediately. Liquidated damages are specific amounts of money agreed to in a contract as compensation for a breach of that contract.

front pay

Defined as prospective payments made to a victim of job discrimination who cannot yet be given the job to which he is entitled. These payments, made until the job comes through, make up the difference between money earned now and money that would be made if the new position were available immediately.

A survey by the company Jury Verdict Research showed that successful age-bias claims in one recent year resulted in an average award of $302,914 compared with $255,734 for sex discrimination plaintiffs, $176,578 for race discrimination plaintiffs, and $151,421 for disability discrimination plaintiffs. The difference in amounts may be explained. The age-bias claimants are typically higher wage earners who usually have been fired from a company after long years of service. Thus, awards based on lost income are typically larger than for other types of bias claims.

No punitive claims and no pain and suffering claims are allowed by the ADEA. The contingency fee paid to plaintiffs' attorneys in age discrimination cases are typically one-third the damages awarded plus all other case costs.

liquidated damages

Specific amounts of money agreed to in a contract as compensation for a breach of that contract.

EMPLOYERS AND AGE DISCRIMINATION

Most employment begins with an advertisement seeking an employee. Whether the ad is in the classified section of a newspaper, on the Internet, or even on a bulletin board, a prospective employer should be careful to avoid the appearance of bias of any kind. For example, both full- and part-time employment should be offered to prospective employees of all ages. An employer should periodically review his hiring practices. Does an employment advertisement shout or even hint that mature workers need not apply? During interviews, does the interviewer try to steer the prospective older employee away from the position? Are comments often made about the youth of other workers? Are the interviewee's past employment experiences seen as a negative that overtrained the interviewee? Are concerns about the interviewee's retirement timetable a large part of the interview? Of course, if being 9 years old is a BFOQ for the leading role in the newest theater revival of *Annie*, it can be made very clear in the audition advertisement that those 10 years and above need not apply.

Most age discrimination claims are for alleged wrongful discharge. Interestingly, the ADEA (even with its good intentions) may have helped put a damper on the hiring of workers over 40. The first decade after the ADEA's passage, employment of males 55 years old and above fell 16 percent while the population in that age group rose.[8]

Defending Against Age Discrimination Claims

Once a worker files an age discrimination claim with the EEOC, the agency puts its administrative wheels in motion. The EEOC must notify all possible defendants in the case as soon as possible and investigate the claims. There is a point following the investigation that the EEOC may dismiss the claim because it has not found the claimed discrimination. This technically is called a **no cause finding**. If the EEOC investigators believe that age discrimination did take place, a **for cause finding** is the result. Approximately 60 percent of all EEOC age discrimination investigations end in a no cause finding.[9] The majority of failure to hire age discrimination claims are unsuccessful.

A for cause finding leads to more EEOC involvement. The EEOC will attempt to bring the parties together to settle the case. The EEOC's success rate at settlement is less than stellar, with approximately 10 percent of settlements orchestrated by EEOC personnel. If settlement does not work, the EEOC may file a lawsuit in federal court against the defendant on the plaintiff's behalf. This happens even less than successful settlements. The complaining employee also has the option of seeking private counsel to file a lawsuit against his former employer. Most age discrimination cases reach the judicial system stewarded by a privately hired attorney. However, prior to seeking private counsel, the EEOC must issue a **right-to-sue notice**. This notice ends the EEOC's active involvement in the case. The complaining employee also may proceed to hire private counsel even when a no cause finding was the result of the EEOC investigation or the EEOC investigation is not yet complete.

no cause finding
When the EEOC dismisses a claim because of no finding of the claimed discrimination.

for cause finding
When the EEOC investigators believe that age discrimination did take place, which leads to more EEOC involvement.

right-to-sue notice
A notification from the EEOC to a claimant that the claimant is permitted to seek private counsel to assist in pursuing a claim.

An age discrimination plaintiff may have to reach technical thresholds when attempting to prove his case. For example, some plaintiffs are forced to arbitrate their age discrimination claim because of employment agreements signed by the plaintiff agreeing to do so.

Besides applying only to employers with 20 or more employers, the ADEA does not permit class action lawsuits (unlike Title VII). There is a strict statute of limitations on age discrimination claims. An important point to remember in the defense against an age discrimination claim is that charging complainants must file their charges with the EEOC within 180 days from the date of the alleged violation. The 180-day filing deadline is extended to 300 days if a charge also is covered by a state or local age discrimination law. Failure to meet the ADEA filing deadlines extinguishes complainants' rights.

fair employment practices agencies (FEPAs)

State agencies responsible for enforcing a state's own anti-employment discrimination laws.

Many states have anti-discrimination laws and agencies responsible for enforcing those laws. The EEOC refers to these agencies as **Fair Employment Practices Agencies (FEPAs)**. Through the use of work-sharing agreements, the EEOC and the FEPAs avoid duplication of effort while at the same time ensuring that a charging party's rights are protected under federal and state law. This means that when a charge is filed with a FEPA and is covered by federal law, the FEPA dual files the charge with the EEOC to protect the complainant's federal rights. The FEPA usually retains the charge for handling. If a charge is filed with the EEOC and is covered by state or local law, the EEOC dual files the charge with the state or local FEPA, but usually retains the charge for handling.

Employers should be aware that temporary workers, part-time workers, or independent contractors are categories of workers not protected by the ADEA.

The ADEA protects workers from age-related discrimination, but only if a worker is able to do his work sufficiently. If a worker can no longer fulfill his responsibilities because of a physical or mental disability, the ADEA does not protect the worker. However, the worker with a disability may find appropriate protection and recourse through the Americans with Disabilities Act (ADA) or a disability claim. The ADA forbids discrimination against persons with disabilities or handicaps.

Waiving an Employee's Rights under the ADEA

ADEA waiver

An employer is allowed to ask an employee to waive any of the employee's rights under the ADEA as part of an ADEA settlement or incentive to terminate employment.

An employer is allowed to ask an employee to waive any of the employee's rights under the ADEA as part of an ADEA settlement or incentive to terminate employment. However, there are strict rules for waiving those rights. An **ADEA Waiver** must:

1. Be in writing and be understandable.

2. Refer specifically to ADEA rights or claims.

3. Not waive rights or claims that may arise in the future.

4. Be in exchange for valuable consideration.

5. Advise the individual in writing to consult an attorney before signing the waiver.

6. Provide the individual at least 21 days to consider the agreement and at least 7 days to revoke the agreement after signing it.[10]

Recent Case Aids Plaintiffs

Two relatively recent Supreme Court cases that made it more difficult for plaintiffs to garner a satisfactory conclusion to their age discrimination claims, *St. Mary's Honor Center v. Hicks,* 90 F.3d 285 (1993) and *Hazen Paper Co. v Biggins,* 508 U.S. 948; 113 S. Ct. 2437; 124 L. Ed. 2d 656 (1993) have lessened in importance. This is because the Supreme Court expanded the potential for age discrimination lawsuits in the more recent *Smith v. City of Jackson, Miss.,* 544 U.S. 228, 125 S. Ct. 1536 (2005) case. The Supreme Court previously had used *Hazen* to instruct that age-connected behavior was not sufficient by itself to prove age discrimination. Instead, the *Hazen* decision forced employees to prove that an employer's behavior was based on age stereotypes either consciously or unconsciously and that the behavior led to the age-connected behavior.[11]

CASE LAW   *Smith v. City of Jackson, Miss.*

544 U.S. 228, 125 S.Ct. 1536 (2005)

Facts: The city adopted a pay plan granting raises to all City employees on October 1, 1998. The stated purpose of the plan was *to attract and retain qualified people, provide incentives for performance, maintain competitiveness with other public sector agencies and ensure equitable compensation to all employees regardless of age, sex, race and/or disability.* On May 1, 1999, a revision of the plan, which was motivated, at least in part, by the City's desire to bring the starting salaries of police officers up to the regional average, granted raises to all police officers and police dispatchers. Those who had less than five years of tenure received proportionately greater raises when compared to their former pay than those with more seniority. Although some officers over the age of 40 had less than five years of service, most of the older officers had more.

     Petitioners, a group of older officers, filed suit under the ADEA claiming (among other issues) that the City deliberately discriminated against them because of their age (a disparate-impact claim). The District Court granted summary judgment to the City. The Court of Appeals held that the summary judgment ruling was premature because petitioners were entitled to further discovery on the issue of intent, but it affirmed the dismissal of the disparate-impact claim. Over one judge's dissent, the majority concluded that disparate-impact claims are categorically unavailable under the ADEA. The United States Supreme Court granted the officers' petition for certiorari on the question of whether their disparate impact claim was available under the ADEA.

Issue: Whether disparate impact claims are available under the ADEA.

(continues)

SAMPLE BRIEF *Smith v. City of Jackson, Miss.* (continued)

Court's
Reasoning:

The ADEA, now codified as 29 U.S.C. 623 (a)(2), provided that it shall be unlawful for an employer *to limit, segregate, or classify his employees in anyway which would deprive or tend to deprive any individual of employment opportunities or otherwise adversely affect his status as an employee, because of such individual's age.* Except for substitution of the word *age* for the words *race, color, religion, sex, or national origin,* the language of that provision in the ADEA is identical to that found in 703(a)(2) of the Civil Rights Act of 1964 (Title VII). Other Provisions of the ADEA also parallel the earlier statute. Unlike Title VII, however, 4(f)(1) of the ADEA, 81 Stat. 603, contains language that significantly narrows its coverage by permitting any *otherwise prohibited* action *where the differentiation is based on reasonable factors other than age.*

In *Griggs,* a case decided four years after the enactment of the ADEA, the court considered whether 703 of Title VII prohibited an employer *from requiring a high school education or passing of a standardized general intelligence test as a condition of employment in or transfer to jobs when (a) neither standard is shown to be significantly related to successful job performance, (b) both requirements operate to disqualify Negroes at a substantially higher rate than white applicants, and (c) jobs as part of a longstanding practice of giving job preference to whites.* 401 U.S., at 425-426. We accepted the Court of Appeals conclusion that the employer had adopted the diploma and test requirements without any intent to discriminate and in good faith.

Our opinion in *Hazen Paper,* however, did not address or comment on the issue we decide today. In that case, we held that an employee's allegation that he was discharged shortly before his pension would have vested did not state a cause of action under a disparate-treatment theory. The motivating factor was not, we held, the employee's age, but rather his years of service, a factor that the ADEA did not prohibit an employer from considering when terminating an employee. While we noted that disparate-treatment claim *captures the essence of what Congress sought to prohibit in the ADEA,* we were careful to explain that we were not deciding *whether a disparate impact theory of liability is available under the ADEA.* In sum, there is nothing in our opinion in *Hazen Paper* that precludes an interpretation of the ADEA that parallels our holding in *Griggs.*

In most disparate-treatment cases, if an employer in fact acted on a factor other than age, the action would not be prohibited under the subsection (a) in the first place.

In disparate-impact cases, however, the allegedly *otherwise prohibited* activity is not based on age. *Claims that stress disparate impact [by contrast] involve employment practices that are facially neutral in their treatment of different groups, but that in fact fall more harshly on one group than another.* (Quoting *Teamsters v. United States,* 431 U.S. 324, 335, 336, n. 15 (1977).

Finally, we note that both the Department of Labor, which initially drafted the legislation, and the EEOC, which is the agency charged by Congress with responsibility for implementing the statute, 29 U.S.C. 628, have consistently interpreted the ADEA to authorize relief on a disparate-impact theory.

Two textual differences between the ADEA and Title VII make it clear that even though both statutes authorize recovery on a disparate-impact theory, the scope of disparate-impact liability under ADEA is narrower than under Title VII.

Turning to the case before us, we initially note that petitioners have done little more than point out that the pay plan at issue is relatively less generous to older workers than the younger workers. They have not identified any specific test, requirement, or practice within the pay plan that has an adverse impact on older workers.

As we held in *Wards Cover,* it is not enough to simply allege that there is a disparate impact on workers, or point to a generalized policy that leads to such an impact. Rather, the employee is *responsible for isolating and identifying the specific employment practices that are allegedly responsible for any observed statistical disparities.* 490 U.S., at 656 (emphasis added) (quoting Watson, 487 U.S., at 994). Petitioners have failed to do

(continues)

SAMPLE BRIEF *Smith v. City of Jackson, Miss.* (continued)

so. Their failure to identify the specific practice being challenged is the sort of omission that *could result in employers being potentially liable for 'the myriad of innocent causes that may lead to statistical imbalances,'* 490 U.S., at 657. [I]t is also clear from the record that the City's plan was based on reasonable factors other than age.

Petitioners' evidence established two principal facts: First, almost two-thirds (66.2%) of the officers under 40 received raises of more than 10% while less than half (45.3%) of those over 40 did. Second, the average percentage increase for the entire class of officers with less than five years of tenure was somewhat higher than the percentage for those with more seniority. Because older officers tended to occupy more senior positions, on average they received smaller increases when measured as a percentage of their salary. The basic explanation for the differential was the City's perceived need to raise the salaries of junior officers to make them competitive with comparable positions in the market.

Thus, the disparate impact is attributable to the City's decision to give raises based on seniority and position.

Holding: Accordingly, while we do not agree with the Court of Appeals' holding that that the disparate-impact theory of recovery is never available under the ADEA, we affirm its judgment.

Case Discussion: The *Smith* case is important because over half the nation's workers could be affected by the decision even though the senior officers' case was dismissed. A key point of the decision is that the court found that plaintiffs do not have to show intent to discriminate on the part of their employers as long as the plaintiffs can show that the employer's actions had a *disparate impact* on older workers. This is in direct contradiction to a decade's worth of stifling decisions and a higher legal threshold. For a quarter century, cases involving race, sex, and religion under Title VII simply had to demonstrate a disparate impact. However, here the court still gave employers an opportunity to defend themselves by proving that an allegedly discriminatory policy was necessary and based on reasonable factors other than age.

ELDER LAW PRACTICE

"It's been one thing after another," lamented Alice. "First, Mr. Jefferson wouldn't let me take the training to be updated on the computers. Then my job performance evaluation was poor because he claimed I wasn't current on the new computer program."

Alice was happy to have a friendly ear to bend and a shoulder to cry on, so she continued, "I'm telling you, Trish, I felt so bad that I took a course on my own at the local college. I even took another course on networking. Mr. Jefferson wouldn't pay for it, so I dug into my own pocket. After all, I really believed I was protecting my job."

"What happened next?" Trish asked

"Well, I really knew my stuff, so when a promotion came up, I thought I'd be the one picked," Alice said dejectedly. She added, "I had seniority, training, experience, and a perfect attendance record."

Trish said, "I guess you didn't get the job, or you wouldn't be here asking about the law firm that my nephew Luke works for."

(continues)

"You got that right," Alice moped. "I got turned down because the company needed a 'dose of fresh air.' By the way, fresh air apparently only comes in with anyone under 25 years old."

Getting angry, Alice exclaimed, "Mr. Jefferson even asked me to train the 'new girl,' as he put it. The next thing I knew I was being downsized for the good of the company. I was being paid twice what the new hire is making!"

Trish inquired, "I suppose you did try to talk your boss out of his decision?"

Alice answered, "Yeah, but it was like talking to a brick wall. He tried to say it was for my own good. Apparently, at this point in my life, I should be taking it easy."

Trish stated, "You should talk to Luke about hiring Tara Jensen to get after that boss of yours."

Should Alice make an appointment with Tara? What are the steps the EEOC insists an employee take when claiming that illegal age discrimination has occurred?

SUMMARY

The Age Discrimination in Employment Act (ADEA) was enacted in 1967 as the federal government's response to age discrimination. The fundamental tenet of the ADEA legislation is that aging varies with individuals and the effect of a stereotype is not only inaccurate but also morally and legally wrong. Forty years of age is the lower age limit; Congress revised the upper limit in 1986 by eliminating forced retirement at any age, with certain exceptions. The ADEA applies to private employers with 20 or more employees, the federal government, and any local government. The U.S. Supreme Court has held that the ADEA cannot be applied to state governments. However, most states have enacted state versions of the ADEA. Other exceptions include high-level executives in policymaking positions and government officials who are appointed or elected and their non-civil service staff. If employment involves a bona fide occupational qualification, an exception may be made to the ADEA. The exception is rare. All of the nation's baby boomers are old enough to be covered under the ADEA. When a person is employed at will, he may be fired or leave the job of his own volition usually at any time.

Age discrimination is usually proved through circumstantial or indirect evidence. The legal standard of proof that the plaintiff must meet in an age discrimination case is by a preponderance of the evidence. There is a strict statute of limitations for an age discrimination case. An employer is allowed to ask an employee to waive any of the employee's rights under the ADEA as part of an ADEA settlement or incentive to terminate employment. The *Smith* case is important because the key point of the decision is that the court found that plaintiffs do not have to show intent to discriminate on the part of their employers as long as the plaintiffs can show that the employer's actions had a disparate impact on older workers.

KEY TERMS

ADEA waiver	disparate impact	liquidated damages
age discrimination in employment act of 1967 (ADEA)	disparate treatment	mixed motive case
	employment-at-will	motions to dismiss
back pay	fair employment practices agencies (FEPAs)	no cause finding
bona fide occupational qualification (BFOQ)		preponderance of the evidence
	for cause finding	right-to-sue notice
circumstantial evidence	front pay	summary judgment
discovery process	indirect evidence	

REVIEW QUESTIONS

1. Should the argument be made by an employer today that age discrimination is only a natural by-product of the making of sound economic business decisions? Explain.

2. What job protections do the federal ADEA statutes intend to provide?

3. Explain when the BFOQ exception may be permitted.

4. Explain the concept of employment at will.

5. What remedies are available to successful age discrimination plaintiffs?

6. What is the EEOC's role in age discrimination cases?

7. When would an employee be asked to sign an ADEA waiver?

8. How can an employer avoid the appearance of age discrimination?

9. How did the *Hazen Paper Co.* case affect age discrimination cases?

10. How has the *Smith v. City of Jackson, Miss.* decision affected the previously applied legal threshold in age bias cases?

ETHICS ALERT

Rena recently learned from a friend at her old law firm that her former boss was retiring.[12]

"It's hard to believe, but the partners have decided to put Mr. Roxbury out to pasture at 65," Rena shared with Tara and Luke.

Tara answered, "Mandatory retirement policies are in place for partners at some law firms. I read that 40 percent of large firms have such a policy."

"Really?" Luke asked. "Why?"

Tara answered, "Well, I know some firms think that's the only way the younger partners can get a real piece of the law firm and make sure clients stay with the firm. She paused and added, "In fact, the EEOC sued a big firm last year for forcing about 30 partners out of their equity positions. That means the partners owned a piece of the firm, but the firm forced them to take salaried positions. It was the first age bias suit against a law firm."

Rena interjected, "I thought the ADEA wouldn't apply to a partner because that person was considered management."

Tara responded, "Yes, it's true that when a plaintiff is in a policymaking position, the ADEA doesn't apply. But the EEOC decided the law partners in the case didn't really have a say in how the firm was managed."

Luke asked, "Would the decision in that case affect different kinds of professional groups?"

Tara smiled and answered, "Sure it would. But I know one place it won't affect, and that's here. I knew I liked going solo!"

What are some of the ethical issues that may arise when a law firm forces out older partners to make room for younger ones?[13]

HELPFUL WEB SITES

EQUAL EMPLOYMENT OPPORTUNITY COMMISSION <HTTP://WWW.EEOC.GOV> This site provides a complete list of EEOC office locations and telephone numbers across the United States.

NATIONAL EMPLOYMENT LAWYERS ASSOCIATION (NELA)<HTTP://WWW.NELA.ORG> According to the Web site, NELA is the country's largest professional organization that is made up exclusively of lawyers who represent individual employees in cases involving employment discrimination and other employment related matters. NELA has 67 state and local affiliates and more than 3,000 members.

ENDNOTES

[1] Segrave, Kerry, Age Discrimination by Employers, McFarland and Company, New York, 2001.

[2] Munk, Nina, Fortune Magazine, 1999.

[3] <http://www.eeoc.gov/types/age.html> The U.S. Equal Employment Opportunity Commission, June 7, 2005.

[4] Harris, Diane, "Simple Justice," AARP Magazine, July–August 2003.

[5] Montana Wrongful Discharge from Employment Act of 1987. Mont. Code Ann. Sections 39-2-906 to 39-2-914.

[6] Vavarette, Ruben, "High Court Ruling Bolsters Rights of Older Workers," The Record, April 7, 2005, page 7.

[7] Gregory, Raymond, F., Age Discrimination in the American Workplace: Old at a Young Age, Rutgers University Press, 2001.

[8] Carter, Terry, "Working Retirement?" ABA Journal, December 2003, page 38.

[9] 29 C.F.R. Part 1625 Age Discrimination in Employment Act.

[10] <http://www.eeoc.gov>

[11] Carnahan, Ira, "Light at the End of the ADEA Tunnel: Landmark Case Protects Workers," Forbes, New York, August 12, 2005, page 2.

[12] Lisante, Joan E., "Thank You and Goodbye," ABA Journal, January 2005, page 31.

[13] A 2001 survey of 197 small and large firms conducted by Altman Weil, Inc., found that 47 percent of the nation's law firms had mandatory retirement. The trend is on the rise.

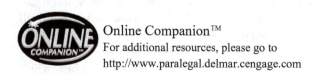

Online Companion™
For additional resources, please go to
http://www.paralegal.delmar.cengage.com

CHAPTER 10

Elder Abuse

> "The world is a dangerous place, not only because of those who do evil, but because of those who look on and do nothing."
>
> **ALBERT EINSTEIN**

■ OBJECTIVES

After completing this chapter, you will be able to

- Describe the extent to which elder abuse, neglect, and exploitation exist in American society.

- Explain the Administration on Aging's role in dealing with elder abuse.

- Define the behavior that should be considered elder abuse.

- Identify the federal and state laws designed to prevent elder abuse.

- Explain the mechanisms available to report and punish elder abuse.

INTRODUCTION

The numbers are shocking and hard to believe. Each year hundreds of thousands of America's elderly men and women are abused psychologically and physically. The abuse is found in all ethnic, financial, and social groups. One study presented evidence of 551,011 incidents of abuse of persons over 60 years of age in just one year recently.[1] Refer to Exhibit 10–1 for the results of this elder abuse survey. Perhaps more shocking are the results of another study that reported that elder abuse statistics were too indeterminate, that they fall far short of reality, and that they are rising in proportion to the increase in the country's elderly population.[2]

Sadly, issues pertaining to the abuse of the elderly usually involve family members. Abuse of elderly family members is considered domestic violence. Statistically, 90 percent of physical and emotional abusers are family members and 75 percent are the victims' adult children or the adult children's spouses.[3] It has been estimated that there may be at least 5 million annual cases of financial abuse among elderly victims.[4]

EXHIBIT 10–1   RESULTS OF ELDER ABUSE SURVEY

National Trends—Abuse of Vulnerable Adults of All Ages

- APS received a total of 565,747 reports of elder and vulnerable adult abuse for persons of all ages (50 states, plus Guam and the District of Columbia). This represents a 19.7% increase from the 2000 Survey (472,813 reports).

- APS investigated 461,135 total reports of elder and vulnerable adult abuse for persons of all ages (49 states). This represents a 16.3% increase from the 2000 Survey (396,398 investigations).

- APS substantiated 191,908 reports of elder and vulnerable adult abuse for victims of all ages (42 states). This represents a 15.6% increase from the 2000 Survey (166,019 substantiated reports).

- The average APS budget per state was $8,550,369, compared to an average of $7,084,358 reported in the 2000 Survey (42 states).

Statewide Reporting Numbers

- APS received a total of 253,426 reports on persons aged 60+ (32 states).

- APS investigated a total of 192,243 reports on persons aged 60+ (29 states).

- APS substantiated 88,455 reports on persons aged 60+ (24 states).

- APS received a total of 84,767 reports of self-neglect on persons aged 60+ (21 states).

- APS investigated a total of 82,007 reports of self-neglect on persons aged 60+ (20 states).

- APS substantiated 46,794 reports of self-neglect on persons aged 60+ (20 states).

- The most common sources of reports of abuse of adults 60+ were family members (17.0%), social services workers (10.6%), and friends and neighbors (8.0%).

Categories of Elder Abuse, Victims Aged 60+

- Self-neglect was the most common category of investigated reports (49,809 reports or 26.7%), followed by caregiver neglect (23.7%) and financial exploitation (20.8%) (19 states).

- Self-neglect was the most common category of substantiated reports (26,752 reports or 37.2%), followed by caregiver neglect (20.4%) and financial exploitation (14.7%) (19 states).

(continues)

EXHIBIT 10–1 RESULTS OF ELDER ABUSE SURVEY *(continued)*

Substantiated Reports, Victims Aged 60+

- States reported that 65.7% of elder abuse victims were female (15 states).

- Of the victims aged 60+, 42.8% were 80 years of age and older (20 states).

- The majority of victims were Caucasian (77.1%) (13 states).

- The vast majority (89.3%) of elder abuse reports occurred in domestic settings (13 states).

Substantiated Reports, Alleged Perpetrators of Victims Aged 60+

- States reported that 52.7% of alleged perpetrators of abuse were female (11 states).

- Over three-fourths (75.1%) of alleged perpetrators were under the age of 60 (7 states).

- The most common relationships of victims to alleged perpetrators were an adult child (32.6%) and other family member (21.5%) (11 states).

- Twenty-one states (40.4%) maintain an abuse registry or database of alleged perpetrators, while 31 states (59.6%) do not.

Interventions and Outcomes, Victims Aged 60+

- Over half (53.2%) of cases were closed because the client was no longer in need of services or the risk of harm was reduced (8 states). Other reasons for closure were the death of the client, client entering a long-term care facility, client refusing further services, client moving out of the service area, inability to locate the client, and client being referred to law enforcement.

- Only four states, Colorado, Connecticut, Louisiana, and Massachusetts, and Guam provided information on outcomes of APS involvement.

Recommendations

- Accurate and uniform data must be continuously collected at both state and national levels so that abuse trends can be tracked and studied. A concerted effort is necessary to create uniform definitions of and measures for reporting abuse. As a baseline, all states need to be able to provide the information that this survey requested.

- States should collect detailed age- and gender-specific information on race and ethnicity of victims and alleged perpetrators. Little is known about the racial composition and ethnic background data of elder abuse victims.

- The inclusion of information on reporters of abuse such as municipal agents, postal service workers, utility workers, and hospital discharge planners suggests that training on the identification of abuse should expand to groups heretofore not known as critical to prevention and intervention efforts.

- It is critical that states collect outcome data on the clients served. This information will be extremely helpful in determining efficacy of APS intervention.

- Increased numbers of reports, investigations, and substantiations lead to the need for increased local, state, and national intervention and education efforts targeted toward the abuse of adults 60+.

(continues)

EXHIBIT 10–1   RESULTS OF ELDER ABUSE SURVEY *(continued)*

- Little information is available about perpetrators and what happens to them as a result of APS intervention. States should collect as much information as possible not only about the victims, but also about the perpetrators. Data collected will inform multiple actors in the elder abuse arena regarding prevention, intervention, and advocacy.

- A national study of APS data, specifically related to the abuse of adults 60+, should be conducted no less than every four years. The increment of every four years is recommended because studies conducted in the past twelve years have been conducted within this time frame. This regularity is desirable for methodological comparability.

THE ROLE OF THE ADMINISTRATION ON AGING

The **Administration on Aging** is the federal agency under the HHS given the job of shepherding elder initiatives and programs through the system. The agency is a treasure trove of information about seniors. The agency deals with the elder abuse problems in the United States through its funding of the **National Center on Elder Abuse (NCEA)**. The NCEA is a partnership of the National Association of State Units on Aging, the Commission on Law and Aging of the American Bar Association, the Clearinghouse on Abuse and Neglect of the Elderly of the University of Delaware, the National Adult Protective Services Association, and the National Committee for the Prevention of Elder Abuse.

The Administration on Aging also supports training law enforcement and medical personnel in the special needs of the elder abuse victim, provides information to the general public, and acts as a liaison for abuse prevention coalitions across the country. However, the prevention, recognition, and punishment of elder abuse typically begins at the local municipal or county level.

Defining Elder Abuse

The Administration on Aging provides an inclusive description of what should be included as a definition of elder abuse. These definitions can be found in Exhibit 10–2.[5]

Self-Neglect

The incidence of abuse described as self-neglect by the elderly may represent the largest number of elder abuse cases. Reports of alleged self-neglect represents 50 percent of all cases brought to the attention of state Adult Protective Services (APS).[6] Interestingly, the question of intervening in a self-neglect case crosses into the area of an individual's constitutional rights. If an

administration on aging

The federal agency under the Department of Health & Human Services given the job of shepherding elder initiatives and programs through the system.

national center on elder abuse (NCEA)

An organization funded by the Administration on Aging and in partnership with the National Association of State Units on Aging, the Commission on Law and Aging of the American Bar Association, the Clearinghouse on Abuse and Neglect of the Elderly of the University of Delaware, the National Adult Protective Services Association, and the National Committee for the Prevention of Elder Abuse.

EXHIBIT 10–2   ELDER ABUSE DEFINED

1. **Physical abuse** is the willful infliction of physical pain or injury (e.g., slapping bruising, sexually molesting, or restraining).

2. **Sexual abuse** is the infliction of non-consensual sexual contact of any kind.

3. **Emotional or psychological abuse** is the infliction of mental or emotional anguish (e.g., humiliation, intimidation, or threats).

4. **Financial or material exploitation** is the improper act of an individual using the resources of an older person without his or her consent for someone else's benefit.

5. **Neglect** is failure of a caretaker to provide goods or services necessary to avoid physical harm, mental anguish, or mental illness (e.g., abandonment, denial of food, or health-related services).

6. **Self-neglect** is the behavior of an elderly person that threatens his or her health or safety.

7. **Abandonment** is desertion of a vulnerable elder by anyone who has assumed responsibility for the care or custody of that person.

individual is considered legally competent, should her self-neglect be considered self-abuse that should be stopped by authorities, or is it a constitutional right to behave as she wishes without governmental interference?

Different factors may lead to self-abuse. Certain individuals may have a history of self-neglect that began in young adulthood. That early self-neglect can stem from causes such as physical impairment, social isolation, malnutrition, substance abuse, cognitive impairment, and limited financial resources. Such abuse may worsen with the onset of age.

The elderly suffering from the early undiagnosed stages of dementia are particularly susceptible to self-neglect. The dementia may make such sufferers forget to eat, wash, or otherwise act to protect themselves. Other signs of self-neglect may be nonworking utilities in the home and little food in the cupboards. A typical case of self-neglect in the case of dementia (similar to Rena's situation with her aunt discussed in Chapter 4) may lead to initiation of a guardianship petition if the problems are serious enough.

Depression also may play role in the incidence of self-neglect among the elderly. Depressed older adults are less likely to seek help. According to mental health advocates, depression should not be considered a natural part of aging. The Centers for Disease Control and Prevention has reported that the suicide rate for people 65 years and older is higher than in any other age group. People 65 years and older accounted for 18 percent of all suicides in the United States between 1999 and 2004. In fact, the rate of suicide for older Caucasian males is 12 times higher than any other age group.[7] Poverty also is another factor that fosters self-neglect by the elderly. Poverty-stricken elders may be forced to decide between food, housing, and medication.[8]

FEDERAL AND STATE LAWS OFFER VULNERABLE ELDERS PROTECTION

The first congressional investigation of elder abuse occurred in 1978. Legislatures in all 50 states have since passed revised elder abuse prevention laws following the publicity of that investigation. State statutes vary, but all states have a reporting mechanism in place. Some states combine protection of any adult with a disability with the protections provided for their state's elderly. In such states, the elder abuse laws are usually found under the heading **Adult Protective Services (APS)**. Nationally, nearly 70 percent of all APS caseloads involve elder abuse.

There are some major differences among the states. Some states require *mandatory* versus *voluntary reporting* of suspected abuse. Some states emphasize the protection of incapacitated or vulnerable elderly residents. Some states provide broad powers to their investigators of elderly abuse reports while other states limit such power.[9]

Many other agencies and nonprofit organizations work to protect the elderly, including each state and area agency on aging; law enforcement on the local and county levels; district attorneys and the court system; medical examiners, hospitals, and medical clinics; state long-term care ombudsman's offices; public health agencies; mental health agencies; and state offices dealing with facility licensing and certification for senior housing.

The OAA had been in effect for over 40 years when Congress reauthorized the Act and added funding for **Title VII, Chapter 3**. The main purpose of Chapter 3 is to work toward the prevention of elder abuse, neglect, and exploitation. The funding provided to the states through Chapter 3 also provides for long-term care ombudsman programs and development of state senior legal assistance across the country. The Act has been instrumental in fostering cooperation between law enforcement and the courts, with the goal of preventing elder abuse.

Reporting Abuse

Reports of alleged abuse can be made to the agencies that are designed to protect the elderly. Again, these agencies include each state and area agency on aging; law enforcement on the local and county levels, hospitals, and medical clinics; state long-term care ombudsman's offices; public health agencies; mental health agencies; and state offices dealing with facility licensing and certification for senior housing. Consumers can reach the Administration on Aging through a telephone hotline operating in each of the 50 states. The Administration on Aging's national toll-free help line at the time of publishing was 1-800-799-7233. The agency also provides a national toll-free help line called the **Eldercare Locator** if a help line is not available in a particular area.

adult protective services (APS)
A heading under which a state's elder abuse laws may be found.

title vii, chapter 3
A part of the Older Americans Act that provides funding to the states to provide for long-term care ombudsman programs and development of state senior legal assistance.

eldercare locator
The Administration on Aging's national toll-free help line to assist a consumer in locating a hotline in a particular state for reporting elder abuse.

Reported claims of elder abuse typically are referred to a local state adult protective services agency. The local agency typically investigates claims of abuse and completes an analysis of whether the alleged elder abuse has violated the particular state's elder abuse laws. An adult protective services agency will provide a caseworker for the senior involved if the senior agrees to the intervention. If the senior is incapacitated and unable to make a decision, the adult protective services agency will usually seek court intervention and the appointment of a guardian for the alleged elder abuse victim.

Data on elder abuse in domestic settings suggest that 1 in 14 incidents, excluding incidents of self-neglect, are reported or come to the attention of authorities. In fact, it has been estimated that for every case of elder abuse, including neglect, exploitation, and self-neglect, five more go unreported.[10] Significantly higher investigation rates have been found for states that require mandatory reporting and tracking of reports.[11]

Moral or Legal Responsibility to Report Abuse?

All citizens can act as a preventive force if they report suspicions of elder abuse. While some may believe that every citizen has a moral responsibility to report abuse, legal responsibility generally is left to mandated reporters. **Mandated reporters** usually are doctors, nurses, home health care workers, guardians, trustees, law enforcement personnel, attorneys, and any other individuals in a fiduciary role to the victim. A minority of states have gone further and made it mandatory for any person who knows of abuse to report it. Additional protections are offered in the federal Elder Justice Act bill. The bill was presented to Congress, but it had not been presented for a vote at the time this textbook was published.

The following cases involve two different families. The first case concerned a 91-year-old victim and highlights the difficulties that prosecutors face in gathering admissible evidence against an alleged elder abuse perpetrator. The second case detailed the claim of alleged fraud and financial abuse by a son who was a trustee for his mother's estate. This case dealt with the question of who has standing (i.e., the right to sue) in the case of financial elder abuse.

■ **mandated reporters**

Doctors, nurses, home health care workers, guardians, trustees, attorneys, and any other individual serving in a fiduciary role to an elder abuse victim.

CASE LAW   *The People of the State of Illinois v. Oehrke*

369 Ill. App. 3d 63, 860 N.E. 2d 416 (2006)

Facts: Ninety-one year old Frieda Oehrke was taken by paramedics to the emergency room at Resurrection Hospital on June 24, 2000. She had a 1 inch bleeding wound on the top of her head, old bruising on the right side of her face and multiple areas of bruising on her body in various stage of healing. Defendant's son lived with Frieda and was her sole caregiver. The State filed a motion prior to trial to admit Frieda's out of court statements through her treating doctor and nurse, 2 police officers and an elder abuse investigator. The state's criminal code permitted admission of certain hearsay statements made by an elder adult in support of a prosecution for

(continues)

CASE LAW *The People of the State of Illinois v. Oehrke* (continued)

elder abuse if the court found in a hearing conducted outside the presence of the jury that the time, content and circumstances of the statement provided sufficient safeguards of reliability. Following a hearing on the motion, the trial court determined the testimony of the doctor, nurse and police officers was trustworthy and reliable and would be allowed as an exception the hearsay rule. However, before the trial the United States Supreme Court in *Crawford v. Washington*, 541 U.S. 36, 53-54, 124 S.CT. 1354, 1366, 158 L.Ed.2d 177, 194-95 (2004), decided the confrontation clause barred the admission of testimonial statements of a witness who did not appear at trial unless he was unavailable to testify, and the defendant had a prior opportunity for cross-examination. Due to the *Crawford* case the State withdrew its motion to admit the evidence. Instead, it offered only the statements Frieda made to Dr. Rachel Burke, an emergency room physician, and Nurse William Babiarz, relying entirely on the common law hearsay exception that permits statements made for the purpose of obtaining a medical diagnosis or treatment. The trial court, over defense counsel's hearsay objection, admitted the statement, holding the common law hearsay exception was satisfied.

Issue: Whether the trial court's admission of Frieda's statements identifying defendant as her abuser was harmless error.

Court's Reasoning: Dr. Burke said Frieda did not seem unreliable when she said her son had hit her. This information would affect Dr. Burke's final disposition of whether "Frieda would be safe to go home or not or whether she would be cared for at home or not." Defense counsel objected to the admission of the hearsay statements on the grounds that they did not fit within a recognized hearsay exception. Defendant relying on *Crawford*, contends Frieda's statements to Nurse Babiarz and Dr. Burke constituted testimonial evidence. Defendant contends the admission of Frieda's statements at trial, in the absence of an opportunity to cross-examine Frieda, violated his 6th amendment constitutional right of confrontation. In this case, Frieda's statements were made 90 minutes after she was admitted to the hospital, and after Dr. Burke had finished treating Frieda's head wound. There is no suggestion in the record that Dr. Burke and Nurse Babiarz questioned Frieda in order to assist in her present or future psychological treatment. Instead, Dr. Burke said she questioned Frieda in order to determine whether it was safe for her to return home to defendant's care. No Illinois court has extended the medical diagnosis and treatment hearsay exception to include an adult physical abuse victim's statements identifying her attacker. In order to find a hearsay exception for statements made during medical treatment and diagnosis to include extending the statements made during a determination of whether a victim will suffer future physical harm would be "exception by judicial fiat, less the exception swallow a rule that has served so well for so long".

Dr. Burke's and Nurse Babiarz's questions were intended to protect Frieda from returning to an abusive environment, not to assist in her medical diagnosis and treatment. The admission of the evidence is harmless error if there is no reasonable probability that the verdict would have been different had the hearsay been excluded.

Based on the record, we cannot say the properly admitted evidence was so overwhelming, without the erroneously admitted hearsay statements, that no fair-minded trier of fact could reasonably have acquitted the defendant.

Holding: We find the trial court's admission and use of Frieda's hearsay statements was reversible error. We are not making a finding as to defendant's guilt or innocence. Retrial of defendant, without Frieda's inadmissible hearsay statements, would not constitute double jeopardy. We find the trial court erred in admitting Frieda's out-of-court statements under the medical diagnosis and treatment exception to the hearsay rule. The error warrants a new trial and Frieda's in court testimony.

Case Discussion: Frieda Oehrke died before she could testify at the new trial.

CASE LAW *Estate of Laura Marie Lowrie, Lynelle Goodreau v. Sheldon Lawrence Lowrie, as Trustee*

118 Cal. App. 4th 220, 12 Cal. Rptr. 3d 828, (2004)

Facts:

Laura Marie Lowrie, the decedent, had 3 children (all of whom are still living) Norma Goodreau, Alan Lowrie, and appellant Sheldon Lowrie. Decedent had 6 grandchildren, including respondent Lynelle Goodreau who is the eldest daughter of Norma Goodreau. In March 1989 estate documents Sheldon was named as the executor of his mother's will, Lynelle was designated as the successor executor, the decedent was designated as the trustee, Sheldon was designated as the first successor trustee, and Lynelle was designated as the second successor trustee. Alan Lowrie and Norma Goodreau were each bequeathed the sum of $10,000. Lynelle was to receive an Edison Boulevard residence. Lynelle had resided at the residence as a child. Sheldon was bequeathed the remainder of the estate (which would be the bulk of the property) and if Sheldon did not survive the decedent Lynelle was to receive the remainder. The 1992 trust amendment was a 1 page document which deleted the bequest to Lynelle of the house and replaced it with a monetary bequest of $10,000.

Unknown to the other family members, the decedent transferred the Edison Boulevard residence and a Kenwood Street residence to Sheldon in 1993 and 1995, respectively. In 1993 decedent transferred all of her personal property to Sheldon. In August 1997, decedent resigned as trustee of her trust and Sheldon became trustee. Decedent died on August 13, 1999, at the age of 89. At the time of her death, decedent's estate was worth approximately $1 million.

The trial court made a specific finding that Sheldon acted with recklessness, oppression, fraud and malice, entitling Lynelle to attorney fees and punitive damages. Damages were awarded to Lynelle as follows: $225,000 for pain and suffering; $665,623 for financial abuse; attorney fees to be determined upon written motion; and punitive damages to be based upon proof of Sheldon's net worth.

Court's
Reasoning:

Sheldon asserts that Lynelle had no standing to bring the elder abuse case. Originally, the Elder Abuse Act was designed to encourage the reporting of abuse and neglect of elders and dependent adults. However, elder abuse lawsuits were seldom pursued as few attorneys would handle the cases, partially because survival statutes did not permit compensation if the elder died before a verdict was rendered. Then, the Legislature shifted the focus. The statutory scheme was modified to provide incentives for private, civil enforcement through lawsuits against elder abuse and neglect. Subject to statutory criteria and limitations, the statutory scheme now permits heightened remedies. These include pain and suffering damages even after the abused elder dies, punitive damages and attorney fee awards.

Sheldon argues Lynelle does not have standing because: 1. under the trust he is the named trustee and thus, decedent's personal representative and Lynelle is not a person entitled to succeed to the decedent's estate because she does not succeed to decedent's estate under the laws of intestate succession, but rather Lynelle is simply a beneficiary who was bequeathed $10,000.

A cause of action for the death of a person caused by the wrongful act or neglect of another may be asserted by any of the following persons or by the decedent's personal representative on their behalf: a. The decedent's surviving spouse, domestic partner, children, and issue of deceased children, or if there is no surviving issue of the decedent, the persons, including the surviving spouse or domestic partner, who would be entitled to the property of the decedent by intestate succession. Sheldon's argument ignores Probate Code Section 259 and the purpose of the Elder Abuse Act. Probate Code Section 259 is a forfeiture statute that deems abusers of elders or dependent adults to have predeceased a deceased, abused elder or dependent adult. The purpose of Probate Code Section 259 was to deter the abuse of elders by prohibiting abusers from benefiting from the abuse. According to decedent's estate plan, if Sheldon predeceased decedent, Lynelle would become the successor

(continues)

CASE LAW *Estate of Laura Marie Lowrie, Lynelle Goodreau v. Sheldon Lawrence Lowrie, as Trustee* (continued)

trustee and the successor beneficiary to the remainder. Thus, Lynelle would become the person entitled to succeed to decedent's estate and Lynelle would have standing to bring this case. Standing for purposes of the Elder Abuse Act, must be analyzed in a manner that induces interested persons to report elder abuse and to file lawsuits against elder abusers. In this way the victimized will be protected. Here, Lynelle's expectancy, her contingent interest, provides her with a strong incentive to pursue this action and gives her standing.

Holding: The judgment is affirmed. Sheldon Lowrie is to pay all costs.

Case
Discussion: The state's forfeiture statute, Probate Code Section 259, is designed to prevent abusers from profiting from their abuse. What other preventive measures should or could be taken before abuse occurs?

How Are Elder Abuse Perpetrators Punished?

Across the country, specific state statutes detail the criminal penalties that abusers will face. Some states have increased the jail time when physical violence is against an elderly victim. Refer to Exhibit 10–3 to read a sample state Adult Protective Services Act. This example deals with the reporting of elderly abuse and is fairly typical.[12]

EXHIBIT 10–3   SAMPLE STATE ADULT PROTECTIVE SERVICES ACT

Reporting of suspect abuse, neglect, exploitation

4a. A person who has reasonable cause to believe that a vulnerable adult is the subject of abuse, neglect or exploitation may report the information to the county adult protective services provider.

b. The report, if possible, shall contain the name and address of the vulnerable adult; the name and address of the caretaker, if any; the nature and possible extent of the vulnerable adult's injury or condition as a result of abuse, neglect or exploitation; and any other information that the person reporting believes may be helpful.

c. A person who reports information pursuant to this act, or provides information concerning the abuse of a vulnerable adult protective services provider, or testifies at a grand jury, judicial or administrative proceeding resulting from the report, is immune from civil and criminal liability arising from the report, information or testimony, unless the person acts in bad faith or with malicious purpose.

d. An employer or any other person shall not take any discriminatory or retaliatory action against an individual who reports abuse, neglect or exploitation pursuant to this act. An employer or any other person shall not discharge, demote or reduce the salary of an employee because the employee reported information in good faith pursuant to this act. A person who violates this subsection is liable for a fine of up to $1,000.

e. A county adult protective services provider and its employees are immune from criminal and civil liability when acting in the performance of their official duties, unless their conduct is outside the scope of their employment, or constitutes a crime, actual fraud, actual malice or willful misconduct.

FINANCIAL CRIMES AND THE ELDERLY

State agencies responsible for investigating elder abuse claims have reported that the largest *explosion* has occurred in financial exploitation.[13] Financial crime and fraud against the elderly have been called a *nationwide epidemic.*[14] There may be at least five million cases of financial abuse annually among elderly victims.[15] A big problem with policing the scams, frauds, and con games that pop up all over the country and plague the elderly is that such fraudulent activities may disappear from one town only to move to another town half way across the country.[16]

One fraudulent scheme directed at older individuals in 18 states involved telemarketing, direct mail, and sales presentations that one mortgage company used to target homeowners with poor credit ratings. All those targeted were over 59 years old. A California company allegedly marketed home loans by touting low or no-fee loans when the fees actually reached 25 percent of the loan. The legal case against the mortgage company was originally initiated by AARP attorneys claiming unlawful lending practices. That case was later joined with another case that the Federal Trade Commission (FTC) brought against the same company. A settlement was later reached.[17]

The enactment of the federal government's Do Not Call Registry is one more way to protect citizens from possible fraudulent activities, not to mention annoying dinnertime interruptions. The Do Not Call Registry should aid those seeking privacy by stopping unwanted telemarketing calls to their homes. Charities and political parties are exempt. Some state governments have gone further by toughening state privacy laws even more. There are stiff state and federal penalties for attempting to circumvent the do not call privacy laws.[18] Information about the Do Not Call Registry can be found by calling 1-888-382-1222 or accessing the Internet at <http://www.donotcall.gov>.

An excellent guide to learning more about senior fraud prevention is provided by the United States Postal and Inspection Service. The guide, called *Senior Fraud Prevention,* gives tips for avoiding illegal telemarketing and mail fraud.

Court Says Protect Your Own

Many laws and agencies may be available to protect elderly crime victims; but in the following case, the Rhode Island Supreme Court was not ready to extend a legal duty to a bank to investigate and report financial abuse of one of its elderly bank customers.

CASE LAW *Santucci et al. v. Citizens Bank of Rhode Island*

799 A.2d 254 (R.I. 2002)

Facts: The plaintiffs, Robert M. Santucci and Rose J. Volpe, as co-guardians of their mother, Assunta Santucci, appealed a summary judgment in favor of the defendant, Citizens Bank of Rhode Island. A long-time customer of Citizens Bank of Rhode Island, Assunta Santucci opened an 18 month certificate of deposit account at Citizens, with an initial balance of approximately $39,000. Assunta began to withdraw an average of $300 per month. Coinciding with Assunta's deteriorating physical and mental health she began to make larger withdrawals beginning in 1996. In August 1996 Assunta withdrew $2,400 and in September 1996 she withdrew over $3,000. This pattern of withdrawals continued until over $27,000 was withdrawn. According to Volpe, a man with a history of drug abuse, David Baccari, was accompanying Assunta to the bank during each withdrawal. According to Volpe, Baccari stole all of the withdrawn money from Assunta. By May 1997, Volpe and her brother were appointed co-guardians of their mother who was declared incompetent by the appropriate court.

Issue: Whether a bank owes a duty of care to an elderly depositor to investigate and report an alleged suspected financial exploitation.

Court's Reasoning: The plaintiffs filed a 4 count complaint alleging the following: 1. a breach of Citizen Bank's statutory duty to report exploitation of the elderly pursuant to G.L. 1956 Section 42-66-68; 2. negligence; 3. breach of contract; and 4. breach of fiduciary duty. Count 1 was dismissed pursuant to Rule 12 (b) (6) of the Superior Court Rules of Civil Procedure. The defendant's summary judgment motion for the remaining counts was granted in February 2001. It is well settled that a defendant cannot be liable under a negligence theory unless the defendant owes a duty to the plaintiff. Whether a duty exists in a particular case is a question of law for the trial or motion justice. In general, unless it is specially agreed to otherwise, a banking institution and its depositors stand in the debtor and creditor relation. It is well established that a litigant opposing a disputed issue of material facts and cannot rest upon mere allegations or denials in the pleadings, mere conclusion or mere legal opinion. The plaintiffs next argues that Citizens breached its contract with Santucci by releasing funds in her account. There was no evidence, however, that Santucci did not request the withdrawals or that Citizens released funds to her after she was declared to be incompetent. The crux of plaintiffs argument is that Citizens had the right to refuse Santucci's withdrawal requests and that the bank was negligent when it did not exercise this right. We disagree. Under the rules that governed Santucci's certificate of deposit account, the account holder could make withdrawals before the maturity date only if the bank agreed to the withdrawal. But the document did not specify the circumstances under which the bank could refuse to allow an account holder to withdraw his or her funds nor did it require that the bank inquire into the reasons for the withdrawal. In these circumstances we are of the opinion that the contract between Citizen's and Santucci did not give rise to the duty advocated by the plaintiffs.

Lastly, the plaintiffs argued that the motion justice erred in failing to find that a fiduciary relationship existed between Santucci and Citizens. In general a depositor relationship does not in and of itself give rise to a fiduciary relationship and the motion justice found that the plaintiffs failed to present facts to demonstrate that Santucci was relying on Citizen's as a fiduciary.

Holding: We deny and dismiss the plaintiffs appeal, and we affirm the judgment of the Superior Court.

Case Discussion: The plaintiffs failed to show that the bank did not meet its limited obligation to Mrs. Santucci. Banks do have obligations to its customers. For example, a bank should permit only the designated renter of a deposit box to have access to the box. There are exceptions to this obligation. For example, a designated renter could give another person a power of attorney with the right to access the deposit box.

Identity Theft

Identity theft is the illegal obtaining of personal information for the purpose of using the stolen information to commit theft and fraud. Identity theft, the largest source of consumer fraud in the United States, is on the rise.

Two federal agencies heavily involved in investigations of identity theft include the SSA and the United States Postal Service. These agencies are involved because theft of an individual's Social Security number can have dire consequences and because stolen mail plays such a large part in identity theft scams.

The FTC is the federal agency empowered to coordinate all federal and state agencies investigating identity theft. The specific federal statute drafted to fight identity theft is the Identity Theft and Assumption Deterrence Act of 1998. Identity theft was made a federal crime in the late 1990s; and by the turn of the twenty-first century, an estimated $3 billion was being stolen annually as a result of identity theft. All 50 states have criminalized identity theft.

Identity theft is often committed by thieves who open accounts under another person's name using stolen personal information such as Social Security numbers. Unfortunately, the largest source of personal information is often the consumer. For example, fraud often begins with a stolen wallet, checkbook, or credit card. A surprising fact is that one in seven cases of identity theft are the result of a trusted friend, family member, or caretaker who stole the personal information from the victim's home.[19] The elderly client utilizing the services of caretakers with continual access to their homes should be warned to lock up important papers as a precaution.

Unsolicited mail offering applications for credit cards, mortgages, and loans has increased by five billion pieces since the federal Do Not Call Registry went into effect. The problem with all of the unsolicited mail is that identity thieves can use those offers to open accounts in another person's name if they already have other personal data about the person (e.g., Social Security numbers and license numbers). In fact, each year more than three million Americans face fraudulent credit card accounts being opened in their name. Many of these fraudulent credit cards can be traced to stolen mail. A locking mailbox can help protect clients.

The United States Postal Service investigated almost 40,000 cases of mail fraud in 2006. The resulting scams cost victims an estimated $27 million. Elderly clients should understand that any mail informing them that they have won a lottery or sweepstakes but the prize requires the winner to pay a fee is usually a scam targeted at the elderly.[20] A person can stop legitimate mail solicitations at the source by writing to the following address and asking for free forms: Direct Marketing Association, Mail Preference Service, P.O. Box 643 Carmel, NY 10512. An individual can stop solicitations for mortgage refinancing and home equity offers by writing to DataQuick, Attn: Opt-Out Dept., 9620 Towne Center Drive, San Diego, CA 92121.

Property Theft

A California judge made history when he sentenced a financial planner to six years in prison. The financial planner committed felonies when he defrauded elderly purchasers of annuities. Apparently, the selling of the annuities involved a financial scam called *churning* or *twisting*. The planner acted as broker of the annuities he sold, and every time an annuity was bought or sold the planner received a commission. Receiving a commission for selling annuities is not illegal, but the sentenced planner misled clients and forged documents that reported profits when the elderly clients were actually losing money. Churning is a misdemeanor under California state law, but the planner's actions were so blatant that authorities charged him with grand theft and *financial elder abuse*. One elderly client in particular was involved in so many purchases and sales of annuities that combined losses totaled $176,000.[21]

Another property theft scam reported by a head of a state Crimes Against the Retired and Elderly Unit centered on an apparently friendly visit by a stranger to a senior citizen's home on a false pretense. The stranger would visit the home, asking for directions, requesting a glass of water, or claiming to be a neighbor's relative. The stranger would direct the senior's attention away from one part of the house while an accomplice would enter and rob small items of higher value.[22]

Yet another scam focuses on the perpetrators using romance in defrauding their victims. The Internet has become a popular tool for this type of scam. Victims are wooed, usually with online photos and profiles that have nothing to do with reality. Eventually, the victims are conned into giving their online lovers money, never hearing from the scammer again. Reports of a suspected scam involving the Internet should be made to the Internet Crime Complaint Center at <http://www.ic3.gov>. Individuals who have been scammed have created Web sites to offer advice about how to prevent such abuse. Refer to "Helpful Web Sites" for one such address.

It has been said that there is no such thing as a free lunch, and the adage is true in the case of certain free lunch seminars masquerading as education-only sessions. Investigators from the SEC have found that the elderly are being targeted at free lunches with high-pressure sales pitches aimed at getting them to purchase new investments and open new accounts. The SEC's investigation concentrated on seven states with large elderly populations and 110 well-known investment firms sponsoring the free lunches. The SEC reported incidences of apparent fraud, such as liquidating accounts without a customer's knowledge or consent, selling bogus investments, providing exaggerated or misleading claims of investment performance, and providing weak supervision of sales staff per SEC regulations.

ELDER LAW PRACTICE

Willie Foster suspects that his brother, Bernie Foster, an attorney, is stealing from their dad, Bill Foster, Sr., by pocketing money from their father's bank accounts.

Bernie has taken over all of his father's finances since his father had a stroke last month; and now all of the addresses on his dad's checking, savings, and IRA accounts have been changed to Bernie's office. Willie also discovered that some checks that Bernie wrote to pay for their father's household aide bounced. The aide told Willie, which is why Willie became suspicious.

Before Willie approached his brother or upset his dad, he decided to find out what his options were by speaking with attorney Tara Jensen. Tara listened to Willie's story and agreed that circumstances appeared questionable and that she could ask Bernie some questions if Willie did not want to face his brother. However, Tara explained that without Bill Sr. giving a power of attorney to Willie, the bank was not going to explain much to Tara or Willie without involvement of the authorities. Tara suggested that Willie speak with his father (if his health permitted) and get his cooperation.

After Willie talked to his father and his father visited his bank, the senior Foster clearly understood what Bernie had done. Both Willie and his father then visited Tara.

"Ms. Jensen, I guess Bernie thought I'd die from the lousy stroke and no one would find out, but I am here to tell the tale and am not ready to meet my maker," the feisty octogenarian commented. "If my son cleaned me out, he needs to be punished," Bill Foster declared.

"I wanted to leave at least some inheritance." Bill added, "Now I don't have much left for anyone, including myself."

Tara learned that Willie's dad had never given permission to Bernie to write checks and that, in fact, Bernie Foster had forged the signature on his dad's checks. A complete review of documents showed that Bernie had no durable power of attorney or other right to his dad's accounts and had indeed forged his dad's signature.

Tara began, "I can talk to your son on your behalf and try to get the money back, but there aren't any guarantees he still has it or will even admit to wrongdoing. If that doesn't work, I can try to claim the bank is responsible for paying unauthorized withdrawals based on a fraudulent signature."

Tara moved ahead with her plan. Not surprisingly, Bernie Foster was in total denial when Tara approached him. However, Tara could smell fear and presented the obvious evidence to Bernie. Bernie capitulated, but Tara's success was short-lived when she quickly realized that he had already gambled away his father's life savings. This forced Tara to ask Bill Foster's local bank to face its responsibility in this familial mess. Again, not surprisingly, the bank capitulated only when faced with litigation and obviously fraudulent checks.

Although thankful to have most of his assets back, Willie and Bill Foster's success was tempered by the sad realization of what Bernie had done to his father. A few months later Bill Foster, Sr., died, but not before Tara had been asked to change Bill's will to provide only for his son Willie and Bill's grandchildren. Bernie might have gotten jail time; but as a first-time offender, he was left instead with the shame of being disbarred from his legal practice. [23]

SUMMARY

Each year hundreds of thousands of America's elderly are abused in psychologically and physically. The abuse is found in all ethnic, financial, and social groups. The Administration on Aging deals with elder abuse problems in the United States through its funding of the National Center on Elder Abuse (NCEA). The Administration on Aging also supports training law enforcement and medical personnel in the special needs of the elder abuse victim, provides information to the general public, and acts as a liaison for abuse prevention coalitions across the country. However, the prevention, recognition, and punishment of elder abuse typically begins at the local level. Elder abuse includes physical abuse, sexual abuse, emotional or psychological abuse, financial or material exploitation, neglect, self-neglect, and abandonment. Legislatures in all 50 states have passed elder abuse prevention laws. There are some major differences among the states. Many agencies and nonprofit organizations work to protect the elderly, including each state agency on aging; law enforcement on the local county level including the county district attorney and the court system; the medical examiners, hospitals, and medical clinics; state long-term care ombudsman's offices; public health agencies; area agencies on aging; mental health agencies; and offices dealing with facility licensing and certification. The Older Americans Act added Title VII, Chapter 3 to work toward the prevention of elder abuse, neglect, and exploitation. Although every citizen may have a moral responsibility to report abuse, legal responsibility is generally left to mandated reporters. Some states have increased the jail time when physical violence is against an elderly victim. State agencies responsible for investigating elder abuse claims have reported that the largest explosion has occurred in financial exploitation.

▓ KEY TERMS

administration on aging	identity theft	national center on elder abuse
adult protective services (APS)	mandated reporters	(NCEA)
eldercare locator		title vii, chapter 3

▓ REVIEW QUESTIONS

1. Where is elder abuse found in American society?

2. What is the typical relationship that an abuser has to her elderly victim?

3. What roles in the fight against elder abuse are filled by the Administration on Aging and the National Center on Elder Abuse?

4. According to the NCEA, what types of behavior are included in the general definition of elder abuse?

5. What are some signs of elder abuse?

6. What are some of the differences in states regarding their treatment of elder abuse?

7. What is the main purpose of Title VII's Chapter 3?

8. What responsibilities does the average citizen have to report suspected elder abuse?

9. What responsibilities does an elder law attorney and her staff have to report suspected elder abuse?

10. What type of elder abuse has been called a nationwide epidemic?

ETHICS ALERT

Luke was passing through the firm's main waiting area when he was shocked to see a man he thought he would never have the misfortune of seeing again. Luke caught himself before he released an "ugh" within earshot of the man. Casually hanging back and straightening magazines in the waiting area, Luke eavesdropped on the man as the man announced himself to Rena.

Yes, it was he, Luke thought. During Luke's paralegal internship at the county prosecutor's office, the man had plea-bargained to lesser counts of elder abuse involving fraud. Luke immediately was suspicious of the man's motives for being at Tara's office. Luke thought, "I wonder if I should tell Tara everything I know about him? Can I even work on a legal matter involving him?" Should Luke be concerned? Explain the answer.

HELPFUL WEB SITES

YAHOO! GROUPS <HTTP://GROUPS.YAHOO.COM/GROUP/ROMANCE>   This site warns of possible romance scams.

LOOKSTOOGOODTOBETRUE.COM <HTTP://WWW.LOOKSTOOGOODTOBETRUE.COM/FRAUD/ ROMANCE.HTML>   This site is sponsored by the United States Postal Service and the Federal Bureau of Investigation.

ENDNOTES

[1] National Elder Abuse Incidence Study, Department of Health & Human Services, Administration on Aging, 1998.

[2] The National Center on Elder Abuse. Data collected for 2000 survey on prevalence of elderly abuse provides quantification of such abuse in the United States.

[3] "The Prevalence of Elder Abuse: A Random Sample Survey," *The Gerontologist*, Vol. 28, 2005, pages 51–57.

[4] Wasik, John F., "The Fleecing of America's Elderly," *Consumer's Digest*, March/April 2000, page 47.

[5] Definitions from National Center on Elder Abuse, pages 1–4, April 20, 2005 <http://www. elderabusecenter.org>

[6] Public Policy Institute of AARP.

[7] Suicide Prevention Action Network USA, November 26, 2007, <http://www.webster.edu>

[8] "Self-Neglect," *Journal of Elder Abuse and Neglect*, Vol. 11, No. 2, 1999.

[9] Bergeron, L. Rene, and Gray, Betsey, "Social Work," *New York*, Vol. 48, Issue 1, January 2003, page 96h.

[10] National Center on Elder Abuse.

[11] Jogerst, Gerald, "Domestic Elder Abuse and the Law," *American Journal of Public Health*, Vol. 93, No. 12, 2003, pages 2131–2136.

[12] New Jersey 52:27D-409, Report of suspect abuse, neglect, exploitation (2005).

[13] Wasik, John F., "The Fleecing of America's Elderly," *Consumer's Digest*, March/April 2000, page 79.

[14] Lewis, Becky, *Sheriff*, Vol. 54, Issue 6, November/December 2002, page 22.

[15] Lachs, Mark S., *Prevention*, Vol. 54, Issue 5, May 2002, page 178.

[16] Rubbinaccio, Michael, "Special Unit Offers Program About Crimes and Scams That Affect Seniors," *Daily Record*, May 15, 2004, page 11.

[17] Pouncey, Maggie, "AARP Advantage," *My Generation*, September–October 2002, page 100.

[18] "The Sounds of Telemarketing Silence," *NJ AARP Member Update*, June 2004, page 4.

[19] Kircheimer, Sid, "Stamp Out Identity Theft," *AARP Bulletin*, February 2005, page 27.

[20] Larini, Rudy, "Con Men Still Seek a Quick Buck the Old Way: By Using the Mail," *The Star-Ledger*, March 28, 2007, page 2.

[21] Guccione, Jean, "Churn Artist Favor Seniors as Victims," *Los Angeles Times*, November, 28, 2003, page B2.

[22] Gordon, Mary, "Probe Finds Investment Seminars Mislead the Elderly," *The Star-Ledger*, September 10, 2007, page 23.

[23] This story is based on an actual case first reported by William C. Smith in the story "Respecting the Elders" in the *ABA Journal's* October 2002 edition, page 45.

Online Companion™
For additional resources, please go to
http://www.paralegal.delmar.cengage.com

Grandparenting Issues

■ OBJECTIVES

After completing this chapter, you will be able to:

- Describe the fundamental liberty and privacy interests of parents.
- Explain the purpose and use of the best interests of the child test.
- Explain the importance of the *Troxel* decision.
- Explain the status of grandparent visitation legislation.

INTRODUCTION

The relationship between a grandparent and a grandchild can be one of life's greatest rewards. Grandchildren, usually enjoyed without the responsibility of day-to-day child care, often bloom under the benevolent and loving eye of mature and patient grandparents.

Unfortunately, harmony and the wholesome virtues of family life can be tragically interrupted by death, divorce, or other personal traumas. Sadly, many parents not only argue in front of their children but also bring their intense hostility for each other or for other family members to the negotiation table when discussing the future custody and visitation arrangements of their children. This hostility can prevent clear heads from prevailing and makes the work of attorneys and paralegals more difficult.

Family harmony also can be interrupted when grandparents strongly disagree with their adult children's childrearing methods. Any of these reasons can negatively affect grandparents' relationships with their children or their children's spouse or partner. Subsequently, grandparents may find themselves shut out from their grandchildren's lives in varying degrees. Of course, this is a cause for concern and without any other effective recourse, a grandparent may seek help from an elder law attorney to explain the applicable law.

GRANDPARENTS' ROLE IN CUSTODY AND VISITATION

The changing reality of family life at the end of the twentieth century saw America's children living with only one parent in 28 percent of the country's households. This reality was evident in the developing role of third parties undertaking traditional parental responsibility in many U.S. households. For example, by 1998, approximately 4 million children lived with a parent in a grandparent's home and 1.4 million children were being raised solely by a grandparent without the presence of a parent.[1]

The end of the twentieth century also saw widespread enactment of third-party visitation statutes recognizing that, in addition to their parents, children also may benefit from relationships with statutorily specified persons who are not their parents. All 50 states ultimately enacted statutes that provided for some form of grandparent. For example, in New Jersey, the state legislature enacted one statute that listed factors to be considered in a dispute case involving grandparent visitation. Refer to Exhibit 11–1 to read the statute.[2] However, New Jersey's Supreme Court has since declared the state's grandparent visitation statute unconstitutional as a violation of parents' due process rights. Instead, grandparents in New Jersey seeking visitation must now allege in their initial pleadings that their grandchildren would be *harmed* in some way if visitation were denied and *must show by a preponderance of the evidence as a constitutional threshold that such visitation must be allowed.*

What Is Best, Grandma's Babysitting or Day Care?

One widely publicized case weighed the benefits of grandparent babysitting versus day care when a young Michigan mother fought her daughter's father for custody. At first glance, nothing seemed unusual about the unmarried teenage parents in the case.

EXHIBIT 11-1 FACTORS *PREVIOUSLY* CONSIDERED IN GRANDPARENT VISITATION

1. The relationship between the child and the grandparent;

2. The relationship between each of the child's parents, or the persons with whom the child is residing and the grandparent;

3. The time that has elapsed since the child last had contact with the grandparent;

4. The effect that such visitation will have on the relationship between the child and the child's parents or the person with whom the child is residing;

5. If the parents are divorced or separated, the time sharing arrangement that exists between the parents with regard to the child;

6. The good faith of the grandparent in filing the application;

7. Any history of physical, emotional or sexual abuse or neglect by the grandparent; and

8. Any other factor relative to the best interest of the child.

Jennifer Ireland, the mother, who had always lived with her toddler daughter, was a full-time student and resident at the University of Michigan. Steven Smith, the father, also was a student and resided with his parents. The case gained notoriety when the father pointed to the fact that the daughter attended daily day care on campus as the reason why he should gain custody. As an alternative babysitting arrangement, the father planned to have his mother care for his daughter. The trial court judge agreed with the father and granted Steven Smith sole custody. The mother appealed.

The appellate court ultimately overturned the lower court and returned the toddler to her mother's custody and the college day care center, but not before the media publicized this case as a possible legal turning point for all of America's working mothers. Should the fact that a parent uses day care, nonrelative babysitters, or grandparents or other blood relatives as babysitters be a factor in determining which parent gains custody? Did the outcome of the Ireland case ultimately serve the best interests of the child?

CHILD CUSTODY AND VISITATION FUNDAMENTALS

It is sad when parties with at least above-average degrees of intelligence lose the ability to make reasonable decisions when it comes to child custody and visitation. Our years of handling such cases have proved the main result of the conflict is unnecessary damage to the children, the most valuable and continuing asset of the marriage relationship.[3]

Justice Lund

The U.S. courts have a long history of supporting a parents' paramount right to decide what is best for their children. Indeed, it may be the oldest of the fundamental liberties recognized. In the early twentieth century, the U.S. Supreme Court case *Meyer v. Nebraska* endorsed the right to marry, establish a home, and bring up children as a fundamental liberty and privacy interest protected by Fourteenth Amendment.[4]

Many parents, grandparents, and extended family members make every effort to ensure that the children know that while their family will be different after a separation or a divorce, a new version of their extended family will be built together. The majority of parents do not leave child custody, visitation, and support issues to a judge to decide, but unfortunately, disagreements between parents may necessitate that a judge make the final decisions on these issues. These disputes can occur whether parents are divorcing or were never married. Whatever the situation, the first issue that must be determined is whether the court in which the custody and visitation matters will be heard has jurisdiction over the parties and their case. This involves determining whether the court has *in personam jurisdiction* over the parties involved in the dispute.

Following the jurisdictional hurdle, the primary legal question that a judge who is hearing custody or visitation matters asks is the threshold question known across the county as the **best interests of the child test**. Married or unmarried, once parents bring their custody or visitation matters into the court system, a family court judge will be asked to approve the parents' mutually agreed-to custody, visitation, and child support decisions. Typically, judges approve what parents decide unless a judge believes inadequacies are present. For example, if it appears that the parents have agreed to unfair visitation arrangements or insufficient financial support, a judge may not approve the parents' decision. Judges must seriously consider the children's best interests—not just the interests of the parents or other family members.

Alternatively, a family court judge will make any custody, visitation, and support decisions if the parents cannot come to some agreement on the issues. Some states have abolished the use of the term *child custody;* instead, they use the term *parental responsibility.*

best interests of the child test

The threshold question that a judge who is hearing custody or visitation matters asks.

Determining What Is Best for the Children

The best interests of the child test is used by all 50 states as a guideline for the courts to follow. However, different state courts can determine the best interests of the child many different ways. Generally, the best interests of a child are determined by analyzing a number of factors, which may include the following:

1. The emotional ties of the child to each parent

2. The amount of child care that each parent contributed in the past

■ **uniform child custody jurisdiction act (UCCJA)**

A model child custody statute that was adopted by all 50 states; it prohibited states from modifying custody orders made by other states and required states to enforce original custody orders from other states.

3. The wishes of the child

4. The lifestyle and moral beliefs of each parent

Exhibit 11–2 provides the lengthy and rather typical list of factors used in Illinois.[5] Obviously, with such general topics, there is great deal of room for judicial interpretation.

Reaching for Uniformity: The UCCJA Is Born

By the 1950s, America's child custody laws were like a patchwork quilt that was sewn together haphazardly. State courts were not required to respect each other's custody decisions, and one state's laws could differ radically from those of another. Judges, lawyers, scholars, and legislators knew that a more uniform way to deal with custody issues was needed for the sake of the nation's children. A group of professionals eventually got together to study the problem. The group, the National Conference of Commissioners on Uniform State Laws (NCCUSL), studied the child custody laws in effect in all 50 states. Following years of work, a list of the most effective and responsible child custody legislation enacted throughout the United States was created.

EXHIBIT 11–2   STATE OF ILLINOIS CHILD CUSTODY FACTORS

Sole or joint custody may be awarded, based upon the best interests of the child and upon the following factors:

1. Preference of the child;

2. Wishes of the parents;

3. Child's adjustment to his or her home, school, and community;

4. Mental and physical health of all individuals involved;

5. Relationship of the child with parents, siblings, and other significant family members;

6. Any history of violence or threat of abuse by a parent, whether directed against the child or against another person; and

7. Willingness and ability of each parent to encourage a close and continuing relationship between the child and the other parent.

Additionally, for an award of joint custody, the court will also consider the following factors:

1. Ability of the parents to cooperate effectively and consistently;

2. The residential circumstance of each parent; and

3. Any other relevant factors.

Ultimately, that was how the **Uniform Child Custody Jurisdiction Act (UCCJA)** was enacted in 1968. The UCCJA was promoted as a model child custody statute that should be put into effect in all 50 states. Eventually, all 50 states did adopt the UCCJA in an effort to bring a more standardized set of child custody laws to the United States. The main purpose of the UCCJA is to prohibit a court in one state from modifying custody orders made by other states; it requires the states to enforce original custody orders from other states. This standardization was intended to eliminate the possibility of parents removing or kidnapping their children to another state and requesting a new custody hearing once they established their new state's jurisdiction over the children on the single test that the children were present in the state. Unfortunately, the UCCJA does not provide enforcement procedures for states to follow, and various sections of the UCCJA have been interpreted inconsistently across the country.

Offspring of the UCCJA

The UCCJA was ultimately revised by the NCCUSL to reduce confusion. The result was the **Uniform Child Custody Jurisdiction and Enforcement Act (UCCJEA)**. The UCCJEA provides newer, more uniform methods for expedited interstate enforcement of custody and visitation orders.

The UCCJEA amended the UCCJA to bring it into conformity with two newer federal statutes, the **Parental Kidnapping Prevention Act (PKPA)** and the Violence Against Women Act (VAWA). The purpose of the PKPA, enacted in 1980, is to provide the necessary authority for states to give full faith and credit to their respective custody and visitation orders. In a nutshell, the PKPA requires courts to refrain from exercising jurisdiction over a custody case while another state is processing a custody case for the same child.

The majority of states have adopted the UCCJEA, and more states are expected to do the same. The UCCJEA requires the first step in a custody dispute to be the *determination of which state court has jurisdiction to hear the custody dispute.* Determining proper judicial jurisdiction is an essential step in the undertaking of any litigation. But before the UCCJA and the UCCJEA were adopted, state jurisdiction in custody matters could be determined by asking where the child's domicile was located at that time or whether there was a significant connection between the child and the proposed court. The newer legislation provides more specific requirements.

The first and most important requirement is to determine the child's *home state.* A state becomes a child's **home state** when the child has lived there for six months. Under the UCCJWA, once the home state is designated, that state has **continuing jurisdiction**. Even the absence of a child from the home state is immaterial since what matters most is that a custodial parent or a person acting as a parent (e.g., a grandparent) continues to live in the state. A parent who is

uniform child custody jurisdiction and enforcement act (UCCJEA)

An act that provides newer, more uniform methods for expedited interstate enforcement of custody and visitation orders.

parental kidnapping prevention act (PKPA)

An act that provides the necessary authority for states to give full faith and credit to their respective custody and visitation orders. In essence, it requires courts to refrain from exercising jurisdiction over a custody case while another state is processing a custody case for the same child.

home state

A state in which a child has lived for six months and where a court has made such a jurisdictional determination.

continuing jurisdiction

The power of a court to continue to control a matter even after the court has decided the case; used especially in cases involving child custody and support.

fighting the current custodial parent for custody cannot alter the home state's designation simply by removing the child from the state and trying to get a new custody order in another state.

The second requirement is to determine whether the state in question has a significant connection with the child. However, under the newer UCCJEA, establishing a significant connection is not as important as determining what state has home state designation. A court with a significant connection jurisdiction under the UCCJEA becomes the primary jurisdictional court only when the home state declines jurisdiction, when there are *forum non conveniens* grounds or misconduct grounds, or when there is no home state. **Forum non conveniens** is defined literally as "inconvenient court." For example, if two or more courts have proper jurisdiction over a case, a judge may rule that a lawsuit be brought in one court or the other for the sake of convenience and fairness to the parties.

The third requirement is whether the situation calls for a state to come forward and declare its jurisdiction over a child living in that state because of some kind of emergency situation.

The Many Options of Child Custody

The mechanics of child custody arrangements are as varied as the families involved. For example, parents may decide to alternate physical custody by the week, month, or year, with the children moving from one parent's home to the other parent's home. Other parents may be concerned about the emotional health of their children having to change homes so often. A small minority of parents alternate living arrangements themselves; for example, the children may stay in the family home while the parents alternately move between the family home and another home. This type of arrangement depends on the former spouses being unusually friendly and flexible.

Joint parental custody appears to be a more balanced alternative to a court granting one parent sole custody and the other parent only visitation rights. Critics of sole custody argue that it forces one parent to become essentially a visitor in his children's lives, having no significant parental influence, while the other parent's role becomes artificially larger with his designation as sole custodial parent. Since the early 1980s, the majority of states have created legislation supporting joint custody arrangements.

As stated earlier, all custody and visitation arrangements are most effective when they are decided by the parents. Some states require that a judge approve joint custody arrangements that parents made voluntarily to ensure that those arrangements will be best for the children involved. Some states support joint custody to such a degree that the courts decide in favor of a joint custody arrangement in spite of objections from the parents who have to live with the arrangement.

▓ *forum non conveniens*

Latin meaning "inconvenient court." If two or more courts have proper venue for a case, a judge may rule that a lawsuit be brought in one court or the other for the sake of convenience and fairness to the parties.

Advocating for the Children: The Guardian *Ad Litem*'s Role

A guardian *ad litem* (GAL) in the context of a child custody or visitation lawsuit is a person who may be appointed by a judge to look after the interests of a child or children during the litigation. A GAL also may be appointed in any matter involving children or adults with special needs. Depending on the state, a GAL may be an attorney, a social worker, a psychologist, or a volunteer who has been trained by the court system to get to the heart of the family's custody issues. The GAL, depending on the state, also may be called an **advocate** or a children's advocate. In a custody or visitation dispute, the GAL should speak with anyone who can help sort out the family's background and give insight into custody or visitation issues. A GAL should speak with the parents, grandparents, child or children, children's teachers, and family clergy (if any). The GAL also should visit the family's homes. In addition, the GAL should look at any psychology reports and speak with the professionals who prepared them. The GAL will prepare his own report to present to the judge. That report should detail what custody and visitation arrangement the GAL believes are in the best interests of the child or children. A judge may use the GAL's report to help him decide the final custody and visitation arrangements. A judge, however, is not bound by the GAL's recommendations.

advocate

A person who speaks on behalf of another person; also called a guardian *ad litem*.

The Psychological Expert's Role

The GAL is not the only non-family member who gets to share an opinion with the court. Battling spouses or grandparents often hire psychologists when custody and visitation are at issue. The psychologists hired by the parties may be formally appointed by the judge hearing the case. A court order may be granted to ensure participation by the parties and the children involved. The judge hearing the custody or visitation dispute may decide whether an independent court-appointed psychologist also should be hired—with one or both of the warring parties paying the bill.

A **confidentiality waiver** allows the psychologists to discuss matters that normally would be privileged information. The attorneys also should make sure that the psychologists conduct interviews with all of the parties. The psychologists should make home and school observations. They also should administer psychological tests and procure any pertinent documents.

confidentiality waiver

A waiver that allows psychologists or others to discuss matters that would normally be confidential or privileged information.

The Child's Role in Custody and Visitation Determination

Judges deciding custody or visitation issues may ask the children involved what their wishes are. However, the age of the children is usually taken into consideration, and there is no guarantee that a judge will agree with the children's wishes or that a child will be asked his opinion.

The Final Judgment

A family court judge does not take kindly to a party ignoring the final decision. A person who ignores a court order regarding custody or visitation may find himself in court to respond to contempt of court charges. A person found guilty of contempt of court may face a monetary fine, jail time, or both.

HISTORY OF GRANDPARENT VISITATION LEGISLATION

■ **grandparents'
rights movement**

A movement that gained
momentum with the
backing of senior advocacy
groups.

■ **grandparent
visitation legislation**

Legislation enacted to
ensure that grandparents
would be able to continue
their relationships with
their grandchildren.

■ **grandparenting
time legislation**

Another name for
grandparent visitation
legislation.

The first documented grandparent visitation lawsuit came from the Supreme Court of Louisiana in the case *Succession of Reiss*, 25 L.R.A. 798 (1894). The court in *Reiss* stated: *It is a law of nature that a child is under the authority of the father or mother and a judge has no right to intervene. The courts have no jurisdiction to interfere as to how and when a maternal grandmother may visit her grandchildren, merely because there is ill feeling between the grandmother and father.* The Louisiana court at that time was not alone in being loathe to interfere judicially with what had historically been considered the penultimate authority of parenthood. As U.S. Supreme Court Justice Sandra Day O'Connor noted over 100 years later in *Troxel v. Granville*, 530 U.S.57, 120 S.Ct.2054, 147 L.Ed. 2d 46 (2000), grandparent visitation has no historical roots in the common law, but rather is a *legislated creation.* Courts began to interfere with the often heavily weighted parent–child bond only when forced to do so by legislatively mandated statutory authority.

The first official grandparent visitation statute was enacted in New York in 1966. This grandparent visitation statute was created after the **grandparents' rights movement** gained momentum with the backing of senior advocacy groups. This is not surprising considering the fact that there was much social flux and the U.S. divorce rate was climbing during this time. Eventually, the states had a variety of **grandparent visitation legislation**, also known as **grandparenting time legislation**, enacted to ensure that grandparents would be able to continue their relationships with their grandchildren.

States Split on Grandparents' Rights

No state has ever given a grandparent an absolute right to definite visitation. Rather, the states have generally given grandparents the right to petition a court for visitation under certain circumstances. For the most part, a state's grandparent legislation is one of two types. First, some states view grandparent visitation as only a small interference or burden on a parent's right to parent. These states *broadly* provide for grandparents to petition the court and ask that the best interests of the children in question be the most important factor, not the parents' fundamental right to parent their own children. These broadly permissive states also permit unrelated individuals (such as a stepparent or significant caregiver to seek visitation).

Other states more *narrowly* provide for nonparents to seek visitation. Usually, these narrowly defining states do not give standing to nonfamily members even to bring a visitation petition. In addition, grandparents have a higher threshold to meet. For example, in Michigan, grandparents must prove by a *preponderance of the evidence* that it is mentally, physically, and emotionally in the best interests of a child that he see his grandparents. The Michigan statute goes beyond what the Michigan Supreme Court said in 2003 in *DeRose*[6] and the U.S. Supreme Court said in *Troxel* that it was necessary to protect a parent's constitutional rights. The Michigan statute holds grandparents to a higher standard. Michigan's *DeRose* court struck down previous grandparenting statutes based only on a best interests test because the statutes failed to require a trial court to give deference to the decisions of a fit parent.

ELDER LAW PRACTICE

Luke was hoping Tara could help his neighbor, Lucille Montgomery, deal with her ex-son-in-law, Jim Smith. Luke could not think of a bad enough word to describe what Smith had done to Lucille, one of the kindest and sweetest people Luke had ever met.

Lucille had lived with her daughter Casey and granddaughter Lucy ever since Jim had moved out of the apartment just three months after little Lucy was born. Lucille had taken Casey and little Lucy into her home. They had been living together happily for five years when tragedy struck. Luke knew this firsthand since he had lived next door to the Montgomery family most of his life.

The problems began when Casey became ill. Months of chemotherapy finally ended in Casey's death. Stunned by her daughter's death, Lucille focused on her only grandchild. A few weeks after Casey's funeral, any hope of getting back to normal ended when Jim did not return with Lucy after one of his rare visits. Jim finally called later that night to tell Lucille that his daughter would be living with him now.

Luke knew about that day too because he had been visiting his parents when Lucille came running over to their house crying hysterically.

(continues)

ELDER LAW PRACTICE *(continued)*

An hour later Luke and his parents had managed to calm Lucille's tears, but not before Luke had promised Lucille and his parents to talk to Tara and see if she could meet with Lucille the next day.

True to his word, Luke arranged for Lucille to come to the office. Lucille asked if Luke would stay for her appointment with Tara to provide moral support. Taking notes on her laptop, Tara listened politely to Lucille's story.

When Lucille was finished, Tara began, "Mrs. Montgomery, does Mr. Smith have a relationship with his daughter?"

"Well, Lucy knows who he is and has visited with him over the last five years, but he's on the road a lot and never had a regular visitation schedule," she answered. "I guess Lucy saw him once a month or so, but not overnight until recently, when Casey got sick. You see, I was Casey's main caregiver and sometimes it just got to be too much caring for two. Jim started to help out a little."

Tara continued, "Did Mr. Smith pay his child support regularly?"

"Casey didn't want to have to track him down all the time, and even though she had a support order, she didn't push it. So no, he didn't pay it regularly. Casey made a good living working in tech support," Lucille answered. "But I guess I should tell you that Jim would send $100 or a new outfit or toy every once in a while."

Tara looked at Mrs. Montgomery's expectant face and wished she could guarantee that everything was going to be okay and that little Lucy would be back in her old room that evening. She had been an attorney long enough to know there were no guarantees when a case involved the law and human beings. Oh, if people would only plan for the worst-case scenario before it actually happened, Tara thought to herself.

Tara's next thought was that it would have been a good idea to have Lucille's visitation rights included in Jim and Casey's final judgment of divorce. That is one way to try to avoid future litigation.

"We need strong evidence and good witnesses to support your claim that visitation and as much as we can get is best for little Lucy," Tara explained. "We have to emphasize that this is especially true after Casey's death. You are the link to her mother and the only world that Lucy knew. The court will likely appreciate the fact that Jim is stepping up to his responsibility."

"Finally!" exclaimed Lucille.

"Well, exactly," Tara agreed. "This is what we have to emphasize. You have an established long-time relationship with Lucy. I'm going to move forward to negotiate your visitation with Jim or, if he hires counsel, with his attorney. I'm hopeful that Mr. Smith will realize that litigation is expensive, time-consuming, and not the best thing for Lucy. Okay?" she asked.

"Okay," Lucille said grudgingly. "How long will this take? He's letting me talk to her on the phone, but I don't know if he'll keep that up," she added.

Asking the Right Questions

An attorney cannot launch a good legal offense or defense without having as much information as possible about a client's case. Grandparents seeking visitation should be prepared to produce documentary evidence, including witnesses' names, to support their claim that visitation is in the best interests of their grandchildren. Of course, grandparents seeking custody of their grandchildren have a proportionately higher threshold to meet due to the seriousness of a custody demand.

Opposing attorneys usually kick off the discovery phase of a case by requesting interrogatories (written questions regarding the facts of a case) of the opposing party. Answers to interrogatories are usually based on client interviews. Paralegals often assist in interviewing clients and preparing the final answers to interrogatories. The parties answering interrogatories are asked to attach their signature, swearing to the truthfulness of their answers. What questions should Tara ask Lucille Montgomery?

Developing interview skills requires practice. A skilled interviewer can question a client and quickly adapt when the interviewee veers away from the interviewer's control of the interview. Many law firms have fine-tuned the art of client questioning by developing generic questionnaires. However, a client's file probably will not be complete if all of the questions are taken from a one-size-fits-all questionnaire. Review Exhibit 11–3 for a sample of the type of interview questions that may be asked in a dispute involving grandparent visitation. These types of questions also can be used as the basis for interrogatories that are sent to the opposing party's attorney.

EXHIBIT 11–3   SAMPLE INTERVIEW QUESTIONS TO ASK IN A GRANDPARENT VISITATION DISPUTE

1. How would you describe your grandchildren?

2. Since they were born, what role have you taken in their care and nurturing?

3. How do your grandchildren perform in school? What are their best and worst subjects?

4. Do your grandchildren play sports or participate in extracurricular activities, sports, or school activities?

5. Do you participate with your grandchildren in their extracurricular activities? How so?

6. Do you know the names of you grandchildren's friends and teachers?

7. Do your grandchildren have any medical conditions? If so, how do these conditions affect the children's behavior, schoolwork, and so on?

8. How do any siblings interact with each other?

9. What activities do you like to do with your grandchildren?

10. In what way do you believe your grandchild will suffer emotional harm, if any, if you are prevented from participating in the child's life?

11. Why do you want the court to allow you visitation over the objections of a grandchild's parent?

12. Why do you think your grandchild's parent or parents are resisting your visitation requests?

13. What is your history of visitation and/or custody with your grandchild?

Courts Vary in Interpreting Grandparent Rights

The following cases demonstrate how the rights of grandparents and grandchildren to visit each other have been interpreted by different state courts. The first case, *Bowers v. Matula*, concentrates on the question of a grandparent having standing to sue for visitation rights. Each case is briefed from the original judicial opinion.

CASE LAW   *Bower v. Matula*

943 S.W. 2d 536 (1997)

Facts:	The maternal grandparents brought an action seeking access to their grandchild. The biological parents' rights were subsequently terminated, and the child was adopted by the paternal grandparents in a separate action. The paternal grandparents then moved to dismiss the maternal grandparents' action because they claimed the maternal grandparents lacked standing to request visitation.
Issue:	Whether the maternal grandparents had standing to request visitation of their grandchild.
Court's Reasoning:	This court finds that, under governing statutes, the line before which grandparents' requests for access to their grandchildren may be made, and after which such requests may not by made, is when all the parental rights have been terminated and the grandchild has been adopted by someone other than a stepparent.
	The statute is clear and unambiguous. The maternal grandparents had standing to request access to their grandchild when they filed their petition requesting access. The subsequent termination of the parents' rights and the grant of adoption to the paternal grandparents did not deprive the maternal grandparents of standing in their action seeking access. No parental rights had been terminated or adoption ordered when the maternal grandparent filed their petition.
Holding:	Reversed and remanded to the lower court to hear the maternal grandparent's petition.
Case Discussion:	What difficulties could occur when the maternal grandparents visit their grandchild? What positive outcome could result because of the child being able to continue a relationship with a second set of grandparents?

Biological Connection Touted

The second case, *Dolman v. Dolman,* explains how simply having the biological connection as a grandparent does not ensure court-ordered visitation without a best interests of the child standard being applied to the facts of the case. Interestingly, a jury heard the *Dolman* case's custody dispute. Texas is the exception in having juries hear child custody trials.

CASE LAW *Dolman v. Dolman*

586 S.W. 2d 606 (1979)

Facts: Carolyn R. Dolman was divorced from Denver Floyd in June 1967. The judgment awarded sole custody of Lise Nicole Dolman, an infant daughter, to Carolyn, with reasonable visitation privileges awarded to Denver.

In May 1978, Louise P. Dolman, the paternal grandmother of Lise, appearing *pro se,* filed a motion to modify the divorce judgment of June 1967 by seeking visitation rights pursuant to a state statute.

The case went to trial and was heard by a jury. The court's charge contained two special issues. The jury answered: (1) it was in the best interest of the child to grant the grandmother access rights to the child, and (2) one day each calendar month for eight consecutive hours was reasonable access. Access rights were defined in the jury charge to mean rights of visitation with the child. The mother appealed and claimed the state statute did not provide a grandparent with an independent cause of action for reasonable access rights to a child if the child was in the custody of a fit parent.

Issue: Whether the court erred in entering judgment for the paternal grandmother.

Court's Reasoning: Generally, an obligation of the custodial parent to permit visitation by a grandparent is a moral obligation, not a legal one, and courts will not enforce a right of visitation by a grandparent so as not to intervene in a relationship between a child and a custodial parent. Evidence in this case included the following: (1) the paternal grandmother had not seen the child, who was almost 12 years old, since the child was 19 months old; (2) she had never learned to pronounce the child's name correctly; (3) she had not written to the child since the child had learned to read; (4) she had once gone to the child's school in an attempt to visit her, but had erroneously determined that another student was her grandchild; and (5) the child's father did not want his mother to visit the child. This evidence was sufficient to show that the welfare and social needs of the child would not be served by the grandmother's visitation.

From our review of the record, we are convinced that the jury's answer is based upon little more than the well-accepted notion that it is just and right for a grandparent to know his grandchild. The paternal grandmother did not demonstrate by a preponderance of the evidence that the welfare or social needs of Lise would be served by the grandmother's visitation. Indeed, there is considerable support in the record that such visitation would not be in the best interests of Lise. Evidence indicated that allowing visitation by the paternal grandmother could be disruptive and emotionally detrimental to the child. In sum, the court, after considering all of the evidence, is of the opinion that the jury's decision was so contrary to the great weight and preponderance of the evidence as to be manifestly unjust.

Holding: Reversed and remanded for a new trial.

Case Discussion: The appellate court's decision clearly states the best interests of the child must be weighed against the right of the grandparent to visit the grandchild. The court went further and wrote that the evidence appeared to show that such a visit in this case could be disruptive and emotionally detrimental to the child. Could a parent negatively influence a child's visit with even the most wonderful of grandparents?

Case Brought Legal Confusion

The third case, *Troxel v. Granville,* was ultimately decided by the U.S. Supreme Court. *Troxel* steps away from statutorily ensured third-party visitation and supports the application of a more stringent fundamental liberty interest before third-party visitation can be provided by a court.

The majority in *Troxel* wrote that the U.S. Constitution still leaves room for states to consider the impact on a child of possible arbitrary parental decisions that neither serve nor are motivated by the best interests of the child. In other words, following the *Troxel* decision, state governments still got involved on a case-by-case basis when their courts thought that parents might make decisions that would harm the children.

CASE LAW *Troxel v. Granville*

530 U.S. 57, 120 S.Ct. 2054, 147 L.Ed. 2d 46 (2000)

Facts: Unmarried parents Tammie Granville and Brad Troxel had two daughters from a relationship that ended in June of 1991. Brad subsequently established a relationship between his daughters and his parents, the Troxels. Brad committed suicide in 1993. The Troxels commenced their case in December 1993 by filing a petition to obtain visitation rights with their granddaughters, Isabelle and Natalie. The Troxels filed their petition under Wash. Rev. Code § 26.10.160(3), which states: *any persons may petition the court for visitation right at any time including, but not limited to, custody proceedings.* The Troxels requested two weekends of overnight visitation per month and two weeks of visitation each summer. The mother, Granville, did not oppose visitation altogether, but instead asked the court to order one day of visitation per month with no overnight stay. The original order gave the Troxels one weekend per month, one week during the summer, and four hours on both of the petitioning grandparent's birthdays.

The mother appealed, and the Washington Court of Appeals remanded the case back to the Superior Court. The Superior Court, on remand, again found quality-time visitation with their grandparents to be in the best interests of the girls.

Again, the mother appealed, but this time the Washington Court of Appeals reversed the lower court's visitation order, declaring the non-parents lacked standing to seek visitation under the Washington statute in question unless a custody order was pending.

The Troxels then asked the Washington Supreme Court to review the case. Although the Washington Supreme Court disagreed with the appeals court and declared that the Troxels had standing to sue without a pending custody action, it agreed that visitation could not be ordered. Citing the United States Constitution, the Washington Supreme Court found that Wash. Stat. § 26.10.160(3) unconstitutionally infringed on the fundamental right of parents to rear their children. The Troxels then sought the assistance of the United States Supreme Court by filing a *writ of certiorari.* The United States Supreme Court agreed to hear their case.

Issue: Whether third parties may petition a court for visitation rights at any time when the visitation serves the best interests of the child.

Court's Reasoning: The liberty interest at issue in the case—the interest of parents in the care, custody and control of their children—is perhaps the oldest of the fundamental liberty interest recognized by this Court. In light of this extensive precedent, it cannot not now be doubted that the due process clause of the Fourteenth Amendment protects the fundamental right of parents to make decisions concerning the care, custody, and control of their children.

The Washington statute in question contains no requirement that the court accord the parent's decision any presumption of validity or any weight whatsoever. Instead, the Washington statute placed the best interest determination solely in the hands of the judge. Should the judge disagree with the parent's estimation of the child's best interests, the judge's view necessarily prevails. Thus, in practical effect, any Washington court can

(continues)

CASE LAW *Troxel v. Granville* *(continued)*

disregard and overturn any decision by a fit custodial parent concerning visitation whenever a third party affected by the parent's decision files a visitation petition. This compels our conclusion that §26.10160(3) as applied exceeded the bounds of the due process clause. First, the Troxels did not allege, and no court has found, that Granville was an unfit parent. The Superior Court judge's comments instead suggest that the grandparents' request should be granted unless the children would be impacted adversely.

The Superior Court gave no weight to Granville having agreed to visitation even before the filing of any visitation petition. Many other states expressly provide by statute that courts may not award visitation unless a parent has denied visitation to the concerned third party. All the factors discussed by the Superior Court showed an unconstitutional infringement on Granville's fundamental right to make decisions concerning the care, custody, and control of her two daughters. The Washington Superior Court failed to accord the determination of Granville, a fit custodial parent, any material weight. The due process clause does not permit a state to infringe on the fundamental right of parents to make child-rearing decisions simply because a state judge believes a better decision could be made.

Holding: Affirmed.

Case   The *Troxel* case provides an excellent lesson in constitutional law. The freedom to parent is described as a
Discussion: liberty interest. This liberty interest is provided by the U.S. Constitution. The Fourteenth Amendment of the
                Constitution states: *No state shall deprive any person of life, liberty, or property, without due process of law.*
                This amendment ensures that the rights provided in the federal Constitution are not taken away by a state
                through its courts or statutes.

However, this case also is a good example of the U.S. Supreme Court putting off for another day the job of defining the precise scope of parental due process rights in the context of visitation. In other words, the 49 other states with grandparent visitation statutes were not instructed the day *Troxel* was decided that their statutes were unconstitutional. Rather, the court simply stated that the constitutionality of any standard for awarding visitation depends on the specific manner in which that standard is applied. That is, the Washington statute was found to be breathtakingly and overly broad in that it allowed the decision of any fit custodial parent to be overturned. In the context of a statute described as overly broad, the fear is that application of the statute will be seen as overreaching and as stepping on people's constitutional rights.

Grandparent Visitation Post-Troxel

In *Troxel,* The Supreme Court specifically left it to the state courts to interpret whether state statutes granting grandparent visitation could withstand constitutional scrutiny. In general, one of three things has occurred in state courts since *Troxel.* State grandparent visitation statutes have been found constitutional, unconstitutional, or unconstitutional as applied. This makes the issue of grandparent visitation very state-specific in the post-*Troxel* world.

How could courts come to such different conclusions? For example, the Indiana Court of Appeals found that Indiana's grandparent visitation statute permitted visitation only if such visitation was in the child's best interests in addition to one of the following:

1. The child's parent is deceased

2. The marriage of the child's parents has been dissolved in Indiana

3. The child was born out of wedlock, and there had been a declaration of paternity.[7]

The Indiana court contrasted the more narrow reading of its state statute with the overly broad statute discussed in *Troxel*.

The Pennsylvania Supreme Court recently found that the state is justified in interfering with parental rights when the health and welfare of a child is at stake and the statute in question is narrowly defined. In *Hiller v. Fausey*, a young boy was living with both of his parents when his mother became ill.[8] The maternal grandmother subsequently cared for the boy on a daily basis until her daughter died and the father refused to allow the grandmother continued contact with her grandson. The grandmother filed for partial custody under a Pennsylvania statute that permitted the parent of a deceased adult child to seek such partial custody or visitation if "it would be in the best interests of the child and would not interfere with the remaining parent's parent-child relationship." The Pennsylvania Supreme Court applied the strict scrutiny test to the statute, (i.e., whether there was a compelling state interest for the statute and whether the statute was narrowly defined). The Pennsylvania court found that the statute narrowly applied only to grandparents whose adult child had died.

Similarly, the Ohio Supreme Court found in favor of grandparents being permitted visitation to a grandchild who had lived with them previously for more than five years. In *Harrold v. Collier*, the Ohio Supreme Court looked to the narrowness of Ohio's grandparent visitation statute and found that *Troxel* only required that the wishes of parents refusing visitation be given special weight.[9]

These cases are contrasted with a long list of cases from across the country that failed to find courts willing to support third-party or grandparent visitation.

SUMMARY

The United States courts have a long history of supporting parents' rights to decide what is best for their children. The primary legal question that a judge who is deciding a custody or visitation matter asks is what will be in the best interests of the child. This threshold question is asked in family courts in all 50 states. A guardian *ad litem* (GAL) is a person who may be appointed by a judge to look after the interests of a child or children when disputes regarding custody or visitation arise. Different states may call the person in this role by different names. Judges who are asked to decide custody or visitation issues may ask the children involved their wishes. However, the ages of the children is taken into consideration, and there is no guarantee that the judge will agree with the children's wishes.

The first official grandparent visitation statute was enacted in New York in 1966. The grandparents' rights movement gained momentum with the backing of senior advocacy groups. No state has ever given a grandparent an absolute right to definite visitation. Rather, the states have generally given grandparents the right to petition a court for visitation under certain circumstances. *Troxel v. Granville* was decided by the U.S. Supreme Court, and *Troxel* stepped away from statutorily ensured third-party visitation and supported the application of a more stringent fundamental liberty interest before third-party visitation could be provided by a court. Ultimately, *Troxel* does not mean that all grandparent visitation statutes are found unconstitutional. The issue remains one for a case-by-case and state-by-state analysis.

KEY TERMS

advocate

best interests of the child test

confidentiality waiver

continuing jurisdiction

forum non conveniens

grandparent visitation legislation

grandparenting time legislation

grandparents' rights movement

home state

parental kidnapping prevention act (PKPA)

uniform child custody jurisdiction act (UCCJA)

uniform child custody jurisdiction and enforcement act (UCCJEA)

REVIEW QUESTIONS

1. What legal question should every court that is deciding a custody or visitation issue ask?

2. What factors are typically investigated when dealing with child custody and visitation?

3. What laws have been passed to combat the problem of enforcing child custody and visitation orders?

4. What constitutional interest do parents have when courts are deciding third-party visitation issues?

5. What is a guardian *ad litem*? When is one usually appointed?

6. Can children make their own decisions about whom they may visit? Explain.

7. When was the first grandparent visitation legislation enacted? Why was it enacted?

8. Has any state ever given grandparents an absolute visitation right?

9. Compare the broad and narrow views the states have had concerning grandparent visitation.

10. What made *Troxel* an important case in the grandparent visitation debate?

ETHICS ALERT

"I'm sure happy it's Friday," Rena murmured. "It didn't come soon enough this week." Rena was feeling a bit burned out by the demands of another busy week at the firm. She commented to Luke before leaving the law office that evening, "Only a full moon could explain our clients' behavior today. I'm off to the hairdresser to wash them out of my hair!"

Later that evening Rena was comfortably ensconced in her new hairdresser Mona's salon regaling her with stories of a certain client's wacky behavior. Laughing, Mona told Rena that her legal client sounded as nutty as her boyfriend's ex-wife. This led Mona to share a story with Rena about a wacky ex-wife. Rena's shared laughter suddenly turned to shock when she realized Mona was probably talking about the same woman! Rena quickly turned the conversation away from storytelling and then breathed a sigh of relief. Mona had not made the connection. Did Rena circumvent an ethical dilemma when Mona failed to realize who Rena's client was? How should Rena alter her behavior?

■ HELPFUL WEB SITES

AMERICAN BAR ASSOCIATION <HTTP://WWW.ABANET.ORG> Users can find a chart of visitation rights for all 50 states by using the key words *family law charts* to conduct a search, clicking on "Family Law Quarterly: Laws in the 50 States Charts" and then clicking on "Chart 6: Third-Party Visitation."

PARENTSRIGHTS.ORG <HTTP://WWW.PARENTSRIGHTS.ORG> This site describes itself as being designed as a coalition for the restoration of parental rights and against what the site describes as unconstitutional third-party visitation. It provides links to state statutes and judicial opinions on third-party visitation.

GRANDPARENTS RIGHTS ORGANIZATION <HTTP://WWW.GRANDPARENTSRIGHTS.ORG> This Web site focuses on all aspects of grandparents' rights.

AARP.ORG <HTTP://WWW.AARP.ORG> This site discusses the rights of grandparents, if the user focuses on the terms family and grandparenting.

■ ENDNOTES

[1] Grandparents Raising Grandchildren: Implications for Professionals and Agencies, Purdue University Cooperative Extension Service, National Conference January 12, 1999.

[2] N.J.S.A. 9:2-7.1 1993.

[3] Justice Lund in re: *Marriage of Bush*, 191 Ill. App. 3d. 249, 138 Ill. 423, 547 N.E. 2d 590 (1989).

[4] *Meyer v. Nebraska*, 262 U.S. 390; 43 S. Ct. 625; 67 L. Ed. 1042 (1923).

[5] Ill. ANN. STAT. ch 5§ 602, 602.1, 603.1, 610 (2005).

[6] *DeRose v. DeRose*, 469 Mich. 320, 666 N.W. 2d 636 (2003)

[7] Gregory, John DeWitt, *The Detritus of Troxel*, *Family Law Quarterly*, Vol. 40 No. 1 Spring 2006.

[8] *Hiller v. Fausey*, 851 A.2d 193 (Pa. Super. 2004).

[9] *Harrold v. Collier*, 107 Ohio St. 3d 44 (2005).

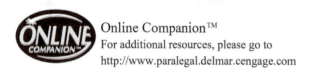

Online Companion™
For additional resources, please go to
http://www.paralegal.delmar.cengage.com

Legal Aspects of Funeral Planning

■ OBJECTIVES

After completing this chapter, you will be able to:

- List the choices available in planning a funeral.
- Describe the financing strategies used to pay for funerals.
- Explain the state and federal laws that regulate the funeral industry.
- Explain the potential for fraud when planning a funeral.

INTRODUCTION

Twenty-first-century Americans use the term **funeral** for an event during which a person who has recently died is honored. The word *funeral* is derived from the ancient Sanskrit term meaning "smoke," which refers to the custom of **cremation**.[1] Cremation is defined as the incineration of a corpse until only ashes are left.[2]

Funeral rites vary widely based on culture, custom, and religion. However, a meaningful funeral brings together a community of mourners to remember the deceased, create opportunities to

■ funeral

The event during which a person who has recently died is honored.

■ cremation

The incineration of a corpse until only ashes are left.

express grief and offer emotional support, allow moments of reflection on the meaning of life and death, and provide mourners with a sense of closure.[3]

Funeral arrangements are a deeply personal choice. The discussion of funeral planning can be one of life's more uncomfortable and emotion-laden discussions that everyone faces eventually, either for themselves or for others. Planning a funeral may be an unpleasant chore, but someone must do it. In fact, Americans arrange more than 2 million funerals for family and friends each year.[4] Those funerals are planned in the nation's approximately 22,500 funeral homes and 100,000 public, private, military, municipal, and religious cemeteries.[5]

CLIENT CHOICES

Clients essentially have two choices when contemplating funeral planning. The first choice is for an individual to *preplan* her funeral arrangements. This choice frees family and friends from the responsibility of making decisions about burial or cremation following the sorrow-filled experience of losing a loved one. Such funeral arrangements also may be prepaid by the planner. The second choice is for an individual to die *without plans* for burial, cremation, or funeral arrangements. This choice leaves the entire matter to family or friends who may or may not know or may not comply with the deceased's wishes.

An attorney can be of assistance to clients who want to preplan their funeral arrangements. An attorney can begin by reviewing the basic decisions that a client must make when planning a funeral. A client may be confused by what is and is not legally permitted. The client may choose whether to have a simple disposition or a more elaborate funeral. For example, some clients may not know that a funeral home's services are not legally required or that a casket can be purchased from an online retailer and sent to a funeral home. Exhibit 12–1 provides a list of basic decisions that a person needs to make to initiate funeral planning.

▨ **direct cremation**

The service of a funeral home in picking up a body from the place of death, transporting it to a crematory, providing a container for cremation, obtaining all necessary authorizations, carrying out the cremation, and returning the remains to the family.

Clients may choose to use the services of a funeral home only for a **direct cremation**. A direct cremation includes picking up a body from the place of death, transporting it to a crematory, providing a container for cremation, obtaining of all the necessary authorizations, carrying out the cremation, and returning the remains to the family. The cremation option was chosen in 26 percent of all deaths in 2000. Cremations totaled 600,000 in 2000.[6]

The decision to be buried involves more choices. A single or double gravesite may be purchased. U.S. cemeteries usually offer an option of a traditional monument being placed at a grave, or they may offer the option of a grave marker being placed flush with the ground at a gravesite. If an individual already owns a gravesite, the cemetery will charge a fee for opening the gravesite when it is needed. Cemeteries also may allow mausoleums on their property by choice or necessity. For example, in Louisiana, above-ground mausoleums are used due to the low water table of the land. There are public, private, religious, and military cemeteries.

Clients may want to add more details to their funeral plans. For example, some clients may want certain music to be played, flowers displayed, and food served. Clients often ask their attorneys to incorporate their wishes into their last will and testament or have them included in a letter of instruction written to accompany their will. An individual who preplans her funeral is considered (in the parlance of the funeral industry) to be making a **pre-need decision**.

▥ **pre-need decision**
Any funeral plans made by an individual prior to her death.

EXHIBIT 12–1   FUNERAL PLANNING DECISIONS

1. Does the client want burial or cremation?

2. If the decision is a burial, will the burial be in a cemetery plot or a mausoleum crypt?

3. If the decision is cremation, what is the decision regarding the disposition of the ashes?

4. Should the ashes be stored in a columbarium niche, be buried, or be scattered? If scattered, where? Is the location legally permissible?

5. An alternative to consider: Does the client want to donate organs, tissues, or her entire body to a medical school?

Anatomical Gifting

Individuals seeking an altruistic option to burial or cremation may opt for **anatomical gifting**. Anatomical gifting is the donation of a person's designated body parts or her entire body to aid medical science. An anatomical gift may reach a patient in need or be utilized for medical research and education. Part of the donation process may provide assistance with processing necessary documents, providing a no-cost cremation, and returning the cremated remains if the next of kin so chooses.[7]

▥ **anatomical gifting**
The donation of a person's designated body parts or her entire body to aid medical science.

Cryonics

An admittedly more unusual burial alternative is **cryonic suspension**. Cryonic suspension is the process of taking a body that has been frozen with care and storing it in tanks filled with liquid nitrogen. The most famous person to have been placed in cryonic suspension was the sports legend Ted Williams. Williams's cryonic suspension became public knowledge when his daughter filed a lawsuit against her siblings seeking to have her father cremated instead of adhering to

▥ **cryonic suspension**
The process of taking a body that has been frozen with care and storing it in tanks filled with liquid nitrogen.

his instructions as stated in his will. The siblings contended that Mr. Williams had the requisite mental capacity when he signed a contract (after signing his will) to be cryonically preserved. The case was settled, and Williams remains in cryonic suspension.[8]

LAWS AFFECTING FUNERAL PLANNING

funeral homes
Business establishments where corpses are prepared for burial or cremation and where funeral services may be held and the body viewed by mourners.

The earliest funeral regulations developed at the turn of the twentieth century when states began to license **funeral homes** and **funeral directors**. Funeral homes are business establishments where corpses are prepared for burial or cremation and where funeral services may be held and the body viewed by mourners. Funeral directors are usually the proprietors of funeral homes. Their job is to manage funerals. Often they are able to prepare corpses for burial or cremation. The rationale used at the time for the initiation of these regulations was the prevention of communicable disease. The argument was successfully made by legislators that dead bodies were infectious and could be safely disinfected only by being properly embalmed.

funeral directors
Usually the proprietors of funeral homes. Their job is to manage funerals. Often they are able to prepare corpses for burial or cremation.

All 50 states except Colorado license funeral directors, and most states regulate their state's funeral industry to some degree. For example, the most prevalent requirement in 33 states is that funeral homes must have embalming preparation rooms. Almost half of the states prohibit funeral homes from offering their services within cemeteries. A small number of states require that crematoriums operate only within cemeteries. This was originally thought to limit the emission of gasses from the crematoriums to the cemetery and surrounding neighborhood. Modern-day cemeteries have limited problems with emissions due to the more sophisticated design of crematoriums.

Funeral Homes and Worst-Case Scenarios

The failure of a funeral home to perform its services adequately can have an emotional effect on a deceased's family. The following cases, *Ingaglio v. Kraeer Funeral Home*, 515 So.2d 428, (1987) and *Perkins, et al. v. Johnson, et al.*, 866 So.2d 1146 (2003), are worst-case examples of what can happen when funeral homes fail to perform adequately.

CASE LAW *Ingaglio v. Kraeer Funeral Home*

515 So.2d 428, (1987)

Facts:	The plaintiffs were the daughter and wife of the deceased, Richard P. Ingaglio. The plaintiffs made arrangements with the defendants to have Richard's body removed from their home and prepared to be sent to Pennsylvania for burial. The plaintiffs traveled to Pennsylvania to view the body and were horrified by the body's condition. The deceased's body had decomposed due to improper embalming. The deceased was also found wearing ill-fitting clothing, unnatural cosmetics, and orange colored mustache and hair, with one eye bulging out and with his mouth hanging open. The plaintiffs sued the funeral home for mental and emotional distress and breach of contract. The funeral home's motion for summary judgment was granted for both claims. The plaintiffs appealed.
Issue:	Whether the plaintiffs' claims should be heard.
Court's Reasoning:	Appellee acknowledges that the trial court erred in dismissing Count II, the breach of contract action. Accordingly, we reverse summary judgment as to Count II. The funeral home's employees claimed that the deceased's remains were prepared properly and denied any wrongdoing. The funeral home was granted a summary judgment on the grounds that plaintiffs could not recover under Florida law for mental and emotional distress alone. Under Florida law, damages for pain, suffering, and mental anguish cannot be recovered absent some impact or physical injury unless willful, wanton or malicious behavior is shown. Malicious behavior can be implied or imputed from an entire want of care or great indifference to others. We conclude the record does contain genuine issues of material fact as to whether Kraeer Funeral Home's conduct exceeded all bounds reasonably tolerated by society from which the jury could imply malice or the entire want of care or great indifference by the Kraeer Funeral Home.
Holding:	Reversed and remanded.
Case Discussion:	This case provides an excellent lesson for when a summary judgment should not be granted. The appellate judges explained that if any fact issues were in dispute between the parties, a trial judge should not have granted a summary judgment motion. The holding that the case was reversed and remanded meant that the case should be returned to the trial level to be heard by a jury.

Personal Preference Laws

Earlier chapters reviewed the importance of memorializing one's major life choices (e.g., drafting a will to specify beneficiaries and advance directives to detail health care decisions). In addition, an individual may want to ensure that her burial wishes are carried out by detailing burial or cremation decisions in a will or in a letter of instructions. Unfortunately, there is no guarantee that such decisions, *even those included in a will or letter of instruction,* will be carried out. The reason is because **state personal preference laws** may permit an individual's next of kin to disregard such instructions and to decide whether their deceased family member will be buried or cremated. For example, in Arkansas, a person who

■ **state personal preference laws**

Laws that may permit a person's next of kin to disregard instructions included in a will or letter of instruction and to decide whether their deceased family member will be buried or cremated.

wants her remains cremated must sign a specific form and have it witnessed by two other people to ensure that the cremation will be carried out. Without the signed and witnessed form, next of kin in Arkansas can override a deceased's wishes. Conversely, Wyoming case law requires survivors to comply with the wishes of the deceased. Exhibit 12–2 provides a list of states with personal preference laws.[9] The case *Birch v. Birch*, 204 N.Y.S. 735 (1924), is an older case that clearly explains personal preference law that is still followed in the majority of states.

CASE LAW *Perkins, et al. v. Johnson, et al.*

866 So.2d 1146 (2003)

Facts:	The plaintiffs, relatives of Joyce Cotton, sued Howard G. Johnson and Johnson Memorial Funeral Directors, Inc., alleging breach of contract, fraud and the tort of outrage. The plaintiffs contacted the defendants regarding a pre-need contract for Joyce Cotton who had terminal cancer. The parties signed a contract allowing the relatives to pay a portion of the fee up front ($1,000) and the balance being due over the course of 12 months ($375 per month). After the contract was signed the defendant presented the plaintiffs with an Irrevocable Pre-Funeral Agreement (IPA) which stated that if their relative died before the 12 months were up then the full amount would be due prior to the funeral service. The plaintiffs neither signed the IPA nor initialed it.
	Two days later Joyce Cotton fell into a coma and the plaintiffs called the defendant to cancel the contract because they could not afford the full amount of the funeral at that time. The defendant allegedly told the plaintiffs that the contract was "a done deal" and there were no refunds available. The plaintiffs then sued the defendants. The defendants responded with a summary judgment motion. The motion stated the parties had entered into a valid contract that clearly stated what would happen in the event the relative died prior to the end of the 12 month period. The motion was granted and plaintiffs appealed.
Issue	Whether the summary judgment motion was properly granted.
Court's Reasoning:	We conclude that a question of fact exists as to whether the plaintiffs assented to the terms contained in the irrevocable funeral services agreement. The terms making the funeral services contract irrevocable do not appear in the document signed by the plaintiffs and Howard Johnson.
Holding:	Reversed and remanded.
Case Discussion:	This case provides a lesson on how to recover on a breach of contract claim. A plaintiff must prove the following:

1. The existence of a valid contract binding the parties in the action

2. His or her own performance under the contract

3. The defendant's nonperformance

4. Damages

The fact that the IPA was neither signed by the plaintiffs nor included in the contract signed by the plaintiffs was the most important point in the case. Contract law usually does not look outside the four corners of a signed contract for additional contract language. To do otherwise would invite (with certain exceptions) contractual turmoil.

CASE LAW	Birch v. Birch		

204 N.Y.S. 735 (1924)

Facts:	The plaintiff, Mary L. Birch, was the widow of John Birch. John Birch did not provide testamentary direction or preferences regarding the disposition of his body or the erection of any memorial monument. The defendant, Charles E. Birch, was the executor of John Birch's estate. The case revolved around a dispute between Charles and Mary regarding the choice of monument. Mary sought an injunction to stop Charles from erecting a monument of Charles' choice.
Issue:	Whether the plaintiff's motion for injunction to stop the executor's choice of memorial monument being erected should be granted.
Court's Reasoning:	In the absence of a testamentary direction on the part of the deceased the right to the possession of the dead body for the purpose of preservation and burial belongs to the surviving husband or wife or next of kin. The rule is subject to modification, depending upon the particular circumstance in each case.
Holding:	Motion for injunction granted.
Case Discussion:	The defendant had the power to settle the estate, but the closest next of kin (in this case, the widow) trumped the executor's powers.

Law Designed to Protect Consumers

The **Funeral Industry Practices Rule**, commonly known as the **Funeral Rule**, was promulgated in 1982 and made effective in 1984. The Federal Trade Commission (FTC) administers the Funeral Rule, which requires funeral providers to provide consumers with information regarding funeral products and services and ensures that consumers pay for only the products and services they want and need.

Under the Funeral Rule, all funeral providers are required to supply an itemized statement of costs for any funeral they are contracting to provide. If the funeral provider does not know the cost of a particular service, she may provide a good faith estimate. Funeral homes are not legally required to mail their price lists but are required to provide their prices over the phone. No one is legally required to use the services of a funeral home.

funeral industry practices rule

The regulation that requires funeral providers to provide consumers with information regarding funeral products and services and ensures that consumers pay for only the products and services they want and need.

funeral rule

The common name for the Funeral Industry Practices Rule, administered by the Federal Trade Commission.

EXHIBIT 12–2   PERSONAL PREFERENCE LAWS

Alabama	No	Alaska	No
Arizona	Yes	Arkansas	Yes
California	Yes	Colorado	Yes
Connecticut	Yes	Delaware	No

(continues)

EXHIBIT 12–2 PERSONAL PREFERENCE LAWS *(continued)*

District of Columbia	Yes	Florida	Yes
Georgia	Yes	Hawaii	No
Idaho	Yes	Illinois	Yes
Indiana	Yes	Iowa	No
Kansas	Yes	Kentucky	Yes
Louisiana	Yes	Maine	Yes
Maryland	No	Massachusetts	Yes
Michigan	Yes	Minnesota	Yes
Mississippi	Yes	Missouri	Yes
Montana	No	Nebraska	Yes
Nevada	Yes	New Hampshire	Yes
New Jersey	Yes	New Mexico	Yes
New York	Yes	North Carolina	Yes
North Dakota	No	Ohio	Yes
Oklahoma	No	Oregon	Yes
Pennsylvania	Yes	Rhode Island	Yes
South Carolina	Yes	South Dakota	Yes
Tennessee	Yes	Texas	Yes
Utah	Yes	Vermont	Yes
Virginia	Yes	Washington	Yes
West Virginia	Yes	Wisconsin	Yes
Wyoming	Yes		

Since the inception of the Funeral Rule in 1984, the FTC has engaged in traditional enforcement actions through investigation and litigation. In 1996, the FTC embarked on a new method of enforcement with the institution of the Funeral Rule Offenders Program (FROP). Since the inception of FROP, FTC agents have shopped a total of 574 funeral homes to ascertain whether the funeral homes adhere to the Funeral Rule. The test shopping that is conducted by FTC and state attorney general staff involves sending individuals to funeral homes to inquire about funeral arrangements. At least 74 funeral home violators discovered by the FROP investigation have been offered the opportunity to pay a fine as an alternative to litigation. Under FROP, funeral homes make a voluntary payment to the U.S. Treasury or appropriate state fund for an amount less than what would likely be sought if the FTC authorized filing a lawsuit for civil penalties. In addition, the funeral homes found to be violating the Funeral Rule must participate in the compliance program of the National Funeral Directors Association (NFDA). This program includes a review of the price lists, on-site training of the staff, and follow-up testing and certification of violators following their compliance with the Funeral Rule. "Helpful Web Sites" includes a link to the state laws for funeral service providers. Refer to Exhibit 12–3 to find a portion of The Federal Rule.[10]

EXHIBIT 12–3   FUNERAL RULE EXCERPT

§ 453.2 Price disclosures.

(a) *Unfair or deceptive acts or practices.* In selling or offering to sell funeral goods or funeral services to the public, it is an unfair or deceptive act or practice for a funeral provider to fail to furnish accurate price information disclosing the cost to the purchaser for each of the specific funeral goods and funeral services used in connection with the disposition of deceased human bodies, including at least the price of embalming, transportation of remains, use of facilities, caskets, outer burial containers, immediate burials, or direct cremations, to persons inquiring about the purchase of funerals. Any funeral provider who complies with the preventive requirements in paragraph (b) of this section is not engaged in the unfair or deceptive acts or practices defined here.

(b) *Preventive requirements.* To prevent these unfair or deceptive acts or practices, as well as the unfair or deceptive acts or practices defined in § 453.4(b)(1), funeral providers must:

(1) *Telephone price disclosure.* Tell persons who ask by telephone about the funeral provider's offerings or prices any accurate information from the price lists described in paragraphs (b)(2) through (4) of this section and any other readily available information that reasonably answers the question.

(2) *Casket price list.* (i) Give a printed or typewritten price list to people who inquire in person about the offerings or prices of caskets or alternative containers. The funeral provider must offer the list upon beginning discussion of, but in any event before showing caskets. The list must contain at least the retail prices of all caskets and alternative containers offered which do not require special ordering, enough information to identify each, and the effective date for the price list. In lieu of a written list, other formats, such as notebooks, brochures, or charts may be used if they contain the same information as

(continues)

EXHIBIT 12–3 FUNERAL RULE EXCERPT *(continued)*

would the printed or typewritten list, and display it in a clear and conspicuous manner. Provided, however, that funeral providers do not have to make a casket price list available if the funeral providers place on the general price list, specified in paragraph (b)(4) of this section, the information required by this paragraph.

(ii) Place on the list, however produced, the name of the funeral provider's place of business and a caption describing the list as a "casket price list."

(3) *Outer burial container price list.* (i) Give a printed or typewritten price list to persons who inquire in person about outer burial container offerings or prices. The funeral provider must offer the list upon beginning discussion of, but in any event before showing the containers. The list must contain at least the retail prices of all outer burial containers offered which do not require special ordering, enough information to identify each container, and the effective date for the prices listed. In lieu of a written list, the funeral provider may use other formats, such as notebooks, brochures, or charts, if they contain the same information as the printed or typewritten list, and display it in a clear and conspicuous manner. Provided, however, that funeral providers do not have to make an outer burial container price list available if the funeral providers place on the general price list, specified in paragraph (b)(4) of this section, the information required by this paragraph.

(ii) Place on the list, however produced, the name of the funeral provider's place of business and a caption describing the list as an "outer burial container price list."

(4) *General price list.* (i)(A) Give a printed or typewritten price list for retention to persons who inquire in person about the funeral goods, funeral services or prices of funeral goods or services offered by the funeral provider. The funeral provider must give the list upon beginning discussion of any of the following:

(*1*) The prices of funeral goods or funeral services;

(*2*) The overall type of funeral service or disposition; or

(*3*) Specific funeral goods or funeral services offered by the funeral provider.

FUNERAL COSTS

Funerals are among the highest-priced purchases that consumers make. In 2007, the typical U.S. funeral cost $6,000. An in-ground burial can add $2,400 to the costs of a funeral. Additional niceties such as flowers, newspaper obituary notices, stationery, and special transportation can add an additional $1,000.[11] Obviously, the high cost warrants careful scrutiny. A general price list should include an itemized list including the cost of the following:

1. Direct cremation/immediate burial

2. Basic services

3. Transfer of remains to funeral home

4. Forwarding/receiving of remains to/from another facility

5. Embalming and preparation (restoration or cosmetology)

6. Use of facilities/staff for viewing or a ceremony

7. Use of equipment/staff for graveside service

8. Use of hearse/limousine

9. Prices of caskets (individual/range)

10. Prices of outer burial container (liners/vaults)[12]

Burial costs vary with the cemetery and the choices that a person makes. *Perpetual care* is a term used to describe the prepaid continuing maintenance of a burial plot, monument, or mausoleum.

Once the total cost of the choices (e.g., cremation or burial, type of funeral service, flowers, and music) are tallied, the question of how to finance the funeral is the next consideration.

Payment Strategies

A person can arrange for her funeral to be paid in one of three ways:

1. Prepaying prior to a person's death

2. Paying after a person's death out of the person's estate

3. Ignoring the issue

Paying for one's funeral ahead of time is considered to be paying pre-need, or **pre-funding** one's choices.

In addition to paying pre-need for a funeral or allowing an estate to cover the funeral costs, an individual has quite a few funding options to consider with regard to the costs of a funeral. These options include but are not limited to the following:

- Pre-need insurance
- Life insurance
- Annuities
- A bank or a funeral trust
- A **payable-on-death bank account**
- A state prepaid funeral trust fund

Pre-need insurance purports to eliminate complicated claims procedures of a regular life insurance policy. It is supposed to ensure that when money is needed to pay for a funeral, the money will be available. Pre-need insurance is also called **burial or funeral insurance**. Some insurance companies require the policy owner to purchase a burial policy in one lump sum. Other companies let the owner pay the premiums over a certain period of time (e.g., three or five years). The only pre-need insurance policies an insured with serious health problems may be able to find are those that limit coverage the first year, then increase coverage the next year. Life insurance or an annuity are other options

pre-funding
Paying for one's funeral ahead of time.

payable-on-death bank account
An option for funding funeral costs.

pre-need insurance
Insurance that may eliminate complicated claims procedures of a regular life insurance policy.

burial or funeral insurance
Another name for pre-need insurance.

▨ **bank or funeral trust**

An option for funding funeral costs.

for funding funeral costs to ensure that beneficiaries will be able to afford the cost of the insured's funeral when needed. A trustee of a **bank or funeral trust** can invest in a certificate of deposit. Some states now offer state-sponsored prepaid funeral trust funds.

A minority of states have passed legislation designed to protect pre-need purchasers. For example, New Jersey's Pre-Need Act requires checks written to purchase burial insurance be made payable only to the insurance company, not to a funeral home. In addition, New Jersey's act stipulates that any money paid to a funeral home pre-need belongs to the consumer and must be made available to the consumer upon request. New Jersey's Prepaid Funeral Trust Fund requires that 100 percent of the principal and interest (minus a 1 percent trustee fee) must accrue for the benefit of the beneficiary and that the money must be deposited in a FDIC-insured bank account. Trust fund monies also are revocable or 100 percent refundable with interest on demand.

Similarly, the state of Illinois requires each funeral home that participates in the Illinois Funeral Directors Association Pre-Need Trust be individually licensed to accept trust funds by the Office of the State Comptroller under the Illinois Funeral or Burial Funds Act, that each member firm be bonded, and that each funeral home annually report to and be audited by the state's comptroller.

Guiding Clients Who Prepay Funeral Costs

Elder law attorneys can advise clients who decide to prepay funeral costs. For example, clients may ask attorneys to review contracts and make sure funds are secured. Attorneys can advise their clients to keep papers in a safe place that is accessible by family. Clients may want to consider an irrevocable prepayment plan when eligibility for Medicaid benefits is a concern. Such prepayment is permitted and does not influence Medicaid's determination of eligibility. Clients should be advised that not all states require funeral homes to make full refunds when clients want to cancel pre-need or prepaid funeral plans.

Veterans Burial Benefits

The U.S. Department of Veterans Affairs (VA) provides a small stipend to assist with the financial costs of a veteran's funeral. All veterans are eligible to receive a free burial flag and may be eligible to be buried at no cost in a national veteran's cemetery. Burial at well-known Arlington National Cemetery is limited to those men and women who meet certain criteria. The following Web site provides that criteria: <http://www.arlingtoncemetery.org>.

Funeral Planning Societies

Farmers in the northwest United States formed burial co-ops in the early 1900s as a way to cut costs through cooperative buying power. These co-ops were an offshoot of the popular farm grange organizations. The concept of burial co-ops spread to other parts of the United States, and the national organization the Funeral Consumers Alliance was started in 1963. The goal of the Funeral Consumers Alliance is to protect a consumer's right to choose a meaningful, dignified, affordable funeral.[13]

Fraud Prevention

Over $20 billion was invested in pre-need funeral and cemetery plans at the start of the twenty-first century, but no federal regulation had been designed to monitor how safely those dollars were invested. Pre-need and prepaid funeral plans are actively solicited to the elderly all over the country via marketing plans sold over the phone, through the mail, and through door-to-door solicitation. It has been estimated that over 50 percent of all funerals will be prepaid and pre-arranged by 2010.[14] According to the American Cemetery Association, at least 90 percent of all cemetery plots are sold on a pre-need basis.

Although pre-need and prepaid funeral plans are not regulated by federal law, most states do regulate pre-paid funeral plans. However, state oversight varies widely, and in different states different agencies regulate the funeral industry. A number of states do not address pre-need burial contracts. In fact, only 10 states have consumer protection laws dealing with consumers recovering funds from pre-need burial contractors.

The following case highlights the difficulties the members of one family encountered in financing the funeral for their husband and father.

CASE LAW *Wilson v. Houston Funeral Home*

42 Cal. App.4th 1124, 50 Cal. Rptr. 2d 169 (1996)

Facts: Plaintiffs were the wife, daughter, and sister of the deceased, Melvin Wilson. They sought damages from the Houston Funeral Home, and its director Willie Houston for breach of contract and fraud in connection with the burial service of Mr. Wilson. Two days after Mr. Wilson's death the plaintiffs entered into a contract with Houston for professional services typically associated with funeral proceedings. At that time Mrs. Wilson informed Houston that she had a check for $5,000 from a mortgage loan she had taken out plus the proceeds of an insurance policy to pay the funeral expenses. Houston assured her that the insurance proceeds would cover the cost of the funeral and there wasn't a need for her to cash the $5,000 check.

(continues)

On the day preceding the funeral Mrs. Wilson received a call from Houston asking if she still had the $5,000 check, she did. Then again on the day of the funeral she received a call from an employee of the funeral home asking if she had the check, she still did. On the day of the funeral the funeral home's limousine driver picked up the family and instead of taking them to the services the driver took them to the bank where Houston was waiting. Houston in a loud manner demanded payment in full from the $5,000 check. After about an hour the family gave Houston the check. The family returned to the funeral home and the deceased had all ready [*sic*] been put in the hearse and Houston refused to allow the family to see the deceased. On the way to the burial site the limousine driver drove at a high rate of speed reaching 90 miles per hour while weaving in and out of traffic. The Wilsons sued the funeral home and its director for breach of contract, breach of covenant of good faith, fraud and breach of a fiduciary duty. The lower court dismissed their claims.

Issue: Whether the lower court erred in dismissing the breach of contract, breach of the covenant of good faith, fraud and breach of fiduciary claims.

Court's Reasoning: Houston contends he complied with the written contract which specifically provided that Houston would transport the body and the family to Riverside for burial service. We disagree with such a narrow view of the contract between a mortuary and the bereaved family of the deceased. A contract for burial services involves more than just driving the family to the cemetery to watch a box being dropped in a hole. Rather, as our Supreme Court has observed, the mortuary defendants undertook to provide appropriate and dignified services of the type that bereaved family members normally anticipate. Those services are not limited to the conduct of the funeral rites, but extend through arranging the commitment of the remains though burial. Contrary to Houston's claim the funeral home did not act reasonably in detaining Mr. Wilson's body until its bill had been paid. Courts in other jurisdictions have described holding a body hostage for payment of a debt as morally reprehensible. As to the conduct of the limousine driver, clearly such unprofessional conduct would be a breach of the covenant to provide an appropriate and dignified burial.

Plaintiffs seek to hold Houston liable on a theory of breach of fiduciary duty by an agent. We have found no case in California or any other jurisdiction holding a mortuary owes a fiduciary duty to the family of the decedent. Nevertheless, the mortuary, as the family's agent for the fulfillment of its statutory obligation, may owe the family a fiduciary duty in connection with the preparation and expeditious disposal of the decedent's remains. We need not decide this issue here, however; because of the funeral home's breach of it's [*sic*] duty to provide the family with an appropriate and dignified burial service.

Holding: Reversed and remanded to the trial court.

Case Discussion: This case helped explain that buying the services of a funeral home involves more than handling the body of the deceased. Rather, the court recognized that family members are purchasing from the funeral home the assurance that a loved one's funeral and burial will be handled with consolation, consideration, and dignity and will provide peace of mind after a loss.

DISINTERMENT

disinterment

The removal of a body from a grave or tomb.

The following case involves the question of when **disinterment** is appropriate and who has the right to request disinterment. Disinterment is defined as the removal of a body from a grave or tomb.

CASE LAW   *In the Matter of Jon A. Briggs, as Executor of Harvey D. Briggs v. Briggs*

681 N.Y.S.2d 853 (1998)

Facts:	Petitioner, Jon A. Briggs, was the executor of Harvey D. Briggs' estate. Petitioner sought the disinterment of the deceased from Fairview Cemetery and re-interment in the family plot in Cobleskill Cemetery. The plot at Cobleskill was where the deceased wished to be buried. He had a plot there along side his first wife and his wishes to be buried there with his first wife were made clear in his last will and testament. However, nine months after the death of his first wife the deceased remarried and 19 months thereafter he died. The second wife buried the deceased at Fairview Cemetery without notification to his relatives or his executor.
Issue:	Whether there were good and substantial reasons for the court to exercise its discretion and permit disinterment of the deceased.
Court's Reasoning:	The standard to use in determining whether a deceased should be disinterred is whether there are good and substantial reasons for such disinterment. A decedent's wishes concerning his or her final resting place are of significant concern to a court in determining whether disinterment should occur. A decedent's wishes can prevail even over those of a surviving spouse. Respondent purchased the Fairview plot after decedent's death and with knowledge of the burial dispute. She surreptitiously buried decedent without notifying decedent's other family members. Because issues of fact have clearly been raised concerning decedent's wishes, the lower court erred in dismissing the application with a hearing.
Holding:	Judgment reversed and remitted for a hearing.
Case Discussion:	The court in the *Briggs* case stated that a decedent's wishes can prevail even over those of a surviving spouse. This is counter to some states that do not adhere to the personal preference philosophy.

SUMMARY

Americans arrange more than 2 million funerals for family and friends each year. Twenty-first-century Americans use the term *funeral* for the event in which a person who has recently died is honored. Cremation is defined as the incineration of a corpse until only ashes are left. An individual may want to pre-plan her funeral arrangements. This choice frees family or friends from the responsibility of making decisions about burial or cremation immediately following the sorrow-filled experience of losing a loved one. An individual may die without having planned any burial, cremation, or funeral arrangements. In this case, family or friends may or may not know or may not comply with the deceased's wishes. Funeral arrangements also may be prepaid by the planner. An individual has quite a few funding options to consider with regard to the costs of a funeral. The Funeral Industry Practices Rule, commonly known as the Funeral Rule, requires funeral providers to supply consumers with information regarding funeral products, services, and costs. The purpose of the Funeral Rule is to ensure that consumers pay for only the products and services they want and need. Prepaid and pre-need programs are actively targeted to the elderly all over the country. An alternative to burial is cryonic suspension. Burial co-ops cut costs through cooperative buying power. Personal preference laws permit a person's next of kin to disregard a deceased family member's burial or cremation instructions. Disinterment is defined as the removal of a body from of a grave or tomb.

◾ KEY TERMS

anatomical gifting	disinterment	payable-on-death bank account
bank or funeral trust	funeral	pre-funding
burial or funeral insurance	funeral directors	pre-need decision
cremation	funeral homes	pre-need insurance
cryonic suspension	funeral industry practices rule	state personal preference laws
direct cremation	funeral rule	

◾ REVIEW QUESTIONS

1. What are the first two choices that a person must make when contemplating funeral planning?

2. What is one example of an altruistic option to burial or cremation?

3. What is one example of an unusual option to burial or cremation?

4. Depending on the state, how can personal preference laws impact an individual's personal choices in the planning of her funeral?

5. What is the purpose of the Funeral Industry Practices Rule, commonly known as the Funeral Rule?

6. According to the Funeral Rule, what information must funeral homes provide to its customers?

7. Over $20 billion was invested in pre-need funeral and cemetery plans at the start of the twenty-first century, but no federal regulation had been designed to monitor how safely those dollars were invested. What problems, if any, may occur when an individual preplans and prepurchases her funeral?

8. What benefits, if any, does the VA provide to the country's veterans?

9. What is a goal of a funeral planning society?

10. What legal standard should be reached before a court permits a disinterment?

◾ HELPFUL WEB SITES

FUNERALPLAN.COM <HTTP://WWW.FUNERALPLAN.COM> This site provide links to the applicable laws for funeral service providers in the majority of the 50 states.

FUNERAL CONSUMERS ALLIANCE <HTTP://WWW.FUNERALS.ORG> This organization is a federation of nonprofit funeral information societies. It has been protecting the consumer's right to choose a meaningful, dignified, and affordable funeral since 1963.

CREMATION ASSOCIATION OF NORTH AMERICA <HTTP://WWW.CREMATIONASSOCIATION. ORG> This organization is an association of crematories, cemeteries, and funeral homes that offer cremation.

COUNCIL OF BETTER BUSINESS BUREAUS <HTTP://WWW.BBB.ORG> Better Business Bureaus are private, nonprofit organizations that promote ethical business standards and voluntary self-regulation of business practice.

FEDERAL TRADE COMMISSION (FTC) <HTTP://FTC.GOV> Consumers can file a complaint with the FTC via the Internet by using the online complaint form. The commission cannot resolve individual problems for consumers, but it can act against a company if it sees a pattern of possible violations. A consumer also can file a complaint by contacting the Consumer Response Center by phone, toll-free, at 1-877-FTC-HELP and by mail at Consumer Response Center, Federal Trade Commission, 600 Pennsylvania Avenue, NW, Washington, DC 20580. A free brochure published by the FTC is available to consumers.

UNITED STATES DEPARTMENT OF VETERANS AFFAIRS <HTTP://WWW.VA.GOV> This site offers information on burial benefits available to veterans .

ALCOR LIFE EXTENSION FOUNDATION <HTTP://WWW.ALCOR.ORG> This Web site provides information about cryonics.

ENDNOTES

[1] *Encarta Dictionary.*

[2] *Encarta Dictionary.*

[3] Funeral Service Educational Foundation, page 2 (2007).

[4] American Cemetery Association.

[5] American Cemetery Association.

[6] Cremation Association of North America.

[7] Life Quest Anatomical's Whole Body Donation Program, July 2, 2007 <http://www.lifequestanatomical. com>

[8] "Ted Williams Frozen In Two Pieces," Associated Press, New York, August 12, 2003.

[9] "Be Careful Where You Die," *Parade*, October 14, 2000, page 16.

[10] Federal Rule, 16 CFR Part 453.

[11] U.S. Federal Trade Commission.

[12] <http://www.ajibay.com> August 27, 2005.

[13] Funeral Consumers Alliance <http://www.funerals.org>

[14] Wasik, John F., "Special Report: Fraud in the Funeral Industry," *Consumer's Digest*, Vol. 34, Issue 5, September/October 1995.

Online Companion™
For additional resources, please go to
http://www.paralegal.delmar.cengage.com

Glossary

401k plans A retirement plan where the employer is a for-profit business.

403b plans A retirement plan where the employer is a nonprofit entity.

A

Acceptance An agreeing to an offer.

Activities of daily living (ADL) Basic tasks essential for day-to-day functioning, such as bathing, dressing, grooming, eating, moving about, and using the toilet alone.

ADEA Waiver An employer is allowed to ask an employee to waive any of the employee's rights under the ADEA as part of an ADEA settlement or incentive to terminate employment.

Ademption A situation when the testator has devised personal or real property to a beneficiary, but that property has been sold, given away to another, or lost.

Adjusted gross income The total gross income minus all allowable deductions on which income tax is based.

Administration on Aging The federal agency under the Department of Health & Human Services given the job of shepherding elder initiatives and programs through the system.

Administrator A personal representative appointed by the state to manage, administer, and distribute a decedent's estate when there is no will.

Administratrix A female administrator.

Adult foster care Care provided for adults when they do not need continual caregiving.

Adult Protective Services (APS) A heading under which a state's elder abuse laws may be found.

Advance directives for health care Documents that specify an individual's health care decisions and identify who will make decisions for the individual in the event the individual is unable to communicate his wishes to doctors.

Advocate A person who speaks on behalf of another person; also called a guardian *ad litem.*

Affidavit in lieu of administration An alternative to letters of administration wherein the estate's monetary value does not exceed a certain statutorily designated amount.

Age Discrimination Act Of 1975 Prohibits discrimination on the basis of age in programs and activities receiving federal financial assistance.

Age Discrimination in Employment Act of 1967 (ADEA) A federal government act that provides protection to certain applicants and employees 40 years of age and older from discrimination on the basis of age in hiring, promotion, discharge, compensation, or terms, conditions, or privileges of employment.

Agent The individual appointed to make medical treatment decisions for another person; also known as a *health care proxy.*

Aging in place The desire of seniors to stay in the comfort of their own home as they age.

Alimony An allowance from one spouse to another that usually continues until the recipient's spouse remarries, dies, or perhaps begins co-habitating with another partner. Alimony is called *spousal maintenance* or *spouse support* in some states.

Alzheimer's Disease (AD) A type of dementia that accounts for 50 to 75 percent of all dementias.

Anatomical gifting The donation of a person's designated body parts or her entire body to aid medical science.

Ancillary administration Additional probate administration required to distribute any property owned by a decedent in a state other than the decedent's domiciliary state.

Annual gift tax exclusion The amount an individual or couple is permitted by federal tax law to gift each year.

Antenuptial agreement Another name for prenuptial agreement.

Assisted living facilities Housing options for seniors based on the level of need for assistance.

Attorney-in-fact The individual who has been given the authority to handle another's affairs.

B

Back pay The pay the plaintiff would have earned had he never been fired.

Bank or funeral trust An option for funding funeral costs.

Beneficiary, devisee, and legatee A person who inherits property through a will.

Beneficiary A person who inherits property through a will.

Best interests of the child test The threshold question that a judge who is hearing custody or visitation matters asks.

Board and care homes Types of group homes that offers 24-hour supervision and some personal care services. Similar to adult foster care.

Bona fide occupational qualification (BFOQ) An exception to the ADEA where an employer must prove that age discrimination is reasonable and necessary.

Bond A document that promises to pay money if a particular future event happens; also a sum of money that is put up and will be lost if the event happens.

Bounty An old-fashioned terms meaning a person's assets.

Burial or funeral insurance Another name for pre-need insurance.

Bypass trust A trust that designates the creator's children as beneficiaries but allows the widowed spouse to withdraw adequate income or dip into the trust's principal for support during his lifetime.

C

Capacity A testator's mental ability to sign a will; the legal term used to identify whether a person is mentally competent.

Capital gains Profits made on the sale of real and personal property assets.

Charitable remainder trust (CRT) A trust that permits the creator to transfer his assets into a lifetime income without incurring capital gains or estate taxes because the creator selects a charity to benefit from a charitable donation upon his death.

Charitable trust A trust created with the express intent and purpose to benefit a charity.

Circumstantial Evidence Evidence that is not obvious. Usually used to prove age discrimination.

Civil marriage A government-sanctioned union that is created when a government employee officiates at a marriage ceremony, after which the participants are declared husband and wife.

Civil union A legal designation given to homosexual partners that confers certain marriage-like rights.

Clear and convincing evidence The legal standard used in a will contest to gain from the will being found invalid. Clear and convincing evidence is stronger than a preponderance of the evidence but not as strong as beyond a reasonable doubt.

Client Interview Questionnaire An information tool used by an attorney. It focuses on *all* aspects of life and estate planning when the attorney conducts an extensive and thorough client interview.

Codicil An addition to a will that changes the will.

Community property A person has a right to 50 percent of all of her spouse's assets from the day the couple is married and can be held liable for 50 percent of all of her spouse's debts as well.

Community spouse resource allowance (CSRA) A designated amount a community spouse is permitted by their state to retain from a couples' total countable asset.

Community spouse The term used by Medicaid to describe a person who does not live in a nursing home, but who has a spouse that does.

Confidentiality waiver A waiver that allows psychologists or others to discuss matters that would normally be confidential or privileged information.

Congregate housing Another term for senior communities.

Conservatee A person who the court has determined requires a conservator to handle personal and financial decisions.

Conservator The individual who handles the personal and financial decisions for another person with the continuing permission of that person.

Conservatorship A voluntary undertaking that requires the appointed conservator to have the continuing permission of the conservatee.

Consideration The promise to do or to forbear from doing something that a party otherwise would have the right to do.

Constructive trust A remedy employed by a court to convert the legal title of property into a trust held by a trustee for the benefit of a third party who in good conscience should have reaped the benefits of the possession of the property put into the constructive trust.

Continuing jurisdiction The power of a court to continue to control a matter even after the court has decided the case; used especially in cases involving child custody and support.

Contract An agreement or a covenant between two or more persons in which each party binds herself to do or not to do an act and in which each acquires a right to what the other promises.

Corpus estate A name for real property placed in a trust.

Corpus The money or property put into a trust.

Creator or trustor The individual who creates a trust.

Credit shelter trust A trust designed with one person named as both grantor and trustee and his spouse as secondary trustee who will benefit from the trust once the grantor dies. It utilizes the tax savings of transferring up to $3 million tax free to any designated beneficiary.

Cremation The incineration of a corpse until only ashes are left.

Cryonic suspension The process of taking a body that has been frozen with care and storing it in tanks filled with liquid nitrogen.

D

Decisional incapacity A term that some states use rather than incompetence.

Deficit Reduction Act of 2005 (DRA) An act that prevents individuals in need of nursing home or other long-term care from transferring their assets to others and then applying for Medicaid-funded long-term care due to self-imposed impoverishment.

Defined benefit plan A pension plan in which benefits are specified in advance, usually as a percentage of salary and related to years of service, with no individual account kept for each employee.

Degree of relationship How closely related relatives are to each other (e.g., brothers are related in the first degree; a grandparent and child, in the second degree).

Dementia A general term used to describe a mental illness. It is a persistent impairment of brain function with a decline of memory and one or more of the mental processes of language, visual spatial ability, personality, cognition, calculation, and judgment.

Dependency and Indemnity Compensation (DIC) Benefits paid by the Department of Veterans Affairs when a military member's or veteran's death is due to service-related causes.

Depression The condition of being sad or despondent.

Direct cremation The service of a funeral home in picking up a body from the place of death, transporting it to a crematory, providing a container for cremation, obtaining all necessary authorizations, carrying out the cremation, and returning the remains to the family.

Discovery process Evidence gathered prior to trial through interrogatories, depositions, and requests for production of documents to support a case.

Discretionary trust A trust that allows a trustee to distribute the trust's assets at his own discretion, giving the trustee a degree of personal choice in how the trust assets are distributed; also called a sprinkling or spray trust.

Disinterment The removal of a body from a grave or tomb.

Disparate impact Occurs when a seemingly innocent nondiscriminatory action results in the reality that older workers will suffer from the action.

Disparate treatment Occurs when one or more employees are treated differently by an employer because of their age.

Distributee The term used to describe a person statutorily entitled to a decedent's property through the intestate statutes.

Divorce complaint The pleading citing the legal cause of action for the requested divorce.

Domestic partner A person who has been designated as another's life partner outside marriage and who may receive benefits of some kind.

Domicile A person's home state. A person can have only one domicile.

Durable power of attorney for health care A document that specifies an individual or individuals to carry out the wishes of the principal regarding medical treatments the principal would want if he was unable to share his wishes with healthcare providers. The document endures even if the principal becomes mentally incapacitated.

Durable power of attorney A power of attorney that remains in effect even if the creator becomes incompetent.

E

Elder Cottage Housing Opportunity (ECHO) A concept of classic multigenerational living accommodations, often small apartments built onto an adult child's home or built independently on the adult child's property.

Eldercare Locator The Administration on Aging's national toll-free help line to assist a consumer in locating a hotline in a particular state for reporting elder abuse.

Elective share statutes Statutes that permit a spouse to take what she receives from a will.

Employment-at-will Refers to a mutual employer/employee relationship where a person may be fired or leave a job of his own volition at any time.

Equitable distribution A legal concept some states use to determine a fair division of marital assets based on a couples' particular set of facts.

Equitable remedy A solution that is just, fair, and right for a particular situation.

Escheat The forfeiture of property (including bank accounts) to the state.

Ethical will or family legacy The offering of the details of a person's belief system to loved ones.

Euthanasia The act of painlessly putting to death a person suffering from an incurable or painful disease without the final decision being made by the suffering person, but rather by the person's physician; sometimes described as a mercy killing.

Exculpatory clause A provision in a trust instrument by which the trustee is relieved of responsibility for things that go wrong or for losses as long as the trustee acted in good faith.

Executor A personal representative who manages, administers, and distributes a decedent's estate according to the terms of a will.

Executrix A female executor.

Express contract A contract with terms stated in oral or written words.

Express trust Such a trust has a specific intent with a clearly stated purpose.

F

Fair Employment Practices Agencies (FEPAs) State agencies responsible for enforcing a state's own anti-employment discrimination laws.

Family And Medical Leave Act (FMLA) Provides a federal safety net for working Americans who need to take time off from work to care for a family member suffering from an illness or who have their own medical condition to deal with. Some states provide a state version.

Fee simple absolute An unqualified and unlimited ownership interest.

Fiduciary A person who manages money or property for another person and in whom that other person has a right to place great trust.

Final order A document determining the outcome of a guardianship hearing.

For cause finding When the EEOC investigators believe that age discrimination did take place, which leads to more EEOC involvement.

Forced share Refers to the situation when a spouse is permitted to take a larger share when mentioned but left very little in a spouse's will.

Forum non conveniens Latin meaning "inconvenient court." If two or more courts have proper venue for a case, a judge may rule that a lawsuit be brought in one court or the other for the sake of convenience and fairness to the parties.

Fraud in the execution Occurs when a person misrepresents the character or contents of the instrument to be signed by the testator, which does not, in fact, carry out the testator's intent.

Fraud in the inducement Occurs when a person misrepresents the facts with the intent to deceive the testator to influence the testamentary disposition of the testator's property.

Front pay Defined as prospective payments made to a victim of job discrimination who cannot yet be given the job to which he is entitled. These payments, made until the job comes through, make up the difference between money earned now and money that would be made if the new position were available immediately.

Full disclosure of assets A complete listing of all real and personal property in which the parties have ownership interest.

Funding of the trust One of the most important trust creation requirements in transferring title to property, through deed or otherwise, into the name of the trust.

Funeral directors Usually the proprietors of funeral homes. Their job is to manage funerals. Often they are able to prepare corpses for burial or cremation.

Funeral homes Business establishments where corpses are prepared for burial or cremation and where funeral services may be held and the body viewed by mourners.

Funeral Industry Practices Rule The regulation that requires funeral providers to provide consumers with information regarding funeral products and services and ensures that consumers pay for only the products and services they want and need.

Funeral Rule The common name for the Funeral Industry Practices Rule, administered by the Federal Trade Commission.

Funeral The event during which a person who has recently died is honored.

G

General bequest Any gift given by a will.

General power of attorney A document very broad in its purpose that allows an individual to appoint a trusted person to handle general business matters.

Geriatric care manager A person who conducts a complete and professional assessment of a patient's condition and provides guidelines as to what type of care the patient requires and, specifically, whether that care can be provided by family members.

Grandparent visitation legislation Legislation enacted to ensure that grandparents would be able to continue their relationships with their grandchildren.

Grandparenting time legislation Another name for grandparent visitation legislation.

Grandparents' rights movement A movement that gained momentum with the backing of senior advocacy groups.

Granny flat Small apartments built onto an adult child's home or built independently on the adult child's property. Can also be a mobile home.

Grantor-retained annuity trust A trust that allows a grantor to pass on his business or company to a chosen beneficiary while the grantor is still alive and gives the grantor an income for a designated period.

Grantor A creator who transfers real estate.

Gross estate All of a decedent's assets that are added together and include all gifts made within three years of the date of the decedent's death plus all business interests, annuities, real estate of any kind, stocks, bonds, personal property, cash, and insurance.

Group homes Residences designed for the relatively self-sufficient senior to provide some household maintenance and companionship.

Guardian ad litem A person who is appointed by a court to take care of the interests of a person who cannot legally take care of himself in a lawsuit involving him.

Guardian A person appointed by a court to make personal and financial decisions for someone adjudged incompetent.

Guardianship A legal management tool put in place by state law to protect and aid individuals who have different abilities to care for themselves.

H

Hardship waiver A waiver that provides for exceptions when the period of Medicaid ineligibility would leave an applicant physically endangered or deprived of food, shelter, clothing, or medical treatment.

Health care power of attorney (HCPOA) A document that specifies an individual or individuals to carry out the wishes of the principal regarding medical treatments the principal would want if he was unable to share his wishes with health care providers.

Health care proxy The individual appointed to make medical treatment decisions for another person; also known as an *agent*.

Health Insurance Portability and Accountability Act (HIPPA) The first federal privacy standards designed to limit the information that health care professionals can share, use, and release to others concerning their patients.

Hearing officer, referee, commissioner, or magistrate A judicial officer who serves in the role of a judge during a judicial hearing.

Heir A person who will inherit property from a deceased person with or without a will.

Holographic will A handwritten will.

Home state A state in which a child has lived for six months and where a court has made such a jurisdictional determination.

House sharing An option that allows seniors to remain in their home by living with another family member or boarder.

I

Identity theft The illegal obtaining of personal information for the purpose of using the stolen information to commit theft and fraud.

Implied contract A contract with existence and terms determined by the *actions* of the persons involved, not by their words.

Implied trust Such a trust is often created by the courts to prevent inequity.

In Terrorem clause A no-contest clause included in a will that warns a beneficiary that contesting any of the other devises made to any other beneficiary will cancel the devise made to the contesting beneficiary.

Indirect evidence Evidence that is not obvious.

Individual retirement account (IRA) An investment account designed for an individual to self-manage and fund his own retirement account.

Instrumental activities of daily living (IADL) Those activities that are less basic than the traditional activities of daily living (e.g., shopping, paying bills, cleaning, doing laundry, and preparing meals).

Intangible Refers to property that is a right rather than a physical object (e.g., bank accounts, stocks, and copyrights).

Intervivos gift A gift given while the grantor is still living.

Intervivos trust A trust written and enacted by a creator while he is still alive.

Intestacy statutes Each state's statutes that designate the beneficiaries of an individual who has died intestate.

Intestate A person who dies without having drafted a will.

Irrevocable life insurance trust A trust created to guard the decedent's estate from increasing in value and subsequently having to pay taxes on life insurance proceeds.

Itemized or standard Two types of deductions, one of which is allowed by the IRS.

J

Joint tenancy Where two or more owners have equal interests in acquired property at the same time and if one owner dies, that person's ownership interests automatically pass to the other owner without going through probate. This is usually known as right of survivorship.

Judicial separation The common legal term used to describe a separation from one's spouse.

L

Lapsed Refers to a devisee who predeceases a testator.

Last will and testament A document in which a person directs how her property is to be distributed after her death.

Least restrictive alternative (LRA) principle Alternatives to traditional cookie-cutter guardianships that stay in tune with the Constitution's Fourteenth Amendment for due process personal liberty protections.

Letter of instruction A decedent's non-legally binding document giving instructions to family and friends after the decedent has passed away.

Letters of administration An appointment by the court granting a named individual as the personal representative/administrator of an intestate decedent.

Life estate An ownership interest in property that lasts until a named person(s) dies.

Limited, partial, or temporary guardianships Guardianships that are more individualized on a case-by-case situation.

Liquidated damages Specific amounts of money agreed to in a contract as compensation for a breach of that contract.

Living will A document describing an individual's wishes regarding medical treatments the person would want if he was unable to share his wishes with health care providers.

Long-term care insurance Insurance coverage that pays nursing home costs.

Look-back period The time period for investigating asset transfer.

Lump sum death benefit A one-time lump sum payment made by the Social Security Administration ($255) to be used toward burial expenses.

M

Mandated reporters Doctors, nurses, home health care workers, guardians, trustees, attorneys, and any other individual serving in a fiduciary role to an elder abuse victim.

Marital trust A trust that allows the amount of the estate tax exemption to be applied to the estate at the first spouse's death, reducing an estate's tax exposure. When the surviving spouse dies, his exemption amount is applied to the remaining estate.

Marriage A personal relationship arising out of a civil contract between a man and a woman, to whom the consent of the parties capable of making that contract is necessary.

Medicaid A federally funded and state-administered health insurance program providing all types of medical care to individuals who cannot afford to pay for some or all of their medical bills.

Medical power of attorney A document very specific in its purpose that allows an individual to appoint a trusted person to make health care choices when the individual is not able to share his health care choices with health care providers.

Medicare Part A Pays hospital bills and is funded from an employment tax on all income.

Medicare Part B Pays physicians' bills.

Medicare A government program that provides health insurance to U.S. residents age 65 and older regardless of income. Coverage for younger individuals with disabilities is also available.

Medigap insurance Insurance coverage for all medical treatment not covered by the primary Parts A and B Medicare coverage.

Mental Health Reporter A book in which appeals from guardianship orders are collected.

Minimum monthly maintenance needs allowance (MMMNA) A designated monthly amount of the institutionalized spouses' income that the community spouse may retain for their own support.

Mixed motive case A case in which an employer seeks to prove that even though age discrimination may have played a part in a worker's dismissal, there still were other legitimate business reasons for letting the employee go.

Money purchase plan A retirement plan in which an employer, an employee, or both has specified that a certain amount of money be contributed to a retirement fund. The money is invested with earnings divided proportionately among all participants in the plan. Also called defined contribution plan.

Motions to dismiss Requests that the court throw a case out of court, or dismiss the case.

N

National Center on Elder Abuse (NCEA) An organization funded by the Administration on Aging and in partnership with the National Association of State Units on Aging, the Commission on Law and Aging of the American Bar Association, the Clearinghouse on Abuse and Neglect of the Elderly of the University of Delaware, the National Adult Protective Services Association, and the National Committee for the Prevention of Elder Abuse.

National Guardianship Association An organization that drafted a model code of ethics for guardians.

Next of kin All persons entitled to inherit from a person who has not left a will.

No cause finding When the EEOC dismisses a claim because of no finding of the claimed discrimination.

No-fault divorce statute A cause of action that permits a spouse filing for divorce not to levy blame within the complaint.

Nuncupative will A type of will accepted by a minority of states but only during wartime conditions or from a testator's deathbed.

Nursing home A general term for different types of medical facilities that provides meals, skilled nursing, rehabilitation, medical services, personal care, and recreation in a supervised and protected setting.

O

Objective standard The principle that a court should resolve most contract issues by considering only the actions, writings, and other objective evidence of what the parties did rather than considering what the parties subjectively meant to do.

Offer The act of making a proposal and presenting it for acceptance or rejection.

Older Americans Act (OAA) A federally created act that provides that states *must* offer eligible seniors assistance with their everyday needs or face federal funding cuts.

Ombudsman A person who has the power to investigate official misconduct, help fix wrongs done by the government, and sometimes prosecute wrongdoers.

Oral will Technically known as a nuncupative will.

P

Palimony Financial support paid between persons who are not and never were married.

Palliative care Care that treats the symptoms of an incurable disease to make them easier to bear. Hospice care.

Parens Patriae An ancient Roman concept meaning that society as a whole should protect citizens who cannot protect themselves.

Parental Kidnapping Prevention Act (PKPA) An act that provides the necessary authority for states to give full faith and credit to their respective custody and visitation orders. In essence, it requires courts to refrain from exercising jurisdiction over a custody case while another state is processing a custody case for the same child.

Parental or spousal appointments Also known as standby guardianship, these are used in situations when a guardian is needed immediately and should be put in place without the need to go for court approval first.

Parole evidence Testimony explaining what the parties meant when they wrote a contract.

Patient's Bill of Rights A list of legal rights that are guaranteed by the federal government.

Payable-on-death bank account An option for funding funeral costs.

Payee spouse The spouse who receives money.

Payor spouse The spouse who pays money.

Per capita **distribution** A method of dividing a deceased person's estate by giving out shares equally to the surviving beneficiaries.

Per stirpes **distribution** A method of dividing a deceased person's estate by giving out shares equally by representation or by family groups.

Personal property All things not considered real property, including intangibles (i.e., shares of stock and bank accounts).

Personal representative The person who administers a decedent's estate and is responsible for carrying out the wishes of the decedent's will or is appointed by the court to follow intestate guideline.

Personalized legal plan The development of a personalized approach to satisfy client expectations by determining the client's goals for the attorney and the law firm handling the client's case.

Pet trust A trust created for the benefit of a beloved pet in order to provide funds for a trustee to maintain a pet's lifestyle even after the pet owner has died or has become incapacitated.

Physician-assisted suicide The voluntary ending of a patient's life when a physician knowingly assists in fulfilling the patient's desire to die.

Plain meaning of the words The principle that if a contract, a statute, or another writing seems clear, the meaning of the writing should be determined from the writing itself, not from other evidence such as testimony.

Pre-funding Paying for one's funeral ahead of time.

Pre-need decision Any funeral plans made by an individual prior to her death.

Pre-need insurance Insurance that may eliminate complicated claims procedures of a regular life insurance policy.

Prenuptial agreement A contract that two individuals make *before* their marriage to each other, which does not take effect until *after* the individuals are married to each other.

Preponderance of the evidence A standard used to determine civil liability. It requires that the weight of the evidence offered by the plaintiff to prove a matter is more probable than not.

Pretermitted child statutes Statutes that give children born after the execution of a parent's will and not provided for in the will a share in the deceased parent's estate.

Pretermitted spouse statutes Statutes that apply to spouses who have *not* been mentioned in their spouse's will.

Principal The creator of a power of attorney.

Principal Any cash or property placed in a trust.

Private guardianship When a private individual is named as another's guardian.

Property settlement agreement Divorcing spouses who agree on negotiated matters concerning marital property, support and/or custody arrangements memorialize those agreed decisions on paper in a property settlement agreement.

Prudent person standard The standard by which courts may review a trustee's behavior. It asks whether a reasonable person would have acted as the trustee did when dealing with another person's property.

Psychosis A mental disorder characterized by symptoms such as delusions or hallucinations that indicate impaired contact with reality; any severe form of mental disorder.

Public conservatorship Provided by the states for elderly adults with no willing or responsible family members or friends who can serve in that capacity.

Public Guardian Government-provided guardianship or conservatorship services when there are no willing and appropriate family members or friends who can serve.

Public guardianship A guardianship of last resort when there are no willing and appropriate family members or friends who can serve. The government is then called upon to act as a surrogate decision maker.

Public housing Usually refers to government-subsidized project based construction.

Public voucher-based Refers to subsidized housing typically portable in nature that can be used by the recipient in any rental unit that is approved by the local Public Housing Authority.

Punitive damages Extra money given to a plaintiff to punish a defendant and to help keep a particularly bad act from happening again.

Q

Qualified plan A retirement plan that meets IRS requirements for employers to deduct payments from an employee's paycheck and place them in a retirement account.

Qualified terminable interest property (QTIP) trust A marital trust that protects money from the creator's creditors and keeps assets separate from a new spouse and protects children from the creator's prior marriages. It can, however, place restrictions on how the trust's assets can be spent to support the widow.

R

Real property Land and things affixed to or growing on the land.

Reciprocal beneficiaries People who have registered and been designated as life partners outside marriage and who may receive benefits of some kind.

Recovery provisions Provisions in state Medicaid programs whereby the states must attempt to recover from a recipient's assets any Medicaid funding provided to the recipient.

Rehabilitation Emphasizes the recovery of the patient and the goal of returning the patient to her home or at least to one of the assisted living alternatives.

Remainderman The beneficiary who receives the remainder interest in a trust.

Required minimum distribution (RMD) The minimum amount of money that individuals with IRAs, 401ks, or 403bs *must* withdraw by a certain age.

Res Any personal property, other than cash, placed in a trust.

Rescission The legal term used for the rewriting of a contract.

Residuary beneficiaries Those individuals who receive the remainder interest in a trust or will.

Residuary bequest A gift given via a will after all general and specific bequests have been made.

Retirement plan A plan set up by an employer to provide financially for employees after they stop full-time employment.

Reverse mortgage A mortgage that allows an older homeowner to receive a monthly payment based on his equity in the home rather than make monthly payments to a lending institution.

Revocation by a physical act A will may be revoked when the testator purposely destroys it.

Revocation by operation of law A will may be revoked subsequent to a divorce or marriage.

Revocation by subsequent writing A will is considered revoked when a new will is written.

Right-to-sue notice A notification from the EEOC to a claimant that the claimant is permitted to seek private counsel to assist in pursuing a claim.

Rule against perpetuities A rule that places a limitation on the length of time a trust can be in effect.

S

Section 83 The IRS Code concerning the taxing of Social Security benefits.

Self-authentication Proof that a document is genuine. Also called self-proved.

Self-paying Paying for nursing home care with a patient's available income, a patient's accumulated savings, a family or adult children who can pay, or a combination of all three.

Self-proved Proof that a document is genuine. Also called self-authentication.

Senior communities Communities designed for more active seniors who can living independently in their own residence.

Separate property A type of property ownership that permits individual ownership of property by a married couple except for property clearly designated as jointly owned.

Settlor A trustor who transfers personal property.

Skilled care facility A nursing home that offers nursing care 24 hours a day.

Social Security Administration The federal agency that provides retired individuals with income.

Sole ownership Ownership by one person. Also known as tenancy in severalty.

Special care nursing Care for patients with specific physical or mental needs that probably will leave the patient in the setting for the rest of her life.

Special medical guardianship A guardianship appointment made so that a medical procedure can be performed.

Special power of attorney A power of attorney created to give an agent one special power that usually ends with completion of the responsibility.

Specific bequest A gift named and identified in a will.

Spendthrift trust A trust that directs a trustee that a specific sum may be disbursed at specified intervals or that states how monies from the trust can be spent to keep an inheritance from being spent unwisely.

Springing durable power of attorney A power of attorney that begins at a later time upon the happening of a certain event.

Standby guardianships Guardianships used when a guardian is needed immediately. It should be put in place without the need to go for court approval first.

State estate tax A tax paid by the estate to the individual state.

State inheritance tax A tax paid by a beneficiary to the individual state.

State personal preference laws Laws that may permit a person's next of kin to disregard instructions included in a will or letter of instruction and to decide whether their deceased family member will be buried or cremated.

State units on aging State agencies that are empowered to administer, design, and advocate programs and services for their elderly citizens.

Step care or progressive communities Also known as continuing care communities (CCRCs).

Successor trustee An alternate trustee named in a trust to fill the role of the original trustee should the original trustee die, resign, or become incapacitated or unable to serve.

Summary judgment A final judgment (victory) for one side in a lawsuit, without trial, when the judge finds no genuine factual issue is in dispute in the lawsuit.

Supplemental Security Income (SSI) Benefits for citizens who are physically or mentally disabled and whose incomes are within extremely low limits.

Support trust or special needs trust A trust established for the support of minor children or an adult child with disabilities.

Survivor income benefits Benefits paid to a deceased worker's surviving spouse, minor children, or adult children disabled before the age of 22.

T

Tangible Property that is capable of being touched; that is, it is real.

Taxable estate The gross estate minus the debts the deceased owed, which may include funeral costs, medical expenses, estate administration costs, mortgages, and credit card bills.

Tenancy by the entirety Legal ownership providing that property will pass solely to the surviving spouse.

Tenancy for years Created when a lessor (landlord) and lessee (tenant) agree on a specific stated period for a lease to be in effect.

Tenancy in common Ownership interest in land by two or more persons that can be passed on to heirs or otherwise disposed of.

Tenancy in severalty Ownership by one person. Also known as sole ownership.

Testamentary trust A trust included in a will and designed to take effect after a testator's death.

Testator The person who writes her own will.

Therapeutic Jurisprudence The melding together of a client's legal and psychological issues by his attorney and the firm's legal support staff to better serve the client's needs.

Title VII, Chapter 3 A part of the Older Americans Act that provides funding to the states to provide for long-term care ombudsman programs and development of state senior legal assistance.

Tortuous interference with an expected inheritance or gift A cause of action that requires the plaintiff to prove that the interference involved tortuous conduct such as fraud, duress, or undue influence.

Trust instrument Any document in which the trust creator creates a trust.

Trust A legal mechanism by which one or more persons hold legal title to money or property for the benefit of another who holds equitable title.

Trustee The person to whom property has been transferred for the benefit of another and who is responsible for the trust's administration.

U

Undue influence The act of misusing a position of trust or improperly taking advantage of a person's weakness to change that person's actions or decision; coercion.

Uniform Child Custody Jurisdiction Act (UCCJA) A model child custody statute that was adopted by all 50 states; it prohibited states from modifying custody orders made by other states and required states to enforce original custody orders from other states.

Uniform Child Custody Jurisdiction and Enforcement Act (UCCJEA) An act that provides newer, more uniform methods for expedited interstate enforcement of custody and visitation orders.

Uniform Premarital Agreement Act (UPAA) Legislation enacted that sets forth the requirements for creating a valid prenuptial agreement.

V

Viatical settlements Involve the purchase of another person's life insurance policy by an investor in return for a cash payment that is a percentage of the policy payout.

Virtual retirement community Web-based assistance that can be used to provide access to social services and social outreach programs.

W

Ward A person who is legally incompetent and becomes the responsibility of a guardian.

Will substitutes Legal mechanisms created to conduct the transfer of real or personal property without going through the probate process.

Will The shortened term commonly used when referring to a last will and testament.

Index

CPSIA information can be obtained
at www.ICGtesting.com
Printed in the USA
BVHW090003201222
654600BV00004B/57

9 781401 842574